CONTEMPORARY THEATER

CONTEMPORARY THEATER
EVOLUTION AND DESIGN

CHRISTOS G. ATHANASOPULOS

A Wiley-Interscience Publication
JOHN WILEY & SONS
New York • Chichester • Brisbane • Toronto • Singapore

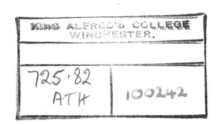
Copyright © 1983 by John Wiley & Sons, Inc.

All rights reserved. Published simultaneously in Canada.
1st Greek edition: Copyright © 1975 Christos G. Athanasopulos
2nd Greek edition: Copyright © 1976 Christos G. Athanasopulos

Library of Congress Cataloging in Publication Data:

Athanasopulos, Christos Giorgos
   Contemporary theater.

   Translation of: Provlimata stis exelixeis tou
synchronou theatrou.
   "A Wiley-Interscience publication."
   Bibliography: p.
   Includes index.
   1. Theaters—Construction.   2. Architecture, Modern—
20th century.   3. Theater—History.   I. Title.
NA6821.A7413   1983   725'.822   82-17508
ISBN 0-471-87319-5

Printed in the United States of America

10 9 8 7 6 5 4 3 2 1

To my father and mother

Foreword

Theater design is rarely the subject of a full-length treatise. In the twenty-four hundred years since the ancient Greeks built the first permanent public theater in Athens on the southern flank of the Acropolis in the fifth century B.C., the number of books that have treated the subject of theater design at all seriously and in detail, either as architectural or as theatrical history, can be counted on fewer than ten fingers.

It is particularly appropriate that Professor Athanasopulos, himself a practicing architect and an Athenian, should undertake to write this treatise on theater design not only from the point of view of his professional specialty but from a depth of understanding of how a theater building fulfills its designed purpose both for the performing artist and for the spectator. The historiography of the subject serves to reinforce the fact that in every age theater design is a complex dichotomy that alternately excites and baffles those who try it.

In our time the practice of architecture and engineering has become a most complicated process, but the essence and meaning of it all, as Professor Athanasopulos shows us, can best be delineated to a lay audience by not being too technically explicit. In the lore of the theater there is a poetic metaphor of uncertain authorship that goes like this: "Theater is two planks and passion." A theater designer construes this to mean one plank for the performer to perform upon, one plank for the audience to be seated at ease upon, and what passes between them is passion. History shows that successful theater design is a balancing act that constitutes reconciliation of the practical planks with the spiritual passion in a successful building for public performance.

Professor Athanasopulos tells this fascinating story not only from the point of view of a practicing architect but also as a sensitive and perceptive participant in the dramatic event of performance which alone can breathe life into the otherwise dead clay of a theater building.

GEORGE C. IZENOUR

Professor Emeritus of
Theater Design and Technology
Yale University
New Haven, Connecticut
Adjunct Professor of
Theater Technology
Lehigh University
Bethlehem, Pennsylvania

Preface

The title of this book, *Contemporary Theater*, reflects a work of research concerning the theater both as a vital element of society and as architecture. My purpose is neither to present yet another concise history of the theater nor to determine its "ideal form," which is, nevertheless, a goal that has been pursued for the past 50 years by everyone concerned with the theater.

My aim is to trace the evolutionary path of the theater from the beginnings of human history, considering the influence of social trends on the evolution of its form, what caused the form to change, and how the theater building was affected throughout the centuries by a succession of styles and concepts.

Theater reflects the history of man himself; it has existed as long as man has existed and has satisfied basic needs of human nature. Its evolution follows that of the human race, from its primitive beginnings to the space age; the two have advanced side by side, and theater adjusts its development to that of the human spirit.

Theater is first of all an art form—one that is eclectic, collective, and compound, that gathers together in itself all other art forms and is expressed through the conscious efforts, not of one individual, but of the collective whole. It is not only the response of a group of individuals—the audience—as it watches and hears the movements and expressions of another group—the performers; more than that, it is a concept that reflects the union and identification of the audience with the spirit, the feelings, and the experience of the playwright, who leads the audience, through the actor, into the midst of a scenic activity and a cultural orientation.

To try to confine that concept, or even to attempt a comprehensive analysis of it, between the covers of a single volume would be a utopian undertaking. Nevertheless, the wide dispersion of material in the international bibliography and my own interest in the theater impelled me to collect all that material here, condensed as synoptically as possible and supplemented by my own observations on a number of distinctive theaters that I have visited in Europe and the United States. I felt it would be redundant to extend my research to the purely technical aspect of the theater since it is extensively covered by a number of excellent works, and to cull from them would be merely a labor of repetition.

The sole aim of this book is, by drawing on the results and conclusions of past research, to determine a trend in the evolutionary path of the theater and to provide a stimulus to researchers for further exploration of its particular aspects, whether these have to do with its architectural form, scenography, or the spoken word, the last in my opinion being the cardinal element of the art called theater. Let this volume be considered, too, as a contribution to the effort to move this art out of the state of stagnancy and uncertainty into which it has again fallen in recent years.

It would be difficult to study the contemporary theater without taking into account the theater of the Greeks and the theaters created throughout the ages by other peoples. What today we call contemporary theater is in effect an evolution of form and style, which, nevertheless, continues to draw on tradition and the remote past for examples and successful achievements and, after adapting them to modern technological standards, endeavors to present them as new and original. A study of the history of the theater and an examination of past forms in relation to the social concepts and philosophy of each period are necessary if one is to perceive the true essence of the theater and the real reasons, conditions, and events that led to its present expression and forms.

This book, reflecting my desire to emphasize that essential relationship between old and new, examines and analyzes the theater from its early beginnings to the present; it defines the components that shaped the theater forms of our era and seeks to identify their resultant direction in contemporary trends and movements. To achieve that goal, the text has been divided into four parts.

The first part deals with theaters of the past and their problems up to the close of the nineteenth century. It opens with the first instinctive appearance of theater among primitive tribes and in Egypt. The discussion next turns to ancient Greece, where theater assumed its true form and reached its culmination. There its progress was speeded by the emergence of tragedy and comedy and by the remarkable cultural development of the ancient Greeks. Tragedy and comedy, the first true dramatic forms, coupled with the great spirit of the Greeks, elevated dramatic performances to the level of an art. This spirit also helped in the creation of an immortal theater form, a form that has survived through the centuries and has been carried forward as a model into later ages and is still considered the direct ancestor of all theaters subsequently developed.

The Roman period, by contrast, marked the beginning of a decline in the theater that ended in its complete extinction during the long winter of the Dark Ages. In exploring the Middle Ages we find that the Byzantine religious drama, which flourished during that period, strongly influenced the later (twelfth century) development of mystery plays in the West and helped lay the foundation for a renaissance of the theater in the very bosom of a church implacably hostile to it. The role of Byzantine liturgical drama, strangely enough in view of its significance, has always been ignored by foreign researchers; their position is that religious drama originated in the West.

The Renaissance, a time of renewed life in the arts, marked the rebirth of the theater. Scholars pursued new realms of intellectual research. Once again channels leading back to classical times were opened; old forms were combined with geometry, the new and fashionable concept

of the era. New forms based on the evolution and refinement of perspective drawing as taught by Euclid and Vitruvius were to appear.

At the same time, the Renaissance failed to comprehend the main characteristic of the Greek demiurge: *spirit.* Having been for the Greeks a religious and social institution, the theater now became for a small privileged caste of nobles and courtiers a means of entertainment. In England, meanwhile, Shakespeare with his poetic genius brought the dramatic structure to new heights and created a new theater form: the Elizabethan. Like that of the Greeks, this form was to be considered a sound basis for future theater development.

The Italian Renaissance was followed by the Baroque period and the creation during the seventeenth and eighteenth centuries of a dominating stage system called "scène à l'italienne," which was to dominate the theater for hundreds of years and has in fact survived, intact but for a few minor changes, to this day. Finally, the nineteenth century was a period once again of decline and confusion for the theater. Artistic movements such as romanticism and realism brought about further depreciation of the importance of the spoken word while strengthening the trend toward entertainment and illusion.

The second part deals with theater in the twentieth century and how it was influenced by the various social upheavals and the consequences of World War I. It examines the relation between nineteenth-century theater and that of the early years of the twentieth, the new movements and trends in theater architecture, scenography, and stagecraft—that new art that was now added to the other theater arts. The 1920s were considered by many as the theater's "golden decade"; during those years the theater pursued new directions in innovation and research. Reaction against the entrenched and dynamically dominant Italian stage amounted to a virtual theatrical revolt. The advance of technology, the emergence of brilliant and strong personalities like Appia, Craig, Reinhardt, Piscator, and Gropius, and the vigorous presence of the Bauhaus school culminated in a latter-day renaissance in the theater and oriented it toward new concepts and new forms appropriate and conducive to its role as an art form and as a functional social instrument.

The third part analyzes new theater forms

produced by the exploratory activity of the period between World Wars I and II. It examines each of these forms separately and, with the help of characteristic examples, investigates the variations and improvements applied to them by the architects of our time. The forms are (1) the proscenium theater, the long-established Italian form readjusted to the needs and demands of our century; (2) the open-stage theater, reflecting the lofty intellectual and spiritual standards of two great periods, the Greek and the Elizabethan; (3) the theater-in-the-round or arena stage, an original form stemming not from tradition but from the hereditary instinct to gather in a circle; and (4) the adaptable or experimental theater, a form that combines the other three and, beyond that, offers itself to experimentation and exploration of new areas in search of theatrical innovations and performance techniques.

The fourth part assesses the resultant trend in the evolution of contemporary theater. It can be considered a summation of the conclusions reached in this study as to the present evolutionary stage of the theater. It determines—in diagrams—the functional needs of each performing art and defines the most appropriate theater form for each one. It also examines the new forms in relation to contemporary functional demands and the needs that produced two new and more complex forms—the multipurpose theater and the theater center—both designed to serve the combined needs of modern cities. The conclusion, nevertheless, is that basically these two forms have not contributed to the development of the theater; they were not created to improve the quality of expression in theater art but to cover the financial needs of costly theater organizations. This concluding section also analyzes the modern theater trends that seek a political-militant theater to serve the political and social needs of our times, a theater that moves out of its traditional space in search of its public in the public's own surroundings—the factory, the school, the street.

There have been efforts to create a new "ideal" space theater equaling the brilliant designs of the Bauhaus. But these efforts either resorted to the easy expedient of combining movie projection with live action or were abandoned because of lack of interest, a fairly common contemporary attitude toward projects involving costly experimentation. In short, the theater is faced once again with the appalling prospect of becoming stagnant, as it was in the nineteenth century; meaning and speech, the two elements that contributed so vitally to the creative development of the theater, are once again in a state of decline.

CHRISTOS ATHANASOPULOS

Athens, Greece
June 1983

Acknowledgments

I hereby make grateful acknowledgments to Professor Jan Despo, who urged me to start work on the subject, as well as to Professors George Izenour, Jannis Liapis, Panagiotis Ladopoulos, and Dionysis Zivas for their assistance and advice. I would also like to thank all the eminent architects whose names occur in these pages and on whose opinions and expert knowledge I have drawn frequently as essential aids to my research.

In the matter of illustrations, my debt is more specific. Some of the pictures I have used are those I have collected or drawn throughout the years. Others come from sources that are acknowledged in the captions. To all, my sincere thanks.

Lastly, I would like to express my sincere appreciation to Loucas Delmouzos, who helped in the accomplishment of this work by assisting me in the translation of the Greek edition. He not only tried to find the right words to express my thoughts in correct English, but he also had to tolerate the great amount of revising required to keep the text up to date.

C. A.

Contents

CONTEMPORARY THEATER

Figure 1. Theater of Epidaurus, during a performance of Sophocles' Antigone. *(Photo by D.A. Harissiadis. Reprinted by permission.)*

Part One

EVOLUTIONARY PROBLEMS UP TO THE TWENTIETH CENTURY

1
The Instinctive Revelations

The Beginnings

Man dances. . . .

After the activities that secure to primitive peoples the material necessities, food and shelter, the dance comes first. It is the earliest outlet for emotion, and the beginning of the arts. . . . Primitive man, poor in means of expression, with only the rudimentary beginnings of spoken language, universally expressed his deeper feelings through measured movement. Nature about him moved rhythmically, in the wave motion of the waters and in the wind-blown fields; the sun and moon rose and fell; his own heart-beats were rhythmic. It was natural, then, that he should create rhythmic movement to externalize any felt joy.

He danced for pleasure and as ritual. He spoke in dance to his gods, he prayed in dance and gave thanks in dance. By no means all this activity was dramatic or theatric; but in his designed movement was the germ of drama and of theater. . . . Wherever "primitive" peoples are found and their customs studied, there is ritual and usually dramatic dance. . . .

Beyond the mere joy of rhythmic movement the actor has been impelled to express, in memetic action, something experienced or imagined, and he has taken on the character of himself in another time, or of an ancestor or an animal or a god. In acting over a period of time, he has fulfilled the first requirement of "drama"; for the word comes from the Greek word δράω, "I do." Primarily it implies "a thing done."[1]

Rhythm revealed new, strong, hitherto unknown emotions; it enabled people to perceive their own great capabilities of expression, which they now felt they must externalize. Words and sounds that rhythmically followed the ritual dance soon developed into speech and music, and these opened up new ways to communicate. Thus the individual began to form new concepts, to discover their importance to the self, to learn how to define ways of living according to them, and finally to create civilizations.

Art, speech, and music became, together with religion, integral elements in human society, exerting a direct influence on the formation of cultures. Expression as a means of communication, movement and gestures as descriptive aids, and sound as a means of transmitting articulated words and tones evolved to the point where they could be used in a unique combination,

either for worship and entertainment or in preparation for war. Thereby a form of primitive drama was created.

This form was indeed primitive and barbaric; the esthetic instincts of nature, which Friedrich Nietzsche attributed to the Greeks,[2] did not appear until much later. The era of the Apollonian and Dionysian spirits, considered by the German philosopher to be indispensable elements in the progressive formation of art,[3] was still far in the future.

Egypt

It is certain that theater as a concept did not exist in the very early cultures. The first evidence of organized movement comes from ancient Egypt, that pre-Greek civilization which is the oldest the Western world knows. It can be said that the Egyptians developed a quasi form of drama and a kind of dramatic presentation that, according to Herodotus, later influenced the ancient Greek rites of the Orphic, Dionysian, and Eleusinian mysteries. Describing the customs of the Egyptians, Herodotus affirms that "at any rate, the festivals, the parades and the formal processions to the temple, these were first instituted by the Egyptians, and it was from the Egyptians that the Greeks learned them."[4]

When we study the theater in ancient Egypt, we realize that the evidence discovered to date is not clear or precise enough to give us a complete and accurate idea of the theater of that era nor to define any particular architectural form that served it. There seem to have been no playhouses or specific play areas.

It is true, of course, that the early Egyptians danced as did all primitive peoples (Figure 2);[5] it is also true that the performances were related to religious ceremonials and pagan feasts, events held in temple forecourts or public squares that could hold large audiences. The populace attended ritual dances, grand processionals, and sacrifices or watched reenacted battle scenes performed on wooden stages, ramps, or raised platforms. The great peristyle courts could be considered as theatrical spaces, but they certainly cannot be classed as theaters and consequently have no bearing at all on the development of theater architecture. Therefore, what remains to be studied is how this Egyptian quasi

Figure 2. Apache war dance: Drawing by George Catlin, showing the Apaches preparing for war against the Navahos. Typical form of round dance to be found in all primitive societies. (Credit: American Museum of Natural History.)

form of drama influenced the concept of "theatrical play."

The Egyptians' principal god, Osiris, his sister-wife Isis, and their son Ap-uat became the central figures in a series of "passion plays," which are considered to be the only established and elaborate form of drama in ancient Egypt. The one performed yearly in Abydos is the most interesting.[5] The dominant structural themes of these passion plays were the adventures of Osiris, his assassination, Isis' campaign for revenge and restitution, and finally the resurrection of the god and restoration of the people's faith in and worship of him.

The aim of this "passion" differs in no great measure from that of religious ceremonies and festivities of today, such as the famous Passion Play performed every 10 years at Oberammergau in Bavaria or the lesser-known performances of the Νιπτήρ (*nipter*, the basin used by Christ to wash the feet of his disciples) that are held yearly on the Greek island of Patmos and in Jerusalem. The primary purpose and theme of these religious plays, notwithstanding the tremendous time interval that separates them, is a people's endeavor to keep vividly alive the memory of the sacrifice, martyrdom, and final triumph of its god.

The setting of the plays was frequently changed, since places and events differed with each episode of the action, as did the type of performance. True drama yielded its place on some occasions to rites of worship, on others to the reenactment of battles. A pagan procession of priests, courtiers, and warriors always followed the king-god, and the sacred barge of Osiris was perhaps the first piece of stage scenery ever contrived and can be considered an unintentional attempt at scenic realism. The structure of each episode differed according to the theme of the action, and the drama was often related to the reality of everyday life (Figure 3).

If there is considerable doubt whether the Abydos passion play series were dramatic presentations in the true sense and not just a widely popularized version of ceremonial rites, the doubts are still greater in the case of the *Pyramid Texts, Memphian Drama,* and other plays.[6]

Figure 3. Maidens performing acrobatic dances: Mural at the acropolis of Memphis. (Credit: Vandersleyen, Das alte Aegyten.*)*

Figure 4. Funerary papyrus from the tomb of Queen Meryet-Amumd at Thebes, conveying an idea of the choric movement, costumes, and use of masks in ancient Egypt. (The Metropolitan Museum of Art, Museum Excavations, Rogers Fund, 1930. Reprinted by permission.)

It is difficult to consider these performances as the expression of a true form of drama, although some hieroglyphs dating from ca. 2000 B.C. (Figure 4) and found in Egyptian tombs, as well as Herodotus' reports from 449 B.C., do suggest that they contained rudimentary forms of dialogue, impersonation, and possibly music. It is of course impossible to evaluate these pagan performances as fundamental elements in the creation of meaning and speech, but they do remain the beginning of everything connected with the theatrical play, which, as it developed through the centuries, assumed significant dimensions and played a serious role in providing intellectual and spiritual nourishment for the individual. And when Greek civilization reached its peak, they influenced, as already mentioned, the Greek mystery cults, which in turn gave birth to the first complete theater we know of, a true theater that combined the early drama still surviving with a method of presenting it and an edifice to serve it.

2
Origin—The Greek Theater

The Meaning of the Term

In studying the development of the theater, it is necessary and useful to give prominent consideration to the Greek theater. In the broad view of the history of art, the Greek theater is not merely a unique form but a terminology, a self-contained body of concepts. When we use the term *Greek theater*, we are apt to think of the famous structures in Athens and Epidaurus or any of the other similar monuments in theater design that abound in Greece. Yet these playhouses, marvelous as they are, do not in themselves exhaust the meaning of the term; other forms of theater emerged later—and are still emerging—in many different places, based principally on the patterns and principles of the ancient Greek theater. It was only natural that this iteration should create a tradition, a terminology still revered today both in the field of architectural research and in the contemporary conception of meaning and speech in drama.[7]

The Greeks were the first to raise the dramatic performance to the level and stature of an art. Breaking away from its primitive antecedents, the Greek theater attained a cultural sublimity that was to bring about a profound and radical change in thought. The great Greek dramatists Aeschylus, Sophocles, Euripides, and Aristophanes, creators of the forms of tragedy and comedy, have been regarded as the prototypes of dramatic expression for centuries, and many modern playwrights continue to model their work on them.

Although the architectural forms of ancient Greek theaters fell into disuse for a long time, they were never overlooked or neglected in later studies of theater design and architectural research; they were variously applied and on different scales in subsequent explorations of ways to use available theater space to the best advantage. This research produced new forms, some of them based on elements of the Greek originals and some of them copies suited to the needs of each era.

Types of Greek Theater

During the centuries when Greek civilization developed and reached its peak, the theater as a concept kept pace with contemporary social and cultural developments. This occurred because it enjoyed widespread popular appeal, having been directly and closely interwoven with religious worship and the way of life of the people. It is nevertheless difficult to define an "ideal" form of the playhouse, particularly when such a thing does not exist. What does exist is a succession of types of theaters arising from changes in social concepts, habits, and customs—; a succession that kept in step with the evolution of Greek civilization from its peak to its decline and into the rise of Roman influence.

According to archeological evidence, this succession went through five main phases: the Minoan; the preclassical, or pre-Aeschylean; the classical Athenian, or Attic; the Hellenistic; and the Greco-Roman.

There is very little information about the Minoan theater. Excavations in Crete brought to light the theaters of Knossos and Phaestos, the

Figure 5. Theater of Knossos.
(Photo by author.)

only discoveries testifying to the form of theater in that period. According to Pierre Cailler, who considers them the oldest theaters in the world, the date of their construction must be placed somewhere between the twentieth and fifteenth centuries B.C.[8] They were probably used as court theaters for holding contests and ceremonial rites. This does not detract in the slightest from their importance as brilliant examples of architectural design. In the power and dynamic character of their form, with the rectangular tier disposition and geometrically shaped orchestra, they differ very little from our present-day conceptions (Figures 5–7).

Figure 6. Theater of Phaestos: general view. (Photo by author).

Figure 7. Theater of Phaestos the tiers (Photo by author).

As to the preclassical or pre-Aeschylean theater, there are no finds and no information. Certain assumptions put forward by Dörpfeld and Reisch lead to the conclusion that pre-Aeschylean theaters must have been wooden structures in the shape of a trapezium and not the semicircle encountered later.[9] Tiers of wooden benches surrounded a trapezoidal space that was later to be known as the orchestra (*drawing*). The date of development of this the-

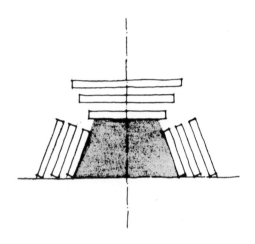

ater form, the existence of which has no interest other than purely historical, is a matter of conjecture. It must have been well before the fifth century B.C., since it is only from that century on that historians have been able to pick up the threads leading to the true dramatic form reflected in due course by the classic Athenian theater, the form that was to become the most important in the history of the theater.

The Hellenistic theater is considered the direct descendant of its classical Athenian predecessor; it evolved during the fourth century B.C., mostly in the Greek colonies, in pace with the developments in Greek culture and the conquests of Alexander the Great, which had a direct influence on its form.

Later, when the dividing line between Greek and Roman civilizations became vague because of the decline of the former and rapid rise of the latter, the Greco-Roman theater emerged. It joined with the Hellenistic to become the basic prototype in the evolution of subsequent theater forms, carrying the Greek conception down the centuries, influencing styles, modes, and playwrights. Although it may seem at first glance

that a Renaissance theater, an eighteenth-century opera house, an Elizabethan playhouse, and a twentieth-century experimental theater have nothing in common with the classical forms, a close study reveals that the roots of the tradition are there.

Before examining these theater types in detail, it is worth noting that, despite the great amount of archeological research and study devoted to the subject, our principal sources of information are still the writings of Aristotle, Pollux, and Vitruvius and the works of the Greek dramatists themselves. As a result, many questions remain unanswered, and many of the arguments advanced are open to discussion and dispute. The ruins of the famous Theater of Dionysus in Athens and other notable Greek theaters have yielded but scant clues to the actual mode of expression of the classical drama when it reached its culmination in the middle of the fifth century B.C.

Tragedy and Comedy

For the same reason, the origins of Greek tragedy and comedy are somewhat obscure. Nietzsche invokes almost all the principles of aesthetics in trying to trace the sources of Greek tragedy. In *The Birth of Tragedy* he writes:

I trust I shall not be thought unreasonable if I argue that not only has this problem of source not been solved, but that so far it has not even been seriously posed, although many have tried to patch together the tattered rags of ancient tradition. That tradition proclaims in the most categorical way that tragedy was born of the dance and that in the beginning it was dance and nothing but dance.[10]

It can be said that the source of tragedy should be sought in the choric dithyrambs sung in honor of the god Dionysus; in their original form these were improvised chants that later evolved into a medium of poetic and literary expression. In turning toward literary expression the dithyramb changed into a kind of choric hymn sung by the god's worshipers and conducted by a leader. Thespis, from Icaria in Attica, later converted the leader into an actor, or ὑποκριτής (*hypocrites*, impersonator), who spoke words that brought forth responses from the faithful.

This was the original form of dramatic dialogue, which, again according to Nietzsche, constitutes the Apollonian element of Greek drama.[11] The dramatic structure began to change; the hymns to the god were no longer the only motif of the performances. Social problems and recent historical events started to figure in the plot, sometimes in connection with religious worship and sometimes reflecting actual political and social events.

With this rather slow development, tragedy was born during the late sixth century B.C. The introduction of a second actor by Aeschylus (525–456 B.C.), and later of a third by Sophocles (496–406 B.C.), was the prime characteristic of this gradual evolution of the tragedy until it reached its culmination in the middle of the fifth century B.C. Lamentations by the actors and the chanting chorus were now interpolated in the performance. They were accompanied by movement, which began to assume a specific dance form. Lamentation and dance were introduced into the tragedy to connect the audience emotionally with the unfolding of the plot.

The performance did not depend on scenic effects; it was based on austerity and plainness of meaning and speech. For a long time, until the advent of Euripides (480–406 B.C.), the only hero taking the stage was Dionysus, the tragic hero who impersonated the great characters of Greek drama, including Prometheus and Oedipus.

The same process, more or less, took place in the emergence of comedy, which in its original form was also based on the worship of Dionysus. The word *comedy* comes from the Greek words κῶμος (*komos*, revel) and ὠδή (*ode*, song)—literally, songs sung by masked and cloaked citizens (the revelers) as they caroused in honor of Dionysus, singing derisive and ribald phallic songs. Apparently the chants of the chorus in comedy were often satiric lines addressed to the crowd of onlookers. This was bound to evoke a response, a sort of backchat that soon became part of the ritual. Thus the audience spontaneously assumed the form of a second chorus. And as these ribald improvisations developed into poetic and literary expression, comedy became distinct from tragedy because it used two choruses instead of one. Extensive use of the double chorus was made by Aristophanes (450–385 B.C.); in fact, it became the outstanding structural feature of his plays.[12]

The Classic Athenian Theater

The strong religious spirit and the direct link between worship and theater left no room for class distinctions and prejudice. As an essential cultural and spiritual nourishment of all classes, the theater was an institution that catered to the whole community. Accordingly, when the first theaters were being built, it was immediately apparent that they would need ample room to accommodate the multitudinous audiences of the time. The number of spectators exceeded 15,000, and the problem of accommodating such a large number of people was a fairly serious one. An equally important problem was the size of the acting area. The presence of the chorus, usually a large group, required plenty of room for the elaborate dance movements that accompanied the lyric verses.

The outdoors provided the only solution that could meet these requirements. At first, performances were held in the ἀγορά (agora, or marketplace) but as the need for room increased, they took place on low hills with slopes from which the spectators could get a better and unobstructed view. A large level area was laid out at the foot of the hill as an acting space for the performers, and the Greek theater, albeit in a still primitive form, was born. The level area was named the ὀρχήστρα (orchestra); a sacrificial altar, the θυμέλη (thymele), was placed in its center. The Greek verb θεᾶσθαι (theasthai, to view) generated a new word for a new concept—the θέατρον (theatron, theater). Starting with this conception of space in relation to the natural environment, the theater was embarked on a course of normal evolution based on rationality, simplicity, and functional need.

In its original form, then, the theater comprised two basic elements: the *orchestra* and the slope of a hill providing ample amphitheatrical space, the *theatron* or κοῖλον (koilon, hollow). Later, stepped tiers were hewn in the shape of concentric circular sections in the hillside around the orchestra to allow the audience a better view of the performers. The theater of Chaeronea (Figure 8)[13] is an excellent example of this arrangement.

It was not long before wooden seats were installed round the inner edge of the orchestra for the use of the archons and honored guests; later in the fifth century the tiers hewn in the rock

Figure 8. Theater of Chaeronea, hewn out of rock. (Photo by author.)

were replaced by wooden benches, or ἰκρία (*ikria*), forming a proper ἀμφιθέατρον (*amphitheatron*, amphitheater or auditorium). The amphitheater, however, had not yet acquired its definitive, truly semicircular shape. The use of wood, a difficult material to work in those days, led to angular shapes and ugly structures that blended poorly with the topography of the hillside; it was only when the use of stone and marble gained ground in the late fifth century B.C. that both orchestra and seats for the audience acquired their circular form. The spectators' seats were laid out concentrically around the now circular orchestra in arcs exceeding 180 degrees and often extended around two-thirds of the orchestra circle.[14]

Dörpfeld's excavations at the Theater of Dionysus (Figure 9) uncovered two orchestras, each of a different period. The older (fifth century B.C.) orchestra was found to be 24 meters in diameter, and its level surface could not have been obtained without banking at the rear to

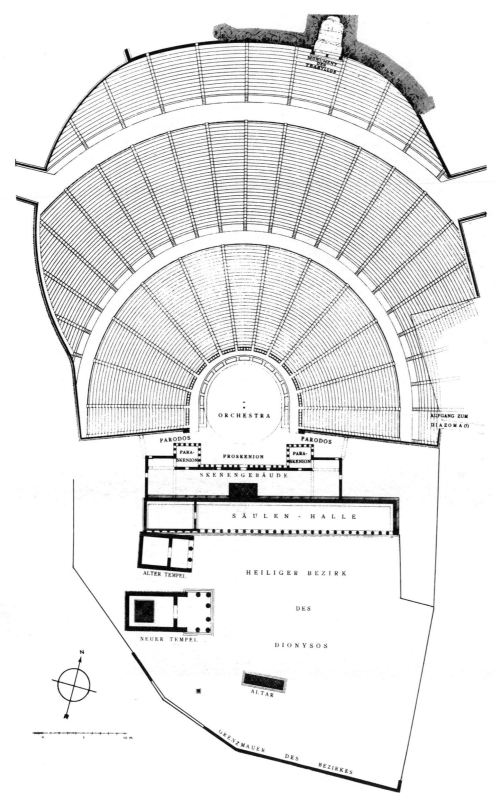

Figure 9. Theater of Dionysus: plan. (According to Dörpfeld and Reisch, Das griechische Theater; *author's archive.)*

Figure 10. Theater of Dionysus. (Above) General view. (Below) The position of the old and later orchestras, according to Dörpfeld and Reisch, Das griechische Theater. *(Photo and drawing by author.)*

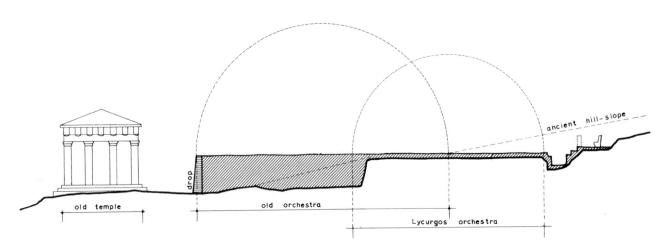

old temple

drop

old orchestra

Lycurgos orchestra

ancient hill-slope

offset the gradient of the Acropolis slope (Figure 10).[15] This created a two-meter drop at the back edge of the orchestra facing the old Temple of Dionysus. According to archeological observation, this orchestra arrangement was retained until 465 B.C., a fact that explains the settings and certain conventions in the earliest plays of Aeschylus. His *The Suppliants* (490 B.C.), *The Persians* (472 B.C.), and *Prometheus Bound* (470 B.C.) are all set in bare, open countryside devoid of any buildings; in *Prometheus Bound* the dramatist actually uses the drop as the edge of the abyss over which the hero disappears.[16]

With the introduction of the second actor and later the third, who according to the requirements of the play had to make their appearances before the audience from different points, the need arose for a roof to shelter them and all others connected with the performance. A wooden shed was the first, primitive form of a stage; it was erected behind the orchestra; it was later improved and added to as required, gradually becoming an important functional element of the Greek theater.[17]

In Athens, however, at the Theater of Dionysus, the proximity of the orchestra to the old temple of the god precluded such improvement and growth; this explains why the orchestra was later (in the fourth century B.C.) moved 15 meters to the north.[18] The new site was its second and final position, as preserved to date. The distance between temple and orchestra was thus increased, allowing construction of a small shed, at first wooden, for the exclusive use of the actors. The structure was named σκηνή (*skene*, scene-building), a covered place for purely practical purposes. It was soon realized that the side of the skene facing the spectators offered many opportunities and could be enhanced by ornamenting it with decorative elements, thereby creating a sort of scenic background. Thanks to this development, playwrights were no longer compelled to set their action in the open country; they could develop their plots in the setting of a palace or temple, using the scene-building as the facade and the orchestra as the area in front of the building.

This first use of scenic background was of course primitive in its initial form. The skene was an improvised wooden structure, and the decorative designs were purely geometric and symbolic. It was only after 425 B.C., during the last quarter of the fifth century, that the skene, though still made of wood, became a somewhat more permanent and elaborate structure, erected on a marble or stone foundation. It consisted of a front wall more than 30 meters long facing the orchestra and auditorium, with projecting wings, the παρασκήνια (*paraskenia*), at the sides (Figure 9). In the wall were doors—first one, then three, then five—through which the actors entered the orchestra. These doors played an important part in the overall structure of the play, whether tragedy or comedy. In the classical period the actors entered the orchestra directly from the skene, whereas in the Hellenistic theater the skene was fronted by a kind of stage known as the προσκήνιον (*proskenion, proscenium*) that extended between the two projecting wings. The floor of this stage was raised one to two meters above the level of the orchestra and was supported by a wall adorned on the audience side either with sculptured designs (Figure 11) or columns (Figure 12). The proscenium was also called λογεῖον (*logeion*, speaking podium) or θεολογεῖον (*theologeion*, podium of the deities); the doors in the front wall of the skene were on the level of the proscenium.[19]

Figure 11. Theater of Dionysus: sculptured proscenium. (Photo by author.)

Figure 12. Sanctuary of Amphiaraeion, Attica (above) and plan of orchestra (opposite). Note the parodi *and the reconstructed proscenium. The decorative supporting wall has been replaced by columns. (Photo by author; plan according to Dörpfeld and Reisch* Das Griechische Theater; *author's archive)*

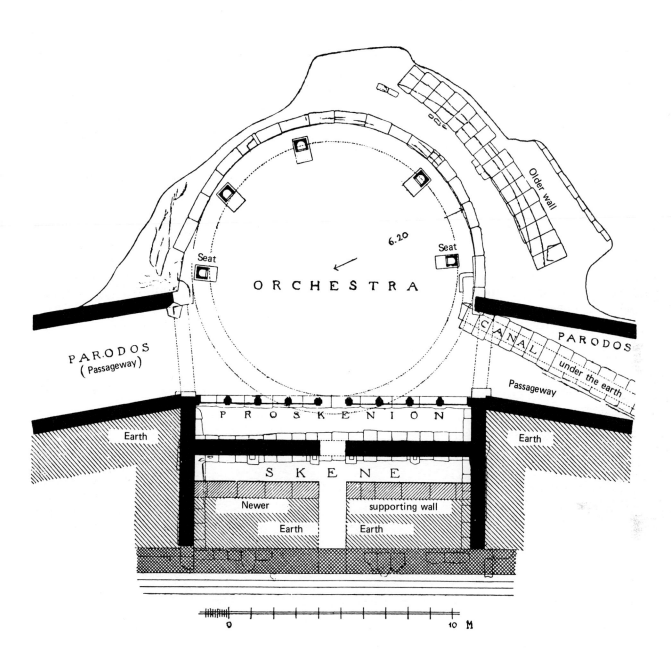

ORCHESTRA

6.20

Seat   Seat

Older wall

PARODOS
(Passageway)

CANAL

PARODOS

under the earth

Passageway

P R O S K E N I O N

Earth   Earth

S K E N E

Newer   supporting wall

Earth   Earth

0   10 M

The proscenium has been used very widely as a basic element of theater space; it is, in fact, the only element preserved almost intact in all subsequent forms of the theater.[20] Because of the proscenium, it is reasoned, the scene-building must have been a two-story structure (Figure 13). The upper story—the top part of the front wall—was called the ἐπισκήνιον (*episkenion*) and was utilized for the μηχαναί (*mechanae*, machines).[21]

Two passageways, known as the πάροδοι (*parodi*), were formed between the scene-building and the supporting walls of the auditorium intersecting the oblique lines formed by the seats. These too were used extensively by playwrights in plotting their action. One *parodos* served as an entrance from the agora and the center of the city; the other was the approach from the suburbs and provinces.[22] The *parodi* later became major decorative and morphological elements, particularly after the fourth century B.C., when marble and stone came into general use; often, as can be seen in the Theater of Epidaurus (Figure 1), they were adorned with richly sculptured gates.

As already noted, in most theaters up to the close of the fifth century B.C., there is no evidence to convince us that the scene-buildings were made of stone. Wood was the staple and predominant material. However, this restriction did not prevent the elaboration and development of the scenic background to a more advanced level. For many centuries the palace prevailed as the dominant scenic illusion; it survived as an almost permanent element until the Renaissance and the rise of the Italian theater.

Figure 13. Theater of Dionysus: ruins of the two-story scene-building. The influence of later periods on the orchestra and proscenium is apparent. (Photo by author.)

The Hellenistic Theater

In the fourth century B.C. Alexander the Great amassed a huge empire that spread Hellenism over vast territories. As a result, Greek civilization was subjected to the influence of the mores and folkways of cultures foreign to it. These events had a considerable and profound effect on established social conditions. Inevitably theatrical form and conception were also affected; the religious influence began to disappear from dramatic works, and a more realistic attitude gradually prevailed in episode and dialogue. Euripides had already brought a realistic note to the theater by using the chorus in a way different from that of Aeschylus and Sophocles.[23] In their plays the chorus played a very active part in the action, to the point, one could say, of dominating the performance. With Euripides the chorus receded to a secondary role, one less vigorous and only minimally accented; sometimes it was confined to merely lyric hymns weakly related to the plot, the purpose of which usually was to bridge gaps in the action. What is more, the imposing tragic grandeur of Aeschylus' written word and the equally tragic intensity in Sophocles' plays began to decline. Tragedy was becoming "civilized," polished; its structure was changing, shedding those attributes that were beginning to lose appeal for the individual. Emphasis and complex action were starting to be used, driving toward new, sophisticated forms of dramatic expression. Nietzsche places the entire blame for this gradual decline of the importance of the written word squarely on Euripides: "What were you trying to accomplish, profane Euripides, when you forced that dying creature to obey you once more? . . . Yet the myth was dead for you, and so music deserted you." Further on he writes: "Greek tragedy did not vanish like the other ancient arts, but in a wholly different manner. It annihilated itself by committing suicide in the most tragic way."[24]

Figure 14. Theater of Epidaurus, during a performance of Euripides' Hekabe. *(Photo by D.A. Harissiadis. Reprinted by permission.)*

Figure 15. Theater of Megalopolis: general view (above) and plan (opposite). (Photo by author; plan according to Fiechter, Antike griechische Theaterbauten; *author's archive.)*

While tragedy deteriorated, comedy showed the same symptoms of decline. The Old Comedy form, in which Aristophanes created his masterpieces, changed gradually until with the plays of Menander (342–291 B.C.) it attained the more realistic form of the New Comedy, which bears the stamp of Euripides' influence[25] and in which, according to Nietzsche, "the degenerated form of tragedy survives as a monument to its painful and violent end."[26] New Comedy had ordinary people as its heroes, it created plot and emphasis, it introduced farce and the unexpected.

As in tragedy, the chorus became something of a burden; Menander used it only to fill gaps in the action.

Naturally, after all these substantial changes in the structure of the play itself, the classic playhouse in its original form no longer served its purpose. The requirements and demands of the times had changed. The theater underwent reorientation, and the concept that its primary aim and function was worship of the gods lost currency.[27] The new social order was no longer satisfied with the simplicity and austerity of a

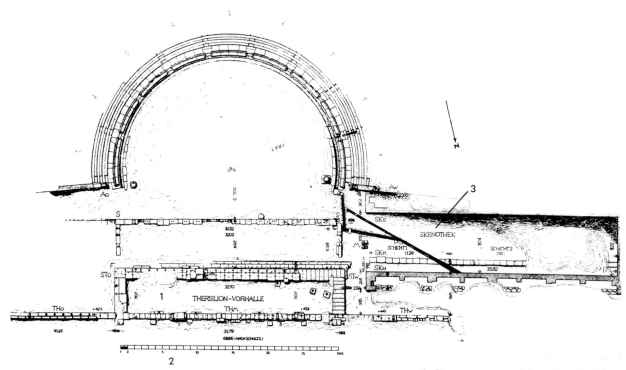

1. *Proscenium and thersileion's lobby*
2. *Thersileion*
3. *Scenery storage*

bare Aeschylean landscape or an imposing Sophoclean choric passage. New demands arose, and new thoughts on scenic presentation influenced theater architecture. Without completely altering the classic form, which remained essentially the same, these changes nevertheless led to the opening up of fresh prospects and the development of new functions and concepts.

Generally acknowledged as the most important and representative examples of this period are the theaters of Epidaurus (Figures 1, 14), Megalopolis (Figure 15), Argos (Figure 16), and Eretria (Figure 17); together with certain other smaller playhouses, such as the theaters of Amphiaraeion at Oropos (Figure 12), and Delphi

(Figure 18), they give us a picture of the period and a clear insight into its problems.[28]

The principal architectural change concerned the scene-building itself. Whereas previously all the weight and importance was given to the orchestra exclusively, in the Hellenistic theaters the scene-building was perhaps the only area to undergo thorough conversion. This is hardly surprising, since it was the natural consequence of the change in the mode of dramatic expression mentioned earlier. The *koilon*, or hollow, of the theater retained its semicircular shape. At Eretria, however, the arc stopped at 180 degrees, and straight sections were added at the ends to form a σφενδόνη (*sphendone*, sling) (Figure 17).[29]

Figure 16. Theater of Argos. (Above) General view. (Below) Plan. (Photo by author; plan according to Fiechter, Antike griechische Theaterbauten; *author's archive.)*

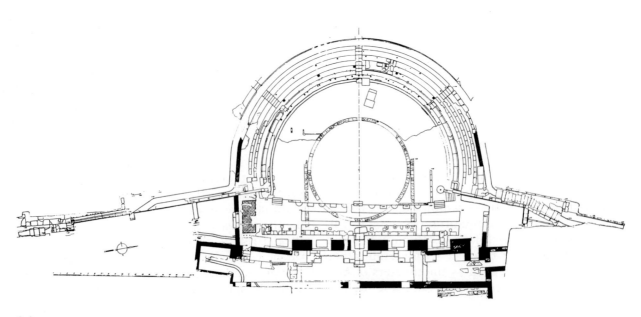

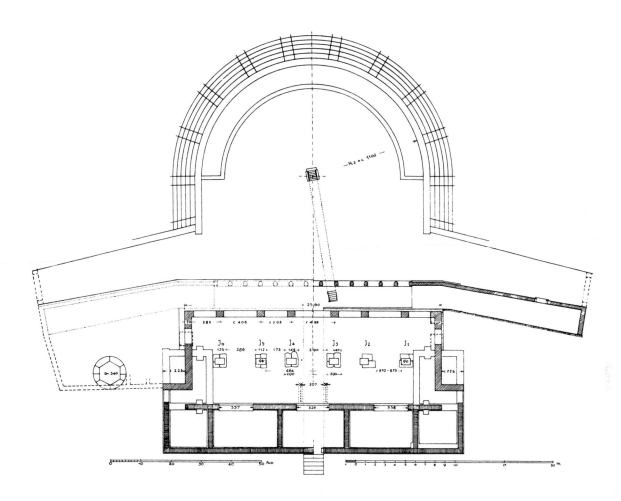

Figure 17. Theater of Eretria: plan. (According to Fiechter, Antike griechische Theaterbauten; *author's archive.)*

Figure 18. Theater of Delphi. (Photo by author.)

The Hellenistic proscenium, like the classic Athenian, was supported by a line of pillars. The spaces between the pillars, however, were closed with wooden panels, the πίνακες (*pinaces*), which were usually painted. The action of the play now took place on the proscenium, and the orchestra was used almost exclusively by the chorus. The front wall of the scene-building behind the actors, as mentioned before, now had decorative designs, and its openings, the ϑυρώματα (*thyromata*, doors), were also boarded over with wooden panels; the attempt to create realistic scenery was evident.[30]

At the same time that the acting area developed, substantial changes were made in the other buildings of the stage. The increased requirements of the plays being presented necessitated additional service areas; storerooms and places where the actors could rest and prepare for their entry were added. Through sophisticated architectural design, the theaters began to acquire a monumental form and character. It can be asserted that in the Hellenistic period the theater emerged from its primeval state and started on its process of development. By the end of the third century B.C. it had reached a point of refined perfection that was an easy target for the alterations soon to come with the advent of the Roman era and its powerful influences, culminating in the new type known as the Greco-Roman theater. This type was to withstand the passage of centuries and the desolate stretch of the Dark Ages, reemerging during the Elizabethan period and becoming the nucleus of playhouse design. Later, in the twentieth century, it served as the basic inspiration for the theater-in-the-round and the open-stage theater.

The Greco-Roman Theater

During the second century B.C. the Greek theater underwent changes imposed upon it by the thinking and concepts of the conquering Romans. These changes, which were to lead directly to the Roman playhouse proper, produced an intermediate architectural type that has come to be known as the Greco-Roman theater. Although it developed chiefly in the Greek colonies flourishing at the time—Termessos (Figure 19), Magnesia, Ephesus[31]—there were examples of the Greco-Roman theater in Greece itself, in

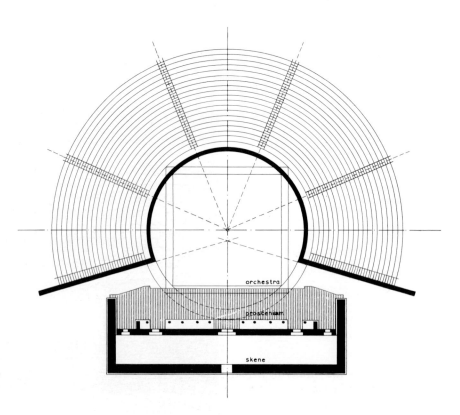

Figure 19. Theater of Termessos: plan. (Drawing by author.)

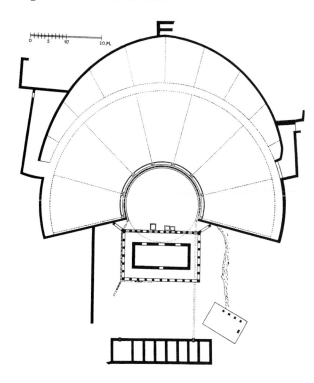

places such as Delos (Figure 20),[32] Messene (Figure 21),[33] Gytheion, Santorin (Figure 22), and other centers. But besides those typical theaters of the period, many Hellenistic theaters also display intermingled elements of later eras, which makes it difficult to draw a sharp dividing line between the two periods.

Figure 20. Theater of Delos: plan. (According to Dörpfeld and Reisch, Das griechische Theater; *author's archive.)*

Figure 21. The small theater of Messene (now Ithomi). (Photo by author.)

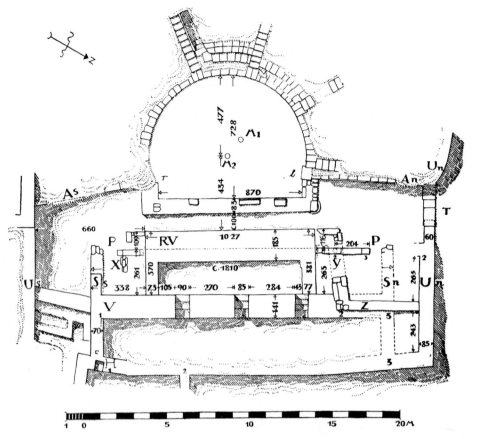

Figure 22. Theater of Santorin: plan. (According to Fiechter, Antike griechische Theaterbauten; *author's archive.)*

The *koílon* kept its familiar shape, but the orchestra underwent a conversion. The entire
scene-building was brought forward, changing
the shape of the orchestra from a full circle to a
segment; now its circumference is no longer tan-
gent to the proscenium but to the front wall of
the scene-building (Figure 19). Thus the proscenium advances into the orchestra to a point
usually midway along its radius (drawing); it
grows more spacious and acquires ample depth,
sometimes as much as six meters or more. Its
height above the level of the orchestra diminishes, and as a functional element it assumes
greater importance. On the audience side the
corridor between the orchestra and tiers is
eliminated, and the lowest row of seats now borders directly on the circumference of the orchestra itself.

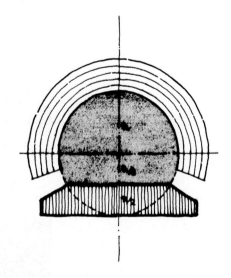

In studying the Greco-Roman theater a nascent trend to endow the stage with greater stateliness can be discerned. Variety and showiness were indispensable attributes of the play, a sign of the changing social attitudes of the times. The theater had long since ceased to serve exclusively as a locus of religious ceremonies and had therefore lost much of the popular appeal it enjoyed in the fifth and early fourth centuries B.C. It catered no longer to all classes of society but only to a certain portion of the urban community. Its size and seating capacity shrank; it was no longer on a scale comparable to that of the theaters of Dionysus and Epidaurus, which could hold 16,000 to 20,000 spectators.

The theater gradually lost much of its erstwhile importance. It became entertainment rather than an end in itself. Plays no longer had their former power, their tragic significance, and their impact on the individual. It must not be forgotten that in the peak period of Greek civilization, particularly the fifth century B.C., the play was a major event attended by everyone from the supreme archon to the humblest citizen, and it lasted from sunrise to sunset. The power of meaning and speech was the only force that held the interest of this multitude; the artificial attractions of scenic devices were unknown and of no concern to theatergoers.

The passage of years, however, with the influence of foreign forces and cultures, wrought changes in people's thinking and in public tastes and trends. The individual was no longer content with simplicity and austerity of expression, desiring instead new sensations, new patterns. Later, when the distinction between plebeians and patricians became sharper, the way had already been paved for the transition of the theater from pure Greek to Roman.

Scenic Conventions—Machines

Before concluding the discussion of Greek theater, some mention must be made of the first attempts to achieve scenic effects, the search for a way to express by means other than movement and speech certain dramatic situations that called for stronger emphasis. The fact that all theaters were open-air edifices made it impossible to develop complex scenic effects or mechanical contrivances. This does not mean there were

no such effects; there was, in fact, a set of devices that were frequently used to enhance the performance and to portray actions that could not be conveyed by verbal description alone.

The earliest permanent theatrical device was, as mentioned, the drop behind the orchestra (Figure 10) that was used by Aeschylus in his early plays. Later, when the front wall of the scene-building became standard, together with the three *thyromata*, or doorways, most plays were performed against a scenic background in the form of a palace or temple. The middle door—the βασίλειος θύρα (*basileios thyra*, royal door)—was generally the main entrance to the palace, and it was from here that the protagonist in the drama or the archon and the members of his family made their appearance on stage.[34] The doorway to the right was used for the entrance of the second actor or was assumed to lead to the palace guest quarters, while the doorway to the left was used by the palace staff and slaves or led to a fictitious desert or prison. These entrances served the action and plot of the play when it took place in and around the palaces, but characters approaching it from the outside used the two *parodi*, one of which, as we have seen, led to the agora and the other to the outskirts of the city or the battlefield.[35]

All these features were permanent symbolic conventions, used in virtually all tragedies. But at the same time there was an attempt to create scenery of a kind readily adaptable to the requirements of the plays. Aristotle attributes the first such attempt to Sophocles, and Vitruvius credits it to Aeschylus.[36] What is certain is that the panels below the proscenium served not only to cover the gaps between the supporting pillars but also as a means of presenting a measure of scenic background.

The περίακτοι (*periakti*) (Figure 23) are described by Pollux and Vitruvius as revolving triangular prisms, each side of which bore a design.[37] The precise position of the *periaktos* on the stage has not been determined; it is assumed that it was installed in front of the flanking doorways and that the one depicted landscapes while the other showed scenes from the life of the city.

The Onomasticon, by Pollux (second century B.C.), is the leading source of information concerning the various devices used for scenic effects during the Hellenistic period and later.[38]

Figure 23. Periaktos. *(Drawing by author, after a suggestion by Frank Whiting.)*

Figure 24. Eccyclema. *(Drawing by author, after a suggestion by Frank Whiting.)*

The ἐκκύκλημα (*eccyclema*) (Figure 24) was a small platform used for the presentation of dead bodies and murder victims; it was used frequently in tragedies, along with a variation known as the ἐξώστρα (*exostra*), the same kind of platform fitted with wheels, which allowed the body to be pushed out.[39]

The μηχανή (*mechané*, machine) (Figure 25) was the most common and widely used of all scenic devices. It consisted of a simple system of ropes and pulleys mounted on the upper left part of the stage wall and was used to lower and raise characters representing the deities. The contrivance appeared often in the plays of Euripides and Aristophanes toward the close of the fifth century B.C. It gave rise to the phrase "god brought by the machine," later adopted by the Romans in the expression "deus ex machina."[40] In some of the tragedies the machine is variously referred to by other names—ϑεολογεῖον (*theologeion*, rostrum of the gods), γερανός (*geranos*, crane), ἀέτωμα (*aetoma*, pediment), αἰώρα (*aeora*, suspension machine)—and, in the comedies, κράδη (*crade*, fig branch), as listed also by Pollux.

The σκοπή (*scopé*, roughly translatable as the watching post) was, according to Pollux, the place from which the master of the play observed the performance; the τεῖχος (*teichos*, wall),

πύργος (*pyrgos*, tower), and διστεγία (*distegia*, literally the second floor) were elevated parts of the stage used by the actor as the plot required.

The κεραυνοσκοπεῖον (*ceraunoscopeion*, literally thunderbolt-scope) has been described as a kind of *periaktos;* its three sides were painted with designs of thunderbolts and streaks of lightning on a black background. An integral accessory to this device was the βροντεῖον (*bronteion*, thunder-making machine), consisting of a jar and a copper tray. The jar was filled with pebbles, and these were emptied onto the tray whenever the sound effect of a thunderbolt was called for.

The στροφεῖον (*stropheion*, rotator) was a revolving contraption painted with pictures of heroes fallen on the battlefield or of persons who had followed the gods. "Charon's staircase" and the *anapiesmata*, finally, were simply trapdoors, probably in the orchestra, out of which emerged the ghosts of dead heroes from Hades.

In concluding this list, the important part played by masks must not be overlooked, the use of which is practically coeval with the birth of ancient drama.[41] The actors used these masks for various effects, notably as a device enabling them to play the parts of two or more heroes in the play or to portray female characters, since the actors in the Greek theater ware always men.

Figure 25. Machine. (Drawing by author, after a suggestion by Frank Whiting.)

and were subsequently adopted for the Greco-Roman theater. The fact is, a trend to create stage effects existed as far back as the ancient period. This supports the theory that the Greek theater, with the passage of the centuries and the changes wrought in the character and attitudes of the people, lost the austerity it had in the sixth and fifth centuries B.C. It is revealing to note that in the early days the playwright was strictly forbidden to present his audience with scenes of violence or murder or even to display the dead body of the victim. It follows that the *eccyclema* and the *exostra* must be regarded as highly revolutionary elements in the history of the tragedy. Before the introduction of these devices, such scenes were narrated by a messenger or a slave who, leaning against the palace door, described the crime in sad, mournful tones. With the *eccyclema*, the playwright could now at least present the victim's body to the shocked and frightened gaze of the spectator. Thus realism was first introduced into tragedy, establishing a new form of drama that, with the passage of the centuries and the ever-diminishing importance of speech, would eventually develop into the drama as we know it today.

It is difficult to determine exactly when these mechanical devices came into use. Pollux claims that they first appeared in the Hellenistic theater

3
The Roman Theater

The Influence of
the Greeks

As trading developed and people began to travel more often to distant places, the Greek spirit and culture, with its advanced civilization and established art forms, gradually flowed beyond the limited boundaries of Greece. As early as the seventh century B.C., Greek works of art were being exported, and influencing the art in other nations, both in Europe and in Asia.

This early influence combined later with the conquests of Alexander the Great to prepare the ground for a gradual Hellenization, a dissemination of Greek culture that gave birth to new civilizations. Though never attaining a full comprehension of the Greek ideal, these civilizations assimilated the elements of that culture, modified its traditions to suit their own needs, and were impelled to evolve new concepts of representation and expression.

One such civilization was the Etruscan, which was the foundation on which the Romans built their own. The Greek tradition was embraced enthusiastically by the Etruscan cities of central Italy long before the Romans created their vast empire and developed, along with their military genius, their own cultural orientation. The Romans had already come into contact in Etruria with Greek cultural themes and modes of expression. When toward the close of the first century B.C.[42] Rome finally gained control over all the Greek kingdoms, the Romans eagerly embraced the Greek tradition and made it the foundation of their cultural and artistic infrastructure.

However, the spectacularly swift growth of the Roman state, its great wealth, sense of power, and arrogant egocentricity of being the victor never allowed the Romans, as they had never allowed the Etruscans, to gain an insight into and an understanding of the aims, the motivations, the deeper meaning and the more profound concepts of Greek civilization. The Romans never sought to identify the prime movers that for centuries had fired and quickened the civilization they so effortlessly took over; they cared only for its tangible benefits. They adopted its architectural forms for use in their own lifestyle, their own *weltanschauung*. But the iterative reproduction of a form merely because it is,

or once was, popular, a form unrelated to the function it is supposed to serve, undeniably leads to its corruption and alienation from the purpose for which it was originally created. Inevitably the Greek tradition, created at different times according to various social ideals or under differing political systems, though irresistibly seductive as a concept no longer satisfied the increased demands of society. The result was a gradual vitiation of the Greek element under the effect of the growing Roman influence.

Purity of architectural form gave way to a strong predilection for elaborate decorative detail. Taste changed in all domains of arts and letters, particularly in architecture. Austerity in speech and writing and geometry and harmony in rhythm were discarded as inapplicable. They were replaced by a florid narrative idiom, spectacular public shows, and hybrid, highly decorated, and fussy architectural styles.

This change naturally affected everything to do with the theater, from the playhouse to the play itself. The religious element disappeared completely from the works of the Roman playwrights, the exact opposite of what we find in the classical works of the Greeks. The Roman drama discarded all elements connected with worship or the temple.

The playhouse emulated the splendor and luxury of the palaces and temples constantly being built around it. Its site was no longer a hollow in the hills but the center of the city, where it stood as an independent monument.[43] For quite some time tragedy and comedy retained traces of the influence of Euripides and Menander, but they were adjusted to the taste of a public that now wanted spectacles, not nourishment for the mind. The plots of the plays began to include spectacular parades of victorious troops, prisoners from conquered nations, processions of horses, and onstage displays of strange, unknown beasts brought from the far-flung empire's subject lands.

Sudden prosperity and newly acquired wealth, perhaps the most telling test of an individual or a nation, had a fateful effect on the mind and character of the people. The theater became a spectacle, and the spectacle had to be splendiferous to impress and sway the masses. Wealthy citizens sponsored free performances, either to show off their affluence or to celebrate victorious campaigns. Meaning and speech all but disappeared from the stage; the actor, who in Greece had been privileged and honored, was disdained and considered socially debased, a person of no repute and unworthy of respect; often the actor was a slave who could be called upon to sacrifice his very life on the altar of entertainment.

In republican and imperial Rome alike, feasts and festivals were the only theme and medium of popular cultural entertainment. At the time when Augustus turned the republic into an empire, there were 76 public holidays a year, and 55 of these were feast days celebrated with theatrical spectaculars. Later the number increased to the point where holidays and public festivals accounted for six months out of the year: 101 days were occasions for theatrical performances, 64 for chariot races, and 10 for gladiatorial contests.[44]

With the advent of this new mentality, the theater, as was to be expected, ceased to have an intellectual or religious function; it· changed from an art form to a medium for entertainment. The subsequent decline of the Roman empire swept the theater with it in its fall, relegating it to obscurity for many centuries to come. To the Christian faith, spreading apace, the theater and all things connected with it were sinful; its every aspect had to be extirpated lest it recall pagan feasts. The Greek and Roman theaters were converted to fortresses or housing for the masses, and many were demolished to provide building materials for more essential structures. The spirit of tragedy and comedy was buried and lost under the new theanthropic doctrines, and many centuries passed before it again surfaced and became the archetypal source for dramatists, from the fifteenth century to the present day, who aspire to master the true expression of meaning and speech.

The Form of Roman Drama

The fact that drama, when Rome was at the summit of her greatness, had been divested of its religious elements does not mean that the same was true during the first years of the Roman state. The Etruscans had developed a form of drama based on the Athenian Dionysian prototypes. This form was influenced by the cere-

monials of predominantly peasant people who paid tribute to their gods at times of harvesting and sowing; its evolution was further reinforced by the feasts and ceremonies that marked social events such as births, weddings, and deaths.

This tradition naturally affected the then-fledgling state of Rome, and it is believed that the first ritual drama was presented in Rome in 364 B.C. in an attempt to propitiate the gods during an epidemic that was decimating the city's inhabitants.[45] This early experience appears to have made a strong impression on the Romans, who from then on were quick to adopt every form of Etruscan drama, thereby creating a mode of meaning and speech that formed the first stage in the evolution of Roman tragedy and comedy.

The process received added impetus from the Greek colonists in Sicily, who had brought with them their native passion for erecting theaters and who staged there all the great Greek tragedies and comedies. The Romans learned a great deal from them. When the Greek city of Tarentum was captured in 272 B.C., the way was clear for the introduction of authentic Greek drama to the newborn civilization of Rome.

The seeds of such highly developed ideas, however, fell on soil that was as yet untilled. In those days the Romans were inflexible and rough-hewn fighting men, materialists insensible to culture or art, and they could not easily grasp the lofty and austere meanings of an Aeschylus or the tragic genius of a Sophocles. Faced with such a wealth of material, they naturally chose those elements most readily adaptable to their intellectual capacities. Euripides, the tragedian, and Menander, the comic playwright, were the Greek playwrights who influenced the Roman drama most directly. So pervasive was their influence that the Roman dramatists of the day were unwilling to introduce original views of their own; as a result, plays written by Romans featured Greek heroes in Greek dress in an Athenian setting. Roman tragedy never succeeded in progressing beyond a poor imitation of the works of the Greek tragedians. Comedy, on the other hand, patterned on the Greek New Comedy, was more successful, but the result was almost totally lacking in originality and was pervaded by Roman qualities.

Although a not inconsiderable number of playwrights appeared on the Roman scene through the years, the only ones worth noting are Seneca (3 B.C.–A.D. 65) in tragedy and Plautus (254–184 B.C.) and Terence (195–159 B.C.) in comedy.[46]

Both forms, however, were very soon to lose even those few elements of Greek influence they had so far retained. It was hardly likely that Seneca, who lived in the first century of the Christian era, a statesman, senator, philosopher, and a contemporary of Caligula and Nero, could master the profundity of Aeschylus' verbal beauty or Euripides' emotional fervor. The austerity of the fifth century B.C. was in disaccord with the magnificence and luxury of the first century A.D., and, although he dramatized the figures of Oedipus, Medea, and Agamemnon, Seneca was unable to give expression to the emotional and spiritual exaltation that inspired the true creators of the original masterpieces.

Poetry was lost in rhetoric, sincerity was replaced by illusion; action became violent, tough, and full of mannerism. The spectator, who according to Nietzsche[47] had been transported by Euripides onto the stage itself and made a true critical appraiser of the play, was now returned to his appointed place, isolated, barred from participating; all communication and identification with the actor disappeared, not to reemerge for many centuries.

Plautus and Terence, perhaps because they antedated Seneca by a couple of centuries and were therefore less in thrall to Roman megalomania, did not succumb to the popular demand for crude humor and farce. Although their plays were patterned after the Greek models, they managed to instill the Roman character and mentality into the borrowed themes of their comedies.

The time when these two dramatists produced their work was, in effect, the only period when Roman comedy can be said to have flourished. But it was inevitable that the kind of comedy performed during this brief hundred-year time span should sink into oblivion and soon be supplanted by a clutter of new plays, spectacularly ostentatious and farcical, that were more readily intelligible and closer to the lowered standards of individual and social thinking.

Tragedy and comedy were never again to attain the monumental form and poetic perfection of the fifth century B.C. The time was past when Greek civilization might have had a more pro-

found influence and carried its achievements intact through the Roman era. Rome, at the peak of her power, was making her own history, creating her own creeds, forging her own culture and thought. The Roman citizen was no longer the crude, hardened warrior who pushed his country's boundaries from the banks of the Tiber to the banks of the Euphrates, the aggressive youth whose first concern and occupation was to train himself in the art of war, to steel his character to feats of bravery and patriotism. Mores and conventions underwent radical change; the all-important task of exploiting and augmenting their great wealth left the Romans with little time—or desire—for education. Intellectual pursuits, the refinements of meaning and speech, were outmoded in an age when the roll of drums and the cries of the gladiators had become daily fare. These developments, together with the rise of Christianity, caused drama to decline into decadence and, finally, into an oblivion lasting many centuries. What is truly paradoxical is that when the Rennaissance brought a revival of the tragic and comic dramatic forms, it was the Roman style that prevailed; it was thought to be the most representative. Seneca was considered to be the best tragic playwright, and Roman drama became the model for all theatrical productions. It was only in the nineteenth century that the Greek tradition again received the attention and esteem it deserved; due and full recognition of the Greek theater followed, and the genius of Aeschylus, Sophocles, and Euripides came into its own.

Architectural Form

The various phases in the evolution of Roman drama were closely followed by parallel developments in the architectural form of the theaters of the time. It has been established that up to the early third century B.C. there were, properly speaking, no theaters in the Roman state save for some makeshift wooden stages-cum-scaffolding used for performances of farces popular with the crowd or for productions of Etruscan drama. It is believed that the first Roman stage, still made of wood, was erected in 364 B.C. at the Circus Maximus for the appearance of a troupe of Etruscan performers.[48]

Later, after Tarentum was captured, Romans came into contact with the advanced forms of Greek theaters, both in the colonies of southern Italy and in metropolitan Greece itself; they developed an avid interest in all things Greek, in everything connected with letters and the arts, including architecture in general and theatrical architecture in particular. Despite all this enthusiasm, it was a very long time before a complete and fully equipped theater building was erected. In Plautus' and Terence's day makeshift wooden structures were still used. As late as 194 B.C. seats were provided only for senators, and when the first stone stage was built in 174 B.C., the spectators still had to bring their own chairs.[49]

The first attempt to build a permanent theater has been dated to 154 B.C., five years after the death of Terence; but by order of the Senate the structure was pulled down before it had been completed. According to the spirit of the times, which prescribed austerity and plain living for the citizens, an establishment of this kind would pose a serious threat to the militaristic way of life and would endanger the strict self-discipline and ascetic self-denial demanded of its populace by the developing state. Moreover, a feeling of abhorrence prevailed in the still republican Rome against anything new or anything considered likely to engender a taste for soft living and luxury. Under a law enacted in 185 B.C., the construction of seating tiers in the amphitheaters was prohibited, and the spectators were not allowed to watch the performance sitting down. These prohibitive measures, basically a result of the contempt felt by the Roman republic for the "effete" conquered Greeks, did not prevent the Romans themselves, with the passage of time, from indulging in a much more debilitating form of luxury, a propensity for ostentation, an overweening and vainglorious self-adulation.

At this time the fundamental difference between the two peoples' conceptions of the function of the theater was already apparent. A cardinal principle of the Greek theater was that the spectators' area "embraces" the orchestra, the acting area, thus functionally uniting the one with the other (*drawing* a); the Roman theater preferred this relationship to be a confrontation (*drawing* b). The action was placed opposite the audience, not among it. The two functions were separated. The Romans retained the general

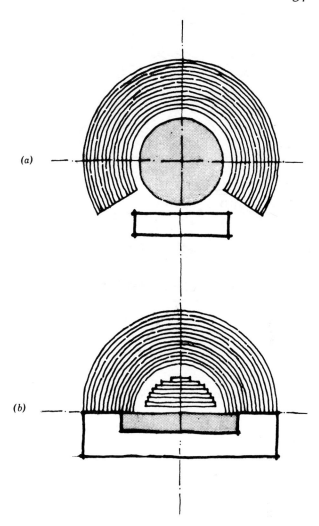

(a)

(b)

shape of the theater hollow, the *koilon*, but for functional and structural purposes abandoned the extended segment in favor of a strictly semicircular section. The orchestra was thus converted to a semicircle; it was no longer part of the acting area but part of the bowl, furnished with seats reserved for members of the Senate and other officials. The *parodi* were dispensed with and the *koilon*, now called the *cavea*, was in direct contact with the scene-building, a structure made progressively more magnificent and ornate.[50]

These differences are characteristically represented and clearly discernible in the plan of a Roman theater given by Vitruvius in his *Ten Books on Architecture* (Figure 26) and in the great Theater of Marcellus in Rome (Figure 27). The term *proskenion*, latinized to *proscaenium*, was

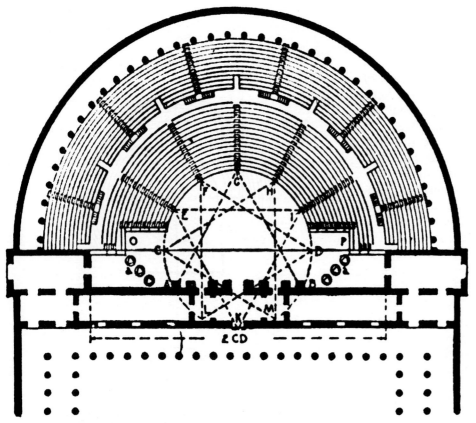

Figure 26. Plan of a Roman theater. (According to Vitruvius; author's archive.)

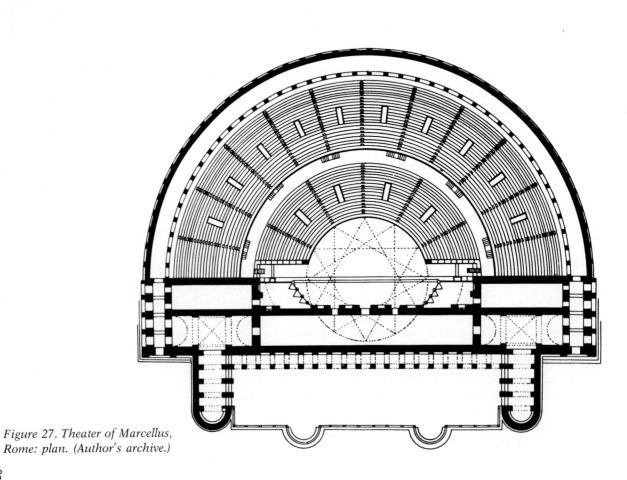

Figure 27. Theater of Marcellus,
Rome: plan. (Author's archive.)

38

now applied to the entire acting area; the floor of the orchestra was considerably lower, and the stage itself acquired greater depth. The front wall of the scene-building, now known as the *scaenae frons*, became a massive structure, ornately magnificent and majestically proportioned. The elaborate ornamentation, the Roman taste for high style in architecture, are prominently displayed in the reconstructed *scaenae frons* of the Theater of Aspendus (Figure 28).[51]

On the subject of these changes to the scene-building, Vitruvius writes: "The platform had to have greater depth than the Greek, since our actors perform on the stage alone, the orchestra containing seats reserved for senators. The height of this platform must not be greater than 1.5 meters so that those seated in the orchestra can see the expression and the movement of all the actors."[52]

The three basic functional components of the theater—the auditorium, the orchestra, and the scene-building—were thus brought together in a single body to form an integral architectural whole whereas in the Greek theater the three elements were independent. From an open space the Roman theater gradually evolved into a building, and it was eventually realized that there was no need to use sloping hillsides as a bed to support the amphitheater. Instead the tiers of seats and the structure as a whole were supported by high surrounding walls.[53]

Figure 28. Reconstructed scaenae frons *of the Theater of Aspendus. (Nicoll,* Development of the Theatre, *p. 28. Reprinted by permission.)*

The imposing theater built by Pompey in 55 B.C.—the first in Rome to be constructed of stone—became the original model for dozens of later structures, among them the Theater of Marcellus in Rome (Figures 27, 29), the Theater of Aspendus (Figures 27, 30), and the Theater of Orange (Figure 31). The towering walls of the facades allowed Roman architects to give full play to their fertile imagination and to decorate them with gorgeous statues, arches, and vaults.

Figure 29. Theater of Marcellus, as it was in the eighteenth century. (Etching by Piranesi; author's archive.)

Figure 30. Etching of the Theater of Aspendus. (Nicoll, Development of the Theatre, *p. 40. Reprinted by permission.)*

Figure 31. Roman theaters and odea: (a) Theater of Orange, first century A.D. *(Nicoll, Development of the Theatre, p. 44. Reprinted by permission.) (b) Odeum of Herod Atticus, first century* A.D., *prepared for a modern performance. (Photo by author.)*

In contrast to the Greek theater, where the spectators used the *parodi* to enter the amphitheater, access to the Roman auditorium was through a number of doors in the outside walls of the building and thence to the corridors by way of various interior staircases and ramps, resembling the way the flow of spectators is handled in a modern stadium. These galleries were given the name of *vomitoria*. Low walls separated the tiers from the corridors, and often each section between two corridors had its own distinct architectural ornamentation. The terminal corridor was roofed and ornamented by colonnades or ranges of pilasters forming a gallery for standees.

To achieve esthetic balance, the height of the *scaenae frons* was increased so that it was on a level with the top of the *cavea;* in this way the Roman theater acquired unity of mass. This is clearly apparent in the Theater of Aspendus, a structure that is yet another example of the grandiose magnificence so greatly esteemed by the Romans. The *scaenae frons,* as we have seen, assumed huge dimensions; it was constructed in conformance with every style in vogue at the time and packed with statuary and sculptured reliefs. The actor was doomed to be eclipsed under the overpowering weight of such a permanently phantasmagorical stage set, but this was of no account in those days, when the actor was likely to be a slave or a prisoner of war. The important thing was to achieve the most impressive effects possible. These theaters, moreover, were not always used for dramatic performances. A low separating wall between the orchestra and the tiers, the *pulpitum,* allowed the former to be used for gladiatorial contests; sometimes it was flooded with water for the mimetic reenactment of naval battles or for the presentation of water ballets.

In striving after ever-greater magnificence and effect, the Romans greatly improved existing construction standards and functional facilities; they were indeed great engineers. During its latter period, the republic succeeded in creating and developing an architectural tradition that was purely Roman. The use of the traditional building materials of central Italy continued without innovation through the imperial period, but in the last century B.C. new building methods and materials came into use at a rapidly growing rate. Domes, cupolas, and vaulted arches, constructed with the help of a kind of mortar very similar to cement, were extensively used. Toward the close of the first century Roman architects were employing the same techniques to build the theaters that were to become such a representative part of Roman architecture.[54]

The trend toward uniformity of mass created an integral architectural whole. Alignment of the height of the *scaenae frons* and *cavea* made it possible for Roman architects to devise a form of roof—a tent or awning that was named the *velum* or *velarium*—to cover the entire theater. This development, together with the use of a stage curtain of sorts during performances, brought the Roman theater another step closer to the indoor playhouses of later periods.

Notwithstanding their opulent splendor, the fact remains that, when compared with the Greek prototypes, Roman theaters were generally ill fitted to meet the needs of the drama and the other performing arts. As mentioned earlier, the Romans were fervently stirred by the achievements of Greek civilization, yet they never managed to grasp the true aims and ideals on which it was built. They were content with the tangible, visible result, but even this they converted or adapted to their own ends and beliefs. In the area of the theater, accordingly, the playhouse diverged from the purpose for which it was created just as the drama itself lost its meaning. Although during certain festivals the Roman theaters may have been used for performances of Greek tragedies or comedies, their principal function was not so much to satisfy the needs of culture and education as to meet the demand for entertainment. If we measure the rapid decline of the drama in the Roman era against the simultaneous and equally rapid development of theater-building, we are bound to conclude that those theaters were designed and built to fulfill a need for vainglorious civic ostentation rather than to improve and perfect the expression and presentation of the drama itself. In effect, when the theater lost its protective shell of meaning and speech, it sought refuge in the magnificence of the instrument—the building—that served it.

4
The Middle Ages

Christianity Versus the Theater

The theater is especially the shrine of Venus. . . . Thou must hate, Christian, those things, the inventors whereof thou canst not but hate. . . . Blush the Senate! Blush all ranks! Let the very women, the destroyers of their own modesty, shudder at their doings before the light and the public, and blush this once within the year. . . . Nay, in all the show, no offence will more meet us, than that very over-careful adorning of the men and women. The very community of feeling, their very agreement or disagreement in party-spirit, doth, by their intercourse, fan the sparks of carnal lust.[55]

These words, redolent of pious fanaticism, are from Quintus Septimius Florens Tertullian's *De Spectaculis*, written in A.D. 198 immediately after his conversion to Christianity. They are representative of the climate of the era, of the hatred in which all things pagan were held, of the way the theater was associated with fear of the devil and God's avenging angels. The quotation, though but a tiny fraction of Tertullian's prodigious writings, reveals clearly enough the prevailing attitudes toward the theater during the first centuries of Christianity, attitudes that prevailed virtually unmodified for 10 centuries to come. A span of a thousand years separates the first primitive emergence of the drama in Athens from the final collapse of Roman civilization. For yet another millennium the Greek and Roman theaters were forgotten, their creative force lost in the obscurantism and fanaticism produced by a new order, a new religious faith. Although Christ never preached hatred and fanaticism, the church fathers of the early Christian era misinterpreted the meanings of His word. They distrusted and condemned all human frailty, all the small joys of life, however innocent. Dressing up was a sin, and sociability a crime that could be expiated only by the fires of hell.

Wielding its weapons of terror, intimidation, and excommunication, the church obliterated every trace of attachment to "pagan events" in any form. Christianity gave the theater its last and mortal blow—not, indeed, out of mere whim or for lack of a feeling for good, but for psychological and religious reasons.[56] The fear of demons and an afterlife in hell, constrained the faithful to live lives ruled by dogmatic imperatives.

From the fourth century on, the great theaters lay empty and desolate; they gradually crumbled into ruins or were occupied by the destitute, who turned them into slums, a condition one can see to this day at the Theater of Marcellus in Rome. Every tradition connected with the performance of the drama was completely obliterated. Roman drama, having died a natural death, was buried by Christianity.[57]

Christianity, of course, was not the only cause of this centuries-long void before the revival of the theater. There were also changes in social conditions brought about by the fall of the Roman empire, the invasions by barbaric races like the Goths and Ostrogoths, and the need for personal survival. Unquestionably, however, Christianity was the single force most hostile to the theater and most militant in its suppression of all forms of dramatic expression.

The Roman drama struggled to subsist in a Rome conquered and ruled by Theodoric the Great through the staging of trashy and demeaning shows, which survived until the middle of the sixth century. In Byzantium it lasted a little longer; up to the close of the seventh century a handful of professional actor-mimes strove to preserve in the capital of the Eastern Roman empire an institution that was already moribund.[58] After the invasion of Rome by the Lombards in 568 all traces of the theater disappeared.[59] Some scholars assert that the last reference to the Roman stage is contained in a letter written in 533.[60]

Evolution of the Medieval Drama

It may be that the drama never did in fact disappear altogether, although there were no theaters. Wandering actors, harried and persecuted,[61] tried to find ways and means of expression that would not aggravate the abhorrence in which they were held. Even before the old tradition died out completely, a new element surfaced: the story recited in verse, which gave rise to a literature that is the most important surviving cultural accomplishment of the early Middle Ages—the chansons de geste, the romans, and the contes. Minstrels and troubadours from every part of Europe roamed the countryside describing the exploits of legendary champions and presenting dramatic episodes, thus developing a form of art acceptable to the period and its spirit and preserving a few—a very few—elements of the old traditional mimetic art.[62] We see here a tolerant attitude on the part of the church toward this form of entertainment: The minstrel was not considered, properly speaking, an actor and therefore was not in danger of hellfire. Nevertheless, he was a connecting link between the old tradition and the new one that was to dawn.[63]

Although it tried strenuously, the church did not succeed in eliminating the spirit of joy from the world, in stamping out the individual's need to rejoice and express innermost emotions. Very wisely it turned to compromise. To counteract the corrupt worldly theater, it attempted to create within its own precincts a religious theater and thereby to satisfy an important social need. At first it selected what it considered the least ungodly of preconversion customs and allowed people to express their feelings on certain traditional festal occasions, such as the succession of the seasons or the time of harvest; it decided to arrogate to itself alone the task of "fortifying the unlearned people in their faith."[64]

The Christian drama began to develop. The more we try to discover links connecting this new form with the old tradition, the clearer it becomes that the birth and growth of the medieval drama was a separate, unrelated process. Its origin must be sought in the heart of Byzantium, in the Eastern church, which conceived of the notion of popularizing the liturgy among its largely illiterate congregation by presenting the events of the life of Christ in a more graphically realistic manner.[65] The Byzantines called their theatrical presentations ϑεανδρικά μυστήρια (*theandrika mysteria*, roughly translated as mysteries of divine man) to avoid using the words theater or drama.

The two great feasts of Christendom—Christmas and Easter—inspired plays and performances depicting the life and death of Jesus. Religious plays like *The Passion of Christ* by Gregory of Nazianzus,[66] *The Three Youths in the Furnace*, or *The Assumption of the Prophet Elijah*,[67] and performances such as the *nipter*[68] or the *Passion of the Palatine Code*[69] had a direct influence on the ritual of the church service. Very soon the mass itself, the symbolic representation of the Last Supper, took the form of a theatrical play.[70] The solemn ceremonial splendor, the feast of colors, the musical accompaniment combined with the responses of the priests were a powerful and stirring factor in influencing the people; the churches once more began to fill. The Byzantine drama produced reverberations that spread beyond the boundaries of the empire and were heard in the West, still sunk in the dark confusion of its superstitions.

In Western Europe religious drama, which the scholars called "liturgical drama," flowered in the early thirteenth century. Its people met and were influenced by the Byzantines; they adopted the liturgical drama and adapted its form in accordance with their own character and religious beliefs. Whereas in the East the plays were performed in the churches, in the West they were less confined; the development was more elaborate and gradually acquired a form closely approximating that of the secular performance—or rather, it developed into secular theater, but its themes and subjects were religious.[71]

The thirteenth and fourteenth centuries saw the culmination of Western medieval drama. Soon the interiors of the churches could not hold the crowds that flocked to watch the great cycle plays, sometimes called mystery plays (*mystères*, *sacre rappresentazioni*), which covered the whole plan of salvation, and the so-called Passion plays, which were confined to the death and resurrection of Christ. The cathedral squares provided the best possibilities for creating space in a theatrical sense; they provided ample space for the spectators and a truly beautiful setting for the plays. In modern times the Passion plays at Oberammergau and in Brittany and several other places give us a good idea of this form and of how these performances were staged.

As the liturgical drama gained popularity, church leaders began to have misgivings. This creation of theirs, which they had endeavored so painstakingly to establish and popularize, was acquiring a tremendous power of its own and slipping out of their control. Interdictions and invidiously virulent criticism by fanatic clerics resulted in a ban on using priests in the performances. Efforts were made to curb the enthusiastic participation by the public, but it was too late. The drama had been reborn and once again had gained the affection of the people. It became too popular and powerful to disappear again; the laity, better educated and more affluent than their ancestors of early Christendom, assumed the role of its guardian and protector.

In England powerful city guilds backed the production of plays. In France and Italy a number of secular organizations were founded, such as the Confrérie de la Passion and the goliardery, consisting of large actors' unions. The subjects of the plays were still taken from the Bible but in greater variety.[72] Performances were given in the vernacular so that people could follow and understand the dialogue. The church continued its bitter opposition against what in effect was its own creation; nevertheless, it must be noted that it was the church that had endowed the drama with unique theatrical virtues, the like of which would never again be forthcoming. The later theater, though richer in literary quality and more refined professionally, could not fill the vacuum left by the passing of the deeply emotional Byzantine piety, the magnificence and idolatry of the church, the loud accompaniment of sacred music, the imposing architectural background of the cathedral, the sincerity and persuasiveness with which the spoken word was delivered. Despite the opposition of the church, the dramatic literature of the Middle Ages remains the most revered, the most moving, and the most pleasing of all in the long history of the theater.

The Medieval Performances

There is no argument whatsoever about the importance of the medieval period to everything connected with the development of drama. It is also certain that no permanent playhouses of any kind were built during the Middle Ages—not a single theater building was produced. Since the nature of the religious drama did not require buildings particularly designed for its purpose, a playing place was chosen and arranged for the occasion of the individual performance, which varied with the type of play presented. Therefore, it is more to the point to consider the basic types of settings and stagings used at various times between the emergence of the first liturgical drama and the spectacles of the sixteenth century.

THE CHURCH AS A THEATRICAL SPACE

In the liturgical plays staged within the church building, the central scenic element was the altar on which the sepulcher of Christ was placed as a symbol. Later this sepulcher acquired the form of a tomb conventionally built of stone or wood (Figures 32, 33) and was placed in the north aisle. As the embryonic drama expanded in incident and dramatis personae, the chancel became inadequate. The staging was expanded into the nave of the church in what might be described as an extension of the acting area.[73]

Figure 32. Sepulcher. (Nicoll, Development of the Theatre, *p. 50. Reprinted by permission.)*

Figure 33. The Resurrection of Christ. (Nicoll, Development of the Theatre, *p. 50. Reprinted by permission.)*

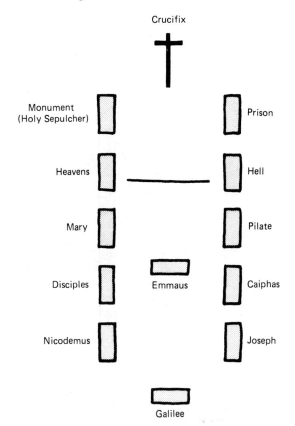

Figure 34. *Position of the mansions for the religious drama* The Play of the Resurrection. *(Drawing by author.)*

THE CHURCH AS A STAGE SETTING

The next step in the evolution of the liturgical drama was its removal out doors to the square or open area in front of the church. With this development, new plays were introduced and the settings acquired greater diversity. At first, seats were placed in two lines to the left and right of a crucifix (Figure 34); these served as stations for the actors representing biblical characters—Jesus' disciples, Mary, Nicodemus, and so on. The seats were later replaced by small canopies with curtains supported by cornerposts. The canopies were modeled on the cubicles, or *cubicula*, of Byzantium; they were called "mansions" and were used by the actors for their entrances and exits. These units of scenery often symbolized the locations of the action: heaven, paradise, Galilee, and so on (Figure 35). This form of setting, with its solemn and imposing ornamentation and the grandeur of the church facade as a background to the entire action, was used to present such notable plays as *The Play of the Resurrection*, a liturgical drama of the twelfth or thirteenth century, and the *Mystery of Adam*, perhaps the oldest drama in twelfth-century French literature.[74]

(1) First door.
(2) Hell.
(3) Garden of Gethsemane.
(4) Mount Olivet.
(5) Second door.
(6) Herod.
(7) Pilate.
(8) Pillar of scourging.

(9) Pillar for cock.
(10) Caiaphas.
(11) Annas.
(12) Last Supper.
(13) Third door.
(14) Cross.
(15) Holy Sepulcher.
(16) Heaven.

Figure 35. *Position of the mansions in* The Villingen Mystery Play *p. 49. (Drawing by author.)*

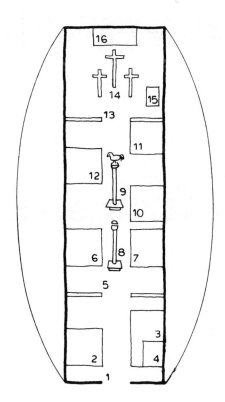

Figure 36. Model of stage setting for The Valenciennes Mystery Play. *(Credit: Cleveland Museum of Art.)*

PERMANENT SCENERY

The demands of the plays created the need for permanent settings. Productions became increasingly sophisticated and elaborate. The mansions changed from canopies to small edifices. Their arrangement depended on the plot of the play and local attitudes.

In many places the playing area became a long, raised stage—often extending for a hundred feet or more—on which were erected the various mansions. Much of the action took place in the open area, the *platea*, *playne* (plain), or *place*, whatever the arrangement of the mansions. Such was the stage for the *Valenciennes Mystery Play*, staged in 1547, with heaven to the left of the spectator and hell to the right (Figures 36, 37). The audience sat on scaffold seats, on the ground, or on balconies or watched from the windows of nearby houses. In Cornwall the mansions were arranged in a circle—or so it is assumed from a plan of the English play *The Castle of Perseverance*[75] (Figure 38).

Figure 37. The Valenciennes Mystery Play. *Reproduction by E. Grasset. (Credit: Cheney,* The Theatre; *p. 144a.)*

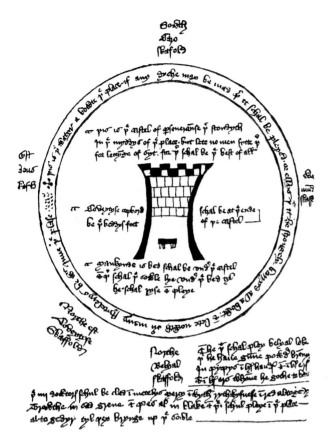

Figure 38. The Castle of Perseverance. (Left) *Plan from the medieval manuscript. (Nicoll,* Development of the Theatre, *p. 58. Reprinted by permission.) (Below) Reconstruction by Richard Southern. (Reprinted by permission of the Richard Southern Accession, University of Bristol Theatre Collection.)*

Figure 39. The Martyrdom of St. Apollonia. *Note the raised mansion and use of the* platea. *(Reprinted by permission of the Bibliotèque Nationale, Paris.)*

In the famous miniature of *The Martyrdom of Saint Apollonia* by Jean Fouquet (Figure 39), the mansions do not quite encircle the playing area. Thus, by comparing these layouts with the modern open stages, we note only minor differences in the actor–audience relationship. In both instances the public is in direct rapport with the action; the spectators surround the actors and participate in the performance.

MOVABLE SCENERY

Movable scenery was developed, in England mainly, around the close of the fifteenth century. The English guilds preferred staging their plays in the manner that became known as the "wagon stage" or "pageant," an innovation featuring wheel-mounted scenery or separate mansions on wheels that could be conveniently moved from one position to another according to the demands of the staging plan (Figure 40).[76] Sometimes the stage area was enlarged by using movable open platforms or more than one wagon stage. This system, a kind of linear stage setting, was perfectly suited to the requirements of the plays of the period; the performance could pro-

Figure 40. Model of an English wagon stage of the late fifteenth century. (Credit: Cleveland Museum of Art.)

gress along the entire length of a street while the spectator stood in one place and watched the passing episodes unfold successively before him, somewhat in the manner of the Eleusinian mysteries of the past and the festive processions and parades of our own times.

THE PLATFORM STAGE

The platform stage was a type of scenography intended for plays of major importance; it was used by itinerant troupes in performances of cheap and trivial acts, not always of a religious nature, at festivals and local fairs (Figure 41).[77] The type, popular in all Western countries during the sixteenth century, may not have much to offer to students of scenography and theater architecture. Nevertheless, it bequeathed a major acting heritage that became a basis for the interpretation of the more refined popular plays of the Renaissance.

This brief description of the five basic scenographic types of liturgical drama presentation brings to a close the discussion of the medieval theater. This period of the "Dark Ages," which lasted nearly a thousand years, may have contributed nothing to the development of the theater in terms of architectural form and style, but it bequeathed two principles that played a useful part in the general evolution of the drama. The first was the close rapport created between actor and spectator, a link that allowed the simple, unlettered folk of the period to share in the action, partake empathetically in the plot, and learn to love the art of expression and its spoken word. The second was the conviction that the effect created by artificial scenery is not always essential to the interpretation of a play. The power of the spoken word, the art and impersonating ability of the actor, the clarity of dramatic purport were enough to stimulate the imagination and transport the audience mentally to the time and place of the play's action without the need of ornament or artifice.

Figure 41. Etching of a sixteenth-century platform stage. (Nicoll, Development of the Theatre, p. 60. Reprinted by permission.)

5
The Renaissance

First Steps

The term "Renaissance" evokes the names of Michelangelo, Leonardo da Vinci, Giotto, Brunelleschi—names that represent a true renaissance in the history of sculpture, painting, and architecture. In each of these arts there was an astounding proliferation of works reflecting the sudden awakening after a millenium of torpor, the abrupt and awesome transition from the superstition of the Dark Ages to the open spaces of spiritual seeking and intellectual expansion where the restless mind roamed free.

In the theater, however, the change did not come in the manner of a universal revival. In the area of theater-speech the drama made a poor and sterile showing despite the admirable achievements of the Middle Ages, particularly toward the close of the period. By contrast, in the area of theater building, there was a renaissance in the true sense of the word. It could be said that this was a pan-European phenomenon, but in actual fact Italy can be unhesitatingly pointed to as its birthplace. Italy was the first country to overcome the stage of uncertainty, to conquer superstition, occult mysticism, and ignorance, and to attain rapidly a new era founded on the till then unknown ideal of freedom of the individual. Other countries followed suit, but they did so much later, and they copied what had been done in Italy rather than creating something new of their own.

In the middle of the sixteenth century, when Italy was producing the first flowers of her renaissance, France was in the throes of dire political troubles, England was seeking cultural consummation through poetry rather than the visual or performing arts, Spain was still in the grip of hidebound conservatism, and the Germanic nations were shaken by Luther's radical and far-reaching religious reforms.

The Italian Renaissance introduced notions that were entirely new and carried man from the medieval past to the threshold of the modern world. In the field of theater, Italy gave birth to the modern stage. The transition from medieval to contemporary theater was accomplished through a complete break with liturgical drama and a return to the glory of imperial Rome and the unrivaled masterpieces of the ancient Greek tradition. The revival of the Greek and Roman written word, the popularization of Vitruvius (70–15 b.c.) through the translation and publication in manuscript of his great work on the theater,[78] and the descriptions of refugees from devastated Byzantium created a passion for research into every form of antiquity.

The ruins of ancient theaters, to which no one had until then given a thought, were excavated, carefully studied, and measured in detail with assiduity and love. Forgotten texts by ancient dramatists were unearthed; works by Plautus, Terence, and Seneca were staged, at first in Latin and then in translated and revised versions. Many painters and architects of the time were fired by the desire to create something new, something till then forbidden. They discovered the beauty and pleasures of perspective, they learned that to fear leaving the established patterns and the beaten path was to betray their own art. And they believed in the theater as a dynamic art and that the theories of the conservative classicists were anachronistic and static, a repetition and a poor imitation of the ancient forms. But the fresh breeze stirred up at the beginning of the sixteenth century by the beauty and allure of classical antiquity was at the same time in danger of dying out, of congealing into petrifaction as a result of the efforts of imitators, whose only aspiration was to accept and preserve all things ancient without regard for contemporary reality.

Two contrary and conflicting trends soon emerged: on the one side the strict advocates of classicism, worshipers of Vitruvius and antiquity in general, and on the other the true and conscientious scholars, the restless intellectuals who believed that antiquity should serve only as a source of teachings and fundamentals and that their own task was not to copy but to develop. Fortunately the second trend prevailed, and the Renaissance thus left a valuable heritage in the conception of the theater, attaining at times realism itself.

Many types of theater stages developed throughout Europe during the Renaissance; each must be studied separately if one is to understand how importantly they contributed to the theater of later times.

The Italian Renaissance Stage

In 1551 Sebastiano Serlio (1475–1554) wrote his *Architettura*,[79] a book on Renaissance theater architecture. Basing his thesis on Vitruvius' work, he describes with admirable lucidity how the Roman architect's principles could be modified to suit the needs of the sixteenth century. Four points of special significance must be singled out in Serlio's work.

First, he accepts the premise that the plan of the auditorium and stage must be rectangular (Figure 42), with the stage at one end and the tiers of spectators' seats in a semicircular layout occupying the rest of the space. This manner of placing the audience is wholly influenced by the *cavea* of the Roman theater; it follows, obviously, that the designs of the Renaissance classicists influenced the development of the auditorium.

Second, drawing inspiration from Vitruvius, Serlio presents three typical perspective scenographic designs—the comic scene, the tragic scene, and the satyric (pastoral) scene (Figures 43–45), all of which faithfully follow the description given by the Latin architect: "There are three types of scenes, one known as tragic, the second comic and the third satyric."[80] These designs by Serlio are not intended only for specific plays; they are meant to serve as auxiliary scenery to enhance the setting whenever a comic or tragic or pastoral scene is performed before the public. As in architecture, here too in the domain of scenography the classic influence is strong.

Figure 42. Sebastian Serlio's theatre: plan and section. Built in the court of the Palazzo Porto, Vicenza, 1539. (Drawing by author, according to Serlio's design.)

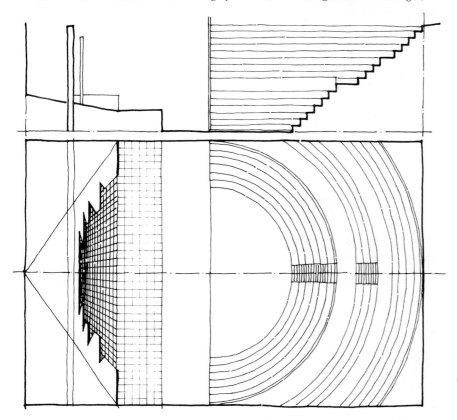

Figure 43. The comic scene, according to Serlio. (Nicoll, Development of the Theatre, *p. 74. Reprinted by permission.)*

Figure 44. The tragic scene, according to Serlio. (Nicoll, Development of the Theatre, *p. 74. Reprinted by permission.)*

Figure 45. The satyric scene, according to Serlio. (Nicoll, Development of the Theatre, *p. 74. Reprinted by permission.)*

Figure 46. Design by Baldassare Peruzzi, probably for La Calandria, *performed in Rome, 1514. (Nicoll,* Development of the Theatre, *p. 73. Reprinted by permission.)*

Third, Serlio's proposition was no innovation. Already in the early fifteenth century the celebrated Florentine architect Brunelleschi pioneered an advanced system of perspective construction[81] that was applied soon afterward to the theater by Baldassare Peruzzi (Figure 46). Comparing it with Serlio's designs, one sees at once that although half a century had elapsed, scenographic techniques remained the same.

Last, a scrutiny of the plan and elevation of Serlio's stage (Figure 42) reveals that here too he begins by reproducing the Roman patterns. The long, low narrow platform in the foreground, intended as the acting area, is reminiscent of the Roman *proscaenium,* but here the similarity ends. The *scaenae frons* gives way to a sloping floor, an extension of the original platform, on which a perspective setting representing a street or square is erected, combining built scenery with painted surfaces. The composition is completed by a flat backdrop painted to represent an extension of the setting, also in perspective. There is always a central vanishing point and a focal plane at a very short distance from the observer to emphasize the perspective effect. Serlio's stage, however, had a number of serious disadvantages. The actors had to perform against it rather than in it, because one step backward was enough to disturb the scale of the setting and destroy the three-dimensional opti-

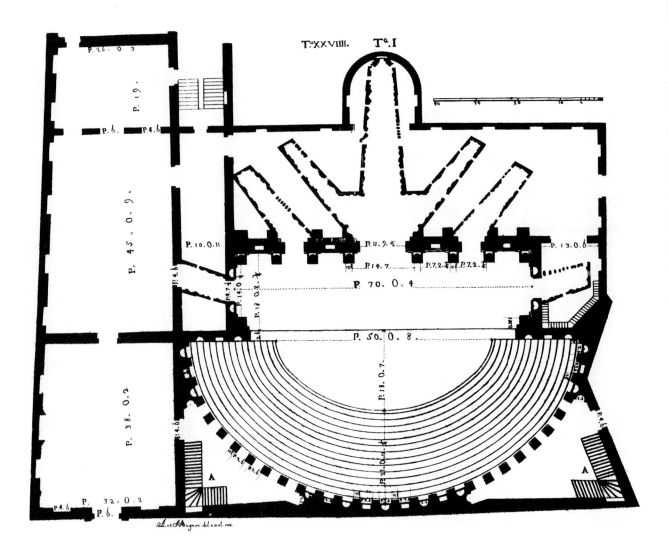

Figure 47. Teatro Olimpico, Vicenza: plan (above) and interior view (left). (By permission of the Victoria and Albert Museum.)

cal illusion, ruining the perspective effect. The composition as a whole lacked flexibility; it could not easily be changed to meet the needs of the play, nor could it be developed in all directions.

Nevertheless, these four views were very popular in their day. Perspectives of streets became the standard scenic background for contemporary performances. Although the stage form created by Serlio was inspired by antiquity, the introduction of perspective was a purely Renaissance feature. Renaissance architects studied Vitruvius to enrich their knowledge of the ancient theater and patterned their designs on the classical models. There were still, however, many among them who were not satisfied with the use of mere detail; they wanted the complete structure, and they wanted it to be strictly Roman. When an academy embarked on the construction of a classical playhouse, its designers read Vitruvius, possibly studied a few ruins, and then constructed a very faithful variation of the Roman classic theater.

The crowning achievement of all these efforts can be seen in the famous theater of the Olympic Academy of Vicenza, also known as the Teatro Olimpico or Teatro Palladio after its designer, the architect Andrea Palladio (1518–1580). Though made of wood, it has been preserved to our day. Construction began in May 1580, but Palladio died in August of the same year and Vincenzo Scamozzi (1552–1616) was assigned to carry on the work, which he finished in 1585 after adding a few variations of his own to the original design.[82]

Generally speaking, the building was designed and constructed along the lines of the best classicist ideas of the period, but it incorporated certain variations worth studying. The general interior arrangement (Figure 47) reveals a number of similarities to any small Roman theater. But a comparison of the plan to that of a classic Roman playhouse (Figure 48) shows that the seating tiers, instead of following the semicircular layout, are arranged in a semielliptical shape, thereby providing greater visibility. Between the front row of seats and the stage is an orchestra at a sunken level. By contrast with the semielliptical configuration of the auditorium, the stage itself, like the Roman playhouses, is an elongated, narrow rectangle with a floor painted to look like marble. The familiar Roman *scaenae frons* faces us

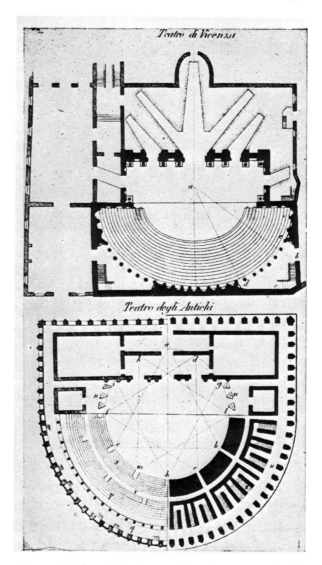

Figure 48. Plan of the Teatro Olimpico compared with that of a Roman theater. (Nicoll, Development of the Theatre, *p. 75. Reprinted by permission.)*

from the back of the stage (Figure 49), elaborately ornamented with pediments and statuary; as in the past, it has three openings: a wide central arch—Vitruvius' *porta regia*—and two smaller flanking doorways to the left and right—the *portae minores*. There are doors in the two narrow side walls too, and over each of these is a loge used either for the play's staging requirements or as accommodation for spectators. At first, all these doorways were closed with wooden or painted panels, but after the death of Palladio, Scamozzi,

Figure 49. Stage wall of the Teatro Olimpico, Scamozzi's vistas are clearly discernible. (By permission of the Victoria and Albert Museum.)

whose fondness for perspective was in line with the trend of his times, added the so-called vistas that could be seen through the doorways, usually pictures of streets or tree-lined avenues (Figure 49), in strict perspective, all converging on a central piazza, the stage.[83]

Although basically the Teatro Olimpico was behind the times compositionally and bore the imprint of many classical influences in form and feature, it is considered a notable monument in the history of the theater.[84] It marked the beginning of the proscenium theater, which was to be the only kind of theater for the next three centuries. In support of this view there is a theory contending that the familiar proscenium arch—the typical form of most modern theaters that has come to be known as the Italian stage or scène à l'italienne—is a direct descendant of the central arch of the Teatro Olimpico as developed by Scamozzi with the addition of the vista.

However, the first theater to be regarded as truly contemporary, by reason of having a proscenium in the form we know today, was the Teatro Farnese in Parma (Figure 50).[85] It was designed by Giambattista Aleotti (1546–1636); completed in 1618 (some thirty-five years after the Teatro Olimpico), it introduced a number of radical changes. Acting no longer depended only on the technique of illusion but began to develop in a real, three-dimensional space enclosed by walls and scenery. The stage was located behind an imposing arch that served as a "frame" for the picture seen by the audience. It was not long before the arch suggested the use of a curtain, behind which it was possible to make, unseen by the audience, quick changes of the now movable and convertible scenery. The typical "Italian stage" form had arrived, and it served as the basic model for most theaters built since then, with very few variations.

60

Figure 50. Teatro Farnese, Parma: plan and view of the stage. (Nicoll, Development of the Theatre, *p. 166. Reprinted by permission.)*

Yet another innovation introduced by the Teatro Farnese is worth noting: the U-shaped auditorium, very similar to the familiar stadium form. This seating layout made it possible to accommodate a much larger audience and also, depending on the requirements of the performance, to use the deep forestage or arena wedged between the ends of the U as an extension of the action or the setting. This innovation was indeed an important departure from tradition, as a result of which the auditorium evolved into the shape of a horseshoe, a form that was to be used in a number of eighteenth-century playhouses as well as in the Grosses Schauspielhaus built in 1919.

To complete this analysis of the Italian stage in the fifteenth and sixteenth centuries, it is interesting to mention something characteristically Greek that substantially influenced the development of convertible, movable scenery. The students of classicism and Vitruvius gave much attention to the *periakti* (mentioned in Chapter 2). They correctly interpreted these machines as triangular prisms with pictures painted on their sides, which were placed in the stage-wall openings. It is very likely that the *periakti* inspired Scamozzi to install his perspective street vistas behind each doorway in the stage walls of the Teatro Olimpico. It is a fact that the theater specialists of that period were fascinated by the *periakti*, which gave them the notion of mobility, a concept eminently appealing to the restless and inquiring spirit of the Renaissance.

No doubt, audiences were at first enthusiastic over the perspective piazzas and vistas, but they soon tired of seeing the same scenes over and over again, and the need for variety became pressing. This need was met by adopting the classic *periakti* on a general scale. Serlio's two-dimensional scenery was replaced by triangular prisms revolving on a shaft fixed to the floor of the stage. The subject was treated at length by Joseph Furttenbach in his *Architectura Recreationis* (1640),[86] in which he attempted to provide definitions and guidelines for scenographic variety and mobility (Figure 51).

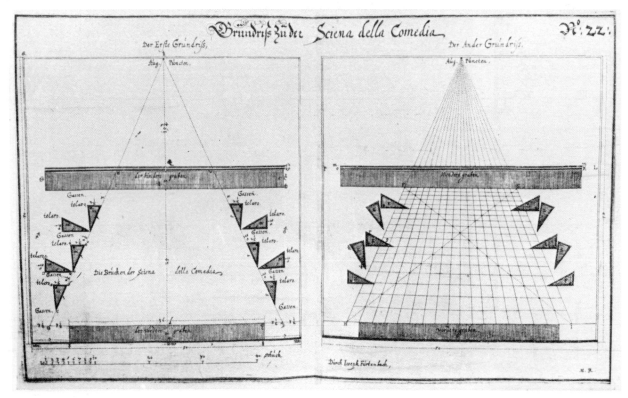

Figure 51. Arrangement of periakti, *according to Furttenbach. (Nicoll,* Development of
the Theatre, *p. 88. Reprinted by permission.)*

The use of *periakti* continued for many years, and these triangular prisms combined with advancing scenographic technology to form the basis for the evolution of setting design and staging techniques.

Booth Stages and Popular Playhouses

Booth stages and popular playhouses are not particularly interesting from an architectural standpoint; nevertheless, they are worth a brief glance because they help us compare the Italian Renaissance stage with the development of the theater in the rest of Europe during the same period.

Booth stages first appeared in 1540 and gradually spread over the whole of Western Europe.[87] They consisted merely of a raised wooden platform with a few crude cloth hang-ings to form the stage and wings (Figure 52). The form survives unchanged today at popular festivals and fairs.

In France the Confrérie de la Passion, an organization engaged in the staging of medieval mystery plays, obtained in 1518 the monopoly on producing theatrical works in Paris. In 1548 it opened its own theater in the suitably remodeled lobby of the Hôtel de Bourgogne,[88] a rectangular room with benches for spectators. The stage was an interesting blend of medieval and Renaissance styles (Figure 53).

In Spain actors for many years had been performing in the capital's *corrales*, small squares or courtyards enclosed by the walls of houses. On one side of the corral they erected a stage, usually with a curtain. The first permanent theater, the Corral de la Cruz, was built in Madrid in 1579, followed by the Corral del Principe in 1583.[89] The stage of the corral theaters was a two-story structure, generally with a balcony, a feature not seen previously. Benches were placed on the ground floor, and often the walls of the

Figure 52. Booth stage at a Dutch fair. Detail from a painting by P. Balten. (Credit: Southern, Seven Ages of the Theatre, *p. 192.)*

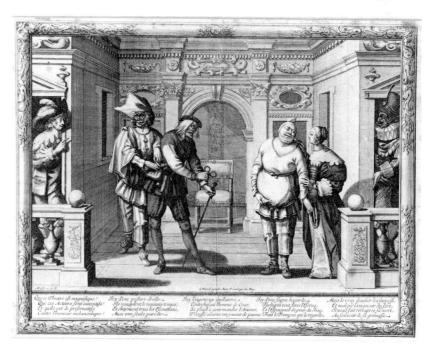

Figure 53. Stage at the Hôtel de Bourgogne. From an etching by Abraham Bosse. (By permission of the Houghton Library, Harvard University.)

houses surrounding the *corrales* had windows or small balconies—*célosias* or *aposéntos*—that were used in the performances (Figure 54). These theaters in many ways were similar to the Elizabethan playhouses in England, and they contributed importantly to the development of drama and dialogue in verse. When Lope de Vega, practically a contemporary of William Shakespeare, began writing his first plays, he wrote for this form of stage, and he carried it to a high peak of development by the power of his rich poetry.[90]

The Elizabethan Public Playhouse

The political conflict between Spain and England during the sixteenth century prevented the development of close cultural relations between the two countries. Nevertheless, the Spanish corral theaters have a remarkable affinity with the English playhouses of Elizabethan times; the similarity, however, applies only to the interior arrangement.

After Queen Elizabeth I succeeded to the throne in 1558, the English theater entered a period of singular intellectual distinction, achievement, and brilliance. Within 50 years it grew and flowered so richly as to be considered, with the Greek theater, the most vital, refined, and philosophically profound theater that has ever been known.

Before Queen Elizabeth's reign not a single theater existed in London. The guilds kept a rudimentary theatrical activity going, but this was confined to performances by small professional or student troupes at ducal courts, inn yards, and public squares. They used booth stages to present Latin plays, translations of Italian plays, or mysteries, still in the medieval manner and style, without settings of any sort.

The performers' only dramatic aid was the spoken word itself. They tried to use its power to capture the spectators, to help them imagine the places where the plot unfolded, thereby creating a close contact between audience and actor.

Under such circumstances scenery is useless, almost superfluous; the spectator's attention is focused on the actor and the words he speaks, not on the setting against which he moves. The cultural level appears so high, the simplicity of external aids so Doric that, when one reflects on the garrulous productions of the Italian stage, one cannot help but speculate about the time and trouble spent, perhaps in vain, during the ensuing centuries on developing and reproducing elegant forms and illusory impressions. These are our purely personal reflections, of course, and they may perhaps conflict with the familiar established views on dramatic expression and on theatrical speech and space. Nevertheless, they spring from the widely different feelings one experiences today when attending performances in the two existing theater trends: the "legitimate" commercial the-

Figure 54. A present-day performance of Lope de Vega's El Acero de Madrid. *(Nicoll,* Development of the Theatre, *p. 102. Reprinted by permission.)*

Figure 55. Sketch of the Swan Theater, London, by John de Witt. (Nicoll, Development of the Theatre, *p. 97. Reprinted by permission.)*

Burbage (1530–1597) outside the east wall of London, it was named simply The Theatre and was the result of the personal success of the professional actors in gaining the recognition and esteem of the difficult London public. No documentation showing the precise design or plans of The Theatre has been preserved, but it is believed that all the popular playhouses that followed—the Curtain (1577), the Rose (1587), and, most famous of all, Shakespeare's Globe Theatre (1599)—were built on the same design.[91] A sketch of the Swan (1596) by Johann de Witt (Figure 55)[92] and a reconstruction drawing of the Globe by Richard Leacroft (Figure 56) furnish very meager information about the Elizabethan playhouse. But a few existing seventeenth-century manuscripts, combined with the staging techniques used at the time, give us a fairly clear picture of how these theaters were constructed.

ater of the boulevard and its superproductions on the one hand (theater as entertainment), and on the other the austere, genuine drama of an Aeschylus or a Shakespeare, a Brecht or a Beckett (theater as edification and intellectual stimulus).

To return to our analysis of the pre-Elizabethan stage, it is worth noting that despite the total absence of theater buildings, the theater as a concept made its reappearance uniquely through the efforts of itinerant actors, helped by a pervading spirit of experimentation in every form.

Although 1558 is accepted as the year that ushered in the era of the Elizabethan stage, it was not until 18 years later, in 1576, that the first playhouse opened in London. Built by James

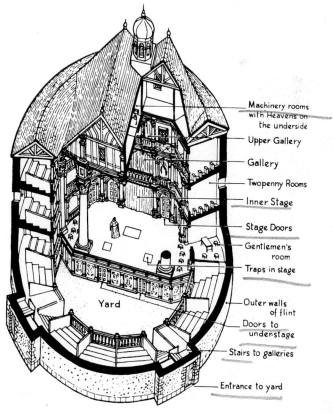

Machinery rooms with Heavens on the underside
Upper Gallery
Gallery
Twopenny Rooms
Inner Stage
Stage Doors
Gentlemen's room
Traps in stage
Outer walls of flint
Doors to understage
Stairs to galleries
Entrance to yard
Yard

Figure 56. Reconstruction of the Globe Theatre by Richard Leacroft (Credit: Roberts, On Stage, *p. 59.)*

Globe is

All were round, octagonal, or square buildings with thatched roofs, constructed around a large central yard. Spectators paid a small entrance fee that entitled them to stand in the yard; if they decided to remain, they had to stand for the duration of the performance. If they could afford to pay for better places, they ascended the stairs to the galleries, which ran almost the entire length of the enclosing walls, where they could sit on benches. Members of the upper classes used the "gentlemen's rooms" or, better still, rented chairs and sat on the stage itself.

The stage was a spacious platform, a large apron projecting into the middle of the yard so that it was almost surrounded by the audience (Figure 57). Two massive pillars near the edge of the stage supported a sloping overhead structure concealing a machinery room that housed the various pieces of scenery and scenic devices; these were lowered onto the stage through a trapdoor. In some playhouses the underside of this structure was painted to resemble a blue sky studded with stars and was called "the heavens." It was topped by a turretlike structure, probably serving as a base for a flagpole bearing the playhouse's distinctive pennant.

hidden

At the back of the stage was a wall with doors, over which a gallery formed a sort of *episcenium*. There were also wings for the actors, but we have no clear evidence as to whether these were permanent adjuncts of the building or movable structures.

Scenery was carried onto the stage from outside, but this was no problem since scenery was very sparingly used; as noted, the English tradition did not depend on scenic effect but on the power of the spoken word.

The origin of the wooden, black-and-white form of the Elizabethan playhouse is unknown. Its many points of similarity to the classical Athenian theater are no proof that it was influenced by it. On the contrary, my contention is that the Elizabethan playhouse arrived at the same result under the pressure of an identical need: the need to communicate, imposed by the poetry of the spoken word. In Athens it was Aeschylus and in London it was Shakespeare who spawned a form of theater unlike any other of that period, a form that allowed full expression to the traditional performances presented in England since the beginning of the sixteenth century.

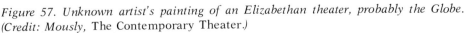

Figure 57. Unknown artist's painting of an Elizabethan theater, probably the Globe. (Credit: Mously, The Contemporary Theater.*)*

A study of the original builder's contract, containing specifications for the building of the Fortune Theatre (1600), provides some further construction details:

The frame of the house to be set square, and to measure 80 ft. square outside and 55 ft. square inside; with sure foundations of piles, brick, lime and sand, both for the outside and for the inside walls; the foundations to rise at least 1 ft. above ground.

The frame to be in three storeys; the first to contain 12 ft. in height, the second 11 ft., and the third 9 ft. Each storey to be 12 ft. 6 in. broad, "besides a juttey forwards in either of the saide twoe vpper Stories of Tenne ynches of lawfull assize," with four divisions for gentlemen's rooms, and sufficient other divisions for Twopenny rooms, with seats in these rooms and throughout the rest of the galleries. And with stairs, "conveyances" [passages] and divisions like those of the Globe.

With a stage and tiring house made in the frame, with a "shadow" or cover over the stage—the stage and staircases to be as shown in the diagram [now missing]—the stage to be 43 ft. "long," and broad enough to come to the middle of the yard. The stage to be boarded in below with new oak planks, and similarly the lower storey of the frame on that side facing the yard, and this to be also "layed over" and fenced with iron pikes. The stage in all other dimensions to be like that of the Globe.[93]

The development of the Elizabethan stage and the study of its influence on the theater of subsequent periods could fill an entire volume. In this study I have confined myself to this brief outline, with the observation that the most important heritage bequeathed to our own times by the Elizabethan theater form is a renaissance of the trend toward a close rapport between spectator and actor, a participation by the audience in the plot, and a mental contact between actors and audience that is often the crowning reward of their efforts.

The Elizabethan theater developed an architecture and a stage design eminently suited to the plays and staging conditions, a wholly functional form that served both the needs of the performance and the trend toward creative imagination and freedom without the exigencies of a setting. It was this freedom that challenged the skill of the actor, who rose to great heights of powerful and effective expression.

The Renaissance theater coming out of Italy influenced only France and Germany, either with its sumptuous *teatri* or the informal theater of the commedia dell'arte, which flourished at about the same time. The former developed the proscenium arch, the painted set, the spectacular effects, the sumptuous costumes—elements that are attributes of what many people today think of as modern theater. The latter, the commedia dell'arte, being primarily an actor's theater, placed little reliance on playhouses and settings, while it achieved a high degree of professionalism in the art of acting. Both types of theater were predominantly secular and developed against a background of virtually incessant strife, invasion, despotic rule, and reformation. In the face of these adverse conditions it is a wonder that so much was accomplished; it is also a wonder how little they contributed to the development of the theater as an art.

By contrast, where the spirit of the Renaissance could move freely and unhindered—as in the more united and comparatively peaceful countries of Spain and England—the accomplishments were much greater. The same thing had happened in Greece during the fifth century B.C., the Golden Age of Pericles. As in that period, the Spanish, and particularly the English, Renaissance era was the greatest of all ages for playwrights, actors, and audiences; its fame has endured to the present day.

6
Baroque—
The Eighteenth Century

Problems of Transition

The period known as baroque generally includes the seventeenth and eighteenth centuries in European art and may be considered an interim between the Renaissance and later times. In a sense it was a "replay" of the Renaissance from its beginning.[94] But it can also be seen as a continuation of what had gone before, as a renewal of creative activity along antecedent lines, as a second turn of the wheel.

The term "baroque" is as difficult to define and interpret as the term "Renaissance"; its chronological limits are not clearly demarcated, and many scholars, in dealing with the history of the period, resort to such distinctions as "early baroque," "middle baroque," and "late baroque." The fact is that in the sixteenth century the word was used to denote any elaborate style or notion or extravagant way of thinking.

Today baroque is used in the stylistic sense to define the art and architecture that emerged in Italy just before the year 1600, flowered luxuriantly there until the mid-eighteenth century, then spread to England, France, Spain, Germany, Holland, and central Europe. These countries, which were so peripheral to the evolution of Renaissance art in Italy, contributed creatively to the baroque, each in its own characteristic way, up to the middle of the eighteenth century, when the scepter of art passed to neoclassicism.

Classicism inevitably had a strong effect on the theater during this period. Scholars studied the techniques of the ancient Greek tragedies and found that music played a fundamental role in the performance. This discovery, coming in an age of constant exploration and ingenuity, opened up a new world of wonders for everyone concerned with the theater and the techniques of play production.

Music and perspective, the latter in constant evolution through the designs of Serlio and his successors, combined to form the foundation of what we shall henceforth call the baroque theater.

The baroque period brought the theater ever closer to the public. The principal financial backers of the Renaissance theater movement—the court, the nobility, the church—may have continued to sponsor the other arts, but in the case of the theater things changed. Theater became popular and public, a feature of everyday life.

This meant that architects were faced with serious problems of function and design, owing to the changes in the mentality and attitudes of the customer.

In most sixteenth-century Italian court theaters, the central axis of their composite functions was directed toward the figure of the local ruler and patron, *il padrone*, with his retinue and guests. With such a small audience to cater to, the size of the auditorium, in terms of volume and area, was in accord with the convenience and comfort of the patron-spectator. The scenes of the play, the settings, the perspective, and the acting were organized and scaled to the requirements of this small group. With the gradual process of conversion from court theater to popular, civic, or national theater accessible to the general public for the price of a ticket, a number of problems arose.

First and foremost was the problem of space. Faced with the pressing necessity of accommodating a larger audience, the auditorium had to undergo radical change. That necessity, certainly, was not the result of any benevolent desire on the part of the management to provide theatrical edification and entertainment for a greater number of people; it reflected a basic pecuniary need to collect more money to cover production costs, building maintenance, and so on. New seating arrangements had to be found; the classical auditorium with its tiers of seats had become unprofitable, so it was gradually abandoned in favor of the pit or orchestra familiar today.

The enlargement of the auditorium created the next problem in architectural design. The need to direct the coordinated efforts of all elements of the performance toward a central figure, the patron (with all the disadvantages attendant on this process during the Renaissance), could no longer be met in an auditorium holding a thousand or more. The stage space, till then considered ample for the deployment of the actors, was now dwarfed by the size of the auditorium. Accordingly the stage began to grow bigger, to extend further back, and the angle of vision in relation to the spectator grew wider to permit adequate visibility from the least advantageously placed seats in the house.

The enlargement of the stage in turn gave rise to a third design problem, or rather a functional need. The depth of the stage, till then not more than two or at most three meters, was now increased, receding further and further away from the auditorium. It left a vacuum that had to be filled, a newly created space that had to be made interesting in order to satisfy the esthetic sense of the theatergoing public. This led to the use of more complex scenery, which in turn required more complex means of manipulation. Scenographic technology became fundamental to the theater. The baroque period saw the emergence of new techniques and ideas for creating impressive and spectacular settings, and technical equipment developed and proliferated. The stage changed form; no longer was it merely part of one of the four walls of a room but an independent and organic functional element, with its lofts, its trapdoors and eventually its organized backstage facilities and workshops.

Finally, an important change during the baroque period was the bringing of the theater indoors. The various types of buildings we have so far encountered, from ancient times through the Renaissance, all had one feature in common: They were open-air structures. From the Greek and Roman theaters to the Teatro Olimpico and the Elizabethan playhouses, at no time was the need for shelter seriously considered. During the baroque period, the three problems outlined here—bigger audiences, enlarged stages, and more sophisticated technical equipment—could never have been solved without a roof to cover all the functions of the theater. The Teatro Farnese (1618), described in Chapter 5, was the first theater ever built with a roof covering the whole; it is unquestionably a connecting link between the two periods.

With the advent of the indoor theater, things changed for both actors and spectators. Actors were faced with the dilemma of having to choose between the strong, brilliant but often harsh light of day and the unsteady, flickering, pale but dramatic and provocative light of candles. They had to adjust the pitch and volume of their voices, which came across so distinctly and richly in the open air, in such a way as to overcome the difficulties of vocal projection in a closed space with its sonic distortions and resonances. With the introduction of music and movement (ballet) into the plot, the spectators were faced with questions of acoustics, visual angles, and comfort.

Both sides raised objections at first. Some argued that the great dramatists of the past would never have written their plays if they had known

that the action was to be confined inside four walls; others contended that the illiterate populace could not possibly appreciate what till then had been intended for the discriminating taste of dukes and nobles. Such views were perhaps extreme. In any case, it is a fact that the new type of theater, the baroque playhouse, became an indispensable feature of social life in Europe, a feature that, though it separated the audience from the reflective thought, nourished by true drama, helped greatly to develop the intellect and critical faculty of the public. Music, movement, and the opera, a new dramatic form that was a product of the baroque period, attracted people from all levels of bourgeois society. The individual was brought closer to art and its achievements and became more discriminating, restless, and inquiring. All technical problems were soon overcome because they were met with diligence and inventiveness. As a result, the seventeenth and eighteenth centuries have given us theater buildings of surpassing charm and advanced design, in terms of both architectural form and technical excellence.

The Scenic Spectacle— Scène à l'Italienne

In our analysis of the Italian Renaissance theater we referred to Serlio, to the *periakti*, and to the first general attempts at evolving a system of stage arrangement—a technique virtually nonexistent until then—that, in combination with the perspective vista, brought to theatrical productions the spectacular quality in such growing demand at the time. These developments, however, were merely the preliminary phase of a movement that was to evolve into the basic element of all theater for at least two centuries to come.

In its final form this stage arrangement was to become known as the Italian stage, or, to use the internationally accepted term, the scène à l'italienne. It was a stage designed not for acting or drama but for spectacle and scenery. It was an invention that made it possible to create every kind of scenic spectacle. An unlimited number of dazzling scenes could now succeed one another rapidly and efficiently, and for the first time playwrights and stage directors had a multipur-

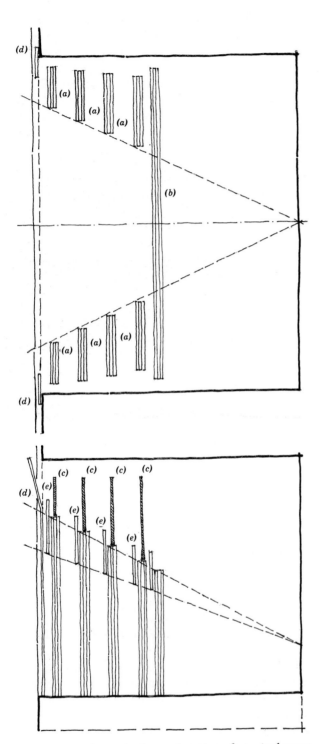

Figure 58. Schematic plan and section of a typical seventeenth-century Italian stage: (a) *wings;* (b) *backscene;* (c) *borders;* (d) *frontispiece;* (e) *corner borders (clouds).* *(Drawings by author.)*

pose weapon at hand that was flexible and adaptable. Last but not least, this technique contributed importantly to the development of a new, purely Italian type of theater—the opera.

Generally speaking, the Italian stage comprised three basic parts: the side wings, the backscene, and the overhead shallow drop curtains known as borders (Figure 58). Each of these was manipulated in its own particular way.[95]

The earlier operas nearly always included in their settings an outdoor scene, so all the early borders depicted skies or clouds. Much later, around 1650, we find scenes set in the interior of palaces, which required some kind of architectural ceiling. The skies or ceilings were reproduced by means of a succession of borders, one behind the other (Figure 58). Then there was the problem of joining them to the wing-tops—a question of the junction itself and of reducing the height of the stage. The problem was solved by fitting small borders in the two corners to suggest clouds or wavelets (Figures 58, 59). Together with the wings and borders, the corner pieces formed something in the nature of an arch. An early eighteenth-century model of this stage system was formerly to be found in the Nuremberg National Museum but has since been destroyed (Figure 60).[96]

The system of wings was given its final form toward the close of the sixteenth century and the beginning of the seventeenth. Serlio's perspective designs were discarded; wings and borders came into general use, arranged in a more sophisticated way and painted according to the requirements of the setting. The onstage edges of the wings were generally cut to match the outline of the object they were meant to represent (Figure 59), and the wings were placed in pairs, one behind the other, all the way to the back of the stage. Each successive pair was lower than the one in front, thus creating a perspective effect similar to that of the vistas described earlier.[97]

The wings were moved and changed by means of an ingenious mechanical arrangement consisting of a tall narrow frame, usually wooden, resting on a chassis mounted on wheels. The chassis, known as the *carretto* in Italy or *Kulissenwagen* in Germany, moved along rails running transversely underneath the stage floor, which had slits to allow movement of the frames (Figure 61).

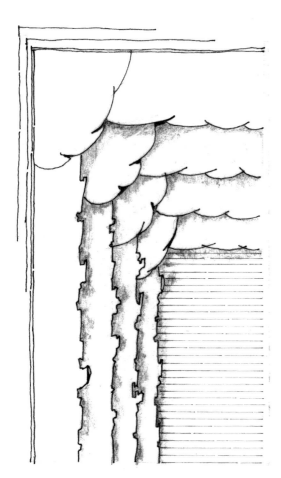

Figure 59. This corner junction of borders and wings with "clouds" was a popular setting in the seventeenth century. Similar clouds were also used on the backscene. The stageward edge of the wings was usually cut to match the outline of the object that they were meant to represent. (Drawing by author.)

Figure 60. Model, now destroyed, of the scenic system used in the seventeenth century. (Credit: Southern, Seven Ages, p. 8.)

Figure 61. Rough sketch of the system for moving the wings: (a) chassis, or carreto; (b) frame; (c) and (d) wings-scenery; (e) stage backscene; (f) shaft controlling the movement. (Drawing by the author.)

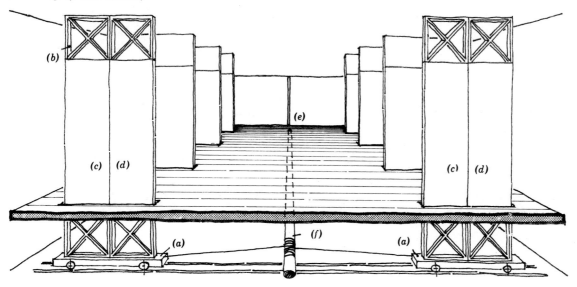

For more efficient use of the available space, two or three frames were mounted on each chassis, making for increased flexibility and speed in changing scenery. A system of pulleys and shafts made it possible to move the carretto-mounted wings simultaneously toward or away from the centerline of the stage and to change them successively so as to form the setting desired by the director. This, or a similar system, is believed to have been used for the first time by F. Guitti in the Teatro Farnese in 1628,[98] but the man who developed and perfected it was Giacomo Torelli (1608–1678). Torelli earned the sobriquet "the great magician" through his creations and inventions, truly remarkable in his day, which helped to carry the principles and ideas of the Italian stage all over Europe and established it as the sole form of spectacle for at least two centuries to come (Figure 62).

The problem of the wings and borders was solved fairly quickly, but the difficulties presented by the back of the stage, the backscene, was a less simple matter. Information explaining clearly how the problem was met in the sixteenth and seventeenth centuries is hard to come by. Indications are that there were three different methods of changing this piece of scenery. The first, generally used only on smaller stages, was to divide the backscene vertically into two halves and to change the sections by means of the wing system just described (Figure 61). This was not feasible for large stages, with their massive, heavy backscenes. Here the backscene was mounted on a one-piece frame that could be lowered on runners and concealed under the stage through a slot in the floor. The third method was to leave the backscene unframed and to have instead a painted or canvas backdrop that could

Figure 62. Design by Giacomo Torelli for The Wedding of Peleus and Thetis, *Paris, 1654.*
(Nicoll, Development of the Theatre, *p. 126. Reprinted by permission.)*

be rolled up around an overhead horizontal pole. Rolling up a cloth can be destructive to its painted surface, but it was only in the early nineteenth century that a solution was forthcoming, which was the most important later development in the Italian stage system. This method, known as flying, involved raising the height of the ceiling above the stage and adding a high loft or tower into which the backcloths could be pulled up and concealed without winding them in a roll. The new system spread quickly, and by the end of the nineteenth century even the smallest provincial theaters had adopted it.

Despite the advances made in Italian stage system, however, one basic disadvantage already evident in Serlio's earlier efforts was not overcome. The disadvantage arose from the desire to achieve illusion through perspective, a goal common to all the scenographic explorations of the Italian stage. The progressively reduced height of the wings and reverse escalation of the borders certainly gave the stage perspective depth, but in most instances it made it impossible for the actors to enter from the back of the stage, for in doing so they threw the scene out of proportion and completely ruined the illusion.

Another invention characteristic of the Italian stage and one that survives to our day was the trapdoor. Many ways were devised of opening sections of the stage floor. The sections were either small squares big enough for a single person or were bridges running the length of the stage into which whole groups of people or large objects could vanish from the audience's view. The technique of raising these traps was so advanced that a person could be made to emerge slowly into the action of the play or catapulted forcefully into the air—which is why actors met with frequent accidents in those days.

Inigo Jones

When the Italian stage spread beyond the frontiers of Italy, it found a fervent advocate, admirer, and scholar in the great English architect Inigo Jones (1573–1652).[99] Jones left a work of immense interest, a work that spanned 35 years, from 1605 to 1640, in every area connected with the theater. Starting as a designer of the Elizabethan stage and masque scenery,[100] he soon came under the spell of the exciting new

theatrical developments in Italy. After two very fruitful journeys to that country in 1606 and 1613, he experimented and studied the work of Palladio and began developing a great many ideas for scenery and for stage and auditorium arrangements.[101]

Combining the style of Serlio with the later discoveries in wing design, Jones evolved a new system of opening a piece of scenery by drawing its two halves apart to reveal another scene behind. Each pair of wings first appeared with its two halves joined (drawing a) to present a single painted picture. The sections slid apart to reveal a second pair of joined wings showing another picture; these in turn opened to disclose a third, and so on (drawing b). Jones continued to elaborate on this, and aptly named the sliding elements "shutters;" the number of shutters varied with the requirements of the play.

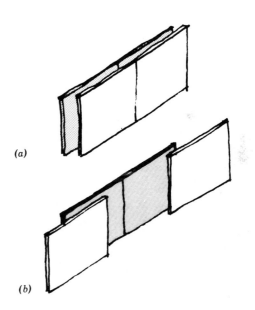

(a)

(b)

To incorporate the new and fashionable effect of the perspective vista so popular at the time, he framed his backscene of shutters in the end of an avenue of diminishing side scenes, in the same way as Serlio (drawing c). These wings had a functional purpose, which was to conceal or "mask" the space at the sides of the stage into which the opening shutters slid when they were opened, and a visual purpose, which was to enhance the perspective depth of the stage.

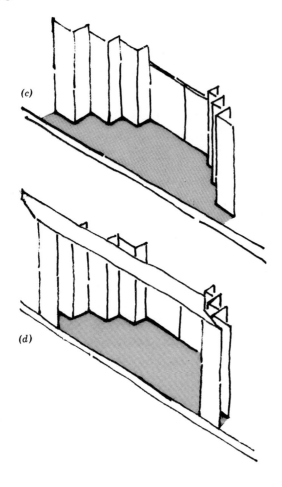

A heaven or sky was needed to complete the scenic composition and with it some means of concealing its leading edge and structural details. Jones's solution was a front frame that provided a mask for the edge by a strip across hung from the ceiling. In this way the setting was set behind a surround, aptly named "frontispiece" by Inigo Jones (drawing d), and viewed through and under that surround (Figure 63).[102]

An application of all these elements can be seen in Jones's design for a French pastoral play titled *Florimène* and produced in Whitehall by a French theater company in 1635.[103] The stage and auditorium arrangement (Figure 64) reveals Serlio's scenery, the shutters and an extension of the proscenium, and the "apron," a relic of the Elizabethan platform stage. The drawing clearly shows Jones's proposed seating arrangement, which bears the distinct influence of the Teatro Farnese (Figure 50). It also shows the special placement of the state or royal seats along the projected centerline of the stage. We must remember that the court theater was still predominant in England, that the centerpiece of every design was the ruler-patron (king or duke) and that the dominant purpose was to create vivid scenic effects. This explains why Jones, while introducing a new staging system, preferred in the audience end of the hall a seating arrangement along traditional lines rather than one that would place the spectators most conveniently facing the stage.

When in 1642 the English Parliament closed all the theaters,[104] the ban continuing after 1648 under Cromwell's Puritans, the life of the theater came to an abrupt and total stop. The playhouses remained closed for 12 more years until the Restoration in 1660; Inigo Jones's, and indeed England's, relations with the Italian stage were completely severed. His work was later continued by his pupil John Webb but without any major variations or developments.

Figure 63. Frontispiece by Inigo Jones for Albion's Triumph, *1609. (Nicoll,* Development of the Theatre, *p. 106. Reprinted by permission.)*

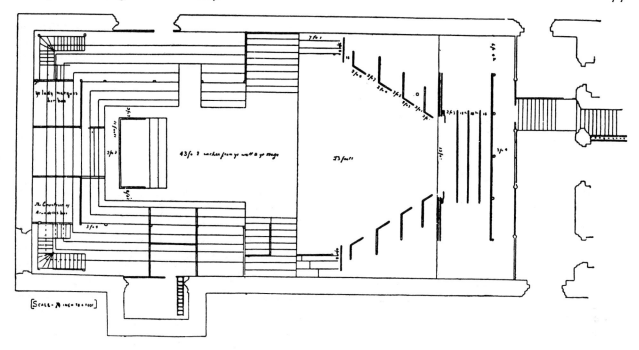

Figure 64. Plan by Inigo Jones for Florimène, *1635. (Nicoll,* Development of the Theatre, *p. 107. Reprinted by permission.)*

The Auditorium in the Italian Stage

The scène à l'italienne affected not only the stage and setting but the rest of the house as well. Corresponding changes had to be made to the auditorium. The main problem was to design a roofed space big enough to hold the greatest possible number of people. The interior arrangement, moreover, had to be conditioned by one key element, the frame through which one looked at the stage in order to enjoy all those marvels of perspective illusion. Thus was born the design of the Italian opera house, the building that, though essentially useless, every self-respecting city still dreams of acquiring.

It can be asserted without hesitation that perspective scenery, which contributed so much to the evolution of the theater, was also the sole factor responsible for the opera house's architectural inflexibility and stagnation, conditions that persisted until the early twentieth century.

This conclusion should by no means be considered extreme. The problem stems from the basic rules of perspective. Frontal perspective has only a single vanishing point. As the spectator moves farther from the vertical axis perpendicular to this single rational point on the stage, the illusion progressively diminishes. To avoid this disadvantage, the audience on the floor had to be a serried mass crowded together in a narrow section. But this was no easy matter. Theaters were now public institutions and not court entertainments concerned only with the visual field of the royal or ducal personage. Public spectacles were open to people of all classes—rulers, patricians, and plebeians alike. These classes had to be segregated; it was inconceivable in the seventeenth century that a nobleman should rub shoulders with the middle and lower classes.

The problem, then, was to keep the spectator's angle of vision in relation to the center of stage as narrow as possible so that the result of variance from the rational vanishing point of the perspective setting would be within a tolerable

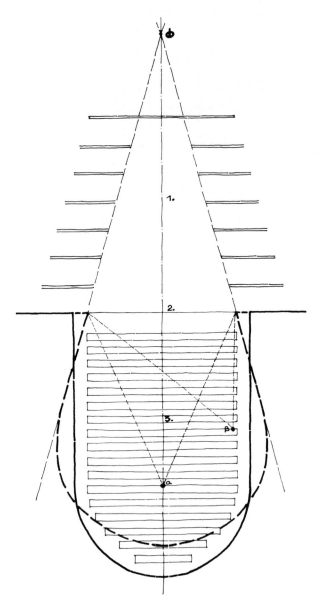

Figure 65. Schematic arrangement of (1) the stage, (2) proscenium arch and (3) stalls of a baroque theater clearly showing the different perspective impressions received by spectator a, who was seated exactly opposite the vanishing point of the perspective composition, and spectator b, who was far to the side. To improve visibility the original U-shaped pit was abandoned in favor of the horseshoe (broken line). (Drawing by author.)

limit (Figure 65). The first step was to enclose the entire stage picture in a "frame" similar to and designed on the same principles as Inigo Jones's frontispiece. The result was the proscenium arch, a feature that became permanent and, with its curtain and ornamentation, is such a familiar part of the stage of every conventional playhouse today that it is the first thing that comes to the minds of ordinary theatergoers if they are asked to describe a theater stage.

To enable the members of the audience to see what went on beyond the arch, they had to be as close as possible to its centerline, and the level of their eyes had to be not too distant from the rational horizon line of the perspective setting. All the forms of auditorium discussed so far fell short of meeting these two fundamental requirements. The floor had to be level; for greater visual convenience of the audience, it was given a slight inclination, and the rows of seats were arranged so that each spectator could see the stage over the heads of the people sitting in front of him.

The word "auditorium" now no longer meant anything; the Italians resorted once again to the Roman period and the Middle Ages. They borrowed the word *platea* for what we would call today the stalls and the pit of a modern playhouse.

At first the *platea* was U-shaped as in the Teatro Farnese; later it was shaped like a horseshoe (Figure 65); shallow, multistoried galleries ran around the back and side walls of the hall, divided into compartments reminiscent of the gentlemen's rooms of the Elizabethan playhouses. The Italians named them "palco," the French "loges," and the English "boxes" (Figure 66).

In light of our remarks concerning visual angles these boxes were the worst seats in the house (Figure 67), but for the upper classes they had other, more important advantages: They symbolized social status, they provided an opportunity to display that status, and they secluded and segregated their noble occupants from the masses. Accordingly, they were the highest-priced seats in the theater. They soon became a permanent architectural feature in all Italian theaters, and today we find boxes not only in opera houses but in most conventional theaters as well.

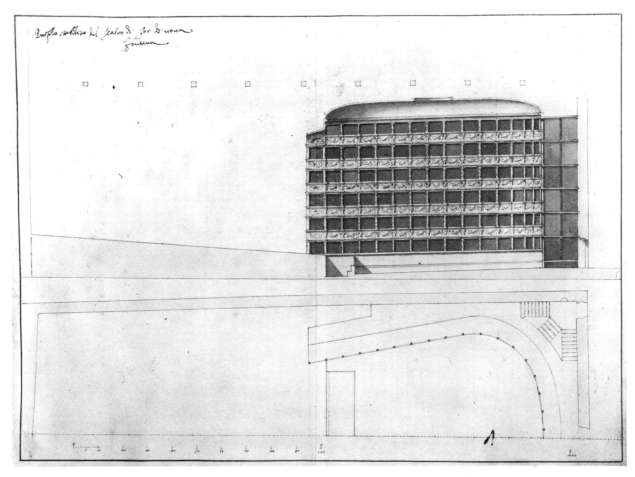

Figure 66. Tor di Nona Theater, Rome: drawing showing the boxes and the horseshoe
shape of the orchestra. (By permission of the trustees of Sir John Soane's Museum.)

Figure 67. The cramped and stuffy
interior of a theater box, from a
print by Honoré Daumier. (By
permission of the Museum of Fine
Arts, Boston.)

It is believed that the boxes were originally separated from each other by wooden partitions at right angles to the wall of the house (Figure 68). This arrangement was soon changed and the partitions slanted obliquely toward the stage for better visibility, as in the Teatro Degli Intronati (Figure 69), built in Siena in 1670, and the Fortuna in Fano (Figure 70), designed by Torelli and built in 1677. Both theaters retained the U-shaped pit.

As we have seen, this shape of pit is not ideal from the standpoint of visibility; therefore, it was abandoned. From the beginning of the eighteenth century on, we encounter the horse-

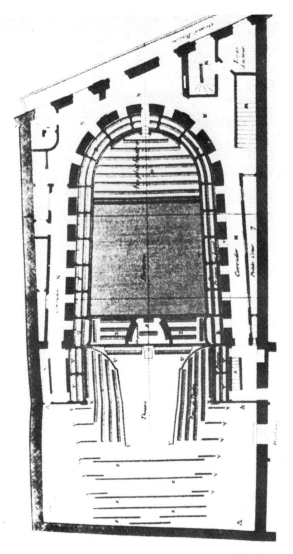

Figure 68. Plan of the first theater of the Comédie Française, showing the perpendicular partitions between the boxes. As in most seventeenth-century theaters, it did not have seats but benches. Benches have also been placed on the stage itself. (Author's archive.)

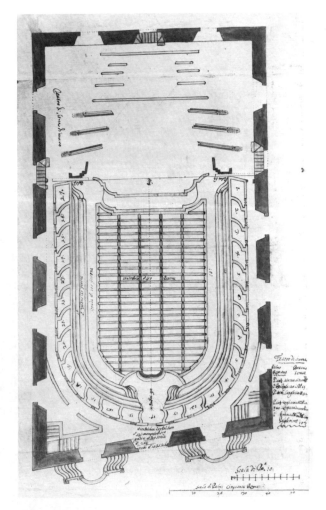

Figure 69. Teatro degli Intronati, Siena: plan. Note the slanting partitions between boxes and the benches for the spectators. (By permission of the trustees of Sir John Soane's Museum.)

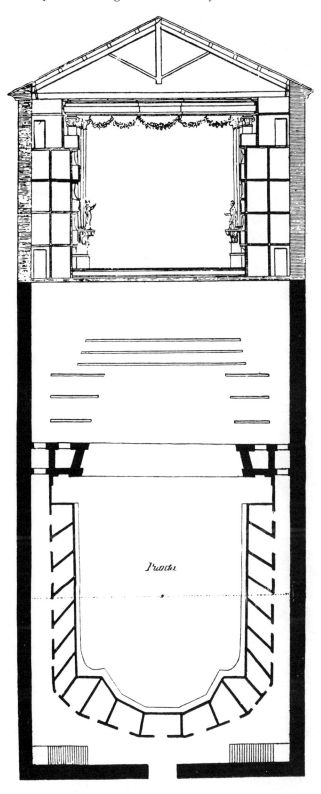

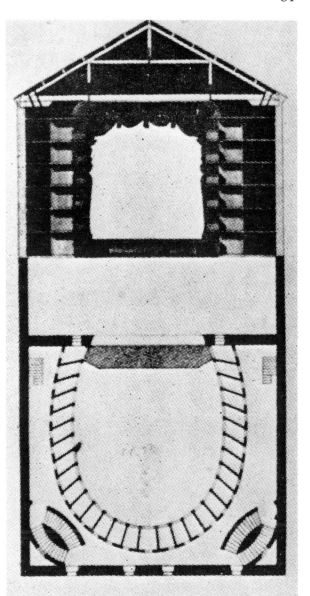

Figure 70. Fortuna Theater, Fano: plan and proscenium arch. (By permission of the Victoria and Albert Museum.)

Figure 71. Argentina Theater, Rome: plan and proscenium arch. (By permission of the Victoria and Albert Museum.)

shoe shape, as in the Argentina in Rome (Figure 71), built in 1732 by Girolamo Teodoli, and the bell shape, as in the famous Teatro San Carlo of Naples (Figures 72, 73), built in 1737 by Angelo Carasale. Another theater with a horseshoe-shaped pit is the celebrated Teatro alla Scala in Milan (Figure 74), built by Piermarini in 1778.

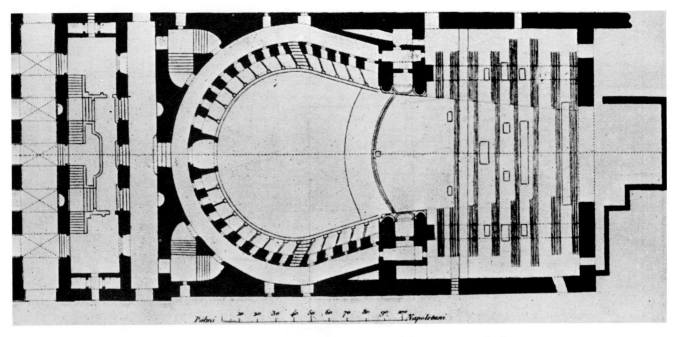

Figure 72. Teatro San Carlo, Naples, 1737: plan. (By permission of the Victoria and Albert Museum.)

Figure 73. Teatro San Carlo, Naples, as reconstructed by Antonio Niccolini, 1817. (Nicoll, Development of the Theatre, *p. 177. Reprinted by permission.)*

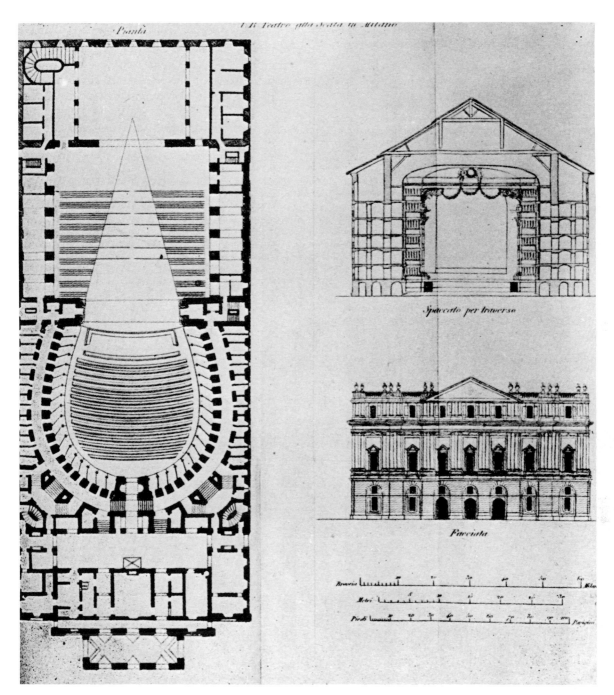

Figure 74. Teatro alla Scala, Milan, 1778: plan, section, and facade. (By permission of the Victoria and Albert Museum.)

Further variations were the near-ellipse used by Alfieri in the Regio Theater of Turin in 1738 (Figure 75) and the oval adopted by Cosimo Morelli in 1779 for the theater of Imola (Figure 76). Here the curve of the oval advanced far into the stage; in place of the standard proscenium Morelli, with two pillars, created not one but

Figure 76. Teatro Imola, plan. Designed by Cosimo Morelli, 1779. (By permission of the Victoria and Albert Museum.)

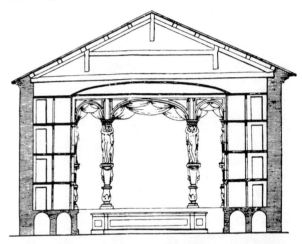

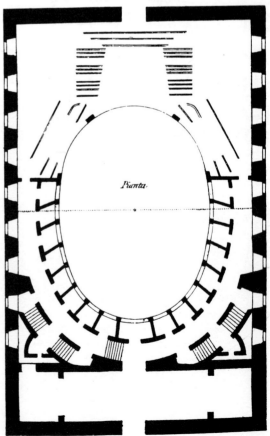

Figure 75. Teatro Regio, Turin: plan. Designed by Vitorrio Alfieri, 1738. (By permission of the Victoria and Albert Museum.)

three stages: the main stage in the middle flanked by two smaller stages. Through the use of wings and shutters this arrangement gave the director greater scope for composition.[105]

We could cite many more examples of the Italian opera houses, which with their variety and sumptuousness endowed the seventeenth and eighteenth centuries with a character all their own. This would be beside the point were it not that not only opera houses but also theaters for true drama or municipal, civic, or national presentations, both in Italy and the rest of Europe, were all built in the same style. Influenced by the prevailing fashion and trends, architects ignored certain fundamental rules of function, scale, acoustics, and other requirements; they emphasized detail and strove for purely visual and decorative effect. The unhappy results are all too obvious, at least to present-day notions. We see how difficult it is to stage a play by Shakespeare or Molière in an eighteenth-century playhouse and how vexatious for a spectator in the twenty-fifth or thirtieth row not to be able to catch the actor's every phrase, expression, and mood.

Inaugurating an exhibition on early Italian stagecraft in 1952 in Venice, Gerardo Guerrieri made the following remarks (as reported by Richard Southern):

One of the paradoxes of theatre history is how the nation least productive of dramatic literature in the whole 17th century came to impose, in that same century, its own conception of spectacle upon all Europe. The theatre building of today, perspective illusion, the frame to the stage and the stage machinery, the auditorium with its boxes, and all which constitutes, even today, the "theatre," do not spring from the England of Shakespeare, nor the Spain of Calderon, nor the France of Molière, Corneille and Racine; but are inventions, elaborated in Italy through nearly two centuries of experiments and projects and provisional schemes. And they were produced—which is no small curiosity—out of the world of architects and decorators rather than that of men of the theatre.[106]

This comment underscores the influence of the Italian stage on the rest of Europe. It is time now to consider theater in other countries before closing the chapter on the seventeenth and eighteenth centuries.

Private and Court Theaters in England

The beginning of the seventeenth century found the theater movement in England fixed on the Elizabethan views concerning public theater. The use of scenery and illusion was almost unknown and little desired by the public. Theatergoers had no use at all for visual effect; what interested and attracted them was the power of the spoken word itself. The achievements of the Italian stage with its perspective scenery, introduced by the designs of Inigo Jones, had a limited appeal through the settings he created for court performances or special festive occasions.

The only development in the Elizabethan public theater during the first 42 years of the seventeenth century was its conversion from an outdoor structure to a closed "private" playhouse, so named because it drew the upper classes of London away from the uncomfortable open-air public playhouses.

When the Globe Theatre burned to the ground in 1613, Shakespeare's company, which owned it, built another on the site, this time an indoor theater.[107] The new Globe continued in the tradition of the old, but the wide public appeal of this enclosed playhouse soon influenced the upper classes to the point where all new theaters built in the early seventeenth century were of the indoor or "private" type. It was now possible to introduce Inigo Jones's scenic inventions in these playhouses, the innovations that had so delighted the court and that gradually became more elaborate and impressive in response to the new tastes and notions of the English public.

While this type of theater was developing and gaining popularity, the English continued building small private court theaters that retained many features of the Roman auditorium as adapted and interpreted in the Teatro Olimpico. Because they were intended for a small and privileged audience, these playhouses were quite small, and the auditorium, often a plain semicircle, was supported by three of the enclosing walls. On the fourth side was the stage, also small, its proscenium arch heavily ornamented with pilasters, arches, and murals.

The private theater is the subject of two rather interesting drawings by Inigo Jones, or possibly his pupil John Webb (1611–1672). The first (Fig-

Figure 77. Drawing of the Cockpit-in-Court: (left) *facade and stage,* (right) *plan of the auditorium and stage. (By permission of the Provost and Fellows of Worcester College, Oxford.)*

ure 77) depicts the Cockpit-in-Court[108] and illustrates how little that playhouse differs from present-day experimental theater forms.[109] The second (Figure 78)[110] clearly reveals the influences of Serlio in the configuration of the auditorium and of the Teatro Olimpico in that of the proscenium.

All contact between the theater and society was abruptly brought to a stop in 1642 by the outbreak of the first phase of the Civil War (1642–1646) between the Royalists and the Puri-

tans. After Cromwell's final victory in 1648, art in all its forms was plunged into darkness; under the Protectorate the theater, once again branded as sinful by the church, virtually ceased to exist for the next 12 years. With the restoration of Charles II in 1660, however, it flourished again and resumed its development. Now, however, it evolved on a new and different pattern; the Elizabethan stage was abandoned, and somewhat belatedly the English theater entered the age of baroque.

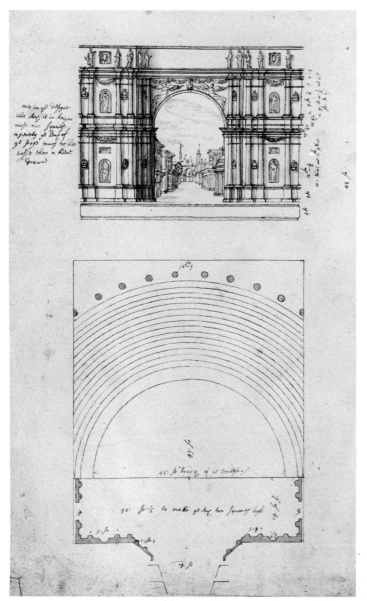

Figure 78. Drawing of a theater by Inigo Jones. (By permission of the Provost and Fellows of Worcester College, Oxord.)

The English Theater of the Restoration and the Eighteenth Century

Between 1656 and 1660 a few bold attempts to revive the theater were made by two ardent supporters of the drama, the playwrights Thomas Killigrew and Sir William Davenant. Both were known to the public; some of their plays had been staged at popular theaters in the past. Davenant, who continued the work of Ben Jonson[111] as a writer of court masques, had worked in collaboration with Inigo Jones when the architect was at the pinnacle of his creativity as a stage designer.[112]

In 1656 Davenant obtained special permission from the authorities to stage the first English opera, *The Siege of Rhodes*, in the hall of Rutland House, and assigned John Webb to design the settings. Webb, a devoted disciple of Jones, adhered faithfully to his master's principles and produced the same scenic arrangement and the same kind of frontispiece in place of the proscenium arch (Figures 79, 80). Both the opera itself and Webb's designs, though primitive, clearly bore the stamp of the Italian tradition.

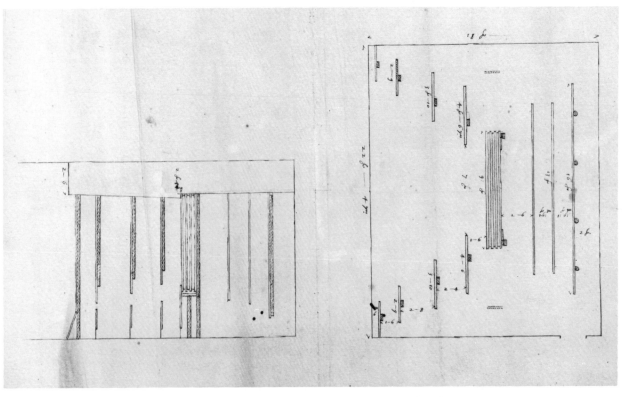

Figure 79. Arrangement of the setting for the opera The Siege of Rhodes. *(By permission of the British Museum, British Library.)*

Figure 80. John Webb's frontispiece and permanent wings for The Siege of Rhodes. *(Nicoll,* Development of the Theatre, *p. 148. Reprinted by permission.)*

It was clear that the English Restoration theater was determined to make a fresh start and to sever all ties with its Elizabethan past, but it did not succeed in regaining the appeal and popularity it had enjoyed in Shakespeare's day. The richly staged spectacles tended to reflect the tastes and pastimes of a highly mannered minority, the exiled court society, which brought over from France in magnified form every fashion and style it could assimilate. An apt description is provided by Vera Mowry Roberts:

Theatre was one of the social activities of a circle brilliantly delineated in Pepys' famous Diary—a pleasure-loving, amoral people, contemptuous of what they conceived to be a narrow Puritan view of the world, and determined to enjoy all the sensual aspects of existence.[113]

Architecturally, too, a final transition from the Elizabethan building to the Italian-type opera house was accomplished during the Restoration. No account would be complete without mentioning the contribution of the great architect Sir Christopher Wren (1632–1723), who worked with both Davenant and Killigrew in building playhouses of the new form to house the two dramatists' theatrical companies.

Very little information is available concerning these theaters. If we accept the view of Allardyce Nicoll[114] that the subject of an uncaptioned design discovered at Oxford is the first Drury Lane Theater of Killigrew's company, then its author unquestionably is Christopher Wren. The design is very typical of the trend then prevailing. The plan (Figure 81) shows a steeply inclined auditorium, the seatbanks arranged in segments of

Figure 81. Plan of a theater by Christopher Wren, believed to be the original Drury Lane. (By permission of the Warden and Fellows of All Souls College, Oxford.)

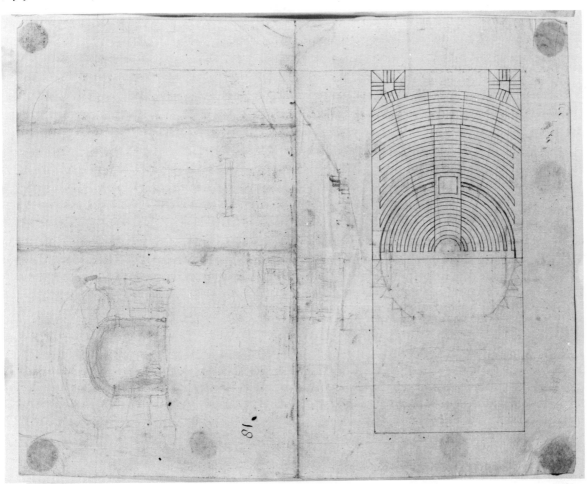

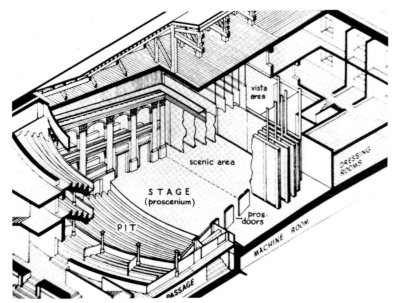

Figure 82. Wren's second Drury Lane, 1674. (Credit: Roberts, On Stage, p. 233.)

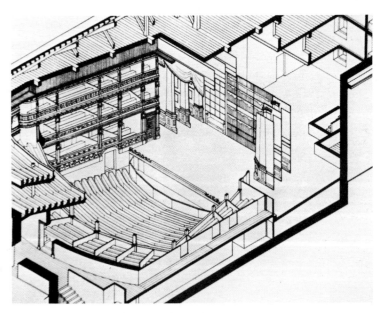

Figure 83. Drury Lane, as reconstructed in 1775. (Credit: Roberts, On Stage, p. 233.)

circles struck from a center almost in the middle of the long, narrow rectangular house. A projection of the semicircle described by the seventh row of seats into a full circle forms a very large, wide proscenium, an apron reminiscent of its Elizabethan forerunner. Behind the apron is a deep stage with a slightly sloping floor.

Strikingly different is the second Drury Lane built in 1674, also by Wren, for the same company (Figure 82). The circular shape is discarded, and the seatbank arrangement is only moderately curved. Galleries and boxes have been introduced, and the building has taken on a

resemblance to an Italian opera house. The proscenium-apron remains as large as in the first Drury Lane, but it has now acquired a slope and connects directly and continuously with the stage, which is equipped with wings, shutters, and borders. Doors on either side of the proscenium are topped by a double tier of boxes. These doors are encountered in practically all English theaters for nearly a century to come; originally, with the oversize proscenium (Figure 82), there were four, the number being reduced to two, one on each side, when the proscenium was shortened (Figure 83).

275834

9568781091011

Conjecture is likewise required in the case of another theater by Wren—Duke's Theatre in Dorset Garden. It opened a little earlier (1671) as the home of Davenant's company.[115]

The use of the two different types of stage in these theaters—namely, the large proscenium and the stage proper—reveals the coexistence of two contrasting notions that then prevailed in England. The foreground—the Elizabethan apron—represented fast action and the austerity that had become a tradition with the English public. It was completely bare of scenery save for the two or four flanking doors that were used by the actors in their comings and goings. At the rear, the stage à l'italienne represented the world of fantasy, a place where the hero would go when the plot required that he do something solemn or mysterious. The painted scenery and understated lighting in this area nearly always produced the desired effect with great success.

In the late eighteenth century the proscenium began growing smaller to make room for more audience seats; during the next century attempts were made to get rid of the actors' side doors. We see this modification first in the reconstructed Drury Lane of 1775 (Figure 83) and later in the Royalty Theatre, which opened in 1787 (Figure 84), and in the 1794 new Drury Lane (Figure 85), which was heralded as the biggest theater in Europe.[116]

Figure 84. Royalty Theater, 1787. (Nicoll, Development of the Theatre, p. 159. Reprinted by permission.)

Figure 85. The new Drury Lane, 1794. (Credit: Roberts, On Stage, p. 262.)

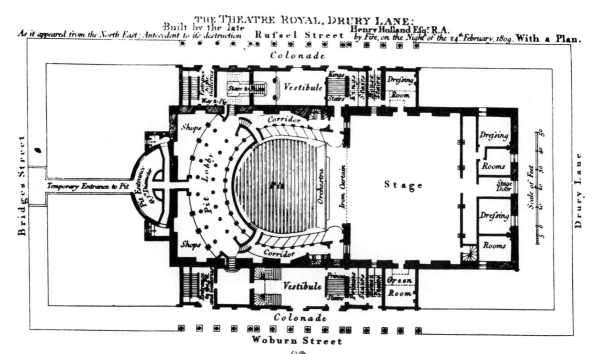

The trend to create sumptuous and imposing buildings was now as firmly established in England as in Italy; the Elizabethan tradition, which had so stalwartly withstood the baroque invasion throughout the eighteenth century, finally retreated before the new notions and lifestyle of the Victorian era.

Figure 86. Vienna Opera House, ca 1690. (Credit: Museum der Stadt Wien.)

The Rest of Europe

The influence of the Italian stage on the rest of Europe resulted in the construction of a number of outstanding theaters in the capital cities. Thus the Salvatorplatz Theater in Munich in 1657, the Vienna Opera House in 1690 (Figure 86), the Opera House at Versailles in 1753 (Figure 87), the renovated Hôtel de Bourgogne in 1765 (Figure 88) in Paris, and in Stuttgart, where the stage assumed unique importance, as one can see from the plan of its opera house (Figure 89).[117]

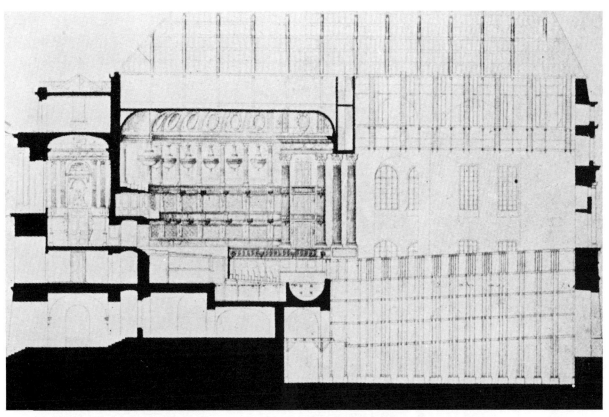

Figure 87. Opera House, Versailles, 1753. (Nicoll, Development of the Theatre, p. 157. Reprinted by permission.)

Figure 88. Hôtel de Bourgogne, 1765. (By permission of the Bibliotèque Nationale, Paris.)

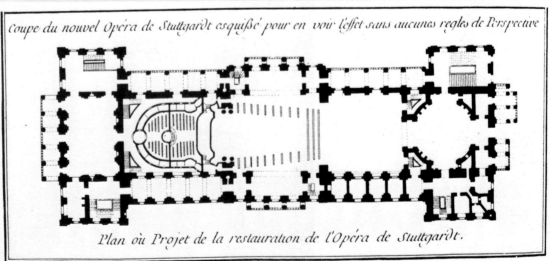

Coupe du nouvel Opéra de Stuttgardt esquissé pour en voir l'effet sans aucunes regles de Perspective

Plan où Projet de la restauration de l'Opéra de Stuttgardt.

Figure 89. Stuttgart Opera House, 1759. (Author's archive.)

94

In 1638 Jacob van Campen designed and built the Schouwburg (show palace) in Amsterdam (Figures 90, 91) in a form that can be compared with no other theater. The elliptical auditorium had two tiers of boxes; the stage, a projection of the ellipse, was adorned by two galleries flanking a central pediment and supported by pillars that framed ornamental painted designs. This style was not copied in any of the succeeding Dutch theaters; thus the 1638 Schouwburg is unique in the history of the theater. When a theater was built on the remains of the old Schouwburg in 1772, the earlier structure was renovated in the established and immensely popular Italian baroque style (Figure 92).

Whereas in Italy there was a trend toward elongating the auditorium, the exact reverse held true in eighteenth-century France. In an attempt to depart from the baroque, French architects began thinking of widening rather than lengthening the audience area. These new ideas ended by combining theory with feasibility. Instead of emphasizing the stage as in Italy, theater design turned to a consideration of the needs of the audience in terms of better visibility and acoustics. The proscenium arch was in most instances discarded, and the stage was brought forward into the audience area, an arrangement clearly seen in the Hôtel de Bourgogne (Figure 88), which was typical of this new notion.

Figure 90. The Schouwburg, 1638: plan. (By permission of the Houghton Library, Harvard University.)

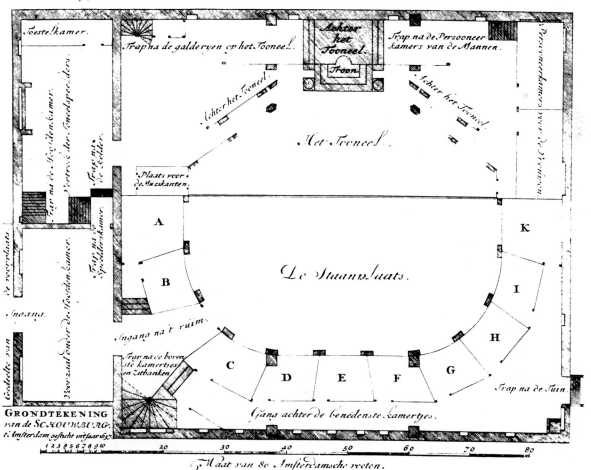

HET TOONEEL VAN D'AMSTERDAMSCHE SCHOUBURG, GESTICHT INT JAAR 1637. EN VERTIMMERT IN 1665.

Tooneelspel kwam in't licht tot leerzaam tydverdryf,   En prikkelt ze tot vreugd, of slaat ons zoete wonden,
Het wykt geen ander spel, noch koninklyke vonden;   Het toont in kleen begrip al 's menschen ydelheid,
Het bootst de waereld na, het kittelt ziel en lyf.   Daar Demokryt om lacht, daar Heraklyt om schreid.

J. v. Vondel.

Figure 91. The Schouwburg, 1638: (above) stage; (below) auditorium. (By permission of
the Houghton Library, Harvard University.)

ZIT EN STAANPLAATSEN VAN D'AMSTERDAMSCHE SCHOUBURG, GESTICHT INT JAAR 1637. EN VERTIMMERT IN 1665.

't Ontbreidelen der Jeugd, noch godloos voedsel van   Die, tot een oeffenschool van Deugd, den Schouburg stichte,
Vervloekte afgodery, en al wat zy verdichte;   Der arme Weezen troost, der Ouden stok en staf.
Maar stichtig tydverdryf wast oogmerk van dien Man   Zo schryft Pompejus niet; maar Kampen op zyn Graf.

J. v. Vondel.

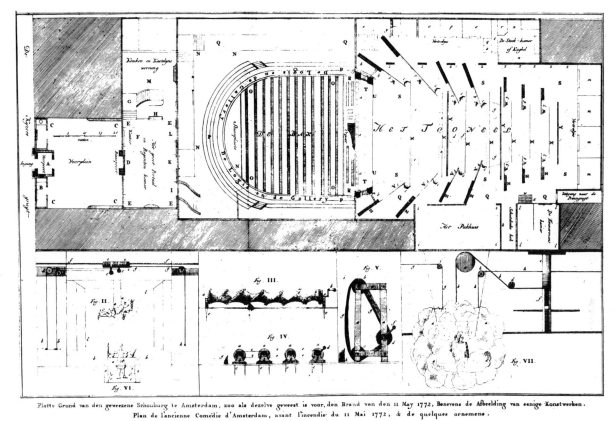

Platte Grond van den geweezene Schouburg te Amsterdam, zoo als dezelve geweest is voor den Brand van den 11 May 1772, Benevens de Afbeelding van eenige Konstwerken.
Plan de l'ancienne Comédie d'Amsterdam, avant l'incendie du 11 Mai 1772, & de quelques ornemens.

Figure 92. The Schouwburg, reconstructed, 1772. (By permission of the Houghton Library, Harvard University.)

In closing the chapter on this period we feel it would be an omission not to mention briefly what happened in Greece during that time. A theater tradition developed mainly during the sixteenth and seventeenth centuries in Crete and was later transplanted to the Ionian Islands by Cretan refugees. It is significant that it was in those islands, which alone in the whole of Greece enjoyed freedom of expression in those times, that the theater was able to survive as a memory of the brilliant past. In the rest of the country, under Turkish rule theatrical activity was reduced to sideshows at local fairs and to primitive forms of presentation, relics of which can still be encountered today in many parts of Greece. It would of course be vain to look for building forms, since for obvious reasons none existed,

but the written word flourished admirably through the works of Kornaros and Hortadjis. With the *Sacrifice of Abraham*, the *Erotocritos*, and the *Erophile*, the seventeenth-century Cretan theater came very close to the standards of ancient tragedy and influenced the later literature of the Ionian Islands.

As late as the nineteenth century these plays were produced in almost the same manner and with almost the same arrangements as those used in the West during the Middle Ages and early Renaissance—clearly a result of strong Venetian influence. At the same time, they contributed to the development of new, independent theatrical presentations that soon evolved into popular custom, mostly of a carnival nature. Outdoor dramatic performances, such as the

Δικαστήριο (*dikastirio*, lawcourt) in Cephallonia and the Ὁμιλίες (*omilies*, homilies) in Zante, not only developed notably from the seventeenth to the nineteenth century but are still regarded with interest from the literary point of view.[118] It is a pity that the political and social conditions of the period prevented the presentation of these pieces in an appropriate architectural frame. If this had been possible, it would certainly have produced yet another architectural form in the history of the theater. Perhaps that form would have affected the theater's evolution; but perhaps this is merely subjective speculation. Nobody can deny, however, that the only people who can fittingly continue a tradition are the people who created it.

7
The Nineteenth Century

The Birth of Democracy

Before considering the evolution of the theater in the nineteenth century, it is essential to examine the climate of the period and the social problems left by the previous century. The problems were certainly neither casual nor superficial; they were the result of situations that changed the entire structure of society, overthrew hallowed institutions, to alter the frontiers of nations, and, last but not least, revived and imposed a concept that for centuries had been forgotten—the concept of democracy.

With the triumph of the French Revolution in 1789 and the fall of the Bastille, there followed the collapse of ideas, concepts, and doctrines that till then had been thought to be God-given and impregnable. For the changes that were to come there was no precedent, at least since the days of the Renaissance. Before that, the Roman Catholic Church had ruled over the destiny of the world "by the grace of God." After the Renaissance, temporal power was vested in the kings and queens, who likewise ruled "by the grace of God" and determined how their subjects must live and what they must think. The French and the Americans rebelled against the old order and established their republics with a democratic system of government that provided a new outlet for the human spirit, a freedom that had been all but forgotten. The intellectuals believed a new renaissance was opening up before them and that the successful revolution in the system of government would be followed by a successful revolution of the spirit and the mind.

The final outcome is not within the scope of this study. One would have imagined, however, that since the theater is so closely and directly linked with the intellect and the spirit, the birth of democracy would have brought a parallel birth of great creations with a social content, great dramatic masterpieces, great and monumental buildings that would leave a deep and lasting imprint for the centuries to come.

Nothing like that happened, or rather what happened was the reverse: The theater fell into a decline or, more precisely, continued suffering a decline that had begun, from the standpoint of dramatic repertory at least, many years previous. No one can seriously consider the Italian type of melodrama of the eighteenth century as a prime form in the theater. And the genius of dramatists like Ibsen, Shaw, and Wagner was still far in the future.

Cheney quotes an artist he considers one of the greatest in theater, who protested: "The old theatre is dead, the new theatre is not born. The stage is in the hands of tradesmen and upstarts. It all started with that damned French Revolution!"[119]

Sad though it may be, the complaining artist was not overstating the case, at least insofar as the nineteenth century was concerned. The drama—and the theater generally—achieved nothing but repetition and a few minor improvements, mostly technical. It certainly did not produce anything that would distinguish it as a period. In contrast with the previous periods, the nineteenth century produced nothing but two concepts, romanticism and realism—two trends that, for the theater at least, were to act as a brake on its evolution and to lead to a needless meandering in garrulous forms and naive scenic innovation.

Romanticism

The militaristic mentality that prevailed in the early nineteenth century, the wave of revolutions, the unstable social conditions, and the priority of other, more pressing problems—all helped to foster and sustain the notion that every form of art was a luxury, a leisure pastime. The prevailing attitude was that art is not a part of everyday life but an escape from it. The art salons, the concert halls, and the theaters were looked upon as private places, refuges where for a few hours one could escape from a dull and routine existence. Accordingly, to be truly an escape, those refuges had to provide something different, something special and unusual. Spectators had to be removed from everyday reality and transported to another world, a world they subconsciously could accept as real. They would identify with the hero. Therefore, the hero must not be a remote and inaccessible being; he must be neither an Othello nor a Hamlet but a d'Artagnan or an Esmeralda, a simple everyday person like the spectator, with similar problems but with the happy gift of overcoming them successfully. It was inevitable that such a trend should very quickly lead to romanticism.

Basically romanticism stood for the picturesque, the vivid detail, the return to nature, the obvious truth. With its abhorrence of simplification and the techniques of classicism, it divested the drama of all grandeur and depth and thus condemned to obscurity the true expression of the theatrical world.[120]

Romanticism catered to a public that was largely "plebeian," a new public enjoying new-found freedoms. The social and economic levels of the people who flocked to the theaters in the early nineteenth century—the period of the Industrial Revolution—have not been researched and pigeonholed, though the quality of the audience differed between major and minor playhouses. Certainly a large proportion of theatergoers were poor and lived under appalling conditions. This is underscored by an incident at the Royal Theatre in Glasgow: After a panic caused by a fire alarm, the total amount of money found on the persons of the 65 victims was 17 shillings and one penny.[121]

Romanticism was a purely French product of the 1830s, and its chief exponents were Alexandre Dumas and Victor Hugo. In striving after the picturesque and verisimilitude, both writers combined the possible with the impossible, good with evil, kindness with cruelty. Their heroes were not always members of good bourgeois society but could be rascals of the underworld, vagabonds, and outcasts. Their works were nearly always melodramatic, and the action built up to a climax, usually toward the end, which kept audience interest at a constant high pitch. Hugo described romanticism as "nothing but liberalism in literature,"[122] but he could not foresee the not-so-brilliant future in store for it. In the drama repertory at least, not a single work by a romantic playwright has survived to our day. The plays' artlessness of expression, the picturesqueness, and the messages without depth did not combine happily with the movement and pace of the theater. Thus even the best of the romantic playwrights never produced anything that could cause a significant change of course in the evolution of the theater.

We encounter a similar failure in English and German literature and drama. Perhaps in Germany the powerful personalities of Johann Wolfgang von Goethe and Johann Christophe von Schiller, with the Sturm und Drang movement,[123] gave the drama a richness and depth that the romantics in France and England were unable to attain. It is interesting to note, in any case, that German scholars refuse to classify these two luminaries with the other romantics—Von Kleist, Tieck, Kerner—perhaps because they think that to do so would be to insult those great names. They may not have left any important dramatic work, but their contribution to German literature and its development is incalculable. Nevertheless, Nietzsche criticized them for failing in their attempt to force their way through "the golden gate that gives access to the interior of the magic mountain of Hellenism" and said of his own period (1844–1900), "Never has there been an era of art in which civilization and art itself were more alien and hostile to each other than in the contemporary era."[124]

Thus it was that romanticism, wandering astray in search of other goals, contributed nothing of essence to the theater either in repertory or in scenographic and architectural development. We can say without hesitation that its only accomplishment was to provide a stepping-stone for a new style that was coming—realism.

Realism

We have seen that romanticism cultivated the trend to return to all that was connected with nature, with the picturesque, with the search for truth. But the truth was always smothered in an emotional fog and idealized in order to tug at the human heart and carry the audience to heights of excitement and emotion.

Realism looked on this retreat from the pure concept of the natural with contempt. For the realists art was something related to the everyday, the familiar, the natural, to what we really see and not what we imagine. This doctrinaire attitude would lead dramatists to reveal the real, the hidden truth, the truth that until then everyone had avoided mentioning. The drama would change form, and its themes would deal with events relating to human weakness, to pathological, criminal, and generally abnormal conditions—in a word, to the truths that had hitherto lain buried deep in the subconscious. Nothing would remain hidden any longer; nobility of character and sentiment, heroism and sublime emotion, would be banished from the stage.

Dialogue would become natural, no different from the talk heard every day in the streets, the marketplace, and the clubs.

The realists were to dominate every form of drama right up to World War I. The theater, after so many centuries, belonged once more to its true and natural moderator, the dramatist. Theatrical speech attained great heights of perfection. Playwrights like Ibsen, Tolstoy, and Chekhov placed their stamp on all theatrical activity; they were the ones who directed the theater to new forms and stage techniques. The stage was turned into a portrait of life itself; illusion was shunned for its distortion of reality, and acting was confined to serving as a medium for the development of the spoken word.

Such detailed, analytical presentations of life, however, had certain adverse effects. The theater as an expressive and performing art became dangerously static again; it lost the magic brought to it by Euripides and Shakespeare. Attention to detail made it look more like a medium of visual enjoyment, a very good photograph, than an art intended to raise people to a higher cultural plane.

This new aberration of the theater is summed up by Cheney:

In the age of scientific inquiry, in the age when social equality apparently was gained for great masses of men, in the age of the clearing away of superstition and pretense, art was brought down to the familiar, the analytical, the microscopic. This was also, we might note, the era when man went farthest toward self-destruction. It was natural that he should almost destroy the theatre.[125]

Self-destruction was indeed close at hand. World War I was approaching, after which the realists were to yield the scepter of the theater to the turbulent twentieth century.

Realism on the Stage

The perspective setting, as we have seen, created a three-dimensional illusion, but the effect was not strong enough to be convincing. This sort of thing, of course, was unacceptable to the true realist, but in the early years of the movement the desire for realism was to some extent satisfied by placing real or natural objects in the setting, sometimes just a single object. A horse and carriage, for instance, would be used in a street scene or a flock of ducks in a farm scene.[126]

Very soon, however, traditional perspective scenery—Inigo Jones's wings and shutters—became irksome. Apart from its anything-but-natural scenic ornamentation, it hindered and cramped the three-dimensional development of the actors' movements and the setting design. The discussion of the development of the stage setting noted that the wings did in fact impart the illusion of depth but that the actor could not approach the back of the stage because the discrepancy in scale completely ruined the effect.

In the seventeenth and eighteenth centuries the actors entered the stage either through the doors on the proscenium (English stage) or through the gaps between the wings (Italian stage). After 1840 the "box set" was adopted, a "room" formed by three solid walls enclosing the acting area and separating the stage from the wings (drawing). The actors entered through doors (soon to be fitted with real doorknobs).

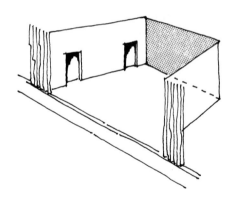

These were often real doors that opened and closed, not merely painted wooden frames. Three-dimensional objects were placed in the box set, such as a rock or a tree (with almost real branches) in the case of an outdoor scene, instead of the painted canvas drops formerly used.[127]

The three-dimensional stage props had the disadvantage of being awkward to handle in a quick scene change when the play called for a second setting. This was the subject of much concern for theater people. A way had to be found to move the props backstage when the

THE MOVABLE STAGE AT THE MADISON SQUARE THEATER. NEW YORK.

Figure 93. Steele MacKaye's two stages in the Madison Square Theater, New York, 1879. (By permission of the British Museum, British Library.)

scene changed. The double stage was first intro-duced in the United States by Steele MacKaye at the Madison Square Theater in New York.[128] The second stage, above the first, was prepared while the performance was in progress and lowered into place at the right time (Figure 93).

Stage technology now began advancing rap-idly, led by the Germans. The entire set was either moved sideways and backward (drawing a) or mounted on a revolving platform together with the other prefabricated sets required for the play (drawing b). Karl Lautenschläger (1843–

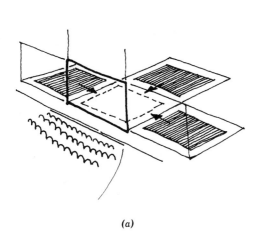

(a)

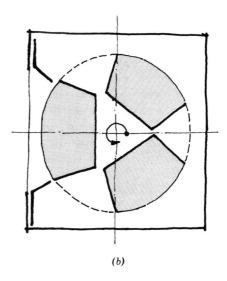

(b)

103

Figure 94. Model of Karl Lautenschläger's revolving stage. (Nicoll, Development of the Theatre, p. 203. Reprinted by permission.)

1906) constructed a revolving stage of this type in 1896 for the Munich Theater (Figure 94).[128]

Another fundamental change wrought by realism was in the technique of presenting the setting to the audience. Until the eighteenth century scenery changes were always carried out in full view of the audience, the wings could be changed—sliding sideways or carried off by stagehands—in a few minutes, thereby providing the audience with yet another interesting sight to watch. With realism the stage curtain became all-important, concealing the entire stage area and leaving only the proscenium arch as a memento of the century that had passed.

Theater theorists explain that the curtain was in effect the "fourth wall" of a room—that is to say, of the box set described above—a wall that opened to reveal a real scene, a scene that would have happened even if the fourth wall had remained closed. Thus the spectator becomes a hidden observer, a Peeping Tom so to speak, watching the life, the loves, and hates of people who appear to be unconcerned by or unaware of being watched.

The stage picture thus became a living photograph that could not contain any bogus painted design. It became like a photograph of a real place, a room, no longer faked but conveying a perfect illusion of reality. Very aptly, the Americans dubbed this type of scenic design the "peephole stage."

Later, when the cinema became established, it was only a small step from this picture stage to a screen. Perhaps, as Arnott claims, that is one of the reasons that impelled the twentieth-century theater to seek a personality of its own—a search that led it to a revival of the historic classical forms and a birth of new forms geared exclusively to its own needs.[129]

Lighting

The most pivotal change of all during the nineteenth century, the change that fashioned an entirely new type of theatrical performance, was the discovery and development of new stage-lighting techniques. When the plays were performed outdoors, of course, the problem did not arise. But the indoor theater required artificial light, and this was provided, at uniform intensity in stage and auditorium alike, by candles.

In 1822 the old Paris Opera installed an innovative system of gas illumination, and some eight years later gas was adopted by the London theaters. By 1850 the theaters of Europe and the

United States, except for a few small and primitive playhouses that retained candles, were adapted to the new lighting technology.[130]

The second step was the use of footlights—lighting fixtures placed along the front edge of the proscenium, invisible to the audience, that provided the stage director with a whole new range of possibilities. The stage could now be lighted with varying intensity, from very bright to total darkness. After 1879 the advent of electricity eliminated all remaining problems. By manipulating a switch or using lights of differing brightness, directors could regulate the lighting on the stage; they could create compositions of illuminated surfaces differing little from those of a painting. New techniques were discovered, and a new scenography developed. Scenery that provided an adequate enough effect by candlelight was useless under a floodlight. The leading actor could with ease be made to stand out from the rest of the cast by means of a spotlight, and color assumed importance as an element of the performance.

To enhance the effect of the stage picture, the auditorium was darkened during the performance; the spectator, sitting in the half-light, watched an illuminated "photograph" in complete detachment from the actors. The segregation of the audience from the players, which had started with the use of the "fourth wall," the curtain, was now complete, and it has lasted to our own time, at least in the commercial theaters.

Nineteenth-Century Theaters

The nineteenth century was above all the age of growth of the commercial theater, an institution that was uninterested in experimentation and therefore preferred to use existing buildings—an attitude that led to stagnation. In England the same form was used more or less as before, as we can see in Richard Leacroft's reconstruction of the Theatre Royal in Plymouth (Figure 95).[131]

Figure 95. Theatre Royal, Plymouth: as reconstructed by Richard Leacroft, 1811. A typical English nineteenth-century theater. (Credit: Roberts, On Stage, *p. 379.)*

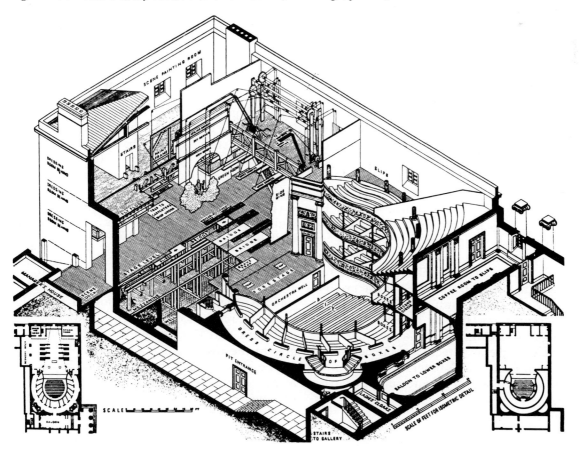

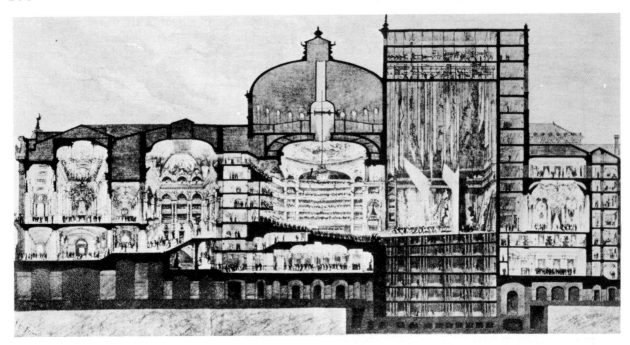

Figure 96. Paris Opera, 1874: section. (Author's archive.)

In continental Europe likewise, except for the Paris Opera (Figure 96)[132] and the Bayreuth Festspielhaus (Figure 97), no building of note was erected. In America, a country still comparatively young and lacking a theater tradition, theater building was nothing but a facsimile of one European form or another, mostly English.

The disappearance of the last remaining traces of the traditional English stage, the growing popularity of the "fourth-wall" technique, the development of new lighting methods, and lastly the severance of the actor–audience relationship—these were the developments that impelled a musical genius, Richard Wagner (1813–1883), to adopt a philosophical approach to the theater and the gulf that by then separated the stage from the auditorium.

Wagner's great dream was to create a theater not only for the musical drama; he wanted to create a truly national theater, free of the prejudices of the preceding centuries. This "philosophical" dream came true in 1876 when, with the backing of the King of Bavaria and in cooperation first with the architect Oscar Brückwald and later with Gottfried Semper, Wagner built his world-famous Festival Theater at Bayreuth (Figure 97).[133]

This theater heralded a new era in theater architecture. It constituted a unique attempt to escape the stagnation that characterized nineteenth-century theaters as a group and that was reflected by a constant repetition of the Italian opera house style.

Wagner's ideas did not include a conversion of the painted scenery, and his stage was designed for settings of the Italian stage type. The two long, narrow passages to the right and left at the rear of the stage were probably used for storing and changing the screens that served as backscenes. The stage was very slightly inclined for better audience visibility and the proscenium was moderately curved. Running the entire width of the front edge of the proscenium and well below it there was now a pit for the orchestra, for the first time distinct and well organized. By using the space below the stage so successfully and providing it with the right design, Wagner and Semper achieved marvelous results: a magnificent quality of sound from the orchestra that was unequaled in any other theater in the world.

The gap between the edge of the proscenium and the first row of seats gave Semper the idea of placing a second proscenium in front of the first,

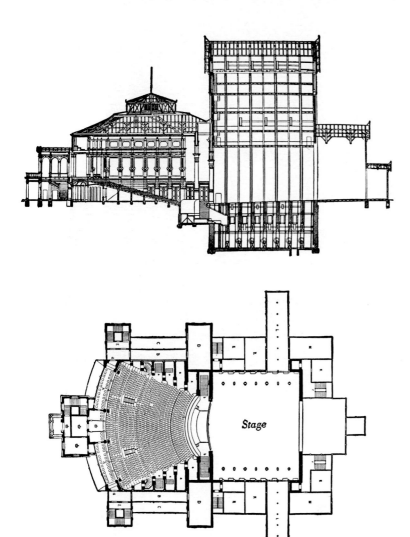

Figure 97. Wagner's Festspielhaus, Bayreuth, 1876: section and plan. (Credit: Cheney, The Theatre, p. 428b.)

the space between the two being left in darkness. The Germans loved this new feature and have been in love with it ever since: the *mystische Abgrund*, the "mystic gulf" separating reality from the ideal dream and illusion.

What was truly a revolutionary break with all established forms was the auditorium. Until then, as we have seen, every theater used a variation of the horseshoe-shaped orchestra and had consecutive rows of boxes reserved for the nobility and high society. At Bayreuth, as can be seen in the plan and section, the seats were laid out on a sharply sloping single floor in a reversion to the amphitheatrical form. The most striking change

of all is that there were no aisles dividing the seats into privileged and nonprivileged zones and no boxes.[134] Class differences were set aside, and every member of the audience had as good a view of the stage as any other. After a hundred years of struggle, democracy was beginning to triumph in the theater.

Bayreuth was the start of an era that in 50 years or so was to transform the theaters of Europe and America and set the tone of the twentieth century: It was an era in quest of new theatrical forms that were to bring the public much closer to the theater—and to the actor.

Figure 98. Man as dancer (Tänzermensch), *Oskar Schlemmer, 1927. (From Gropius and Schlemmer,* Theater of the Bauhaus, *p. 16. By permission of Mrs. Walter Gropius.)*

Part Two

THE THEATER IN THE TWENTIETH CENTURY

8
The Period of Peace

General Social Conditions

The interval of 43 years between the Franco-Prussian War of 1870 and the outbreak of World War I in 1914 was for Europe an unprecedented period of peace, an era free of bloodshed and major conflicts. Taking advantage of the long respite, Europeans set about enjoying the blessings of peace with great optimism and zest. Restrictions on movement between countries had been all but abolished and people began traveling, getting to know one another, admiring one another's works and exchanging ideas and goods. It was the period of far-flung colonies and empires, a time of general prosperity for Europe and America that raised the standard of living to a high level and produced a new type of national hero, the businessman. The person who made a lot of money fast was looked up to by all and regarded as an example to be emulated.

The result was the phenomenon we know as the Industrial Revolution, which was nothing more or less than the outcome of the new hero's efforts. Industrialization brought a wave of inventions that helped the advance of science. Steam, steel, electricity, all of them key products of the period from 1870 to 1914, brought the railroad, the automobile, the telephone, and the motion picture—novelties that rapidly became staples. Interest in all things scientific reached a high peak. Scientific methods were worshiped and adopted in every field of activity, including even the theater. Emile Zola was hailed as a naturalist writer whose novels, with scientific precision and in meticulous detail, analyzed people in relation to their heredity and environment.[135] The old laissez-faire attitude became the dominant philosophy of the period, notwithstanding the efforts of a vigorous minority that since the middle of the nineteenth century had been struggling to impose the principles of socialism. When Marx's *Communist Manifesto* first appeared in 1848, it impressed almost no one. Only in 1886, after it had been translated into English, did it begin to attract notice. The International Workingmen's Association, founded in London in 1864, was disbanded in 1876 without having had any influence at all on contemporary society.[136] A similar fate befell various movements protesting the appalling living conditions of workers in the cities and the corrupt practices of local governments. Such movements were unimportant when measured against the universal spirit of easy living; they were nothing but the yapping of anarchists and could not be allowed to disturb society. The twilight of Victorianism, enhanced by the opulent trappings of material prosperity, the prevailing optimism, and the panacea of misguided internationalism, came to an abrupt and final end in the bitter conflicts of World War I and its aftermath.

At war's end in 1919 people searched in vain among the ruins to find and pick up the thread of their prewar bliss. It was gone forever, all traces vanished; the romantic era of peace was a thing of the past, leaving nothing but a nostalgic memory.

The Revolution in the Theater

It is difficult to determine a point of transition in the evolution of the theater from the nineteenth to the twentieth century. The nineteenth-century theater continued well into the twentieth, while the twentieth-century theater began, on the theoretical level, immediately after the War of 1870, driven by a strong impulse to escape from the fetters of the Italian stage tradition.

At the turn of the century the theater shared the attitudes and notions of society, the blissfulness just described. It was a gilded and sparkling world of irritatingly noble heroes, cloyingly sweet heroines, romantic stories of love and gallant exploits, with no deeper meaning or message. "It was smothered," writes Denis Bablet, "by the spell of the axial view, the magic of the red curtain; it had become view-theater, mirror-theater, painting-theater, which reduced the spectator to a passive observer since no one ever asked him to use his imagination."[137] This kind of theater became the symbol, not of cultural and spiritual uplift, but of business enterprise. Inevitably the theater was drawn into the maelstrom of frenetic commercial activity; since the kind of drama it dispensed attracted such large numbers of people, it could hardly help turning into a thriving and profitable business.

The genuine commercial theater had arrived. In the United States it was to become known as the "legitimate" theater, evidently in contradistinction to the "illegitimate." A street in New York City became the heart of a district filled with such theaters, which grew into a theatrical type; the Broadway theater. In Paris another street spawned the boulevard theaters. They were all ordinary playhouses, and their purpose was to provide the public with entertainment and keep it in unconcerned ignorance of the real problems besetting a declining art that hid its impoverished dramatic content behind lavish spectacle.

Meanwhile, the struggle for ascendancy that was started in the middle of the nineteenth century by the realist writers and playwrights had not flagged. After decades of effort romanticism had been ousted at last from many of its strongholds, and the realists were hailed in the theater as liberators. Unfortunately their victory, when universally recognized, was no longer of much value; the theater, the art form they had fought so hard to conquer and preserve, was in full decline. They discovered that realism, the cause they had so ardently championed, was in fact nothing but a cheap dogmatic fad that produced drama without depth, drama devoid of meanings or messages conducive to reflective thought.

While the realists were absorbed exclusively in their own struggle, the rest of the world forged ahead. People with new ideas, independent groups outside the established theater, amateurs, and enthusiasts of the drama and the theater generally came to the fore. They were ready and eager to take over the job of reviving it, and they laid the foundation of a movement that was to become worldwide, a movement away from realism. Their movement gave birth to naturalism and the "free theater," and also to a new trend known as neorealism. The first fruits of their efforts were the production of new, untried plays, till then considered unacceptable by the legitimate theater. Although at first very few such plays were produced, in other sectors of the theater the movement progressed by leaps and bounds.

Revolutionary changes appeared in the form of the stage and settings. The role of the stage director took on a new dimension and rose to the dignity of an art. Acting adapted to the new plays, which demanded a different kind of expression and a suppression of the pompous and the melodramatic. Lastly, the techniques of organizing theater space conformed to the requirements of the industrial society.

It is useful, perhaps essential, to mention briefly some of the gifted amateurs whose sole motivation was their love of the theater and who did so much to bring about its revival. Theirs is an example to be emulated by every truly dedicated worker in the realm of the theater.

One such—the pioneer of them all—was André Antoine (1858–1943),[138] an amateur pure and simple. In his early years a clerk employed by the gas company, a volunteer soldier for five years, and a reject of the Paris Conservatoire, he was also a student and admirer of all things theatrical and literary pertaining to his time. In his endeavor to rescue the theater from stagnation, he searched and found among piles of unpublished manuscripts four one-act plays, including one by Zola. Despite strong opposition from various quarters he produced his bill of one-act plays on March 30th, 1887, founding the Théâtre Libre[139] before he was 30 years old. Antoine believed that naturalism on the stage should be a perfect imitation of life itself; a setting, he thought, whether a landscape or the interior of a room, must mirror an existing environment. Perhaps it was not mere necessity that the furniture for the first performance at the Théâtre Libre was brought, as we are told by Arnott and Woodruff, "straight from the parlor of his own home."[140]

His success as an actor and director was unique. Enthusiastic reviews, including plaudits by Zola himself, impelled him to carry on his battle against the established theater, which he waged in three phases: the first, from 1887 to 1895 at the Théâtre Libre, against the "adherents of the theatre of the past"; the second, from 1896 to 1906 at the Théâtre Antoine, "to win the general public"; and the third, from 1906 to 1914 at the Odéon, as "a last battle against formal traditions and routine management."[139] At this point we must disagree with Cheney, who maintains that Antoine's movement ended in failure nine years after it began, namely in 1896.[138]

Antoine's stage successes in France inspired a similar movement in Germany. In September 1889 the Freie Bühne (Free Stage) opened in

Berlin. Its purpose was to create a stage free of censorship, financial problems, and outworn shibboleths. Supported by intellectuals and subsisting on the contributions of its subscribers, its productions were nearly always limited to very short runs because its policy was to acquaint the public with the greatest possible selection of neglected plays and to encourage young playwrights by inspiring them with confidence in their own ability and innovative audacity. The venture was successful and was succeeded by the Freie Volksbühne, which catered to large audiences of middle-class and working people and became extremely popular in Germany, particularly after World War I.

In 1891 an English version of the Théâtre Libre—the Independent Theatre, founded by J. T. Grein[141]—produced George Bernard Shaw's first play, and in 1901 the Stockport Garrick Society sought recognition and popular acceptance by staging revivals of the forgotten plays of Shakespeare.[142] In 1898 the celebrated director Konstantin Stanislavski founded the Moscow Art Theater. His theories, dedicated to "the inner truth, the truth of feeling and experience,"[139] have been adopted by the contemporary theater and its people as the springboard of all action and the basis of every theatrical creation.

In the United States the going was not so easy for the free theater. The legitimate Broadway theater was big business, an impregnable citadel that stood in the way of all attempts to start anything resembling the movement in Europe. It was only in 1915, with Europe totally at war and every form of European art in suspension, that the first American "little theater" sprang into existence in New York City, in the form of an amateur production group calling itself the Washington Square Players. In 1919 the group became the powerful New York Theater Guild and staged successful productions of plays by Eugene O'Neill and Ferenc Molnár.[143]

After 1915 American free theaters—or "little theaters," as they came to be known—began springing up all over the country. Their inspiration was drawn from the success of the free theater in Europe, and their attitude was one of total opposition to the commercial theaters of the vested interests. Their popular success was indisputably due to the pioneering efforts of college production groups. Working with dedication and enthusiasm in this new form, American college students created a tradition so vital and enduring that every new theater trend in the United States since then can be traced back to the college campus.

The persevering efforts of the avant-garde pioneers were not left unrewarded; the revolution in literary style, in acting, and in production did not fail to gain a following. In a very short time the movement was so successful that the commercial theater, attracted by the profit-making potential, began adopting these new forms and backing them with its tremendous financial and technical resources. The avant-garde amateurs suddenly found they had acquired a powerful sponsor whose abundant means allowed them to devote themselves without distraction to the development and expression of their ideas. Thus all the fundamental elements that make up the contemporary theater as we know it today were first introduced during the 40 years of peace that preceded World War I.

The Architecture of Repetition

In contrast to the revolutionary changes that occurred in other sectors of the theater, the theater building itself in the early twentieth century was so standardized as to be almost repellent. The architects of the period, singularly lacking in creative imagination and with a fine disregard for the fundamentals that go into a correct architectural form, confined themselves to elaborating on the decorative element alone. Their principal concern was to copy the traditional features of the past and to create an exterior in as conventional a style as possible, unrelated to the function of the building it adorned. Every theater designed after 1875 had to be a reminder of that apotheosis of bombastic French taste, the Paris Opera (Figure 99). Rather wistfully, Cheney says of this monumental masterpiece of French architecture that it is terribly difficult, contemplating its exterior, to distinguish "an honest, cleanly built wall."[144]

A masterpiece is not required to serve as a model for all subsequent designs, as a prototype to be slavishly copied by future generations. The passage of time brings changes in all things.

Figure 99. Paris Opera, 1875. (Photo by author.)

Figure 100. Royal Theater, Wiesbaden, 1894. (Credit: Cheney, The Theatre, *p. 456b.)*

Technology, social needs, function—these keep pace with the progress of time. The repetition of a form that was once successful is bound to have unhappy results.

The early twentieth-century theater architects fell into the same error as their colleagues in other building fields. They were afraid to make bold use of the possibilities offered by the new materials of the period—steel, glass, and concrete. They preferred to dress their structures in ornamental finery, going so far as to construct pediments and rococo curlicues over a straightforward organic steel beam.

The result can be clearly seen in the Royal Theater of Wiesbaden, built in 1894, and the Municipal Theater of Lille, finished in 1910 (Figures 100, 101). The French style, the court style, predominates in both these buildings; contemplating them, one would think one were back in the seventeenth century, not in a period when the Eiffel Tower had been standing since 1889 as a proof of the validity of steel, in itself productive of an infinite variety of forms.

Figure 101. Municipal Theater, Lille, 1910. (Credit: Cheney, The Theatre, *p. 456c.)*

There were no notable changes, either, in the interior of the theater, the floor plan. Most buildings conformed to one of two accepted arrangements. In England and France it was the Italian opera plan, with its horseshoe-shaped auditorium and superimposed tiers of boxes. In Germany and the United States it was the Bayreuth plan, with a few variations. Typical of this latter arrangement were the numerous exits in the side walls of the auditorium and the ample distance between the rows of seats, which allowed the members of the audience to move with greater convenience from seat to exit and vice versa. In the United States fire regulations necessitated the separation of specified blocks of seats by broad aisles running lengthwise through the auditorium.

In Germany the initiative of two fairly avant-garde architects, Max Littmann and Oskar Kaufmann, resulted in a trend to rid the theater of superfluous ornamentation and to weaken the hold of the Italian stage. A new relationship gradually developed between stage and auditorium, and the outer form of the theater building began to adapt to the new building techniques.

In the Prinz Regent Theater in Munich, 1901 (Figure 102), Littmann followed Wagner's Bayreuth example with its unbroken rows of seats and numerous side exits. But he gave the stage greater—one might say disproportionate—importance in relation to the auditorium. The stage was a typical example of nineteenth-century scenographic notions, crammed with machinery and providing ample room for shifting the complicated scenery.

Figure 102. Prinz Regent Theater, Munich, 1901. (Credit: Cheney, The Theatre, *p. 496a.)*

Figure 103. Munich Art Theater, 1914. (Credit: Cheney, The Theatre, *p. 456d.)*

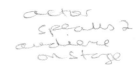

Beginning with the Prinz Regent, theater exteriors broke with tradition and shed their elaborately ornamental features. The break was even more apparent in the Munich Art Theater, completed by Littmann in 1914 (Figure 103). To compare this building with the Royal Theater of Wiesbaden (Figure 100), which antedated it by only 20 years, would be redundant; a glance at the two pictures is enough to demonstrate the striking difference.

The buildings used by the free theater during the period before it was adopted by the organized commercial theater were rudimentary. The Théâtre Libre, the Freie Bühne, and nearly all the other pioneering groups were served by small playhouses, often built of wood, with a capacity of 200 or 300, and they are of no interest to the researcher. The same holds true of the scores of playhouses built at this time in Europe and the United States. They were all repetitions of the old, familiar and successful models and they contributed nothing to the development of the theater. After World War I most of these buildings were torn down or taken over by the theater's great rival, the cinema.

The New Esthetic Trend in Scenography

We have seen how the stage curtain was adopted as a scenographic element by the nineteenth-century theater and how this "fourth wall" cut off all contact between audience and actor. This abrupt severance was a development without precedent in the history of the theater. In the theaters of ancient Greece the audience virtually embraced the orchestra. In the Middle Ages the spectators mingled with the actors, and in the Elizabethan period, as in the Greek, the apron, like the orchestra, brought the actors into direct contact with the audience.

With the notion of scenic design brought by the nineteenth century, all this vanished. The new theaters, with the curtain going up and down and the differential lighting accenting the separation between stage and auditorium, suggested to the spectators that they were watching the show through a peephole. This effect, combined with the fact that realism and naturalism had developed to the point of creating a stage picture, little different from a good photograph, brought reaction at the turn of the century.

Far-seeing people, concerned with rescuing the theater from stagnation, argued that this apparent truth, this fidelity, was not the real truth and not the way to communicate the essential spirit of truth. No matter how well made, scenery had its limitations. It could not substitute a real wall for a painted one or show a paper forest with the texture and color of real foliage. Therefore, such scenery had to be discarded and something else found, something that, as Arnott and Woodruff put it, "would reflect reality through a symbol, or by stylizing reality itself."[145]

Two leading directors of the period, Adolph Appia (1862–1928), a Swiss, and Edward Gordon Craig (1872–1968), an Englishman, made decisive strides toward scenographic simplicity by discarding naturalistic detail and dispensing with effect. They were the pioneers of a new esthetic notion.[146] After the war their work was continued by the renowned Max Reinhardt; the theater changed course to a wholly new direction, acquired a personality entirely its own, and became twentieth-century theater in the true meaning of the phrase.

Appia believed in the importance of the human body. Instead of showing the audience a forest with an actor moving through it, he preferred to create the impression that the actor was in the forest. The aim, he felt, should be to project emotion, the fundamental point of contact between audience and actor. With the proper combination of color and light, he thought, with a neutral scenic background of floating surfaces lighted according to the actor's movements, the central dramatic truth could be achieved: the creation of an atmosphere.[147] What Appia and Craig contributed to the new movement was nothing more or less than to use the value of the actor, to make his acting stand out in relief and to create a truly dramatic tension between him and the audience, reestablishing the contact destroyed by naturalism.[148]

The purely architectural setting made it possible for the first time in the theater to create three-dimensional compositions. Clean geometric surfaces (Figure 104), architectural shapes that come alive only when suitably lighted (Figure 105)—these were the elements that stirred the spectator's imagination, with the spoken word completing the dramatic effect.

Figure 104. Appia's setting for Christoph Willibald Gluck's Orfeo. *(Nicoll,* Development of the Theatre, *p. 209. Reprinted by permission.)*

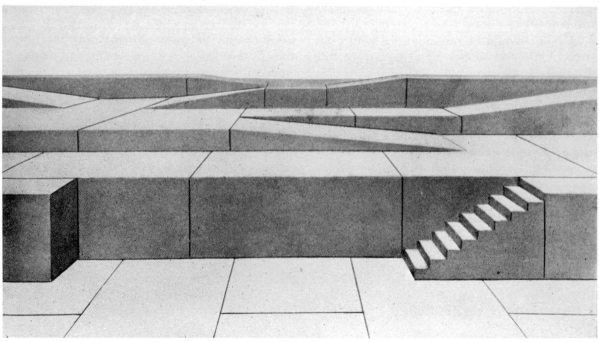

Figure 105. Edward Craig's setting for Hamlet, *Moscow Art Theater, 1910. (Credit: Rowell,* Stage Design, *p. 19.)*

One discerns here a return to the mentality of the Elizabethan stage. The new esthetics had widespread public appeal and were taken up by many imitators in the theatrical world. Although Appia and Craig were both primarily theorists whose ideas were often impossible to put into practice, their influence was far-reaching; they created a school that banished the fallacy that the theater must copy reality. The difficult times of the coming war, the shortness of funds, and the scarcity of technical equipment and man-power were factors favorable to this simplified and low-cost staging technique, factors so strongly affecting its evolution that by war's end it succeeded as an established form in the theater.

9
The Substance of the Contemporary Theater

The Period Between the Wars

The period between the two world wars (1918–1939) can scarcely be called a time of peace. The universal impoverishment that invariably follows in the wake of war, the distrust, the rise and in some countries the total dominion of totalitarianism nazism, and all the other ill-sounding "isms"—these things intensified the differences between nations. The Russian Revolution, the colonial wars, the rise to power of Benito Mussolini in Italy and Adolph Hitler in Germany, the failure of the Versailles Treaty, and the great Wall Street crash in 1929 forced every nation to look out for itself alone, to tend to its own problems. The blissful insouciance of prewar days was gone forever. People looked at each other with suspicion and hostility. The hatred and slaughter of four years of global war were not easily forgotten. Frontiers were only reluctantly opening, and the exchange of cultural achievements was beset by all but insurmountable difficulties. Chauvinism, strict censorship in many countries, constant political conflict and unrest—these were barriers that kept social communion, art, literature, and theater suffocatingly confined within national boundaries.

World War II and the long period of cold war that followed led to the separation of the world into two great and powerful camps and perpetuated the mistrust, the tension, and the fear of a fresh global conflict. Future historians would be perfectly justified in describing the first half of our century as a period of continuous war.

Despite these adversities, during this period the progress of the theater was fairly constant. International exchanges of views may have been limited, but, depending on the political environment, individuals appeared in each country to carry forward the theatrical tradition; they gave the twentieth-century theater its distinctive stamp, the stamp of variety.

Every kind of building, architectural technique, play, and form of setting was tried; all kinds of acting and costume styles saw the light of day and found acceptance to a greater or lesser extent. New forms emerged; they were discussed and criticized, prevailing finally as theories. Lastly, old notions were adapted to contemporary requisites.

At the end of World War I the theater was confronted by several powerful competitors, products of an advancing technology and a changing social outlook.

The rapidly developing talking picture, on the one hand, and, on the other, radio, followed shortly before the outbreak of World War II by television, had a direct effect on the evolution of the theater-building form. Many commercial playhouses were converted into movie houses, an easy switch accomplished by merely replacing the stage curtain at the proscenium arch with a screen. In the United States alone the number of theaters dwindled from 1500 in 1920 to 500 in 1930. A new trend in building design began developing—the small playhouse.

The simplified settings and the desire to give greater emphasis to the actor than to his scenic environment affected the form of the auditorium. The long, narrow shape of the Italian theater with its many rows of seats, so suitable to operatic performances, and the Bayreuth type of festival theater, originally designed to meet Wagner's musical requirements, were architectural forms that could not be adapted to the needs of the modern repertory. However, there were quite a few people who still believed in grandiose structures that could meet the needs mentioned above and also accommodate several thousand spectators.

The obvious solution, then, was to widen the shape of the auditorium so that the greater part of the audience could have a comfortable view of the stage and actors, even with an oblique angle of vision from the sides.

This requirement was taken into account by Reinhardt in 1919 when, with the architect Hans Poelzig, he converted the old Schumann Circus in Berlin and constructed the famous Grosses Schauspielhaus,[149] one of the biggest theaters of the time. The auditorium (Figure 106) and general layout of the theater were the outcome of Reinhardt's long and exhaustive study of the ancient Greek theater. Wishing to bring the action closer to the audience, he created a large platform, an apron or "thrust stage" (Figure 107) in front of the proscenium, while providing the usual deep stage, which he equipped with a dome and a revolving platform; the stage proper would thus be used only to create the appropriate scenic background. The audience seats enclosed the thrust stage on three sides, and once

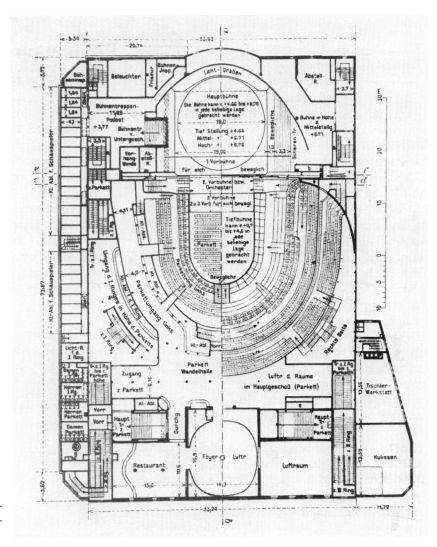

Figure 106. Grosses Schauspielhaus, Berlin, 1919: plan. (Author's archive.)

Figure 107. Grosses
Schauspielhaus: stage. (Author's archive.)

again, as in ancient times, the spectator was "in-side" the action.

However, any attempt at intimacy is doomed to fail in a space so vast; very soon Reinhardt's big theater stopped being used for dramatic performances and became a stage for major spectacles. But a lesson was learned—that modern plays are virtually submerged when staged in mammoth theaters—and a distinction as to kind came to be applied in the performing arts.

Drama was gradually confined to smaller playhouses with capacities not larger than 1000 people. This type of theater proliferated with astonishing rapidity after World War I, especially in the United States, and it was the point of departure for new forms of contemporary theater buildings.

Music and the dance acquired homes of their own, either in buildings created exclusively for concerts or through conversion of old theaters into concert halls. In many instances the deep stages, unnecessary in concert performances, were used to accommodate additional audience seating or as areas for the huge choirs required by large symphonic works.

Opera was confined to the buildings built specifically for it during the two preceding centuries. After World War I, however, a movement got under way to construct buildings serving exclusively as opera houses, erected in accordance with modern technology and the demands of modern audiences. The Metropolitan Opera House in New York City and the opera houses of Berlin, Essen, Salzburg, and other cities are typical products of that movement; most imposing of all is the Theater Center in Sydney, which opened in 1973.

All the other performing arts—musical comedy, vaudeville, big spectacles—were served by existing Broadway-type commercial theaters, all more or less conforming to the last century's notions and contributing nothing of value to the development of the theater except entertainment, pure and simple. The outcome was stagnation and a gradual decline of the commercial theater, in contrast with the other theater forms that developed in a truly remarkable way.

Production as an Art— Political Theater

Before examining the purely architectural developments of the twentieth century, we must look at the social changes that followed in the wake of World War I and that resulted in the creation of yet another art in the theater—the art of production.

When the new movement to rid the drama and the theater generally of the dominance of the romantic playwrights gained the ascendancy, a new and dynamic figure came to the force: the artist-director.

Craig wrote in his first book, published in 1905:

The art of the theater is neither acting nor the play, it is not scene nor dance, but it consists of all the elements of which these things are composed: action, which is the very spirit of acting; words, which are the body of the play; line and color, which are the very heart of the scene; rhythm, which is the very essence of dance. . . . One is no more important than the other, no more than one color is more important to a painter than another, or one note more important than another to a musician. . . .

If you were for once to see an actual piece of theatrical art, you would never again tolerate what is today being thrust upon you in place of theatrical art. The reason why you are not given a work of art on the stage is not because the public does not want it, not because there are not excellent craftsmen in the theater who could prepare it for you, but because the theater lacks the artist—the artist of the theater, mind you, not the painter, poet, musician.[150]

Despite strong opposition, the artists visualized by Craig, the stage directors, assumed their due place in the theater, filling the serious void left by the absence of the playwright-creator. From being mere subordinate employees of the theatrical entrepreneur or the acolytes of a temperamental leading lady, they rose to become the key figures in contemporary theater, the coordinators of all the different preexisting styles who shaped them into a complete and finished form. After 1915, producing and directing were recognized as the leading creative functions in the theater. The school established by Appia and Craig gained the ascendant, and since then the history of theater production has accumulated a roster of great names—producers and directors who originated styles and left artistic legacies. They gave the contemporary theater a true social function that, under the guidance of the director, reflected the social currents of its time.

Reinhardt won fame through his directing techniques, his introduction and use of technology on the stage, and his approach to the play itself. Continuing the work of Appia and Craig, he became the unchallenged master of the stage, using methods that had astounding artistic results.

His dream was to create a theater truly of the people, a theater for the production of powerful plays that could touch the innermost sensitivities of the masses, a "theater of the 5000." He sought to revive the potency and efficacy of the ancient theater, where he could project the action to the public, mix the actors and audience together, and fuse them within a single, indivisible space.[151]

The Grosses Schauspielhaus was his attempt to realize his dream. The underlying principles of this great theater inspired a great many future architects, but unfortunately Reinhardt's dream went wrong. He had counted on the cooperation of contemporary dramatists to provide him with plays of a stature commensurate with the frame he had created. In the end he was forced to admit his dream had failed since the playwrights of the period did not respond; they preferred to play it safe and stick to the Italian stage rather than risk committing themselves to the impulses of this great innovator.

Fleeing Nazi persecution, Reinhardt ended his days in Hollywood, embittered by a further defeat: his failure to transfer his theatrical ideas successfully to the screen.

Germany produced the greatest directors. After Reinhardt, Leopold Jessner at the Berlin State Theater and Jurgen Fehling at the Volksbühne attained great artistic heights in theatrical production.

These three directors succeeded in combining the German theater with pure art, but it was Erwin Piscator who fused pure art with politics for the first time. Standing politically far to the left of the Volksbühne, he founded his own theater, first in Königsberg and later in Berlin. Because of its extremist Communist outlook and unorthodox staging technique, the Piscator Theater was the object of much controversy.

Social conditions in postwar Germany provided a fertile soil for Piscator's theories. The destitution of the people, the parallel rise of nazism and communism, and the political instability of a country in ruins—all fostered to the emergence of this new form of theater, which came to be known as "political theater."

Analyzing the reasons that led him to form his theater, Piscator wrote:

For a long time, until 1919, art and politics were two parallel roads with no meeting point. It is true that until then there had been only one revolution of the feeling (Gefühl). Art alone could not satisfy me as an end. On the other hand I could not yet discern that meeting point which could be the source of a new concept of art, an art become active, militant, political. To this emotional change there had to be added the theoretical knowledge which clearly formulated what I sensed. For me, that knowledge brought the revolution.[152]

When Piscator opened his first theater in Königsberg in 1919, aptly naming it Das Tribunal, he designed a stage that differed from that of Berlin, a "stage of change" (*Wandlung*) as he called it, on which presentations were more realistic than ever before—"exactly as I lived them in the war," Piscator said.[153] The controversy raised by these performances and the opposition from the middle class, the students, the critics, and the press were so intense that the theater very soon was forced to close down.

Despite heated opposition, however, Piscator's theater became self-sufficient, and for 10 years it vigorously dominated the German intellectual scene. For Piscator, as Bertolt Brecht said,[154] the theater was a parliament, the public a legislative assembly. The great issues that concerned the nation and demanded a solution were presented before this parliament in pliable form. His stage did not seek applause but hoped beforehand for a debate. It was not content just to give spectators an experience of some sort; it also wanted to impose on them a practical decision that could be linked to an effective intervention in real life.

Piscator collaborated with and was influenced by the Bauhaus, the Dadaists, and every other progressive trend that appeared in his country, but his sole purpose was to propagate his own absolutist theories. How his theater was used exclusively as a propaganda weapon is apparent in an admission he made himself: "Finally I reached the conclusion that art is merely a stepping stone to the goal I pursue. A political instrument, a propaganda medium."[153] These are ruthless reflections, one would say, by a great artist who spent his gifts one-sidedly, an artist who devoted his art to an ideology that would forsake him.

Piscator divided his political theater into the Theater of the Proletariat, the Theater of Proof, and the Epic Theater. Only the last, as represented by *The Good Soldier Schweik*, survives as a memento of this theater form that was part of German theatrical life from 1919 to 1929 (Figure 108).[155]

Figure 108. Wandlung *(change) stage, created by Piscator for* The Good Soldier Schweik. *It reflects his austerity and realism. In three of the pictures the background is a screen on which slides are projected. (Credit: Piscator,* Das politische Theater, *p. 128.)*

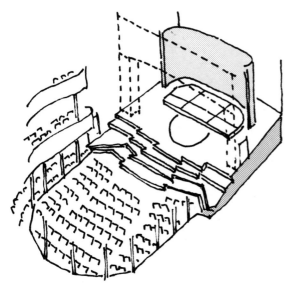

Figure 109. Gray's Festival Theatre, Cambridge (England), 1929. (Design by author, after a suggestion from Richard Southern.)

During those postwar years, few directors in other countries attained the stature of the Germans. In France Jacques Copeau was the first to gain international repute, and in England Terence Gray, following in Reinhardt's footsteps, created the Cambridge Festival Theater (Figure 109). There he constructed a stage that included, in his own words, "a wide fan of fore-stage with multiple levels gradually merging into the auditorium, a revolving middle-stage, and a raised and sliding back-stage. . . . This and its cylindrical cyclorama[156] lit with prismatic lighting will make it possible to practice a type of stagecraft never before seen in England."[157]

In the United States staging had received full recognition as an art but there was no director whose reputation was more than nationwide. We cannot say that names like Duncan or Hopkins did anything for the theater beyond the staging of some fairly successful shows. America was lying fallow, so to speak, awaiting the coming of fugitives from nazism like Reinhardt, Piscator, and their fellows, who were to enjoy the latitude of their adopted land to experiment and in so doing to stimulate the growth of the still adolescent American theater.

In Russia, where during the early interbellum period there was still a great deal of flexibility in the bureaucratic party line, experimentation reached its most revolutionary and fruitful heights. Three bold figures, disciples of the Stanislavski school—Meyerhold, Vakhtangov, and Tairov—tried stage experiments more extreme than any attempted in Western Europe. They introduced new ways of organizing the theater, a new relationship between actor and audience, a new kind of music drama, naked settings uncluttered by scenery (Figure 110), and a fresh approach to the classics. These three, with Meyerhold in the lead, were the pioneers of the avant-garde. Like Reinhardt, Meyerhold created his own theater (Figure 111), which he called "biomechanics." He intended this term to signify the scientific relationship he envisaged would be created between the technique of the artist and industrialization, once the latter was no longer regarded by society as a curse but accepted as a "congenial vital need."[158] For Meyerhold, once the artist enters the work process, "he is converted to a worker, but a worker who must never for a single moment stop feeling himself an artist."[159]

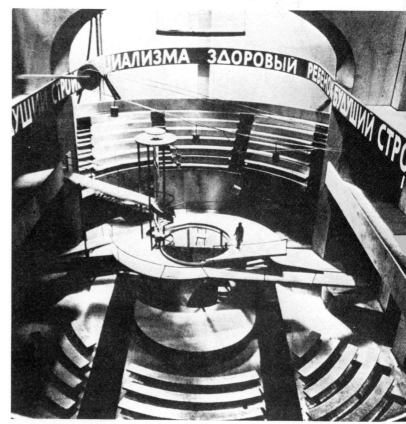

Figure 110. Setting designed by El Lisickij for Vsevolod Meyerhold. (Credit: VH 101, No. 7–8, 1972, p. 105.)

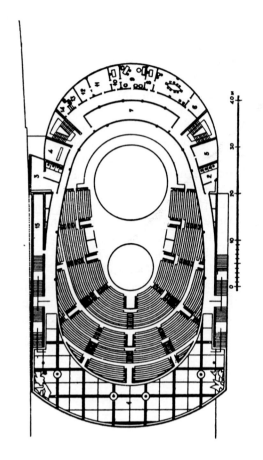

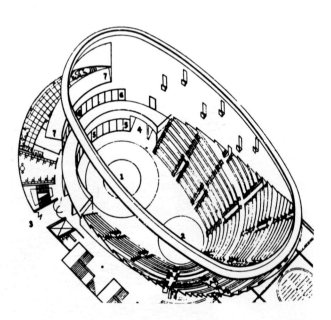

Figure 111. Meyerhold's theater, Moscow, 1935: plan and isometric. G.B. Barkhin and Eugene Vachtangov, architects. (Credit: VH 101, No. 7–8, 1972, p. 105.)

Perhaps that is why Meyerhold, more than any of his contemporaries, attempted in his theater to establish communication between the artist—the actor, designer, playwright, or director—and the public, the "industrial" public. The two orchestras projecting deeply into the audience, the steeply sloping auditorium, and the frugal use of space are features that returned the theater to its original classic Greek form.

This period of experimentation in Russia from 1917 to 1935 contributed much that was valuable to the development of twentieth-century theatrical production.

Political theater made its appearance in England, too, with the opening of the Unity Theatre in London in 1936. With no director to guide the staging, the performances were put on by a group of amateur actors who liked to call themselves the "people's theatre." The more gifted of these enthusiasts soon found their way into the professional theater, where in the course of time they became leading figures of the English stage.[160]

The rise of directing as an art forced a change of form in the theater. The successes of the directors we have mentioned quickly grew and found many worthy successors who continued in their footsteps. The result is clearly apparent in our own time.

Contemporary Trends in the Theater

Once the task of organizing production was concentrated in the hands of a single artist, it was inevitable that the theater should share with the other arts every change of style that came about, according to the innovations espoused by each director. For 75 years or more new trends had been appearing in everything connected with painting and sculpture; unpopular at first, these gradually gained acceptance with both a restricted circle of intellectuals and the wider public.

These exploratory searchings in the arts all had a common feature: an abhorrence of any form that reproduced reality, that had the slightest connection with photographic naturalism. Expressionism, the most extreme antirealist trend, together with all its by-products—cubism, futurism, surrealism, attempted to achieve effective visualization by removing all nonessential and delusive elements.

In the theater these trends exerted an influence as early as the First World War; they led to the development of various setting designs that were adopted and used by stage directors in much the same way and with the same degree of passionate partisanship as were the trends embraced by painters and sculptors.

On the stage, expressionism was achieved through distortion rather than removal of elements, though both were to a certain extent coexistent. Theoretically it was closer to music, the purest art form; it sought to achieve with light what the composer achieved with sound (Figure 112). But the result was static, since this scenographic technique requires a single, permanent setting, an inflexible setting that imposes cramping limitations on the presentation of a play.[161]

Many other modern art trends, such as surrealism and dadaism, found their way onto the stage, particularly through the dance, and became associated with great names like Pablo Picasso and Salvador Dali (Figure 113); these trends failed, however, to attract sizable followings and soon died away. But there were two trends that gained greater ascendancy in the theater than in painting: constructivism and formalism.

Figure 112. Expressionism through lighting. Setting by David Mark. (Credit: Whiting, Introduction to the Theatre, *p. 285.)*

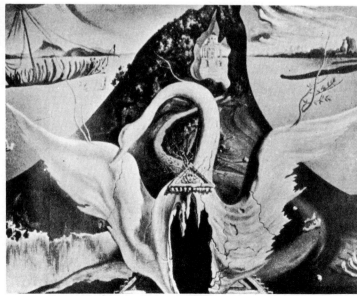

Figure 113. Surrealism. Design by Salvador Dali for Bacchanale, *1939. (Credit: Whiting,* Introduction to the Theatre, *p. 287.)*

Constructivism first made its appearance—albeit unsuccessfully—in czarist Russia in 1911; later it became the basic type of setting used by Tairov and Meyerhold (Figure 114). Soon it spread to the rest of Europe and to the United States. It was accepted enthusiastically and is still in use today under the name of "neoconstructivism" (Figure 115).[162] As a visual background, the constructivist setting in itself has little or no meaning. With the appearance of the actors and with their movements in and among ramps, platforms, steps, and acrobatic equipment, the entire setting comes alive. The constructivist set is meant to be used rather than seen (Figure 116).

Figure 114. Early Russian constructivist setting. (Credit: Rowell, Stage Design, *p. 23.)*

Figure 115. Neoconstructivist setting by Ralph Koltai for Cul de Sac, *London, 1965. (Credit: Rowell,* Stage Design, *p. 23.)*

Figure 116. Alexander Nikolajevitch Ostrovski's setting for The Forest, *Meyerhold's theater, Moscow, 1924. (Nicoll,* Development of the Theatre, *p. 216. Reprinted by permission.)*

Meyerhold, devoted to his concept of the "machine," created an inflexible, rigid constructivism governed by the law of the machine and industrialism. He applied his views not only to the stage but to theater architecture generally.[163] He did away with the boxes, the Italian stage, and the linear, axial arrangement, and adopted the semicircle; for him it was the only shape that could restore the association between actor and audience.

The success of his undertaking is easily discernible in his theater. In this way he provided the stimulus for the birth of architectural constructivism; it was not, however, a trend of purely Russian origin but a simultaneous and parallel movement by all European adherents of the avant-garde theater.

All experiments in the theater have one and the same aim: to attract a new public in one way or another. Thus the emergence of formalism was a reaction against the chaos created by the multifarious settings described above. Recalling the two great ages of the theater, the Greek and the Elizabethan, the formalists maintained that "the actor must perform in front of an acceptable background that will differ only slightly from scene to scene, from play to play and from period to period."[161]

Perhaps the best example of a director who used the formalist stage to recall the days of Sophocles and Shakespeare was Jacques Copeau. In his Vieux-Colombier Theater he constructed a formal scenic background (Figure 117) that remained the same in all the plays he staged; only the stage props and a few other minor details were changed. The stage and auditorium projected into and around each other with no architectural division; the actor and the audience were enclosed "by the same cocoon," as Bablet describes it.[164] This type of stage, however, lacked flexibility, a disadvantage that caused it eventually to be abandoned.

Figure 117. Jacques Copeau's Vieux-Colombier Theater, 1924: stage. (Credit: Centre National, Le lieu théâtral, plate IIIb.)

The permanent stage setting led to architectural formalism, which involved the construction of costly and elaborate designs made up of steps, platforms, blocks, and pillars. These features were deliberately neutral, with no specific purpose or character, so that they could be used again and again in different plays (Figure 118).

As we have seen, the revolutionary mood of the early twentieth century, which brought directors to the fore and made their function an art, was followed by a pronounced renaissance in the organization of the theater. During the comparatively brief period between the wars, theater organization was the subject of diver-

Figure 118. Architectural formalism. Design by Al Sensenbach for Hamlet. (Credit: Whiting, Introduction to the Theatre, p. 289.)

sification and experimentation; essentially these were the processes and elements that form and make up the theater of our own time. The staging techniques just described are in use today, in developed and renewed form to be sure but always patterned after the prototypes created by the pioneers who worked in the theater between 1918 and 1939.

The celebrated stage designer Robert Edmond Jones went a step further than his contemporaries; his aim was to present a stage completely empty and bare of scenery. Supporting his ideas, he wrote in 1941:

> It is a truism of theatrical history that stage pictures become important only in periods of low dramatic vitality. Great dramas do not need to be illustrated or explained or embroidered. . . . The reason we had the realistic stage "sets" for so long is that few of the dramas of our time have been vital enough to be able to dispense with them. . . . Actually, the best thing that could happen to our theatre at this very moment would be for playwrights and actors and directors to be handed a bare stage on which no scenery could be placed, and there told that they must write and act and direct for this stage. In no time, we should have the most exciting theatre in the world.[165]

The Proscenium Controversy

The radical changes in staging and set design during the early decades of our century were concerned first and foremost, as we have seen, with revising the relationship, established for many centuries, between the stage and the auditorium. One specific reaction against that relationship was a movement to do away with the proscenium once and for all.

Soon after the turn of the century, dislike of the stage à l'italienne assumed the dimensions of a crisis. Competition from the movies, the difficulties encountered by directors as they struggled to develop their ideas, and the advances of technology set artists and architects alike searching for solutions. A reexamination of the old forms became essential. Restoration of the close and intimate connection between actor and audience became imperative. Accordingly, the theatrical form had to be adjusted and, if possible, new forms created. But if the proscenium were abolished, what would be left to replace it?

As we have seen, during the Renaissance the proscenium was the stage itself, while an illusion of depth was provided simply by a backscene painted with a perspective design, an arrangement very similar to the Greek *proskenion* and the Roman *proscaenium*. With the advent of Italian opera the stage acquired depth, and the proscenium receded correspondingly. In its final position this recession brought forth the proscenium arch, the frame of the picture seen by the spectator. Southern says of the proscenium arch:

> All this sounds very dynamic and very moving; it is like pressing something with one's thumbs and turning it inside out. And the interested spectators lean forward and press close together to peer more closely at what you are doing. You persevere until suddenly you succeed, and pop!—you have it in the box! At a blow you have created the glass lid, the picture frame, the peep show, the fourth wall. The little, safe, removed, jigging player doing his business in a box of tricks—an illusionist and an illusion in one. (During all this, you have turned the auditorium into a cave of darkness).[166]

Perhaps these remarks are overly caustic; it is a fact, nevertheless, that they accurately reflect the thinking of a number of people in the early decades of our century. All who felt an aversion for realistic scenery concentrated their attack on the proscenium arch, which they felt imposed a limitation on dramatic development. They claimed that it formed a barrier, a trap in which the actor was caught and that made him feel isolated, remote from the audience, a mere moving element, albeit an animate element, of the setting as a whole.

It is true that this fourth wall precluded any contact between spectator and actor; each was compelled to sit on his or her own riverbank and "watch" the other experience feelings and emotions, without being able to share them and participate. For those who were bothered by this situation, there was no other solution: the proscenium must go!

This view did not fail to produce a counterargument. In the opposing camp there were two factions: the financially interested supporters of the commercial theater and those who genuinely loved the true theater but believed that it would be enough simply to seek closer contact between actor and audience.

The ultimate result of this controversy proved beneficial to the theater. The search for a solution led to research and study, which produced new forms; with the help of every branch of science and art, the theater broke free from its centuries-old monolithic state and acquired an unprecedented flexibility and pliancy.

This is discussed at greater length in a subsequent chapter, but first we must look at a phenomenon of major significance in the history of architecture—the Bauhaus school—in combination with the development of technology.

10
The Development of Technology— The Bauhaus

Technology in the Theater

With the discovery of electricity, people's lives underwent radical change.

With the use of steel, concrete, and glass, the architect's profession acquired a new significance.

With the development of the "machine"— meaning anything that helps move an object— the world became infinitely smaller, particularly through the advent of rapid transportation and telecommunications.

The application of these technological advances to the theater wrought an unprecedented change in the building and its contents.

Professor George Izenour of Yale University, a leading authority in theater technology, wrote in 1963:

Today we demand the best conditions for the audience, as well as the best performance from the artist. We still need improvisation, but of another, higher order. Soon, inevitably, we will be compelled to use to its fullest potential that unique hallmark of our age: technology. The machine first changed and then produced a commercial, industrial, and then even a domestic architecture—an architecture with no prior model. And it is unthinkable, at least to me, that our technology will not also produce a unique architecture for the performing arts.[167]

According to Izenour, there is no mystery about technology, which is nothing more than a combination of the rules of science and the human imagination; in the case of the theater, however, the imagination must be very highly developed. It must be the result of the concerted efforts of all the specialized agencies at work in a theater: the architect, the director, and, above all, the businessman financing the project.

During a discussion with me in 1967, Izenour said:

I believe that theater architecture is still in its infancy. If one reflects on the various achievements of modern science, if one thinks that very soon man will go to the moon, then one realizes how trifling an accomplishment it is to be able to rotate a stage, to raise and lower a ceiling, to change the arrangement of seats in a theater by pushing a button. I believe the deterrent lies only in

the cost and the time required for amortization of the needed funds. When people manage to overcome this financial barrier, we will see a real transformation of the theater.[168]

For the theaters of the 1920s, however, the outlook was not so optimistic. Every new thing or technique was followed by reaction, controversy, and sore trial; every innovation had to be tested and tried, often arduously and at length, and it had to prove successful before it could be adopted on a larger scale. Scene-changing methods, revolving platforms, hydraulic lifts, and like devices were invented, but there was as yet no coordinated experimentation that would move theater technology into mass development.

Nevertheless, Craig's geometrical settings, Reinhardt's revolving platforms, and Meyerhold's biomechanics all contributed determinatively to the transformation of the theater. Piscator too drew his ideas from the technical advances of his time and made use of technology, not for the purpose of creating scenic effects, but as a functional element that he incorporated into the drama itself.

Piscator's theories were the same as those promulgated by the Bauhaus school, which tried to deal with the subject on a broad and general level, combining not only technology and theater but also technology and art, art in all its forms, and every product of human hands. Architecture, painting, sculpture, the graphic arts, industrial design—the Bauhaus saw in all these fields a risk of stagnation and inflexibility unless they availed themselves of the aid of technology.

The Theater of the Bauhaus

The Bauhaus was a creation of the post-1918 crisis in every form and function of society, in everything connected with construction and the consumer public. Walter Gropius, with all the enthusiasm and energy of his 36 years, founded the Bauhaus school in 1919 for the purpose of teaching the importance of technology in art and the relation of proportion and design to construction. To help in his task he recruited men whose names today dominate the history of every field of art: Vasili Kandinski, Paul Klee, Lázló Moholy-Nagy, and Oskar Schlemmer.

The school was established at Weimar. In 1925 it moved to Dessau where it continued until it closed in 1932.[169] It drew people of all ages from every part of Germany and Austria. They came to study there because they saw it as an island of creativity amid the chaos of the post-war world.[170]

The Bauhaus quickly attracted numerous supporters, but it also was showered with a storm of criticism. Its adherents were censured; they were called mad when they removed furniture upholstery to make way for steel and glass or when they replaced rococo windows with large organic openings, or even when they stripped away the involuted neoclassical curvilinear decorations for the sake of simplicity and esthetic austerity. Teachers and pupils united in a working community, determined to create a new synthesis of art and modern technology. According to Gropius, "The phenomena of form and space, based on the study of the biological facts of human perception, were investigated in a spirit of unbiased curiosity, to arrive at an objective means of relating individual creative effort to a common background.[171]

The Bauhaus brought a new climate and a new art style. Its principal aims—to pursue the union of the artistic ideal with practical craftsmanship and to understand in all its ramifications the essence of *der Bau*, of creative construction—touched on all artistic creations; naturally it also had valid application in the field of the theater. For, like the concept of *der Bau* itself, the stage is not a self-contained element but an orchestrated complex achieved only through the cooperation of many different forces; it is an end product created, as in any other structure, through the union of the most heterogeneous assortment of creative elements. Schlemmer said that not the least of the functions of the stage is to serve metaphysical needs by creating a world of illusion, by creating the supernatural on the basis of the rational. Concerning the theater, he wrote:

The history of the theater is the history of the transfiguration of the human form. It is the history of man *as the actor of physical and spiritual events, ranging from naïveté to reflection, from naturalness to artifice.*

The materials involved in this transfiguration are form and color, the materials of the painter and sculptor. The arena for this transfiguration is found in the construc-

tive fusion of space and building, the realm of the architect. Through the manipulation of these materials the role of the artist, the synthesizer of these elements, is determined.[172]

Schlemmer also taught that the emblems of his time ought to be abstraction, mechanization, and technology and that these must not be ignored by the theater. The theater must serve as the image of its time and is perhaps the only art form that is distinctively conditioned by it.

With the Bauhaus, the concept of space was given a new approach. Schlemmer's most characteristic contribution to art was the way he interpreted space; he studied and approached it not through vision alone but with the whole body, with the sense of touch of the actor and the dancer. He transformed into abstract geometric terms his observations of the human figure moving in space (Figure 98), and he came to the conclusion that the individual, the human organism, stands in the cubical, abstract space of the stage in obedience to laws of order different from those that apply to the space itself.

The laws of cubical space are the invisible linear network (Figure 119) determined by the relations between the shapes of plane and space. These relations correspond to the inherent mathematics of the human body alone: mechanical and rational motion. It is the geometry of calisthenics, gymnastics, and eurythmics that find expression in gymnastic displays and acrobatic precision acts; these involve physical attributes (Figure 120). The laws governing organic man, however, are different; they are determined by the functions of the inner self: heartbeat, respiration, circulation, the activity of the brain, and the impulses of the nervous system. If these are to be the determining factors, then their center is in the human being, whose movements and emanations create an imaginary space (Figure 121). It is a fluid space, and the cubical-abstract space of the stage becomes only the horizontal and vertical framework for this flow. The movements are determined organically and emotionally. They constitute the physical impulses, which find expression in the great actor and in the mass scenes of great tragedies. Consequently the stage, according to Schlemmer, is the scene of a struggle for dominance between the individual and space; the outcome determines the theatrical form.

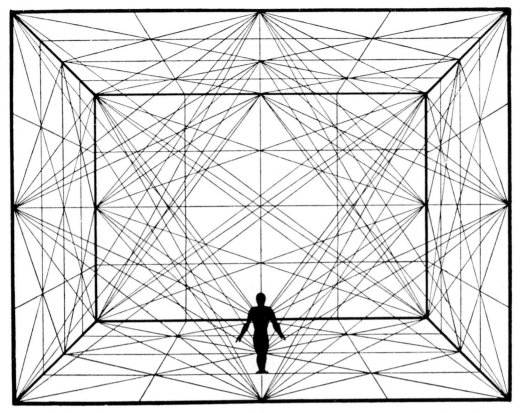

Figure 119. *Linear network of planimetric and stereometric relationships in cubical space. (From Gropius and Schlemmer,* Theater of the Bauhaus, *p. 23. By permission of Mrs. Walter Gropius.)*

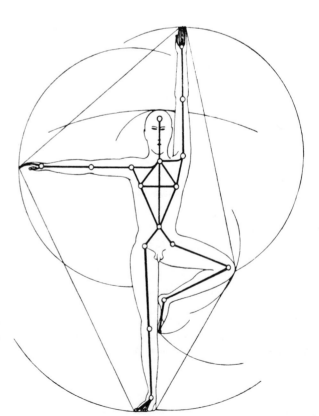

Figure 120. *Mechanical and rational human movements. (From Gropius and Schlemmer,* Theater of the Bauhaus, *p. 24. By permission of Mrs. Walter Gropius.)*

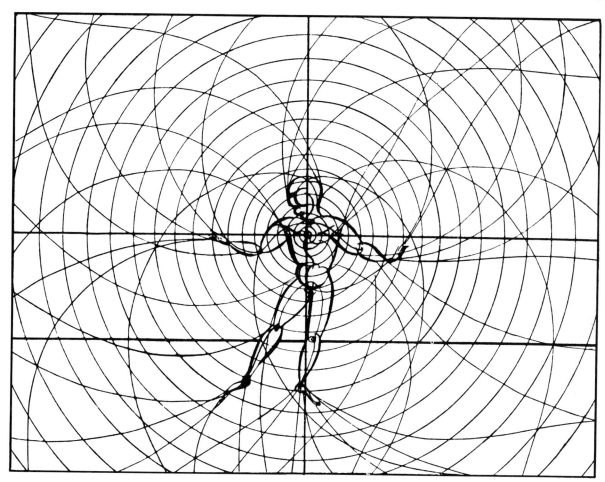

Figure 121. Organic man's fluid space. (From Gropius and Schlemmer, Theater of the Bauhaus, *p. 24. By permission of Mrs. Walter Gropius.)*

When cubical space, irrespective of the physical person, adapts and converts to nature or an imitation of nature, illusionistic realism appears in the theater.

When, to the contrary, the physical being irrespective of cubical space, is recast to fit its mold, then the abstract stage appears in the theater.

These theories were, and perhaps still are, unintelligible to many people; their application in theater, where the dominant element is not motion but speech, was very limited. Schlemmer himself admitted as much when he wrote:

Invisibly involved with all these laws is Man as Dancer [Tänzermensch]. *He obeys the law of the body as well as the law of space; he follows his sense of himself as well as his sense of embracing space. As the one who gives birth to an almost endless range of expression, whether in free abstract movement or in symbolic pantomime, whether he is on the bare stage or in a scenic environment constructed for him, whether he speaks or sings, whether he is naked or costumed, the* Tänzermensch *is the medium of transition into the greater world of the theater* [das grosse theatralische Geschehen].[172]

Although Schlemmer's theories were meant to apply primarily to the dance, they sparked the creation of a "space theater," a theater divorced from the patterns of the past, where the three-dimensional actor, assisted by every theory and every available technological medium, emerged from his "Italian box" to approach and identify with the spectator.

The Space Theater

One answer to the question of how to visualize a space theater was provided by Andreas Weininger, also a Bauhaus follower, who designed the "spherical theater" (Figure 122).[173]

Instead of the customary cubical structure, Weininger used a sphere as the architectural shell, and, by placing the spectators on the inner wall of the sphere, he gave them a new relation to space. The entire structure revolves around an axis supporting the stage, which is free in space. Because of the centripetal force that rotates the structure and because of the all-encompassing view afforded by the ample spherical curvature, the spectators enjoy new experiences and find themselves in a new optical, acoustical, and physical relationship. The static synthesis of architecture disappears: Space, the body, the line, the point, color, light, and sound—all primary media of motion—are brought together in a new mechanical synthesis. The space stage and the space theater become the home of the mechanical play.

At the time, of course, Weininger's design was no more than a hypothesis and a wish that it could be realized some time in the future, when technology would have reached a sufficiently high level of advancement. Nevertheless, it was a praiseworthy effort, and one that could well be realized today. However, the cost of such a structure, to recall what Izenour had to say on the subject, would be enormous; Weininger had the wish, but he could not have foreseen that 50 years later, when his project would be technically feasible, people's interest in the theater would not be sufficiently keen to permit financing such a costly venture.

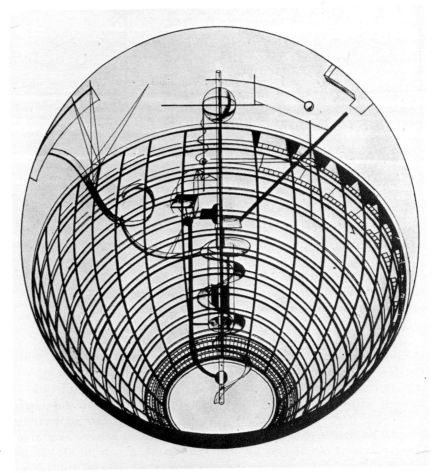

Figure 122. "Spherical theatre". Designed by Andreas Weininger, 1924. (From Gropius and Schlemmer, Theater of the Bauhaus, *p. 89. By permission of Mrs. Walter Gropius.)*

Gropius' "Total Theater"

An outstanding example of theater architecture in which technology, science, and mechanics converge to provide a solution to the search for adaptability and flexibility—essential features of a twentieth-century theater—was Walter Gropius' design for a "total theater" (*Totaltheater*).

The theater was designed for Erwin Piscator in Berlin in 1927, but the project had to be abandoned after "Black Friday," shortly before the Nazis came to power in Germany.

Piscator wanted a theater designed to resemble a machine;[174] he took his idea to Gropius, who at that time was the architect best qualified to undertake a project of this kind and who saw the assignment as a chance to express the new Bauhaus concepts concerning the theater. In 1935 he presented his *Totaltheater* to a convention of playwrights and theatrical producers in Rome and explained the reasons that inspired his powerful pioneering design (Figures 123, 124).

Figure 123. Variations of the Totaltheater: (top) *plan showing the use of the deep stage;* (bottom left) *plan showing the use of the proscenium-thrust stage;* (bottom right) *plan showing the use of the arena stage. (From Gropius and Schlemmer,* Theater of the Bauhaus. *By permission of Mrs. Walter Gropius.)*

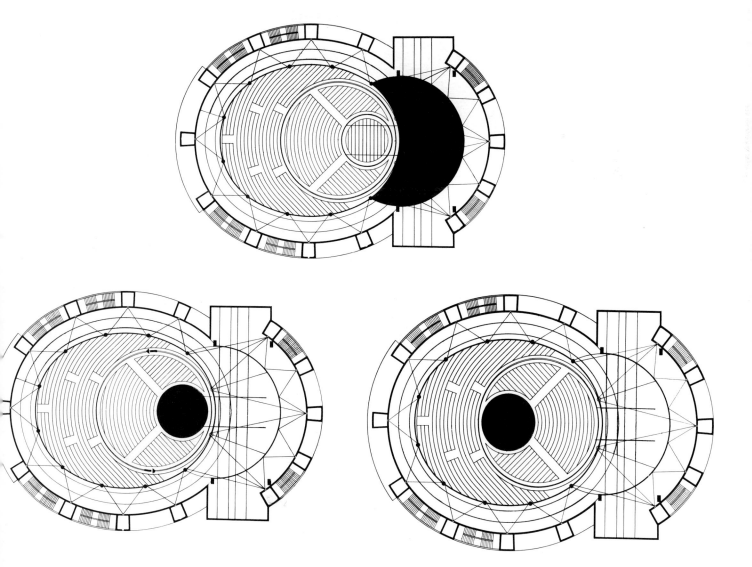

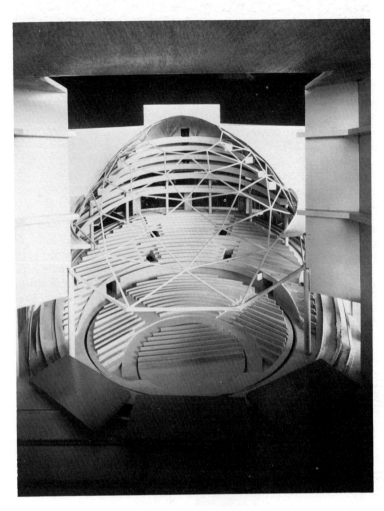

Figure 124. Totaltheater: (left) model; (below) isometric of the auditorium from above. (From Gropius and Schlemmer, Theater of the Bauhaus. Courtesy of Mrs. Walter Gropius.)

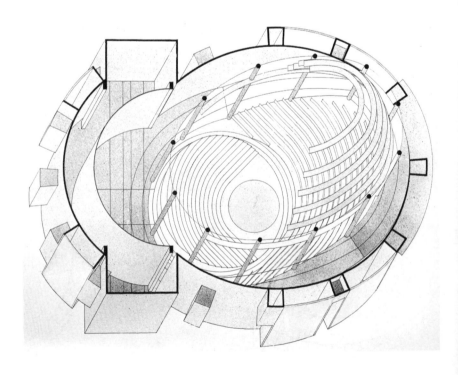

The contemporary theater architect should set himself the aim to create a great keyboard for light and space, so objective and adaptable in character that it would respond to any imaginable vision of a stage director; a flexible building, capable of transforming and refreshing the mind by its spatial impact alone.

There are only three basic stage forms in existence. The primary one is the central arena on which the play unfolds itself three-dimensionally while the spectators crowd around concentrically. Today we know this form only as a circus or a sports arena.

The second classic stage form is the Greek proscenium theater with its protruding platform around which the audience is seated in concentric half-circles. Here the play is set up against a fixed background like a relief.

Eventually this open proscenium receded more and more from the spectator, to be finally pulled back altogether behind a curtain to form today's deep stage which dominates our present theater. . . .

In my Total Theater . . . I have tried to create an instrument so flexible that a director can employ any one of the three stage forms by the use of simple, ingenious mechanisms. The expenditure for such an interchangeable stage mechanism would be fully compensated for by the diversity of purposes to which such a building would lend itself.

An audience will shake off its inertia when it experiences the surprise effect of space transformed. By shifting the scene of action during the performance from one stage position to another and by using a system of spotlights and film projectors, transforming walls and ceiling into moving picture scenes, the whole house would be animated by three-dimensional means instead of by the "flat" picture effect of the customary stage. This would also greatly reduce the cumbersome paraphernalia of properties and painted backdrops.[175]

Gropius' introduction has been quoted almost in its entirety because no other attempt at description could give so lucid and conceptually accurate a picture of this architectural masterpiece.

It must be accounted a grievous misfortune that Gropius' *Totaltheater* was never built and that the ideas of one of the greatest contemporary architects were never given material form. It would have been the right idea at the right time, as Gropius himself once said.[176]

The example of the *Totaltheater* served and still serves as a model for every architectural researcher concerned with the contemporary approach to theater design. It has provided a terminology and an example of how theater building, so constructed as to respond to the imaginative faculty, can become in and of itself a field of action and a force that activates the imagination of the playwright, the director, and the spectator.

The startling results arising from the experience of space transformed—through the changing of scenes, the incorporation of film projection[177] and the three-dimensional revivification of inanimate objects—opened up new vistas for the human mind; for, to quote Gropius' introduction again, "It is true that the mind can transform the body, but it is equally true that structure can transform the mind."

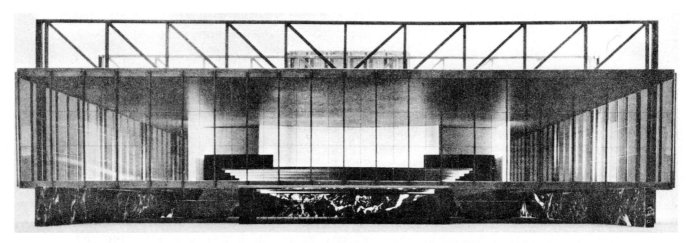

*Figure 125. Ludwig Mies van der Rohe's proposal for the Theater of Mannheim, 1953.
(Credit: Centre National,* Le lieu théâtral, *plate V.)*

Part Three

CONTEMPORARY THEATER FORMS

II
New Forms

The Trend Toward Change

Thus far we have seen that from its birth as an art and an expression of the human spirit, the theater has been in constant evolution. Evolution, of course, involves change—the kind of change we see in people themselves as they go through life's succeeding phases from birth to death; the kind of change we see in science when a theory, once formulated, is developed stage by stage into an industrial process. And we find the same process of change in the theater, with its long history, old as that of mankind itself, a history full of exploration and creative, problem-solving thought.

Dramatists sought new literary figures and new forms of drama; actors endeavored to adapt their style and expression to the words they spoke; the directors and the stage designers tried new ways of presentation. All in their own ways worked to develop the art of the theater and to increase its power to move and to challenge the audience.

The role of architects was never subsidiary to that of the playwrights, directors, or actors; the architects' share in the development of the theatrical form has always been primary and determinative, although it might be held that their part should have been confined to orchestrating all these functions into a single unit of space. From its very beginnings, the theater has been indebted to architects for their help in the development of the drama and for the guidance and motivation they have provided to its other specialists. It was the architects who sought and found more accessible, more feasible configurations, dimensions, and installations. They established dimensional standards, visual angles, circulation-flow patterns, acoustic methods, lighting techniques, and solutions to many other problems; and they tried to find the architectural form appropriate to the trends of each period and to adapt it to the latest technological developments and to current social conditions.

The primary problem for all who were concerned with the theater was the audience–performer relationship—that is to say, the auditorium–stage relationship. The desire to create the most and best possible areas for "action" and "response to action" led to a search for the "perfect" auditorium and the "perfect"

stage. Paradoxically, for a very long time these two theatrical functions were approached separately, each as a different feature that should have no connection with the other.

For 400 years every connection between the auditorium and the stage stopped at the proscenium, as if it were the boundary line between two different worlds that must on no account be overstepped. On one side was the world of the theater, mysterious, esoteric, hinting at obscure and secret doings; and on the other, the world of the audience, the secular lord, the simple citizen, the customer, the consumer. The cause of this separation lies in the fact that the Italian stage—the "optical box" as it is called[178]—while ideally suited to opera (for which, indeed, it was devised) did not reflect any message or stimulate the intellectual process; all it offered was visual enjoyment and illusion.

When, as we have seen, a movement started during the interbellum period to do away with the proscenium, architects went to their drawing boards in search of new theater forms to replace the discredited and besieged classic Italian stage. The Bauhaus explorations in Germany, the creative discontent of college and amateur theater groups in the United States, the developing political-social theater, all of which pursued the goal of reestablishing the actor–audience relation and restoring simplicity of style, were looking for new theatrical forms through which to develop their ideas; in their search they turned to the classical prototypes, particularly those of the ancient Greek theater.

First attempts are not always successful; the old is not easily ousted by the new. Theater people—which means everybody concerned with the theater, including the audience—found it quite difficult to detach themselves from the traditional. They all had to get used to the new trends, the new esthetic, the new way of thinking, the new materials—all the things, in short, that go to form the fundamentals of theatrical evolution. This was not easy to do in a short period of time; one can readily visualize the difficulties they faced in the inspiration, creation, and understanding of the new forms that have emerged in the contemporary theater between then and now.[179]

The Performing Arts

The term "performing arts," as it is commonly used, means every manifestation represented by the theater, every art that requires for its expression and presentation the collective endeavor of many individuals and for its consummation the support of a public that understands and appreciates it. It is the drama, music, the dance, the big spectacle, the circus, with all their offshoots and variations.

In our analysis of the problems of the theater we have seen that from the Renaissance to the beginning of our century the dominant theatrical forms were the spectacular dramatic performance and the opera. The drama based on purely psychological premises and on the power of the spoken word, which requires a direct relationship between actor and audience, made its first appearance toward the close of the nineteenth century, with the exception, of course, of the Greek and Elizabethan periods. The same holds true of music and the dance; for centuries these arts were reserved for the enjoyment of a small, privileged segment of society and were generally presented at the courts or in the salons of princes and noblemen.

The big spectacle, and above all opera, led to the creation of the huge theaters of the eighteenth and nineteenth centuries, which, however, in the period between the two world wars, were found to be unsuitable for any other performing art that tried to claim its place in the world of the theater.

Some solution had to be found, either something that could be adapted to tradition or a totally new form, if any remained to be found. Space had to be arranged in such a way that speech—the words and meanings of O'Neill, Shaw, or Brecht—could reach the audience unrestrained; that, in the same way, the rhythm and movement of the dance would become equally accessible to everyone; that music would find its proper space where the sound and the instruments could be synchronized. The Bauhaus ideas for a space theater did not remain unexploited; Gropius's *total theater* became the model for every future form, and Schlemmer's theories concerning the relation of the actor to cubical space were studied seriously and without derisive intent. Farkas Molnár's U-theater (discussed at greater length at the end of this study) was designed in 1924, but it is still studied today as an original concept, a form uniquely eloquent in revealing what the true space theater should be like.

The successful creations of Reinhardt, Meyerhold, Mielziner, Robert Edmond Jones, and many other directors and designers between the wars proved, first of all, that the proscenium theater prevailed for so many years because of directors' inability to present their work open on all sides, and secondly because of the playwright's difficulty in attracting and holding the interest of his audience by the power of his written word alone. Thus they found it necessary to turn for support to strong illusion, to nice pictures framed by the proscenium arch, that element which, fundamental as it was to opera, also became, because of the weaknesses mentioned, a tool used indiscriminately in every kind of dramatic presentation and in every form of theatrical expression.

However, the most characteristic development in the evolution of contemporary theater forms was the emergence of two dominant but conflicting trends that, in the view of Siegfried Melchinger,[180] must be seriously considered by every student of the theater.

The first of these trends had a negative as well as a positive aspect. Its negative expression was opposition to the proscenium, the "fourth wall" of the eighteenth- and nineteenth-century stage. Its positive, constructive aspect aimed at a return to the Greek and Elizabethan traditions in reaction to the Italian stage. This was the trend that led to the creation of the theater-in-the-round, or arena theater, which differed from the Greek prototype only in that the audience surrounded the orchestra on all sides.

The second trend was the very opposite of the first. Never before in the long life of the theater was its history studied so carefully and given such importance as at this time. All its periods were scrutinized; every kind of play ever written was analyzed in detail and every view concerning the stage was minutely examined, both as to functional building details and as to what may be termed the philosophical base of theatrical evolutionary endeavor in each period of the past. Instead of attacking the proscenium, the followers of this trend wanted to research it. Instead of abolishing it, they tried to adjust it to contemporary needs. At the same time they did not overlook the possibilities offered by the forms that the first trend wanted to impose. The result of all this was the "adaptable" or "experimental" theater, a form that since then has been explored very thoroughly by architects engaged in studying modern theater forms.

With these conflicting trends at work, the first steps of the contemporary theater were made in the middle of a tug-of-war pulling in two different directions at once. On one side was the powerful influence of the Greek and Elizabethan

stages and on the other a fervent search for a form that would disengage the theater from that influence.

The conflict had a happy effect. It resulted in the emergence of not one but four different theater forms: the proscenium theater, adjusted to contemporary needs; the open-stage theater based on the Greek and Elizabethan traditions; the theater-in-the-round; and last, the adaptable or experimental theater, which can be described as an attempt to combine all the previous forms in a single pattern.

12
The Proscenium Theater

Preservation of the Form

It may seem odd that in considering contemporary theater forms we begin with an analysis of one that is so preeminently traditional and that generated such sharp controversy during the first half of our century.

The fact is that the proscenium theater—the focus of the second trend mentioned in the preceding chapter—had numerous supporters among those who felt that a return to tradition was not the sole avenue of salvation open to the theater. This faction held that the proscenium, notwithstanding the arguments of its opponents, did not obstruct the development of contact and unity between actors and audience. Some insisted that the emotional response is actually heightened by remoteness,[181] others contended that the Italian stage appeared, at a given time, to be the ideal type for communication.[182]

If we concede, however, that true drama, old and contemporary alike, is directly dependent on this response and communication, it is difficult to see how such pronounced material obstacles as the proscenium arch and the difference in lighting between stage and auditorium can preserve those relations intact.[183] It is difficult to be convinced that a darkened auditorium combined with a lighted stage can induce greater emotional receptivity and help suspend rational judgment.

Apparently there is some confusion on this point, since the proscenium was not created in response to any emotional need but rather for constructional reasons. It was a frame invented to conceal the imperfections of the Italian stage, and it immediately became a line that separated the actor from the audience. It had no connection at all with Aeschylus' proscenium, which was behind the actor and did not act as a dividing line between him and the audience but as an element that completed the unity of the stage. The acting area remained free, and the actor, not remote from his audience, was the only source of emotion, which he induced by the reality of his three-dimensional presence and by direct participation with the spectator. With the Italian proscenium, on the contrary, the acting area is itself smaller; it acquires definition and becomes remote. This is a serious limitation that posed a constant problem for all thinking people of the theater. It has been noticeable in recent years when directors, in an attempt to avoid the proscenium, developed their plays in front of it or transformed it or sometimes even caused the actors to come forth from the back of the auditorium.[184]

This compromise was the one chosen by Bertolt Brecht, Germany's premier playwright, who used the proscenium in its traditional and orthodox form. For him, one way of eliminating the proscenium was to retain it. Why eliminate it, he reasoned, when you can accomplish what you want by ignoring it? What really needed to be eliminated was the inordinate importance attached to it, and this was one of the major problems faced by the contemporary theater.[185]

Brecht maintained that the difficulty did not lie in the existence of the dividing line but in what would happen when the actor or the director tried to cross it. To circumvent that difficulty, he used a new expedient of his own devising: the chorus. The chorus, as conceived by Brecht for this purpose, consisted of one or two actors who emerged from the proscenium, crossed the demarcation line, and placed themselves between it and the audience. Their presence did not pass unnoticed; it was a positive presence that restored the link between the two functions. These actors were not an integral part of the performance; they were just *there*. Sometimes they did not utter a word, sometimes they exchanged comments about the plot or explained the phases of the play in song.

The success of this technique in *The Caucasian Chalk Circle (Der Kaukasische Kreidekreis),* 1954, originated something fresh and produced a new experience that, gradually developed and was adopted extensively by the contemporary theater. The underlying principle was that the performance should not be given *in front of* the audience but for the sake of realistic interpretation *to* or *for* the audience (Figure 126). Instead of the acting methods of the past, which required the actors to pretend they were oblivious of the public that watched them, the new way was to emphasize the presence of the audience quite openly and without reticence and to acknowledge what was in fact its true role.

Thanks to the widespread support it enjoyed, the proscenium theater survived. However, the proscenium itself, either in its original form or in the attenuated versions adopted by other schools of contemporary theater, was generally reduced

Figure 126. Two chorus singers in Bertolt Brecht's The Caucasian Chalk Circle, 1954, sitting at the foot of the proscenium. (Credit: Southern, Seven Ages, plate 18.)

to an innocuous feature, a vestigial part. Others accepted the proscenium out of a regard for tradition[186] or as a feature essential to the existing repertory.[187]

Adaptation to Contemporary Needs

Against the background of all these conflicting views, it was inevitable that the proscenium theater should be affected · by the considerable forces generated by changing concepts. For one thing, its use in the performing arts was confined to the opera, the operetta, the ballet spectacular, musical comedy, and vaudeville. For these genres the conventional playhouse was moder-

nized with every technical facility needed to make it more flexible while retaining the old, tried and proven features. But where the proscenium form was chosen for theaters used exclusively for drama, the size of the building was considerably diminished. The auditorium was modified to a strictly human scale, since by this time it was commonly acknowledged that, while the proscenium could be retained, no drama could be properly performed and assimilated in a huge house containing as many as 3000 people. Thus in the drama theater the auditorium became smaller, so that it accommodated no more than 600 or at most 700 spectators.

The greatest step forward in modern proscenium theater design unquestionably was made in Germany. Since that country was strongly oriented toward the opera and therefore toward the Italian stage, it was the scene of several important developments in the use of technology on the stage. One outstanding feature that gave the German type of theater a great measure of stage flexibility when applied to the performing arts was the movable proscenium. Based on the Bayreuth tradition, the music area (orchestra pit) was equipped with two platforms that could be raised and rotated hydraulically, a device that gave it great flexibility and adaptability in an auditorium of determinate shape and layout.

The four sectional drawings of the orchestra pit show how the proscenium could be converted in four different ways.[188] In the first position (drawing a) the platforms are so placed as to

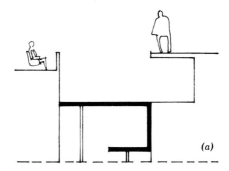

(a)

create a deep and spacious pit that can accommodate the large symphony orchestras required for operas by Wagner or Strauss. In the second

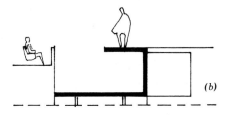

(b)

position (drawing b) the main platform is turned upside down and aligned with the others so as to form a deep, covered pit, narrower than the first, and a projecting apron, a forestage that permits the actor or dancer to come closer to the audience. The third position (drawing c) reduces the

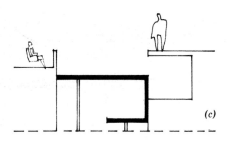

(c)

depth of the pit by half for performances of operettas and musical shows. Finally, in the fourth position (drawing d) the main platform is raised to form a big apron reminiscent of the Elizabethan stage.

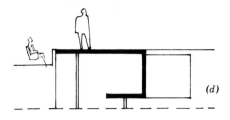

(d)

Before concluding this analysis of the proscenium theater form and turning to its leading examples in various countries, we must for a moment place ourselves in the role of supporters as we examine certain points, the indisputable advantages of which have yet to be equaled by other contemporary theater forms.

Because the audience is facing the stage, everyone has the same view of it and shares the same dramatic experience. Furthermore, this type of theater helps the director control and hold the interest of the audience by minimizing any possible distractions that might divert attention from the plot. The stage lighting, too, can be used and exploited to best possible effect; the audience's eyes are all turned in one direction, and with the lights all aimed at the same point no single spectator risks being dazzled by their beams. And problems of acoustics are easier to solve in this form of theater, since the source of sound is fixed in relation to the auditorium as a whole, a condition that makes it easier to control and coordinate reverberation and sound absorption.

Distinctive Examples

Since Germany was cited as the pioneer in the development of the proscenium theater, it is logical to begin the consideration of outstanding examples with that country. We must always bear in mind that the Germans by tradition are inclined toward opera houses and buildings in the grand style rather than toward the small, independent, and intimate drama playhouse. At bottom, the contemporary theater forms in Germany are nothing but variations of the old Italian opera house where the stage is concerned and of the Bayreuth Theater as regards the auditorium. Considering that more than 90 theaters have been built in Germany since 1950, selecting the best and most representative examples from among this multitude is no easy task.

The designs of two characteristic opera buildings, those of Hamburg and Berlin, and three drama theaters, those of Münster and Bonn and the Kammerspiele Bochum, are the most representative of the contemporary concept of proscenium theater.

The Hamburg Opera represents a wedding of the old and new notions. Totally destroyed in World War II, it was rebuilt in 1955 by architects G. Weber and W. Lux with a seating capacity of 1679.[189] The influence of the Italian opera house is decidedly apparent throughout the building design. The consecutive tiers of separate boxes (Figure 127) have been transferred from the

Figure 127. Hamburg Opera, 1955: auditorium. (By permission of the Hamburgische Staatsoper and Gerhard Weber, the architect.)

eighteenth century to the twentieth unchanged as to function and form. The stage is vast, occupying an area almost equal to that of the auditorium and permitting the use of the most complex settings, and the plan and section of the auditorium (Figures 128, 129) are strikingly similar to the Bayreuth model in the continental-style curvilinear arrangement of the seats, the sharply sloping floor, and the large number of side exits absolutely necessary for access to the foyer. Worth noting is a feature already described in connection with the flexible relation between proscenium and orchestra pit: The distance of the front row of seats from the proscenium is large enough to allow conversion of the pit area into any of the four combinations described above.

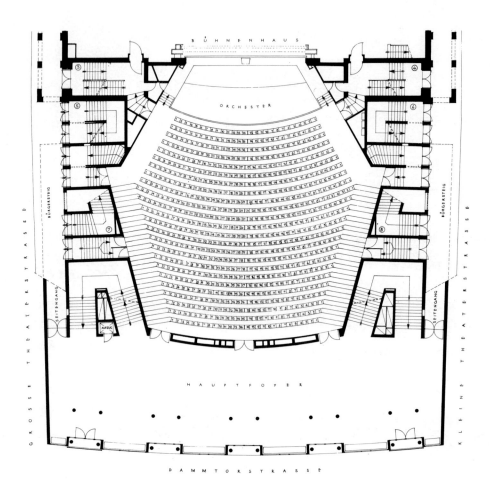

HAMBURG, IM OKTOBER 1955.

PROFESSOR
GERHARD WEBER
ARCHITEKT BDA

Figure 128. Hamburg Opera: plan. (By permission of the Hamburgische Staatsoper and Gerhard Weber, the architect.)

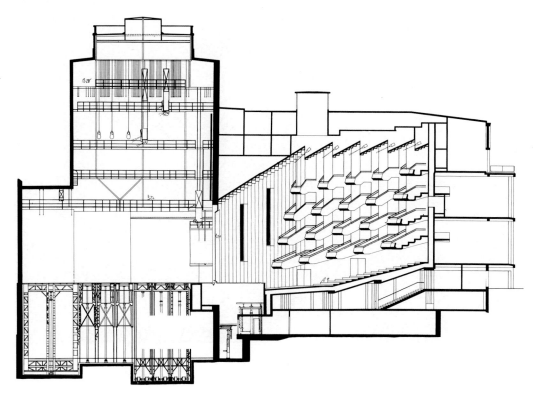

Figure 129. Hamburg Opera: section. (By permission of the Hamburgische Staatsoper and G. Weber, the architect.)

Figure 130. Berlin Opera, 1961: auditorium. (By permission of the Deutsche Oper Berlin.)

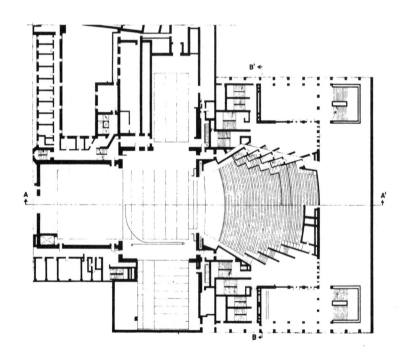

The Berlin Opera, likewise, departs in very few respects from the classical tradition. Designed by Fritz Bornemann, it opened in September 1961.[190] Although the building is of postwar design and completely modern, the influence of the Italian theater is very pronounced (Figure 130). In comparison with the Hamburg Opera, of course, many features have been simplified. The auditorium is largely rid of the weight of superimposed rows of boxes, which are used here as cohesive elements in the synthesis of space rather than as functions serving the spectator in the eighteenth- and nineteenth-century sense. There is in fact only one row of separate boxes, the upper; the lower row is more like an extension of the first gallery. The result is eminently successful, and the effect created by this vast space with its 1900 seats is unique. The Wagnerian seating layout has been retained (Figures 131, 132), but the question of access to the seats has been most successfully dealt with.

Figure 131. Berlin Opera: plan of the auditorium. (By permission of George Izenour).

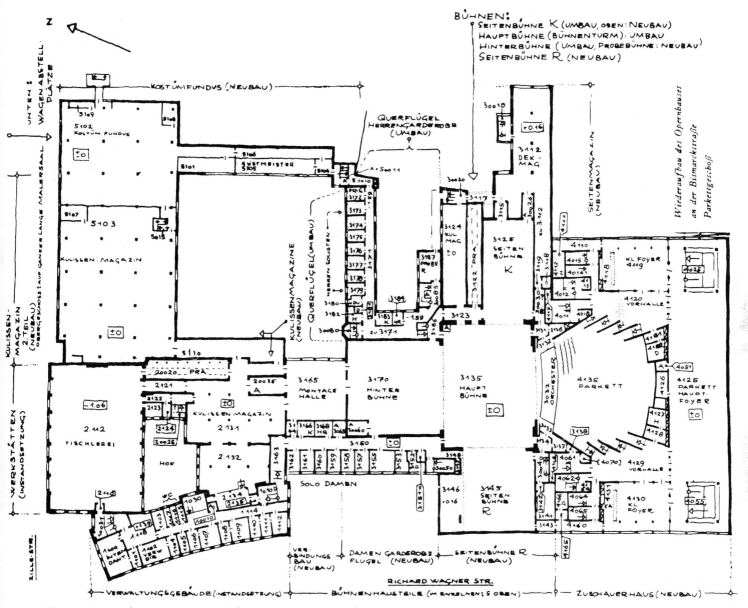

Figure 132. Berlin Opera: general plan. (By permission of the Deutsche Oper Berlin.)

The continental-style seating is thus efficiently served, since the side doors open directly into a foyer that encircles the auditorium, allowing a better flow at peak times. This convenience of access is lacking at the Hamburg Opera, with its two exterior aisles.

The stage area, however, conforms in every respect to the traditional opera pattern. The only notable difference is that here the available space is nearly tripled in relation to the au-

ditorium if, in addition to the main stage, one takes into account the three auxiliary stages that surround it. Moreover, one cannot help but be impressed, in studying the plan of the theater, by the proportion of the auditorium to the rest of the space—production areas, performers' accommodations, administration offices—which has been provided to serve it and the audience; it is a characteristic example of the modern opera house.

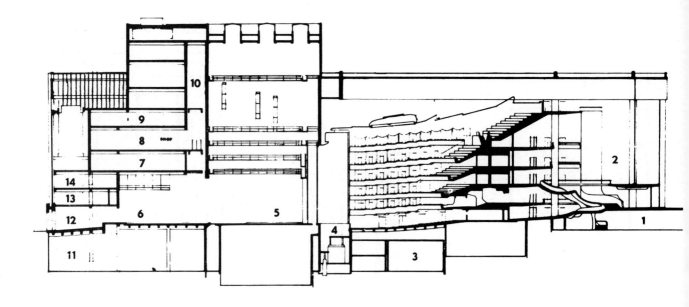

Figure 133. Metropolitan Opera House, New York, 1966: (above) *section;* (below) *plan.*
(Credit: L'Architecture d'aujourd'hui, *No. 122 [1965].)*

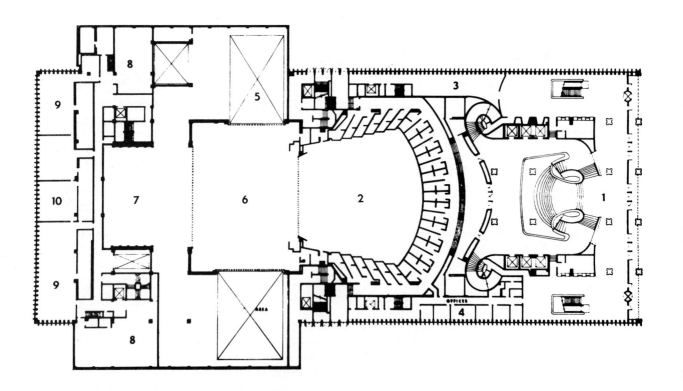

Those who go to the Berlin Opera, though it has less than half the capacity of the Metropolitan Opera House in New York (Figure 133), which seats 4000 and opened five years later (1966), have no cause to envy the latter. Quite the opposite: The Berlin Opera's functional organization is much more rational and efficient since all principal service areas are located on one main level, whereas at the Metropolitan the smallness of the site compelled architect Wallace Harrison to arrange its functions vertically.

The Municipal Theater of Münster, by contrast, is an example of a smaller house that can be used with equal ease for opera and legitimate drama. Here we see one of the first attempts to create a truly modern proscenium theater that is adjusted to contemporary needs (Figures 134, 135).

Designed by architect Harold Deilmann, it opened in 1956 and was one of the first theaters with a capacity of less then 1000. It seats 955 and the auditorium is only 23 meters deep, which makes it considerably smaller than the Hamburg and Berlin Operas (28.5 and 32 meters deep, respectively).[191] Its limited mass perfectly suits the requirements of drama without creating any problems, other than financial, in the presentation of opera. It is through such performances, indeed, that the Münster playhouse made a name for itself in the theater world; along with the small experimental theaters of Mannheim and Gelsenkirchen, it is one of the few theaters in Germany that has engaged systematically in the search for new methods of theatrical expression and dramatic development.[192]

Figure 134. Municipal Theater, Münster, 1956; auditorium. (Photo by Wilhelm Heller. Reprinted by permission.)

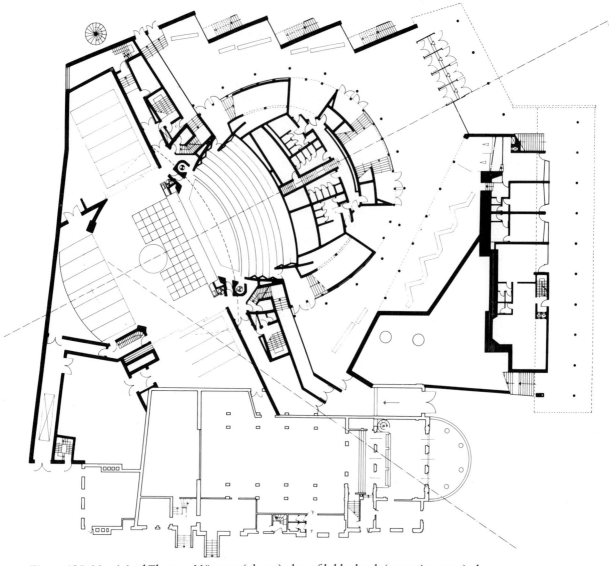

Figure 135. Municipal Theater, Münster: (above) *plan of lobby level;* (opposite page) *plan of foyer level. (By permission of Harold Deilmann, the architect.)*

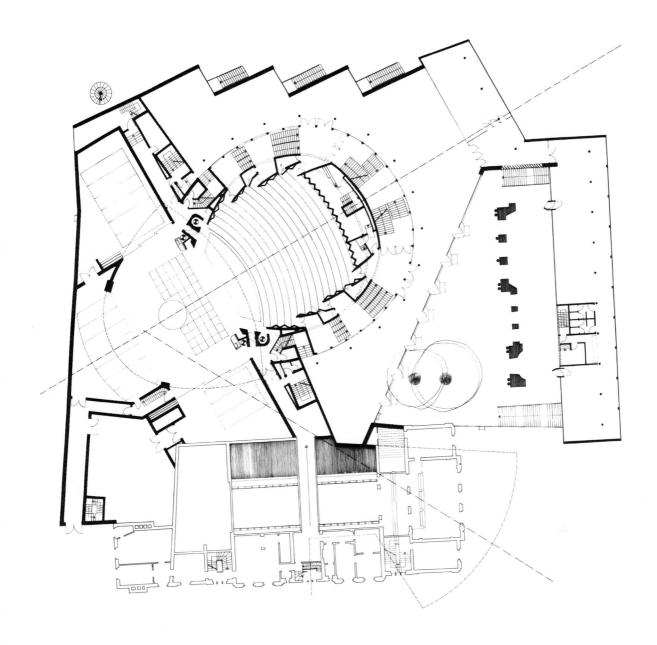

163

The stage is quite small in comparison with those of the Berlin and Metropolitan houses; in this theater opera does not hold first place. The auditorium, while smaller in area, features the successful continental seating arrangement with side exits opening into a surrounding foyer. This layout, which, as we have seen, was adopted by the Berlin Opera, became popular with architects. It eventually evolved into a type characteristic of postwar German theater architecture, and today it can be found in most major theaters in Germany—in Kassel, Cologne, Düsseldorf, and elsewhere. Repetition has not made it tiresome or diminished its value, since it is an arrangement that does not break up the unity of the audience mass with unnecessary aisles, and it provides the best possible convenience of access and circulation.

The Bonn Municipal Theater opened in 1965. Designed to serve as many of the performing arts as possible, it has been used primarily for drama, although it has full facilities and equipment for opera and ballet. It was designed by K. Gessler, P. Frohne and W. Beck and has a capacity of 896 seats.[193] A special feature of this playhouse is the revolutionary design of the auditorium, which has no relation whatsoever to any antecedent pattern (Figures 136, 137). The partially truncated auditorium and asymmetrical gallery make for an unusual architectural austerity not often seen in a theater. Another characteristic feature is, as in the Berlin Opera, the proportion of the auditorium to its service areas; the inequality is so pronounced as to be remarkable because the seating capacity here is lower than that of the Berlin Opera, which means a proportionately higher cost of running the house.

The examination of the German proscenium theater can be closed with the mention of the small art theater (the Kammerspiele), which opened in Bochum in 1956 (Figures 138–141).

Figure 136. Municipal Theater, Bonn, 1965: auditorium. (Photo by Rüdiger Dichtel. Reprinted by permission.)

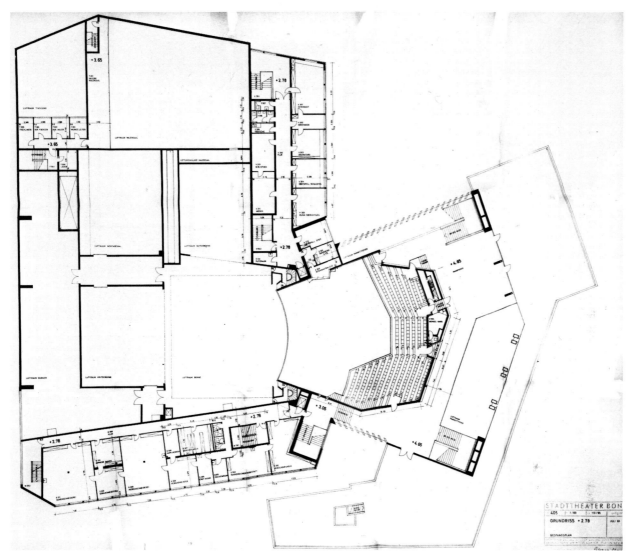

Figure 137. Municipal Theater, Bonn: plan of foyer and balcony level. (By courtesy of the architects Wilfrid Beck-Erlang, Peter Frohne and Klaus Gessler.)

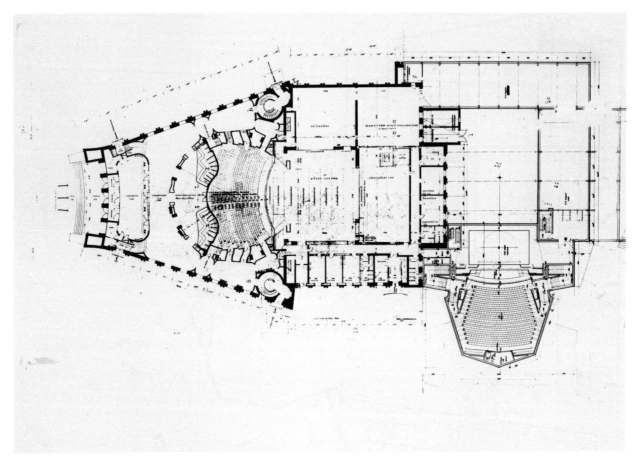

Figure 138. Bochum Theater: general plan. Left, *the old theater, 1953;* right, *the drama theater, 1966. (By permission of the city of Bochum.)*

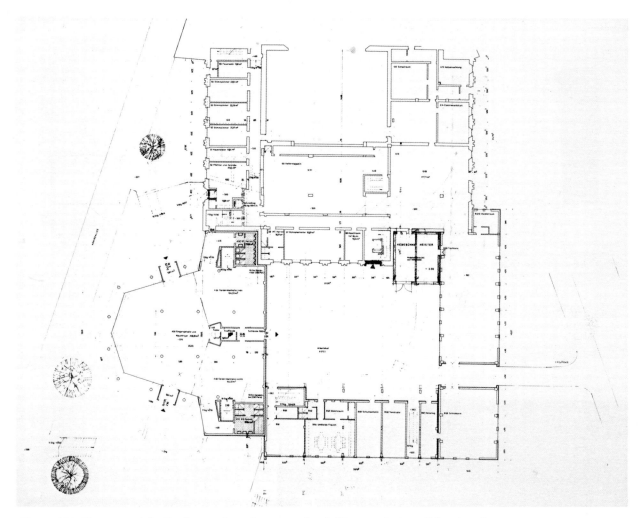

Figure 139. Kammerspiele, Bochum: plan of entrance level. (By permission of the city of Bochum.)

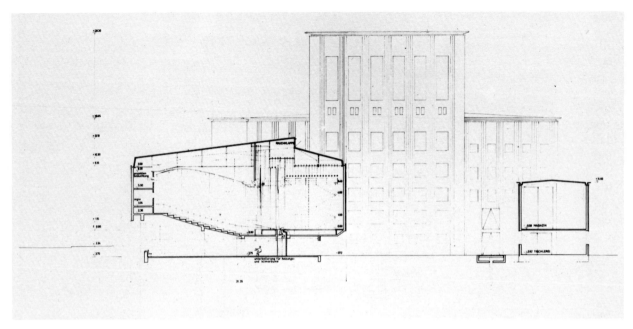

Figure 140. Kammerspiele, Bochum: section. (By permission of the city of Bochum.)

Figure 141. Kammerspiele, Bochum: auditorium and stage. (By permission of the city of Bochum.)

Built as an extension of the old Municipal Theater of Bochum (which had been restored in 1953) to provide a theater center, it seats only 401 spectators and is dedicated exclusively to drama.[194] This small playhouse—its auditorium is a mere 12.5 meters deep—deserves to be considered one of the best examples of modern proscenium theater. The auditorium, simple as can be, serves its purpose completely. The stage, with its strictly essential minimum dimensions, is only for drama and is served by the working areas of the complex. An interesting feature is the arrangement of the public areas, especially those serving as channels of access. The two side staircases and a sort of tunnel in which the lighting is dim and subdued help ease the transition from the outside world to the interior of the theater; the psychological effect is unique.

Apart from Germany, the Scandinavian countries made an early start in the construction of small proscenium theaters devoted to drama alone. In 1952 a small cultural center seating 500 was built in Turku, Finland (Figure 142), and in Stockholm the Folkets Hus (Figures 143, 144), completed in 1961, conformed to the German pattern but with a smaller stage area.

Figure 142. Cultural center, Turku, 1952: plan. (Nicoll, Development of the Theatre, p. 230. Reprinted by permission.)

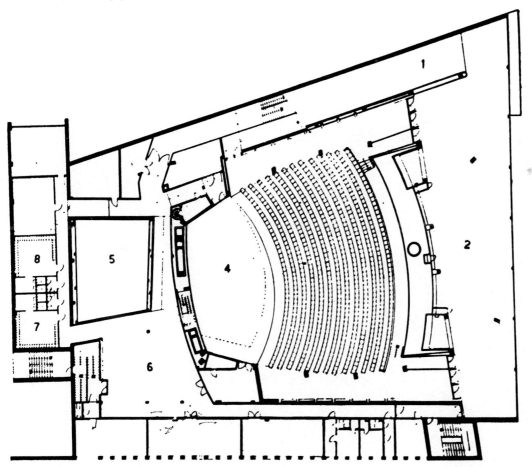

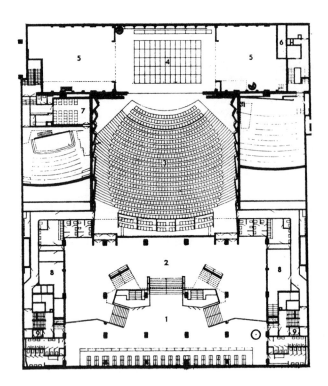

Figure 143. Folkets Hus, Stockholm, 1961: plan. (By permission and courtesy of Arkitekturmuseum, Swedish · Museum of Architecture.)

Figure 144. Folkets Hus: auditorium. (By permission and courtesy of Arkitekturmuseum, Swedish Museum of Architecture.)

In the United States the proscenium theater did not develop to any notable extent. The pressure of the commercial theater and the dominance of Broadway caused dissenters to turn to new forms in which the proscenium had no place. That is why the other contemporary theater forms developed so spectacularly in America. It would serve no purpose here to mention examples of major American proscenium theaters of the Metropolitan Opera House or Broadway type, since all such buildings constructed up to now differ in no essential respect from those already discussed.

Before closing this chapter, however, mention must be made of a remarkable creation by the great Frank Lloyd Wright that I had the opportunity to study during a visit to Tempe, Arizona. The Grady Gammage Memorial Auditorium of Arizona State University is one of the architect's lesser-known works, built in 1964, in which he applied radical designs to the plan and the building volumes alike (Figures 145–147).[195]

Figure 145. Grady Gammage Memorial Auditorium, Tempe, Arizona: plan. (By permission of Arizona State University.)

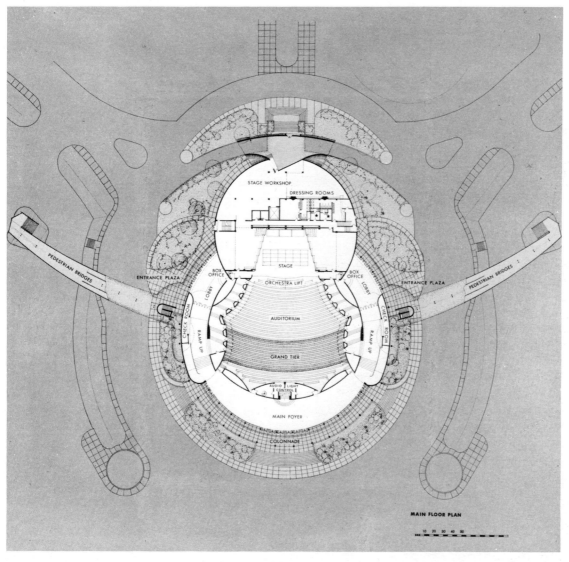

Figure 146. Grady Gammage Memorial Auditorium. (By permission of Arizona State University.)

Figure 147. Grady Gammage Memorial Auditorium: free space between the grand tier and the rear wall of the auditorium. This space considerably enhances the theater's acoustics. (By permission of Arizona State University.)

The building is basically a composition of two overlapping circular forms. The dominant circle contains the auditorium with its surrounding public areas, lobbies, and promenades, encircled by a lofty colonnade. The second circle contains the stage and working areas, four floors for rehearsal, and classrooms of the university's music and drama departments.

The stage, designed by George Izenour, can be adapted to any of the performing arts. The circular plan that predominates in the overall design makes possible a remarkably easy flow of traffic, which is particularly important in a theater with such a large capacity.

A unique feature of the auditorium is the grand tier spanning the theater from side to side but making no contact with the rear wall. This open space behind the balconies assures an even flow of sound to every seat.

The exterior of the building is not up to the standard of the dynamic interior, particularly when one gets one's first sight of the slender columns marking the perimeter of the building, which rise 17 meters to support the disproportionately weighty circular outer porch. But any further criticism of the work of such a great master would be an impertinence.

13
The Open-Stage Theater

The Importance of the Spoken Word Revived

The second form of contemporary theater, the open-stage theater is in fact anything but contemporary. In our century it may admittedly have seemed like something new, reappearing as it did after hundreds of years of predominance by the proscenium arch. Perhaps, too, the fact that it was regarded as the forerunner of the other two forms, the theater-in-the-round and the experimental theater, was not conducive to an investigation of its origin. Yet a look at the history of the theater reveals that it was the only form known in ancient Greece and Elizabethan England, when speech was the most important element in dramatic presentation.

The open-stage theater, a direct descendant of those earlier forms, reappeared to serve speech again, and it has stayed on since then as the most promising architectural form for the presentation of drama. Created by enthusiasts who wished to revive the spirit of Shakespeare, the open stage is the contribution exclusively of England—or at any rate, of the English-speaking world—to the modern theater.

The restoration of speech as a primary element of dramatic theater went through several phases in the last century and remains one of the outstanding literary accomplishments of our era. It began with an attempt to revive the verse-drama of Shakespeare; it continued later with the attempts of T.S. Eliot and Christopher Fry to persuade the audience that words in verse could provide a fountain of sparkling entertainment. When these efforts elicited rather negative reactions, English playwrights began using the form of general speech,[196]—that is, the spoken word used as precisely and evocatively as poetry and not restricted to a particular form ruled by meter and rhyme.

James Joyce, under the influence of Ibsen, was the first to adopt and try out this style of writing but without conclusive success. Samuel Beckett, however, with his plays *Waiting for Godot* and *Endgame* opened up new prospects for the literature of the theater. With the satire of Jean Anouilh, the bizarrerie of Eugène Ionesco, and the revolutionary innovations of Berthold Brecht, a school and a style were created that induced young dramatists like Harold Pinter,

N.P. Simpson, and John Arden to follow its underlying theory: that speech, quite simply, is—and must be—the primary means of interpretation of the drama.

It was for theater of this sort that the open stage was originally created. This theater form does not lend itself to illusion of any kind, just as poetry itself is not based on illusion of any kind. One reads poetry because of the desire to do so. One goes to the theater to be in it. Those who wish to deceive themselves and think they are not in a theater but on a trip to imaginary places with the hero, find the open stage is not for them. Those who are unable to sit through two hours of celebration over the performance of a handful of actors before them or in their midst, who use no means of attracting the audience but the playwright's word and their own interpretative expression of it, similarly find the open stage unappealing. They would do better to seek their intellectual enjoyment, or rather their entertainment pure and simple, in the boulevard or Broadway theater. The open stage and its playbill do not present the rich decor and illusion because it is based on the belief that the audience should not forget for a single moment that it is in a theater watching and hearing a work of art. That was the belief Brecht expressed when he wrote: "The stage decor must not be such that the public believes itself to be in a room in medieval Italy or in the Vatican. The public must remain always clearly aware that it is in a theatre."[197]

Theater historian Richard Southern explains the true interpretation of the term *open stage* as follows: "Let us have no misunderstanding here: by open stage I mean a stage unenclosed by any frame, projecting boldly forward from its background and open to the spectators on three of its sides. In other words the form of the "booth stage."[197] The explanation is necessary because many people believe the open stage evolved from the theater of director Norman Bel Geddes (Figure 148), as presented in 1914, or that of Jacques Copeau (1920), discussed earlier (Figure 117). Some also maintain that the German type of extended proscenium was another predecessor of the open stage. In my opinion, these views are incorrect, since all three forms, though they were attempts to free the actor from the restrictions of the proscenium arch, were nothing but variations of the proscenium theater.

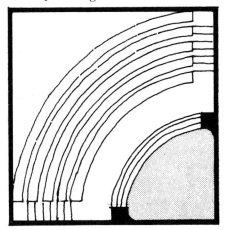

Figure 148. The stage of Norman Bel Geddes. (Drawing by author.)

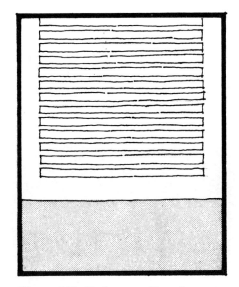

Figure 149. End stage. (Drawing by author.)

To be specific, the theater of Norman Bel Geddes—namely, a stage tucked into a corner of the plan with a 90-degree fan-shaped auditorium—is an arrangement that still uses the stage and setting as a background for the action. The proscenium and its technique are still there, and its inconveniences, particularly insofar as visual angles are concerned, are in fact augmented.

As in the case of Copeau's Vieux-Colombier, again the stage and auditorium still confront each other face to face, with a fixed setting as background. This concept was adopted somewhat more extensively and later evolved into the form known as the end stage (Figure 149). By eliminating the proscenium wall and arch altogether, the entire stage area was exposed to view at "one end of the same room"; but the relationship between stage and auditorium remained unchanged.

Although there is no longer a frame between stage and auditorium and although the angles of vision have been improved, this form, nevertheless, is still a variation of proscenium theater. In addition, the fact that there is no space for side stages (Figure 150) makes the house somewhat inflexible; all the settings have to be brought from the back of the stage, an inconvenience that greatly reduces the scenographic facilities.

The same holds true of the German forestage, the apron stage we have just discussed (Figure 150). As we have seen, Reinhardt used it in the Grosses Schauspielhaus (Figure 106), and it was

adopted (though considerably reduced in size and equipped with raisable floors) by German architects in nearly every proscenium theater built after World War II. Like the other two types discussed, the apron stage is a form of proscenium, where the main stage accommodates a formal setting, and the forestage is used only when needed to develop certain scenes of the play. No massive object can be placed on it that would obstruct the view of the main setting at

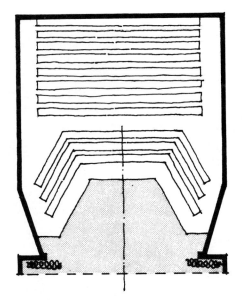

Figure 150. Apron stage. (Drawing by author.)

the rear. In many theaters the forestage can be lowered to the level of the main floor of the auditorium for use as additional seating space or depressed still further to form a pit for the orchestra. In all cases the proscenium arch is retained almost intact (Figures 151, 152). This supports my assertion that this form, though strongly resembling the open stage, is, like the others, but a variation of the proscenium theater: While it does nothing to restore the actor–audience relationship, it forces the director to feed the play through fixed and limited accesses.

Figure 151. Pheonix Theatre, Leicester: end stage. (Credit: Ham, Theatre Planning, p. 25.)

Figure 152. Nottingham Playhouse: apron stage. (By permission and courtesy of the architect Peter Moro.)

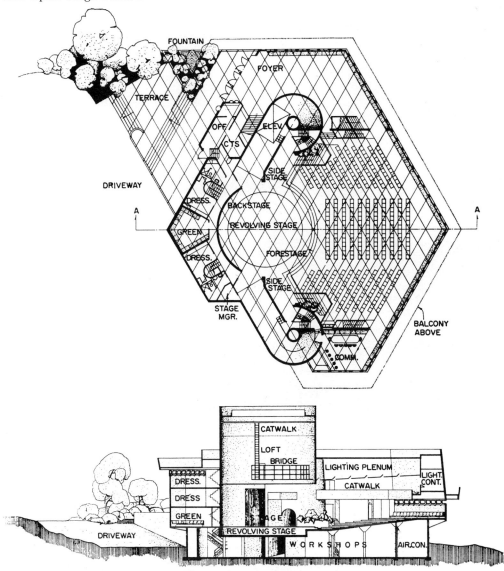

Figure 153. Kalita Humphrey Theater: plan and section. (Author's archive.)

Two interesting examples of how the apron stage can be developed and modified to a smaller scale are Frank Lloyd Wright's 300-seat Kalita Humphrey Theater in Dallas, 1960 (Figures 153, 154), and Marcel Breuer's theater, built in 1952, at Sarah Lawrence College (Figure 155).

With his usual skill, Wright flanked the main stage with two smaller side stages, thus creating an "extended" stage; a big revolving platform on the floor of the main stage provides the director with additional scope and flexibility in the use of the settings. The entire design, in my opinion, bears the stamp of a masterpiece. It is a quiet space filled with an air of expectancy. The quietness—as one critic described it—is owing partly to the gentle angling of the walls, floor, and ceiling, partly to the broad surfaces and continuous materials, partly to the lack of axial movement between auditorium and stage; but principally it is owing to the unity shared by auditorium and stage—a unity of space, of shapes, of character.[198]

Figure 154. Kalita Humphrey Theater, Dallas. Frank Lloyd Wright, 1960. (Author's archive.)

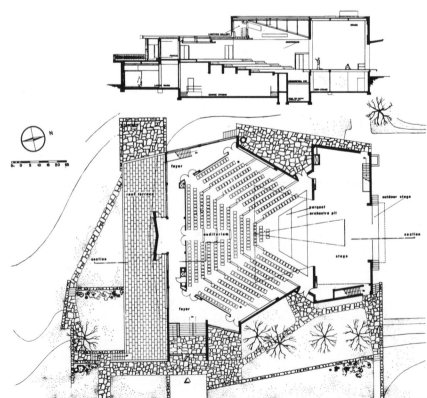

Figure 155. Sarah Lawrence College Theater, Bronxville, New York: section and plan. Marcel Breuer, architect, 1952. (Author's archive.)

Precisely because of this form, the Kalita Humphrey Theater acquired a major reputation in the presentation of a repertory of classic ancient drama and dance. Breuer's theater, on the other hand, was used more as a university school of drama. The forestage of this 500-seat theater can be lowered to make room for an additional 33 seats.[199]

In contrast to Wright, Breuer opted for the functional simplicity appropriate to an educational theater. Nevertheless, the two theaters have a feature in common: They both reflect an attempt to combine the advantages of the proscenium and the open stage, to establish contact between actor and audience but at the same time provide generous latitude for the use of settings that would give greater variety to the performances and preserve the traditional power of illusion inherent in the proscenium.

Form and Purpose

As distinct from the variations described above, the open-stage theater, with its roots going back to ancient Greece and Elizabethan England, has as its identifying feature a stage located at the center of gravity of the auditorium, an "orchestra" like that of the Greek theater, with the audience surrounding it in a 210–220 degree encircling layout. Three sides of this orchestra-stage are thus freely exposed to the audience while the fourth abuts on the wall separating the stage from the backstage area, through which the actors enter and exit exactly as they did in Shakespeare's Globe Theatre.

Designed to serve the spoken word, the open stage is suitable mainly for drama. The use of settings and scenery is virtually eliminated except for a few pieces of furniture or symbolic props low enough to avoid obstructing the audience's view. If there is a tower, its function is confined merely to flying a limited number of backcloths. The strictly unalterable architectural outline, the fixed accesses for the actors' entrances and exits, and the impossibility of concealing any mechanical scenographic aid make this kind of stage entirely unsuitable for performances of formal ballet, opera, or concerts. On the other hand, apart from drama, it is ideal for modern ballet or chamber music. In particular, the dance—the kind of dance that does not depend on the elaborate scenery of classic ballet but on movement and mimetic art—derives, in my opinion, from the open stage quality expounded a few years earlier by Oskar Schlemmer, namely a concordant relation of the actor to the cubical space that surrounds him, the achievement of harmony in three dimensions.

Three-dimensional motion in space is equally important in the performance of drama. On the open stage the actors are no longer face to face with the audience but surrounded by it. Their movement here should not be linear, as on the proscenium stage, but three-dimensional, calculated to be pleasing from any visual angle. Their facial expressions—a fundamental element in the performance of modern drama—should be seen with equal clarity and sharpness by all the spectators. In fact, the actor performing on an open stage can be likened to a piece of sculpture viewed and appreciated from all sides, not the painting or photograph to which audiences have been conditioned for centuries by the proscenium. Simplification of scenic elements diminishes illusion and places the utmost emphasis on the actors, who now become the fundamental factors in the successful projection of a play.

If the actors' efforts to convey this kind of three-dimensional presence are to be successful, they need the assistance of an architectural arrangement of the auditorium that will ensure an unobstructed view of their performance from anywhere in the hall. Since modern drama depends solely on speech, movement, and expression, the spectators' enjoyment and interest diminishes in direct ratio to their distance from the stage, with a commensurate attenuation of emotional involvement. This adds two more limiting factors to the open-stage form: the size of the auditorium and the layout of the seats.

As for the seating layout, it was mentioned that it should conform to an arc of 210–220 degrees, but an additional requirement is a sharply sloping floor; to ensure unobstructed visibility, each row of seats must be considerably higher than the one in front. Both these requirements were basic features of the classic Athenian theater, as noted in the analysis of the Theater of Dionysus. But when we come to the question of auditorium size, the analogy stops. Whereas the ancient theater generally had 50 or 60 seatbanks, a properly proportioned modern open-stage theatre designed on a scale appropriate to our times should be limited to a number of rows ranging from 10 to 16; anything over that number would increase the distance between spectator and stage to the point where intimate emotional involvement would become impossible and the spectator's interest and enjoyment would flag.

Another fundamental defining element of the open-stage form is lighting. Since there is no setting in the familiar sense of the term, directors have to rely for their effects solely on lighting technique—the manner in which they illuminate the actors and the stage. Unlike the proscenium, the open stage must be lighted from the sides to create a sculptural effect and accentuate the third dimension. Vertical lighting from directly overhead must be avoided because it casts deep shadows on the actors' faces; at the same time, care must be taken to avoid dazzling the spectator with the laterally positioned lights required to illuminate the actor at an obtuse angle. As a result of these problems, the art of lighting developed into a science. New systems were perfected; the architect works in cooperation with the scientific lighting consultant long before calling in the structural engineer.

In consequence of these basic features and requisites, the open stage became the theater of the intellectuals and the poor. Small repertory companies and amateur theater groups, students and zealous young directors found in this form a vehicle that could be constructed cheaply and quickly by following Richard Southern's ironic "recipe":

Take any room:
Put a stage against one wall:
Open the four traditional access ways to it in the wall (left, right and center doors, and an "above"):
Add the "booth" or players' rooms behind the stage:
Rake the seating floor:
Provide a gallery for looking diagonally down on the stage.[200]

Things did not long remain as primitive as that, of course, but Southern's facetious recommendations do suggest how simply an open-stage theater can be created (Figure 156). Today there are numerous directors and producers who believe that apart from the scope it gives them to create

Figure 156. Area converted for open-stage performances by the Cockpit Theater Company, 1952. (Credit: Southern, Seven Ages, *plate 23.)*

a work of art, this kind of theater, with no settings to design and construct, allows them to cut production costs to a minimum. Perhaps that was the consideration that motivated the American spirit of business enterprise, when new theaters were needed on a large scale in the 1950s, to adopt this form in most of the playhouses that were constructed.

Typical Examples

One of the finest examples of the open-stage form is the Stratford Shakespearean Theatre in Ontario, Canada. It combines the Greek seating arrangement with an Elizabethan stage, an exact replica of that of the Globe Theatre. Routhwaite and Fairfield, the architects who built it in 1953, were guided by the recommendations of the eminent director Sir Tyrone Guthrie; they were totally successful in their aim to create a theater devoted exclusively to the performance of Shakespeare's plays.

Although its facilities for productions in the other performing arts are limited, the Stratford theater served as a model for all subsequent construction in this form, thanks to the dynamic vitality of its design and the beautiful simplicity of its interior. In contrast to the small, improvised amateur examples that had dominated the form until then, this was the finished product, so carefully organized and designed that its every detail reflected the builders' deep and perceptive study of the Greek and English traditions.

The Stratford theater is clearly a product of the first trend mentioned at the beginning of this section—the trend in the evolution of new theater forms that emerged in our century and that advocated eliminating the proscenium and restoring the theater to its true form, the original form given to it when drama was in its prime.

In conformity with the Greek model, the auditorium is a segment of a circle (Figures 157, 158), similar to that of the theaters of Dionysus and Epidaurus. At its two extremities the bowl of the theater abuts walls resembling the supporting walls used in Greece, the only difference here being the absence of the classic Greek *parodi* for the actors' entrances. The backstage facilities adjoin the ends of the auditorium and complete the

overall circular composition. Besides appearing from the stage, the actors make their entrances by way of the auditorium itself, through tunnels passing under the tiers of seats and giving onto the stage, a feature reminiscent of the *vomitoria* in the big Roman theaters.

The auditorium, of course, is not as large as the ancient model, but the circular arrangement of the tiers and the use of a gallery made it possible to install 2258 seats, a comparatively large number in view of the scale appropriate to modern drama. The size, however, is not a disadvantage here, precisely because the circular seating layout concentrates the audience around the stage so closely that even the spectators in the last (sixteenth) row enjoy good visibility and audibility—they are, after all, only 16 meters from the action. This illustrates the basic financial advantage of the open stage over the proscenium theater, where the limitations of width and depth imposed by modern drama confine the auditorium to a capacity of 700 or 800 seats.

Figure 157. Stratford Shakespearean Theatre: old Elizabethan stage and auditorium. (Credit: Centre National, Le lieu théâtral, *plate VI.)*

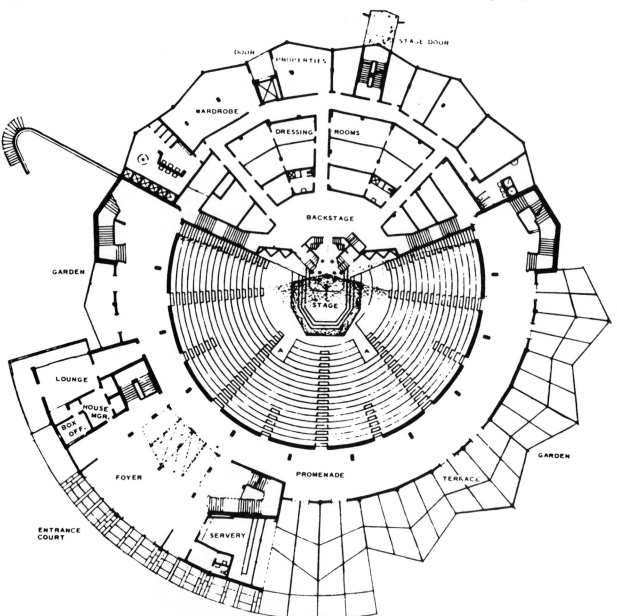

Figure 158. Stratford Shakespearean Theatre, Ontario, 1953: plan. (Author's archive.)

The stage, lastly, is a striking illustration of the influence of the Elizabethan playhouse (Figure 159). The canopy supported by pillars is here, as it was in Shakespeare's own Globe, a permanent feature, the only difference being that it has been placed a little farther back to provide a larger space in front for the action. A noteworthy expedient used by the architects, moreover, was to design the floor of the stage at the same approximate level as the front row of seats and adopt the proper amphitheatrical shape, thereby mitigating the disadvantage of lateral lighting. Thanks to this arrangement the spectators is always at a higher level than the

Figure 159. Stratford Shakespearean Theatre: model of new stage. Designed by Tanya Moiseiwitsch, 1952. (Credit: Centre National, Le lieu théâtral, *plate VII.)*

illuminated actor; their eyes are turned downward, away from the dazzle of the lights directly facing them.

A later and more modern example of an open-stage theater is the Mark Taper Forum, a unit of the Los Angeles Music Center, designed by architect Welton Becket and completed in 1967. The auditorium of the Forum has a 750-seat capacity in 14 rows; there is no balcony.

Thirteen years separated the construction of the Forum and the Stratford theater, during which the open-stage form underwent considerable modification. We still have here the pentagonal thrust stage as the focal point of the room, but the shape of the auditorium is different (Figure 160). Becket chose a semielliptical seatbank arrangement and designed the stage wall marking the boundary of the auditorium so that it

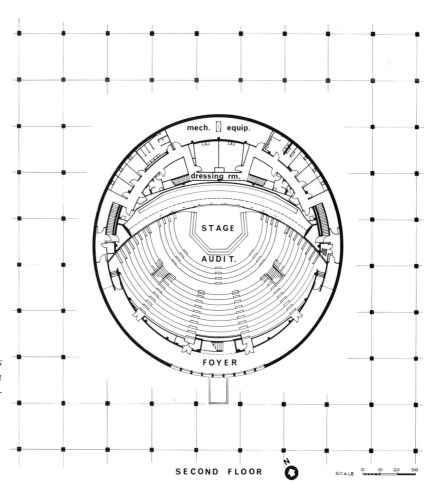

Figure 160. Mark Taper Forum, Los Angeles: plan. (Courtesy of Welton Becket and Associates; author's archive.)

SECOND FLOOR

curves in toward the audience. The 210-degree ratio mentioned earlier does not hold good here. In fact, the auditorium is so designed that no member of the audience is behind the actors, and the disadvantage of lateral lighting is greatly reduced since there is no direct contraposition of spectator and light source.

Another innovation is the revival of the Greek *diazoma*, a wide corridor running the length of the seat rows. The access tunnels give onto this corridor, and their principal function now is not to serve the actors but only the coming and going of the public.

In the big theater of classical antiquity this transverse corridor had a functional purpose, but in a small playhouse like the Forum, in my opinion, it has a disruptive effect on the unity of the auditorium, the unity so successfully achieved through two other features: first, the absence of a second level—a balcony like that of the Stratford theater; and second, the modular ceiling with its attractive and original pattern of movable elements (Figure 161).

Modular ceiling elements of this kind, in the form of panels or prisms, are widely used in modern theaters because they are an excellent means of improving the acoustics. The ceiling of the Forum is made up of 262 fiberglass panels suspended at an average height of 9 meters above the floor. A total of 300 lights are located in the ceiling above and between the acoustic panels. A projection booth and a light-and-sound control booth are located in the domed ceiling above the panels.[201]

Enhancing the stage is a combination of a 29-meter long arc-shaped cyclorama projection wall at the rear of the stage; movable, open aluminum screens 3 meters in front of the cyclorama projection wall; and a movable floor system between the screens and the wall. According to the director's intentions and the requirements of the play, the screens slide open to reveal the cyclorama, creating an "extended" stage reminiscent of Frank Lloyd Wright's design for the Kalita Humphrey Theater in Dallas.

Figure 161. Mark Taper Forum during a performance. Note main corridor and modular acoustical ceiling. (Courtesy of Welton Becket and Associates; author's archive.)

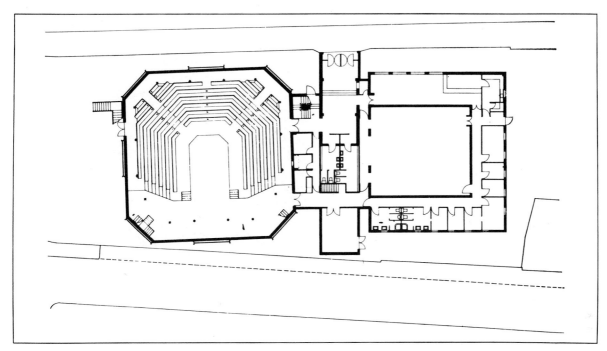

Figure 162. Young Vic Theatre: plan. (Credit: L'Architecture d'aujourd'hui No. 152, 1970.)

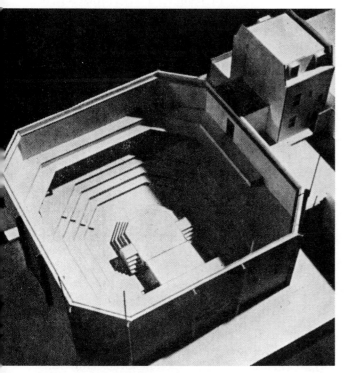

Figure 163. Young Vic Theatre, London: model. (Credit: L'Architecture d'aujourd'hui, No. 152, 1970.)

An example of the open-stage form on a still smaller scale is the Young Vic Theatre in London (Figures 162, 163), designed by architects Howell, Killick, Patridge, and Amis as an annex of England's famous Old Vic.[202] Everything here is simplicity itself. The house is in the shape of a square with the corners lopped off. It seats a mere 450 spectators, and apart from the open stage in the middle it has none of the usual facilities of a theater—no rudimentary proscenium, not even a backstage area. Such scenery as may be required is constructed in the backstage workshops of the Old Vic and transported to the Young Vic when needed. Three sides of the square are occupied by six rows of seats; the fourth sides together with the platform of the open stage, is the acting area. A gallery surrounding the auditorium on all sides connects with the platform of the stage at the same level, which is the level of the last row of seats. This makes for an original arrangement where the stage actually surrounds the auditorium, and the spectators, no longer neutral outside observers, find themselves literally in the midst of the action.

The Young Vic is an example of modern space theater in its fullest application. The stage area acquires incredible flexibility; according to the requirements of the play and the director, the actor can use the peripheral gallery to make his entrance from any point, to appear suddenly behind the spectator, speak to him, make him a participant in the plot. In this small theater, with its original use of space as a principal aid, the director can work wonders and the spectators can experience primitive emotions, the likes of which they could never get from the proscenium.

Sir Tyrone Guthrie and His Theater

The open stage was not taken up to any notable extent by the commercial theater. Although it was generally acknowledged that there was considerable financial benefit to be derived from its low production costs, the limited adaptability of the form, which meant that it could not be used by all the performing arts, discouraged the organized and established commercial theater, which saw greater profit in staying with the old and time-tested proscenium. As we have seen, moreover, the open stage, with the Doric austerity of its setting and the mental effort required by the plays it presented, did not have a strong box-office appeal. By and large, therefore, it was, and continues to be, a form of theater favored by a segment of the public composed of intellectuals, students, and people who looked upon the theater as art and not mere entertainment.

There were, however, some groups among the multitude of commercial theaters that ventured to give the new form a try; they were willing to risk endangering their sound and secure business operations for the sake of a belief in the necessity of furthering the progress and development of the theater. One such group was the Minnesota Theater Company, which commissioned architect Ralph Rapson to design a theater dedicated to a great director. And in 1963 the Tyrone Guthrie Theater (Figures 164–169) opened in Minneapolis, named after the gifted British director in recognition of his outstanding services to the theater in his own country and later in his adopted country, the United States.

Figure 164. Tyrone Guthrie Theater, Minneapolis: stage and auditorium. (Courtesy of the Walker Art Center; author's archive.)

Guthrie, who with designer Tanya Moiseivitch was the principal creator of the Stratford Shakespearean Theatre in Ontario, brought his brilliant abilities to the Minneapolis project and helped to create an admirable, eminently functional building, a model open-stage theater in the true concept of the form. Its prime consideration was the relation of performer to audience, in an effort to put Shakespeare's plays into appropriate surroundings. Guthrie believed that trying to put Shakespeare's plays into the conventional framework for opera was wrong. The plays had been written by a master craftsman for a theater of altogether different design. It was certainly possible to adapt them to the requirements of conventionally planned theaters, but it seemed more desirable to adapt a building than to adjust a masterpiece. This led him to an examination of the whole premise of illusion, which is the basis for the proscenium stage.[203]

In planning the Tyrone Guthrie theater, Guthrie and his collaborators decided that the stage should be an open stage like that in the Elizabethan theater and the ancient Greek and Roman theaters for the following reasons. First, their intended program was of a classical nature,

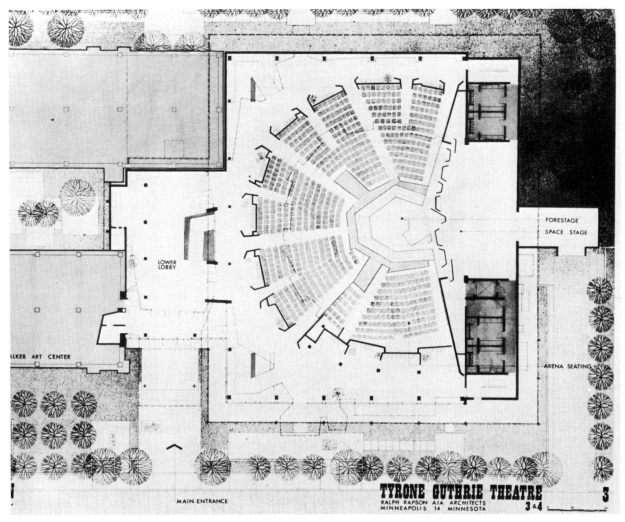

Figure 165. Tyrone Guthrie Theater: plan, stage level. (Courtesy of the Walker Art Center; author's archive.)

and they believed that the classics were better suited to an open-stage theater than to a proscenium one. Second, the aim of their performances was not to create an illusion but to present a ritual of sufficient interest to hold the attention of, even to delight, an adult audience. Third, an auditorium grouped *around* a stage rather than placed in front of it enables a larger number of people to be closer to the actors.

Figure 166. Tyrone Guthrie Theater: performance of The Three Sisters. *(Courtesy of the Walker Art Center; author's archive.)*

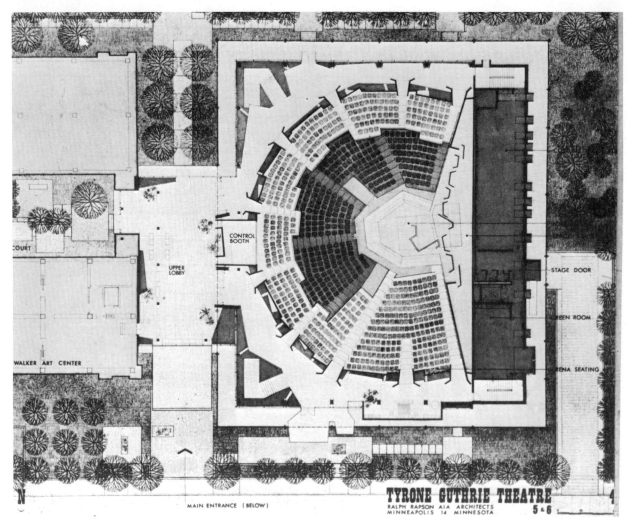

Figure 167. Tyrone Guthrie Theater: plan, gallery level. (Courtesy of the Walker Art Center; author's archive.)

Fourth, in an age when movies and television are offering dramatic entertainment from breakfast to supper, from cradle to grave, it seemed important to stress the *difference* between their offerings and the theater's. Theirs is two-dimensional and is viewed upon a rectangular screen. The proscenium is analogous to such a screen and forces a two-dimensional choreography upon the director. But the open stage is essentially three-dimensional, with no resemblance to the rectangular postcard shape that has become the symbol of canned drama.

Based on the Stratford prototype and guided by Guthrie's ideas, the theater created by Ralph

Rapson is now generally accepted in the United States to be one of the finest and most successful open-stage theater buildings in the country. Rapson endeavored to produce an original design that would give material form to his own ideas and Guthrie's purposes and views. Although his auditorium has a capacity of 1400, no spectator is more than 17 meters from the center of the stage (Figure 165). To dispel any implication that the balcony patron is a "second-class citizen," he attempted to eliminate this distinction by fusing the orchestra and balcony into an unbroken slope on one side. Elsewhere, seating is designed in broken sections, which lend variety

Figure 168. Tyrone Guthrie Theater: western face. (Courtesy of the Walker Art Center; author's archive.)

and dynamic form to the interior (Figure 167) and preserve the effect of spatial unity, in contrast to the Stratford Theater, where the disparity is very pronounced.

Rapson sought to design the interior of the theater so that, in his own words, "it should dramatically set the scene for the performance, anticipating and enhancing a stimulating event without overpowering the actual performance."[204]

This is no mere figure of speech; I found that the interval of waiting in my seat until the curtain rises is time interestingly spent. Everything helps to generate interest—the asymmetrical but very well balanced seating plan, the confettilike color pattern of the seats (it was the first time I ever saw a chromatic design created by using 10 different colors in the upholstery of a theater), the acoustical ceiling "clouds," the free and irregular shape of the stage, and a host of other little details that almost elude description.

The lighting is very well designed and its attendant problems solved with total success (Figures 166, 169); the plane surfaces of the ceiling, apart from providing excellent acoustic properties, are arranged so as to screen the blinding dazzle of the lights.

Figure 169. Tyrone Guthrie Theater: section, showing stage lighting system. (Courtesy of the Walker Art Center; author's archive.)

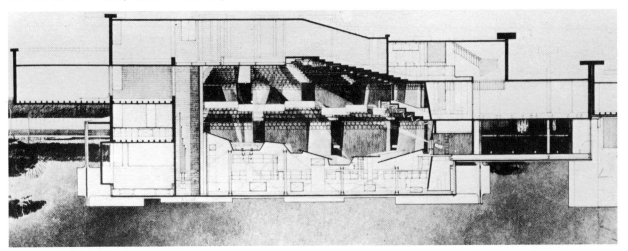

The only point, a minor one perhaps, on which I disagreed with the architect was the exterior design of the Tyrone Guthrie Theater (Figure 168), which displays a pronounced disposition toward ornamentation and a seemingly unconsidered choice of building materials. It may seem odd to many people, but it is worth noting that in an important theater the elements of the exteriors, those distinctive stuccoed screens that envelop the building, have nothing to do with its structure; they are merely decorative screens independent of the building, reflecting an attempt to convey the excitement of theater with bold shapes and unorthodox rhythms. This kind of construction may reflect the American attitude toward permanence and durability; at any rate, further discussion of the subject would be outside the province of this work. What matters is that the design of this theater should be carefully studied by every contemporary architect who wishes to gain an understanding of the open stage in its pure and proper form.

14
The Theater-in-the-Round or Arena Stage

Definition

A circle is the natural shape people unconsciously form when they gather to watch something (Figure 170). The circle formation was used by primitive peoples—African tribes and American Indians, for example—when they assembled to celebrate victories or to worship their gods (Figure 2). Similarly a circle is formed at country fairs around the performing conjurer and at the arena around the wrestlers. It seems rational that the theater, too, should have turned to the circle as a solution to some of its problems.

Although there is no precedent in the history of the theater for the pure circular form, one should not overlook a certain similarity between the examples just cited and the causes that compelled the theater to turn to the circular or arena form. The similarity lies in the spatial relationship between audience and actor, the compulsion that causes the first to gather round the second. It arises from the spectators' need to participate rather than merely to watch and from an urge to eliminate the distance that separates them from the performer so that they can really participate.

Accordingly, if one is to define this contemporary theater form, one might say that the theater-in-the-round is a theater in which the audience surrounds the scene of the action. Richard Southern provides a more distinctive definition:

Theatre-in-the-round means three things; the first is obvious—it is a theatre where the audience completely surrounds the action on all sides. The second follows from this but is not so immediately obvious—it is a theatre where it is quite impossible to give the effect of a painted picture come to life. The third is that, speaking in general, it is a theatre which has no stage. Thus it can properly be called an arena theatre.[205]

The theater-in-the-round is acknowledged to be the latest form produced by the contemporary theater in the course of its evolution, since, as we have said, at no period in theatrical history is a precedent to be found. It is a new architectural conception that organizes within a space this notion of a circle ever sought instinctively by human beings. This conception has attracted many supporters among followers of the contemporary trend in search of novelty in the presentation of drama.

Figure 170. Circle instinctively formed by a crowd to watch a street performance, El Fana Square, Marrakesh, Morocco. (Credit: L'Architecture d'aujourd'hui, No. 152, 1970.)

Origin—First Attempts

The theater-in-the-round first made its appearance in the United States as a reaction against the Broadway-type commercial theaters. It developed there with spectacular rapidity to become, along with the open stage, the leading theater form for the presentation of modern drama.

Sometimes it was called "arena theater" because the central acting area was reminiscent of the wrestling, circus, or bullfight arena. However, because the term suggested all these spectacles, which have nothing to do with true theater, the term that finally, and rightly, prevailed was "theater-in-the-round."

The first theater created for the specific purpose of "presenting plays in circus style" as Percy Corry puts it,[206] was the Penthouse Theater of the University of Washington in Seattle (Figure 171), built in 1940, but it was elliptical in shape, not round. At any rate, the seats in the auditorium—there are only three rows—completely surround the acting area. A similar design was used by André Villiers in Paris in 1954, when he converted a cabaret into his Théâtre en Rond (Figure 172), a playhouse that created a stir in the theater world with its bold and successful experiments.[207]

Figure 171. Penthouse Theater, University of Washington, Seattle, 1940. (Credit: Selden and Sellman, Stage Scenery and Lighting, *p. 198.)*

Figure 172. Théâtre en Rond de Paris. Founded by Paquita Clande and André Villiers, 1954. (Credit: Centre National, Le lieu théâtral, *plate X.)*

Figure 173. Stephen Joseph's movable theater-in-the-round. (Credit: Corry, Planning the Stage, p. 87.

Both these playhouses have certain features in common, which have come to distinguish the theater-in-the-round form. For one thing, the familiar stage was gone; in its place was the arena mentioned by Southern. For another, settings were eliminated. The number of audience seats was reduced to a minimum. One distinctive common feature of both theaters was also a common disadvantage, or rather a mistake, and this was the way the audience seats were laid out. In both cases the difference in elevation between seat rows was very slight, which proved disastrous to the proper functioning of the form.

This mistake was avoided by the British director Stephen Joseph, who devised a movable theater-in-the-round (Figure 173) that could be adapted and set up in any large room. Joseph used his theater to present, in addition to existing plays, new works written expressly for the theater-in-the-round.[208]

In Italy, too, home of the proscenium theater, this traditional native form came under attack by people who aspired to see a renaissance in the theater. Two such pioneering spirits, Antonio Carminati and Carlo de Carli, came out with a new conception of theater-in-the-round in 1952.[209] In their 250-seat Teatro Sant'Erasmo in Milan (Figure 174), the audience does not surround the stage area in a complete circle but is placed on opposite sides, leaving the other two sectors free to serve as access ways for public and actors.

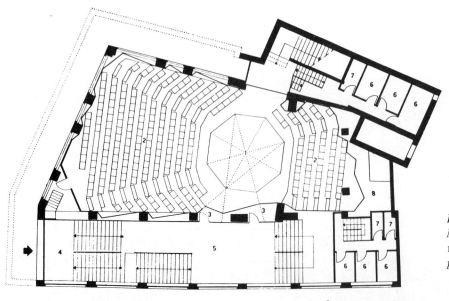

Figure 174. Teatro Sant'Erasmo, Milan, 1952. (Nicoll, Development of the Theatre, p. 233. Reprinted by permission.)

These theaters, however, were but the first tentative steps in the fresh approach to a new form; they could hardly be expected to be anything but early attempts devoid of cohesive architectural virtue or beauty. Rapid growth of the form came later, in the 1960s, when architects, searching for new ideas and helped by new materials and a desire for structural permanence, started building organized theaters based on this contemporary form, theaters claiming and deserving recognition of the way every functional problem has been given due attention.

Functional Requirements of the Theater-in-the Round

The fundamental requirement of the theater-in-the-round, of course, is an area of action centrally located and enclosed throughout 360 degrees by the audience.

The shape of the plan is of no importance. To take the four theaters described above, the Penthouse was elliptical, the Théâtre en Rond circular, the Sant'Erasmo rectangular, and Joseph's theater a perfect square. The shape is determined by the intention of the architect or the director, but the stage area must always be centrally located inside that shape.

We have seen that Southern and Joseph attach major importance to the arena concept when they refer to the stage area. This area, then, which in the theater-in-the-round is not a stage, properly speaking, but an arena, must be at the lowest level of the theater. The rising seatbanks start from that level, and they must be tiered fairly steeply to provide every spectator with a good unobstructed view.

The theater-in-the-round should be small—350 to 500 seats—so that all members of the audience can see the actors' slightest movement, discern every nuance of mood, and hear their speech as clearly as possible. A small theater stays within the scale of the drama; any attempt to increase its capacity beyond the desirable limit would turn it into a circus or sports palace.

The seats must be so arranged as to ensure balanced density of the audience. Regardless of the shape of the plan and the number of seats, a notional diagonal drawn through the plan

should separate it into two parts, each of which has the same audience density (see drawing). This is essential to the relationship of the actors with their audience so that, when performing, they can feel an equal obligation toward all the spectators and expect an equal response from all directions.

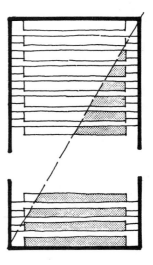

The actor–audience relationship is particularly important in the theater-in-the-round; here, in much greater measure than on the open stage, the major burden of responsibility for a successful presentation of the drama falls on the actors. They become for their audience leading figures, not merely characters interpreting the playwright's words. Their three-dimensional presence in the theater, combined with movement, enhances the sculpturesqueness of their forms and gives the spectator a strong sense of identification, participation, and intimacy.

The actors' responsibility is made greater by the complete absence of scenery, an element that provides variety to take up the slack in the spectator's interest should it flag momentarily. Audience interest must now be kept at a high pitch for two hours solely by power of word and expression, a terribly demanding task that requires from both playwright and actor a high measure of ardor, dedication, and faith in the ideal of the theater.

Those three qualities, when their product is crowned with success, can reward the performers with a feeling of great inner satisfaction, and that is the only reward they will get. The theater-in-the-round's low material returns are the reason it has never been, or ever will be, adopted by the commercial theater. It will always remain a vehicle of the little-theater groups, the people who maintain that the theater is primarily an art; it is a preserve for the cretive development of actors who work for their art alone and not for the acquisition of personal fame and fortune.

In the theater-in-the-round there is no leading man or leading lady; the protagonist is not the actor but the company, and success in performance or box-office receipts is the result of the efforts and power of appeal not of a single performer but of the group as a whole.

Let us return to the functional problems of the theater-in-the-round and to the characteristic features that make up the rudimentary settings in this form of theatre.

As a general rule there are no settings, but in certain cases many directors use the arena as an area in which to develop several scenes at once. They might, for instance, use a section of the area as a bedroom, another as a street corner, and a third as a living room, all at the same time. To separate and identify the scenes, they use furniture, low scenic props suggestive of the intended scene, and slight elevations of the floor level of sections of the arena—all carefully designed to avoid obstructing the audience's view. One device originally used was varying the color of the arena floor with the aid of carpets or painted canvas.[210] These separations, however, hampered the actors who, as we have said, must be able to move freely and easily over the arena in any direction and change their positions quickly, so that their expressions and gestures may be fully seen by every member of the audience; this cannot be done when the actors are confined to a specific area, and this device was eventually abandoned.

Lighting

A piece of furniture or a low decorative stage prop can hardly form or even suggest a setting; therefore, as in the open-stage theater, the director's only aid in creating scenic effects is the use of lighting. Although the open stage and the theater-in-the-round are two entirely different forms, they share the same advantages and disadvantages and are often faced with the same problems. With regard to lighting, in theater-in-the-round and open stage alike the design, choice, placement, and operation of the lights are matters for careful study. More than any other theater form, the arena theater is wholly dependent on lighting for its effects, and angles of incidence are therefore very carefully calculated and planned.

In a theater-in-the-round—states the English director Stephen Joseph—the lighting of the acting area is governed by the general principles that apply to any stage. The light must be confined to the acting area and not spill into the audience. Lighting from directly overhead is of limited use because it casts severe shadows on the actors' faces. Spotlights should be arranged round the acting area so that they shine down on the actors at an angle of about 45 degrees. The spotlights must be easily got at, and a balcony around the theater is the best solution. Besides this outer circle of spotlights, there should be an inner circle that could if necessary be reached from a platform ladder in the acting area.

The overriding consideration in designing the system and arrangement of lights is that the beams should not dazzle or distract any member of the audience. A rule that reduces this risk is that no light source should face the spectator inside a visual angle of 30 degrees (Figure 175).[211]

Unlike the proscenium theater, where the light sources are concealed and invisible to the audience, in the theater-in-the-round and the open stage things are not so simple. Architects spent a lot of time and effort struggling with the problem of how to conceal the lights and their accessories (cables, supporting brackets, etc.) in a way that would be esthetically pleasing.

In the end the problem was solved by ceasing to regard it as a problem. Instead of trying to conceal the lights, the entire system, with its fixtures and accessories, was left frankly exposed to the audience's view. The result, in my opinion, is not an entirely successful one. However well designed the interior of such a theater may be, the ceiling presents an unfinished appearance. Looking upward, the spectators get a shock; they see a forest of lights, cables, catwalks, and beams, a sight that is anything but attractive.

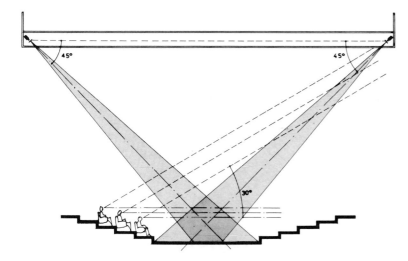

Figure 175. Theater-in-the-round: light-source arrangement. (Drawing by author.)

Another major concern is how to avoid lighting the front row of spectators sitting round the arena, which is quite common in this form of theater. It is disagreeable to the illuminated spectators themselves and disconcerting to those opposite, who view the actors against a background of well-lighted, varicolored legs and knees.

Finally, concerning the floor of the arena, Roderick Ham notes that the reflected glare produced by light falling on a shiny floor is most disturbing to the audience.[212] Shiny surfaces, therefore, should be avoided for the floor and the few stage props placed in the arena. Nonreflective flooring materials should be used, and all objects in the arena should have a mat, lusterless finish; a mirror or well-polished desk can be a source of distress to a section of the audience.

Disadvantages

The theater-in-the-round is a form that creates problems challenging to actors and directors alike. The actors' weak points, as they perform in the middle of a large group of people who will judge them, are constantly under scrutiny from all sides of the theater and from every angle of vision. They are compelled to play to all the audience at once, which is physically impossible. They must move, as noted, in all directions because this is essential if they are to put their expressions across so that they can be seen by every member of the audience. The constant pressure of these exigencies often causes a nervous irritation that makes their performance strained and erratic to the point of losing credibility.

A criticism often leveled at the theater-in-the-round is that when at a given moment the actor is playing to one side of the house, his or her back is turned to all the others, something that on the open stage occurs to a less noticeable extent and in the proscenium theater not at all. Yes, reply the champions of the theater-in-the-round, but that disadvantage is greatly outweighed by the advantage of strong actor–audience identification and the experience of seeing the actor as a three-dimensional presence, which only this form of theater can give. Supporting this view is Stephen Joseph's belief that the success of a performance in the round depends on the actor and the actor alone, whose relationship with all types of open stage Joseph sums up as follows:

I believe that the actor is capable of three-dimensional expression . . . , further, his use of the space on the acting area should be dynamically related to the total space, and not restricted to the consideration of "picture." It is only a flattened actor who needs to face his audience all the time, and if you put such an actor on any open stage he may rush into restless movement. But as he grows into a three-dimensional actor, he will realize that the only movement necessary on the open stage is the movement that is necessary to his part.[213]

In the opposing camp the attitude of the critics is often sarcastic rather than understanding. David Itkin once said of a performance in the round: "I have seen one-half of the show; now I will buy a ticket on the other side of the house and see the other half of the show."[214]

Another disadvantage of the theater-in-the-round is poor acoustics. It is very difficult to obtain the right acoustic result when sound—the sound of the actors' speech—is emitted in a single direction each time they speak; the section of the audience that sees their faces naturally hears them better than those to whom their backs are turned. The problem is further aggravated by the high sound absorbency of the spectators' clothes. The sound produced by the actors is in large measure absorbed by the spectators facing them, only a small part is reflected toward the rest of the audience. This is one of the major reasons the audience must be kept small. A shorter distance between sound source and listener reduces the disadvantage; therefore, the right size for the auditorium is one where there are no more than eight or nine rows of seats. A great deal of sound is also absorbed by the ceiling lighting system with its many unevenly positioned rough surfaces and the considerable height required for these installations.[215]

These are the reasons—despite the intimacy it provides, despite its novel form, its originality, its vitality, and its low production costs—the theater-in-the-round cannot be considered the ideal theater form. Moreover, confinement of the action to an area in the middle of the house causes tricky staging problems that sometimes mar the performance itself. If, for instance, the plot calls for powerful scenes, the overly strong identification generated in the spectators may be unpleasant to them. Likewise, the restrictions imposed on the actors' entries and exits by the inflexible and architecturally predetermined accesses at the four corners of the arena are an added limitation on a director already burdened with the major problem of being unable to use anything but a rudimentary setting.

It is, nevertheless, acknowledged that the theater-in-the-round, properly designed and discriminatingly used, can be the ideal theater form for a large number of plays in the modern drama repertory where identification and intimacy between actor and audience are essential to the performance. Plays of this kind, however, are not alone numerous enough to ensure the financial viability of a theatrical organization, whether private or state-sponsored, that uses the arena stage. In consequence, the theater-in-the-round has not developed significantly as an independent, self-contained building; it has been used rather as an experimental subsidiary stage annexed to big theater complexes or as an alternative layout in the fourth contemporary theater form, the one known as adaptable or experimental theatre.

Examples from the Organized Theater

Perhaps the only existing example of an organized and independent theater-in-the-round is the Arena Stage in Washington, D.C., which was, in fact, built to serve the commercial theater. As in the case of the Tyrone Guthrie Theater, the idea for the Arena Stage was inspired by the sponsor of the project herself, Zelda Fichandler, who was looking for a theater form to house her well-known dramatic company.[216]

The architect of the Arena Stage was Harry Wesse. Although it was his first design for a theater building, he succeeded in creating a dynamic and functionally correct form, one that, irrespective of the esthetic result, is a distinctive example of an independent theater-in-the-round (Figure 176).

The building, completed in 1962, was designed to seat 752 spectators, and an attempt was made to overcome as many as possible of the problems arising from the disadvantages inherent in the form.

The shape of the auditorium (Figure 177) is approximately a square with the corners lopped off. In all its details the structure reveals its function; the bushhammered reinforced concrete, the gray Roman brick masonry, the steel trusses of the ceiling—all make you feel as if you were in a workshop seeking magic in the structure.

In the auditorium the height difference between the seating tiers is sufficient to ensure a good view of the performance for every spectator. With this steep inclination, this deep amphitheatrical concavity, an attempt has been made to mitigate the disadvantage caused by the actor's movement in the space of the arena. The

Figure 176. Arena Stage, Washington, D.C., 1962. (Courtesy of the Arena Stage; author's archive.)

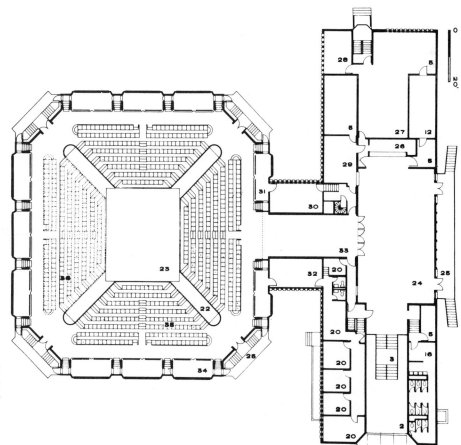

Figure 177. Arena Stage: plan. (Courtesy of the Arena Stage; author's archive.)

Figure 178. Arena Stage: interior, showing actors' entrance ramps. (Courtesy of the Arena Stage; author's archive.)

higher the spectators are seated, the better their perception of the third dimension and the less frequently they are confronted by the actor's back. The steep inclination also makes for better visibility since it keeps every member of the audience within a distance of 15 meters from the center of the arena; it makes for better acoustics, too.

The accesses used by the public are completely separate from those used by the actors to avoid cross-interference between the two functions. A perimeter passageway running around the auditorium at the top of the seat tiers communicates, on the same level, with the foyer of the theater. In this way it serves as access only for the public, while the actors enter through passages at each of the four corners of the stage at stage level. These passages, very much like the Roman *vomitoria*, are often used to identify localities in the play (Figure 178).

Stage and auditorium lighting is provided by a complete system of lights, catwalks, grids, air ducts, and accessory fixtures, an integrated structure frankly and fully exposed to the view of the audience to show how a theater works (Figures 179, 180).

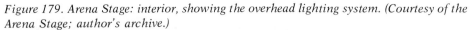

Figure 179. Arena Stage: interior, showing the overhead lighting system. (Courtesy of the Arena Stage; author's archive.)

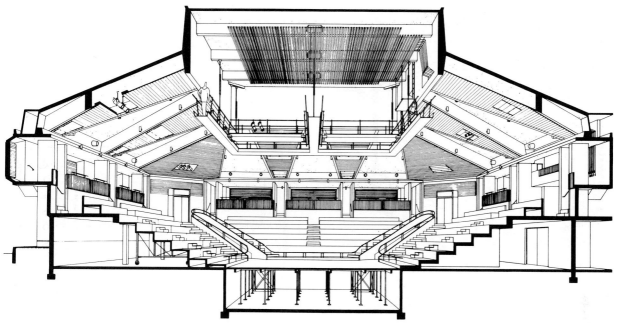

Figure 180. Arena Stage: section. (Courtesy of the Arena Stage; author's archive.)

In spite of this elaborate setup, the lighting problem has been solved, in my opinion, with less than total success. Although the arena floor is some 15 centimeters lower than the front row of seats and there is ample latitude in the choice of light-source positions, the front-row spectators are often lighted as strongly as the actors, resulting in a disturbing effect.

The Arena Stage has been designed so that it can be converted to an open-stage theater. This is done by removing the section of seats facing the main entrance, reducing the theater's capacity to 575. In combination with the arena—which is trapped and divided into sections, any one of which can be raised or lowered separately or in combination with another—and with the corresponding section of the perimeter passageway, an open stage is formed. This flexibility increases the range of the company's repertory and also, of course, its revenue.

The Arena Stage has been considered in such detail because, as pointed out at the beginning, it is to my knowledge the only organized, self-contained theater-in-the-round in existence. The next two examples are treated more briefly, primarily for the purpose of noting the many and varied trends and the absence of limitations on shape that prevail in the design of the form.

The Octagon Theatre in Bolton, England, was built by architect Geoffrey Brooks in 1967.[217] Designed primarily to function as a theater-in-the-round with a capacity of 240, it can nevertheless be converted, by moving the seats, to a 320-seat open-stage theater or a 400-seat proscenium theater (Figure 181). Its flexibility allows it to be used for more of the performing arts as well as for social and educational events, a functional multiplicity in line with the fact that it is part of a cultural center.

With such flexibility it could be classed as an experimental theater, but it is also a good example of the unimportance of shape in a theater-in-the-round.

Looking at the octagonal plan of the auditorium, we find the same perimeter passageway running behind the topmost row of seat tiers as in the Arena Stage, differing only in that it encircles only three quarters of the house. Here, too, audience access is provided by this passageway, but it is served only by two narrow exits, which seems a rather inadequate arrangement.

The second example is part of the Berlin Academy of Arts, built for studio and experimental performances and also as a conference hall for its members.[218] The theater was designed by

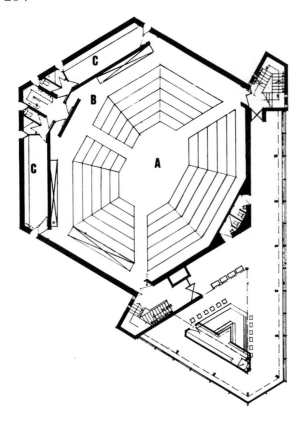

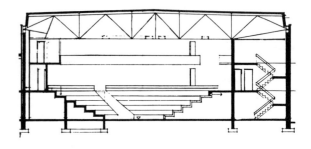

Figure 181. Octagon Theatre, Bolton, England, 1967: plan and section. (Credit: L'Architecture d'aujourd'hui, *No. 152, 1970.)*

architect Werner Düttmann in 1960 (Figures 182, 183), and we have included it because it is an evolved architectural sequel to the Teatro Sant'Erasmo in Milan, discussed earlier (Figure 174), and because it reflects an attempt to find new solutions to the problems of the theater-in-the-round.

The theater's 650 seats do not surround the stage; two sections of seats, asymmetrical and of unequal density as in the Sant'Erasmo, face each other from opposite sides of the stage, the larger section seating 450 people and the smaller 200. The interesting thing here is that either section can be isolated, thus forming two smaller theaters of the end-stage type described in the chapter on open-stage theater.

Figure 182. Berlin Academy of Arts: studio theater. (By permission of Werner Düttmann, the architect.)

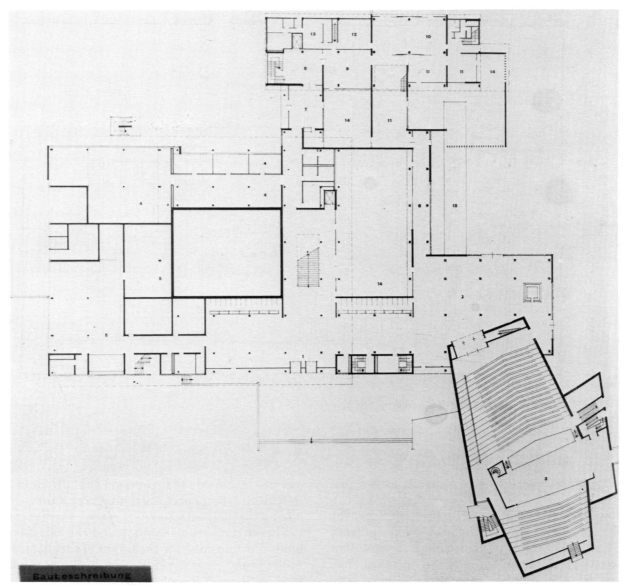

Figure 183. Berlin Academy of Arts, with its studio theater: general plan. (By permission of Werner Düttmann, the architect.)

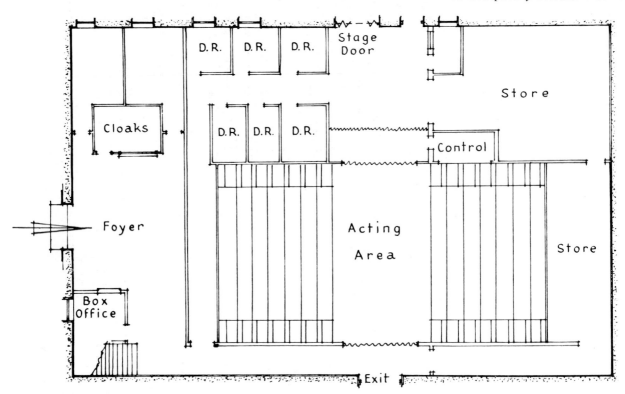

Figure 184. Plan for a theater-in-the-round by Stephen Joseph. (Credit: Corry, Planning the Stage, *p. 88.)*

This arrangement would appear to give the best audience distribution since it mitigates to a considerable extent the disadvantage faced by the actor when he is surrounded by the audience on all sides. Acting on two fronts instead of four allows greater freedom in the performance and enables the director to stage the play with greater latitude. The actors here do not labor under the compulsion of perpetual motion; they can use as a mode of expression that prolonged immobility that, according to Percy Corry, is often extremely effective.[219]

This arrangement seems to be the one that holds most promise for the future of the theater-in-the-round. It is a vindication of the position held by Stephen Joseph, who for many years has maintained that it is the right layout for this form of theater (Figure 184).

15
The Adaptable or Experimental Theater

A Compromise Solution

Many critics of contemporary theater forms concede that both the open stage and the arena can produce astonishingly effective performances of a certain type of drama. Conversely, a fair number of the supporters of "unorthodox" stages admits that the comparative inflexibility of these forms is a source of difficulties.

The search for a middle ground, namely a flexible and adaptable theater that can be converted to meet the requirements of any kind of performance, led—after many compromises—to the birth of a new form, the "adaptable theater." This creation, in effect, was nothing but a combination of all the known forms in a single space and in a building functionally unaffected by that combination.

Nicoll quotes Sean Kenny on the subject:

It is necessary to have the baroque proscenium stage, just as it is necessary to have theatre-in-the-round. But please let us have all kinds of theatres. Square, round, triangular, oblong, and whatever you like. A completely flexible theatre giving all forms of staging.

With the minimum of scenery and machinery one could present different styles of play by altering the interior relationship of the house to the relationship required between actor and spectator for the particular play, the writer and director creating the space they need to work in. [220]

Whatever the form, the underlying principle remains the same. The physical relationship and the spatial relationship between the audience area and the performers' area are unchanged. The only feature that distinguishes the new form is that these two fundamental areas are now movable and convertible, so that any desired arrangement can be produced.

Gropius, with the "total theater" he designed in 1927 (discussed at some length in Part 2), was the first to attempt a theater design where 2000 spectators, under different conditions for each form, could see proscenium, arena, or open-stage performances. We cannot say, of course, to what extent Gropius managed to solve all the difficult and complex technical problems created by such adaptability in a theater of this size. However, since his idea went no further than the design stage, we should not take it as being conclusive of the best size for the adaptable theater. In fact,

a review of the attempts that have been made so far indicates that such theater buildings should be fairly small and that the success of an adaptable theater is wholly dependent on building size. As size increases, the attendant problems increase with it in geometrical progression to the point where they can become insolvable. Lines of vision, acoustical problems, adaptation of the lighting, adaptation of the space after shifting sizable architectural elements—these are some of the difficulties faced by the technical specialists involved in the design of an adaptable theater. Consequently a compromise is needed between some of the functions in each different adaptation.

The Problems

Adding a forestage, an apron, to a conventional proscenium is not a particularly difficult undertaking, as we have seen in the variations used in German theaters and in more advanced form in Breuer's theater at Sarah Lawrence College (Figure 155), where it is used in converting the proscenium to an open stage. The only essential alteration to the auditorium is the removal of the first few rows of seats or the elimination of the orchestra pit (if there is one). With the aid of raisable surfaces, this conversion can be accomplished quite easily without changing the rest of the layout in any way.

However, when the stage has to be thrust still further into the auditorium and enclosed by seats on three sides to form a true open stage, things are a little more difficult. If the existing auditorium has a steep inclination and stepped seatbanks, it will be necessary to adjust the floor at the position of the sides of the stage; otherwise, visibility will be very bad. The raisable surfaces of the stage, too, must be used to create movable surfaces for these sections of the auditorium. The ceiling arrangement must provide for adjustment of the lighting and the acoustical panels that help reflect sound laterally. If the conversion is pushed one stage further to create a theater-in-the-round, the difficulties are still greater.

To make such conversion possible and keep the cost within reasonable limits, all these elements must be restricted to a small scale, even a scale allowing certain sections of the auditorium to be shifted by hand. This is why all adaptable theaters constructed to date have adopted feasible solutions and have been confined to experiments by small theater groups; these small theaters have become workshops where every theatrical notion is tested, a hotbed of study and research inspired by the belief that the theater is an art that must grow and expand. Accordingly the adaptable theater acquired a second name and today is better known as "experimental theater"; it has found its place in the theatrical domain as an essential adjunct, a studio indispensable to every organized theater complex or cultural center.

An experimental theater must be free of all the old conventions; the audience's and performers' areas must be designed so that they can be arranged in any relationship pattern and so that they are neutral in space. This arrangement should not be defined by a static architectural frame but by a design determined on each occasion by the play, the director, and the actors.

Adaptability, it should be noted, must not be confused with flexibility, a quality that any theater, whatever its form, may possess. A proscenium theater or even a classic Italian theater can well be flexible if it has certain technical facilities for expanding the proscenium or shifting the scenery. The purpose of the adaptable theater is to provide a house that can be converted as required to any and all forms—traditional, contemporary, or experimental. It is, in fact, very difficult to give this theater form flexibility, since the compromises required to make it convertible to proscenium, open stage, or arena mean that it must forgo all but the strictly essential functional requirements of each of those forms; it must therefore do without the variations and facilities it could have if it functioned as an independent unit.

Norman Bel Geddes maintains that: "the proper theatre for an educational institution is one where the auditorium and the stage are in one large empty room. . . . Consequently everything within the room can be moved about mechanically or manually but in any event easily."[221] This view appears to be shared by André Veinstein, a leading French theater theorist, who endorses the proposal of Weber and Rubinov for an experimental studio attached to the National Theater in Budapest (Figure 185), which he describes as a successful effort displaying novelty and originality.[222] In this proposal the floor of a hall in the shape of a 28 × 28–meter square has been divided into 20 modular 5 × 5–meter units,

Figure 185. National Theater, Budapest: experimental studio. Designed by Weber and Rubinov, 1965. (Credit: L'Architecture d'aujourd'hui, *No. 129, 1966.)*

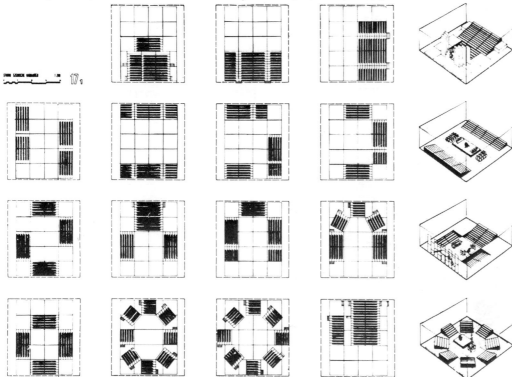

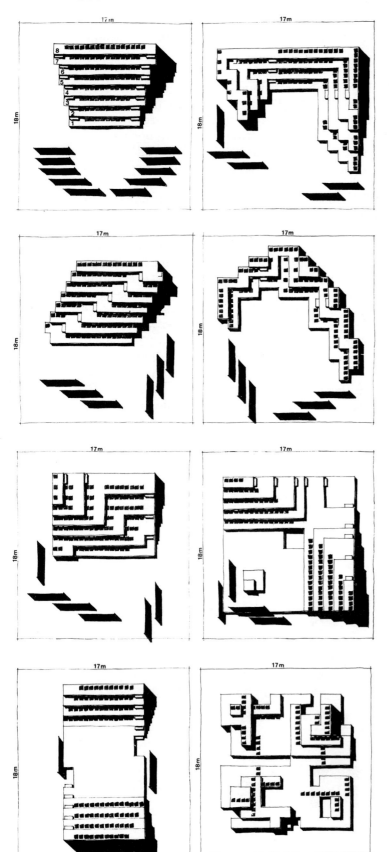

each of which can be hydraulically raised or lowered 83 centimeters from the main level of the floor. The sections serve as bases on which to place eight modular seatbank units, also 5 × 5–meter square and 83 centimeters high at their topmost point, that can hold 42 seats each, giving the theater a maximum audience capacity of 336. In this way each element fits in with the next at matching levels, providing an astonishing number of possible layout combinations; the system permits easy conversion not only to any of the three known theater forms but also to any variation visualized by a director experimenting with ways of staging any kind of drama.

The same notion of a large empty space as visualized by Bel Geddes can be seen, with somewhat less impressive results to be sure, at Tampere, Finland, where architect Toivo Korhonen built an experimental theater for the local university in 1962 (Figure 186).[223] It does not provide the 15 alternative arrangements of the previous example, but it does reflect the same simplicity of design and the same trend toward standardized modular elements. The standard seatbank units can be used simply and handily in the free space of the plan to form a proscenium, a theater-in-the-round, and two alternative open-stage layouts.

Long before these two projects, in 1950 to be specific, Robert M. Little and Marion L. Manley were among the first to turn to this new form when they designed the experimental theater of the University of Miami.[224] They, too, adopted the notion of a large and uniform space, but they chose a circular shape for the house (Figure 187). The only fixed elements in it are a revolving platform and a peripheral passageway that, in combination with modular seatbank units, can be made to form five different stage-and-auditorium arrangements (Figure 188).

Figure 186. Toivo Korhonen's experimental theater, Tampere, Finland, 1962. (Credit: Toivo Korhonen.)

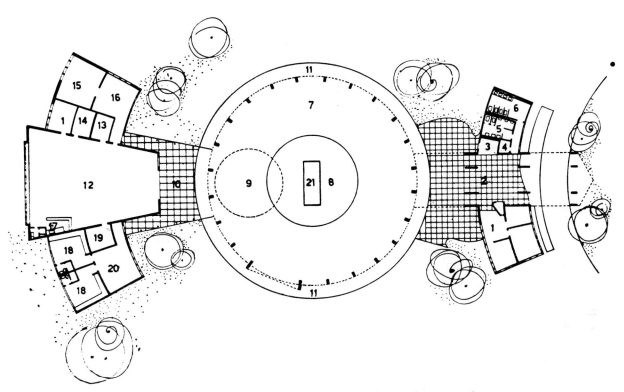

Figure 187. University of Miami's experimental theater, 1950. (Nicoll, Development of the Theatre, *p. 236. Reprinted by permission.)*

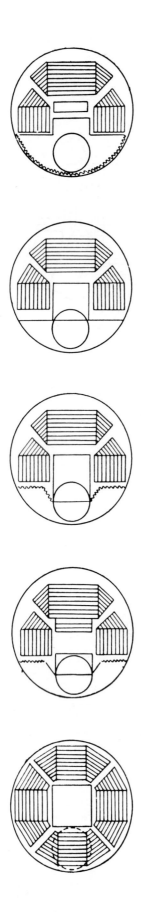

The experimental theater, however, was created not only for the sake of serving universities and schools but also for the benefit of a larger public interested in keeping abreast of developments in the contemporary theater. This public naturally did not relish a constant fare of Doric austerity in a test workshop, functional to the highest degree no doubt but totally lacking in comfort and architectural design. The adaptable form therefore had to assume a different character in the organized theater; it had to integrate all the other essential functions of a building properly designed for this purpose.

One who worked with marked success in this field was an American technologist, George Izenour. His contribution is such as to merit fairly extensive treatment; accordingly the following section of this study is devoted to his ideas and the work he has accomplished to date.

Figure 188. University of Miami's experimental theater: alternative stage and auditorium arrangements. (Nicoll, Development of the Theatre, p. 236. Reprinted by permission.)

George Izenour's Contribution

The name of George Izenour will not be found in the directories of architects, directors, or other professionals connected with the theater in an "artistic" capacity. When he finished college in 1938, Izenour could have become a successful mechanical and electrical engineer had he not decided at an early age to devote his outstanding technical ability and inventive mind to the theater. As a result, he is considered the best and most widely known theater technologist in the United States today and the leading authority on all technical subjects connected with the theatre.

He started teaching at Yale University in 1939 and since then has produced numerous inventions for use in electronic lighting systems, synchronized pulley systems, stage and seatbank raising systems, and stage machinery. He is the principal creator of a large number of theaters in which the character of his technological devices is strongly dominant, so much so that, as I found during my travels in the United States, when people speak of one of those theaters, the name they mention is not that of the architect who designed it but that of George Izenour, who gave it life and movement. As a theater consultant, his services are indispensable; no architect can translate his own ideas into a workable theater design without the technical help of such a specialist. As Izenour himself modestly puts it:

In my judgment three specialists—the architect, the acoustician, and the theater design and engineering consultant—must collaborate in order to achieve the optimal result in any building to be used for the performing arts. To be successful this collaboration must start with the design concept. It is in the concept itself that the skill of each specialist effects the basic conditions leading to a design solution. The architect is still the master builder, but specialized techniques require specialized knowledge, and here the other men can offer their ideas. It is just this kind of collaboration—with its continual give and take—that must characterize such projects. . . . I wish to point out that necessary compromises have to be made without penalizing the artist who is to perform nor the audience who is to watch. This is most crucial, for when the lights go down and the performance begins, the building and the production facilities are of secondary importance. If the performer is seen and heard easily, and if he is in a satisfactory and comfortable relationship with his audience—a relationship that has been provided by the design and its execution—then the build-

ing works. If not, the building fails. And no kind of magic or extreme unction can correct the mistakes. [225]

Experimental theater was a field that could scarcely fail to attract Izenour, and it was in this form that he worked for many years, improving its adaptability with such successful inventiveness that it has made remarkable progress in the United States, far beyond the boundaries of the university campus.

Izenour's particular concern was to develop a refined form of adaptable theater that would look like a theater and not merely be an indifferent space in which a few standardized elements are arranged to form a layout of some sort. As he writes:

Mechanization (hydraulic or mechanical) and control (analogue or digital) can achieve a fluid movement of surfaces and masses so that large spatial relationships can be changed with ease and accuracy with little or no expenditure of human muscle power, not that this kind of fluidity is in itself a special virtue. But if a conversion involving spatial relationships is wanted, it can be achieved most perfectly through mechanization. Any other means is impractical, and sometimes even impossible. Mechanization represents a saving in both capital expenditure and operating costs. [225]

From among Izenour's designs, we have selected one that illustrates how an adaptable theater can be organically integrated in a building serving a wider public and not just a small group of students.

The design is for a drama theater seating 500 to 600 people, which can be converted into a proscenium theater, an open-stage theater, or a theater-in-the-round. Explaining the reasons that led him to this design, Izenour wrote:

My experience thus far in this field has led me to address this problem in the abstract rather than to consider the space as building or architecture. In doing this, one is immediately struck by the fact that once the geometry is decided upon (that is, the geometry of the space module), this gives the cue to the architecture and, consequently, the flexibility of the relationships between the actor and the audience. From a study of this problem over twenty years I have come to the conclusion that almost any geometry can be made to work, if the proper methods are used to control it, and that some geometries are (size and shape of people being what they are) simply more efficient than others. [226]

To understand how this proposal works, it is necessary to give some attention to the plan (Figure 189), the sections (Figures 190, 191), and the three axonometrics (Figures 192–194). They combine to give a clear picture of the final result of each possible alternative arrangement.

The numeral 1 designates the auditorium's fixed seats; numerals 2 and 2' designate the movable seatbank sections, which by means of hydraulic pistons can be raised, rotated, and lowered in different positions to form new arrangements. A look at the plan, which for the sake of illustration has been divided to represent two different arrangements, shows that in the lower part (B-B') section 2 has been combined with 1 to form a proscenium theatre; in the upper part (A-A') section 2 has been turned 90 degrees and combined with 2' and 1 to form an open stage. The sequence of rotary shifts can be better understood by observing the six different phases in a change of arrangement (Figure 195).

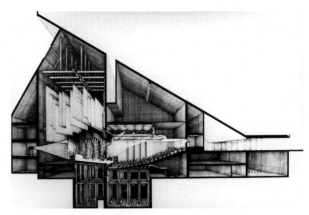

Figure 190. Izenour Theater: section B-B'. (By permission of George Izenour.)

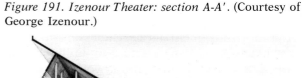

Figure 191. Izenour Theater: section A-A'. (Courtesy of George Izenour.)

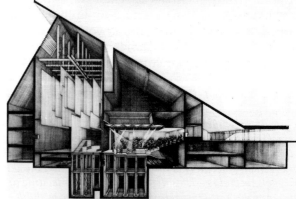

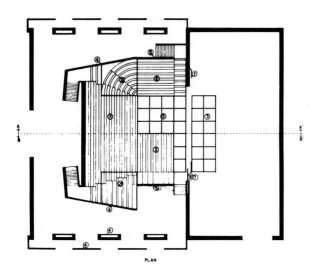

Figure 189. George Izenour's design for a drama theater: plan. (By permission of George Izenour.)

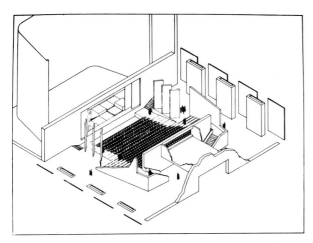

Figure 192. Proscenium theater arrangement, George Izenour. (By permission of George Izenour.)

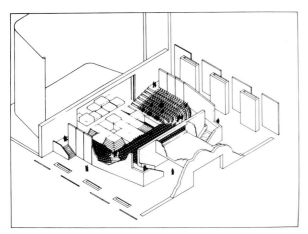

Figure 193. Open-stage theater arrangement, by George Izenour. (By permission of George Izenour.)

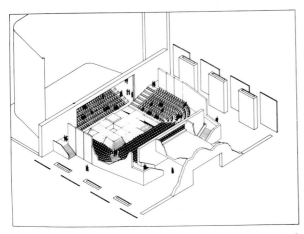

Figure 194. Theater-in-the-round arrangement, by George Izenour. (By permission of George Izenour.)

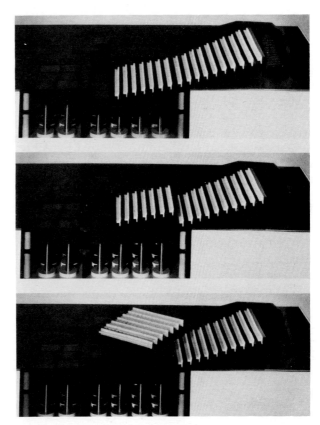

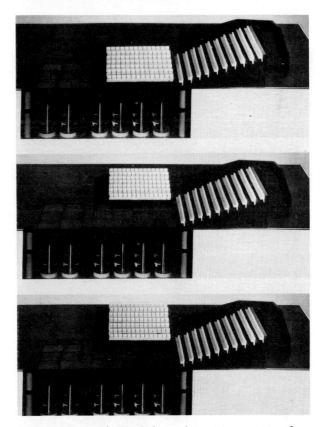

Figure 195. Seatbank shifting phases in converting from proscenium theater to theater-in-the-round, by George Izenour. (By permission of George Izenour.)

The numeral 3 identifies the open modular lift system, which can be raised or lowered to any desired level; it serves as a space modulating system for all three forms of theater. In the theater-in-the-round arrangement the main stage is used for seats, the raisable sections of the floor having been formed into stepped banks to give the required amphitheatrical elevation to the seats (Figure 191).

The numeral 4 designates the fixed walls of the auditorium and numeral 5 the movable partitions whose position can be changed to suit the desired arrangement. Last, numerals 6, 7, and 8 designate, respectively, the actors' staircase leading backstage and the stage curtains used with the proscenium form.

Everything about the proposal is eminently rational; the project seems to have been designed expressly and uniquely for the purpose of housing all these contrivances, as though the protective cortex of a brain rather than an architectural work. Notwithstanding the modesty of Izenour's views on the role of the technical consultant, one is compelled to admit that in creating a building of this sort the architect cannot do without the contribution of an ingenious inventor whose design will give it all its functional vitality.

Examples in Different Countries

The Loeb Drama Center at Harvard University, which is nothing more or less than an application of this proposal, was designed by the architectural firm of Hugh Stubbins and Associates, in collaboration with George Izenour (Figures 196, 197).

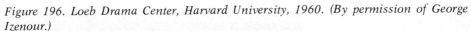

Figure 196. Loeb Drama Center, Harvard University, 1960. (By permission of George Izenour.)

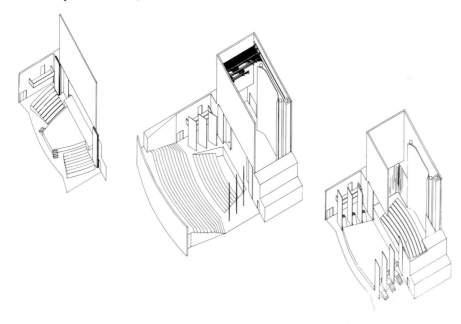

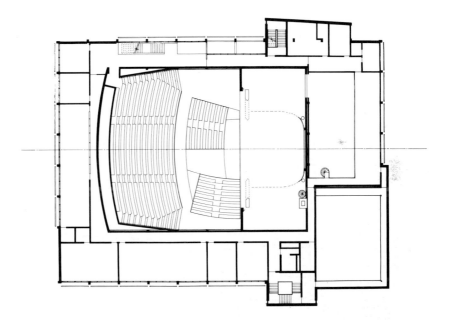

Figure 197. Loeb Drama Center: plans, showing alternative arrangements of stage and auditorium. (By permission of George Izenour.)

When it first opened in 1960 the theater was hailed, in the words of one reviewer, as "such a mechanical marvel that many people who would otherwise care may not notice that it is first rate architecture first of all."[227]

Izenour incorporated in this theater all the things just described. One person at the controls of the electronic systems can convert the theater in 15 minutes from proscenium to arena or to open stage. Such adaptability cannot fail to encourage all students and lovers of the theater. Here experimentation is not confined within the narrow boundaries of the campus; it is shared with the whole community, since that is the purpose for which the theater was designed.

Its 600 spectators enjoy all the facilities expected in a modern theater, and the stage is backed by a full range of essential service areas on a scale that is commensurate to the size of the building.

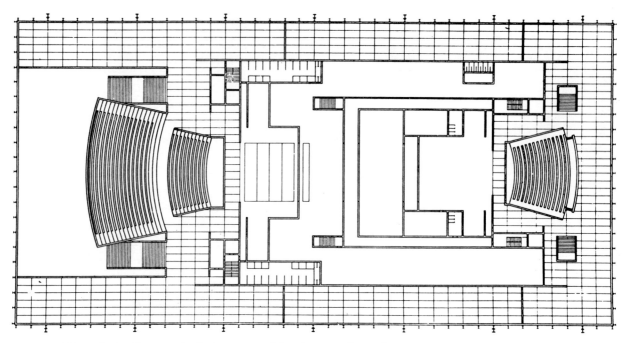

Figure 198. Ludwig Mies van der Rohe: proposal for the Mannheim theater, competition drawing, 1953. (Author's archive.)

Figure 199. Plan of the final design by Gerhard Weber for the Mannheim theater, showing (right) the traditional opera house and (left) the little experimental theater. (By permission and courtesy of the architect Professor Gerhard Weber.)

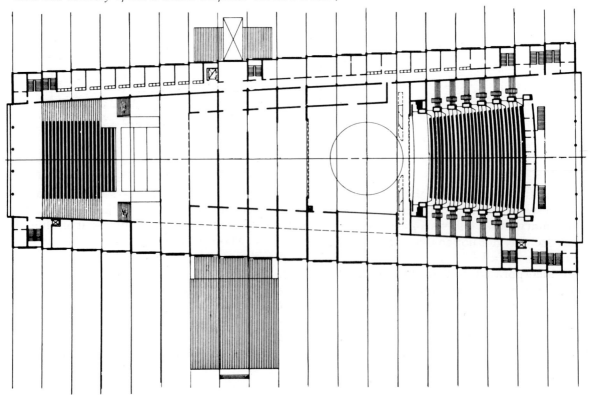

The Little Theater (Kleines Haus) in Mannheim, West Germany, part of that city's National Theater Complex, is another interesting example of experimental theater. The clean-cut cubical structure is modeled on a proposal entered in the architectural competition by Mies van der Rohe in 1953 (Figures 125, 198). Gerhard Weber[228] worked from Mies's idea to create, in 1957, one of the most important and distinctive theaters in Europe (Figs. 199–204).

Figure 200. Mannheim theater: isometric of the entire building, showing the experimental theater arranged in arena form. (By permission and courtesy of the architect Professor Gerhard Weber.)

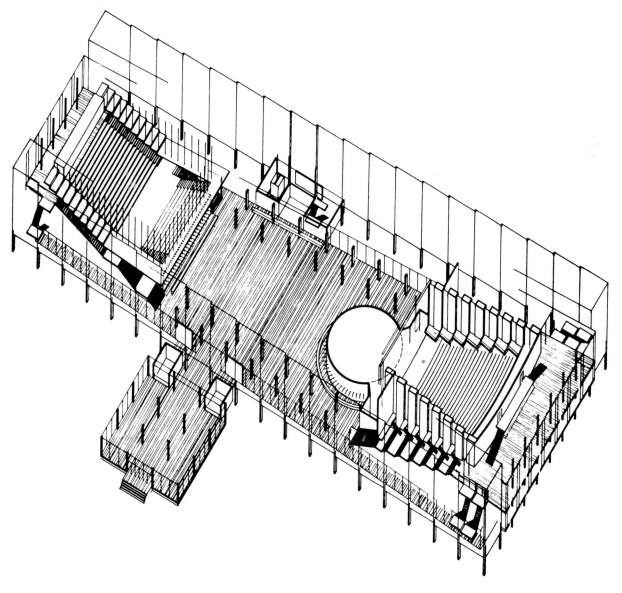

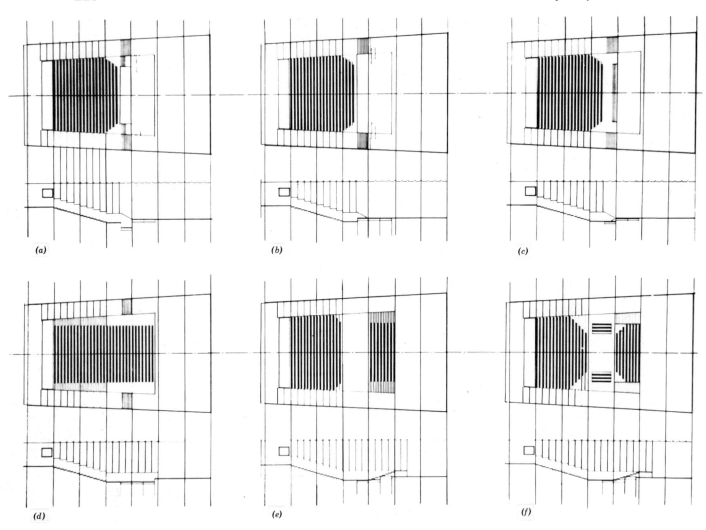

Figure 201. Mannheim experimental theater: stage and auditorium arrangements. (By permission and courtesy of the architect Professor Gerhard Weber.)

The small experimental theater is a particularly striking example of how an organized theater interior can be transformed at minimum cost. With comparatively simple mechanical devices, the stage and auditorium can be adapted quickly and easily to suit the requirements of the director and the play. The proscenium theater form (Figs. 201*a–c*) can accommodate 600 spectators; arrangement *a* in Figure 201, provides the traditional orchestra pit, arrangement *b* extends the proscenium to form an apron, and arrangement *c* provides steps connecting the proscenium with the auditorium. By raising or lowering sections of the stage and auditorium floors, the capacity can be expanded to 870 seats for conventions or concerts (Figure 201*d*). By using the same movable sections, the interior can be converted to a theater-in-the-round, with the seating arranged circumferentially (Figure 201*f*) or on two opposite sides of the arena, the pattern of the Teatro Sant'Erasmo in Milan.

The latter arrangement was used for a performance of Piscator's play *The Robbers*, which is shown in Figure 202; Figures 203 and 204 show the arena and proscenium arrangements, respectively.

Figure 202. Mannheim experimental theater: arena form used for Piscator's The Robbers. *(Photo by Robert Häusser. Reprinted by permission and courtesy of the architect Professor Gerhard Weber.)*

Figure 203. Mannheim experimental theater: arena form used for Max Frisch's Biedermann and the Firemen. *(By permission and courtesy of the architect Professor Gerhard Weber.)*

221

Figure 204. Mannheim experimental theater: proscenium form. (By permission and courtesy of the architect Professor Gerhard Weber.)

Figure 205. Gulbenkian Center in Hull, England, 1969: interiors. (By permission and courtesy of the architect Peter Moro and the Architect's Journal.)

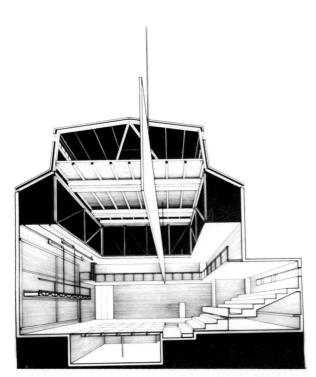

Figure 206. Gulbenkian Center: section and interior perspective. (By permission and courtesy of Peter Moro, the architect.)

Another example that can be classed as purely experimental is the theater known as the Gulbenkian Center, at Hull University in England, which was designed by architect Peter Moro (Figures 205, 206) and built in 1969.[229] The emphasis here is wholly on the acting area, since the 260 spectators accommodated by the small house (17 × 17 meters) are considered to be nothing but guinea pigs in this theatrical laboratory. The interior form was selected so that none of the alternative arrangements should have ascendancy over the others, and the acting area was placed permanently in the middle of the house. Its floor consists of 56 hydraulically operated movable square sections. Movable platforms of seats permit arrangement of the audience seating at will to form an arena (Figure 207e), an open stage (Figure 207d), and three alternative forms of proscenium (Figure 207a–c). Conversion from one form to another does not take more than 25 minutes. Functionally dominant in converting to each form are, first, the flat central surface (Figure 206) which can be lowered to divide the interior into two sections, and, second, the four triangular prisms, reminiscent of the *periakti* of the ancient Greeks and of Serlio,

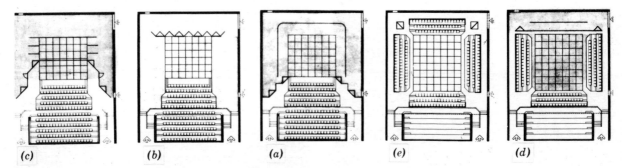

(c)   (b)   (a)   (e)   (d)

Figure 207. Gulbenkian Center: interior arrangements. (a) *Classic proscenium form, 192 seats;* (b) *proscenium with apron, 192 seats;* (c) *proscenium with end-stage;* (d) *open stage, 261 seats;* (e) *arena, 200 seats. (By permission and courtesy of Peter Moro, the architect.)*

which are particularly important in the three proscenium arrangements. In the first, the classic version, they form the necessary arch and frame; in the second, the backscene of the forestage; and in the third, the familiar end-stage proscenium.

The preceding are some outstanding examples of adaptable theater; but the one that stands preeminent as an illustration of experimental theater is the small studio installed in the basement of the Municipal Theater in Ulm, Germany (Figures 208–211). It adapts as required at no cost whatever, and it offers the greatest possible degree of audience–actor identification.

The building, completed in 1969, was created by architect Fritz Schäfer,[230] who based his en-

tire design on the geometry of a hexagon, a shape that enabled him to create better relationships between people and surrounding masses by eliminating repetition of the right angle. Although our subject is the small experimental theater, the Podium as it is called, it is useful to reproduce the other floor plans as well because it helps one understand the relation of this small space to the rest of the complex.

The Ulm Municipal Theater successfully combines in a single building two elements different as to form, function, and purpose: a traditional proscenium theater of the purely German and Wagnerian Bayreuth type, and an experimental studio where any deviation is possible and any original notion welcome.

Figure 208. Municipal Theater, Ulm. (Photo by author.)

Figure 209. The Podium, Ulm's experimental theater, 1969: (above left) *main layout in arena form with revolving seats;* (above right) *during the performance of* Time out of Mind; (right) *during a performance of Peter Weiss's* The Persecution and Murder of Paul Marat. *(Photos by Wilhelm Pabst. Reprinted by permission.)*

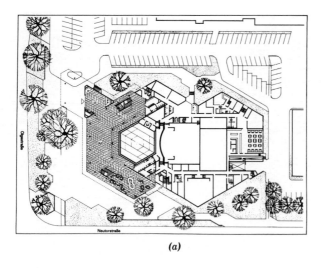

(a)

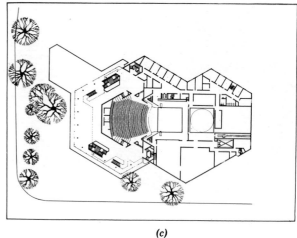

(c)

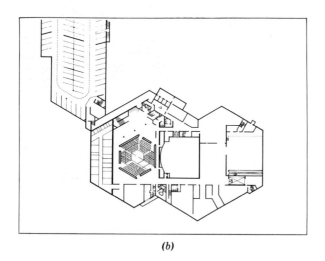

(b)

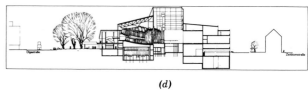

(d)

Figure 210. Municipal Theater, Ulm: (a) *plan of ground floor, entrance lobby;* (b) *plan of basement, experimental theater;* (c) *floor plan, opera house;* (d) *section. (By permission and courtesy of Fritz Schäfer, the architect.)*

The one feature most distinctive of the Podium is that there is no auditorium, no familiar seatbanks, no immovably mounted seats that keep the spectator turned in a single direction. The seats here are freely movable; they swivel, and the spectators sit comfortably as they do in their homes, in their own intimate surroundings, among family and friends, relaxed and at ease (Figure 209).

Thanks to this novel system of seating, every kind of layout is possible at the Podium. Adding to its versatility, the floor of the house is divided into two immovable sections and 16 smaller movable sections (Figure 210d) that can be raised or lowered independently through a 1.80-meter travel (0.00 to ±0.90 meters). These facilities make it possible to set up a large number of alternative space arrangements, creating various different theater forms that can accom-modate up to 200 spectators. Some such arrangements are shown in Figure 211, but several more are possible. An imaginative director could create something quite new in this eminently adaptable neutral interior, where all the styles of the past can be applied and all the trends of the future tried.

This is an appropriate point at which to close the discussion of examples of adaptable or experimental theater, because the Ulm Municipal Theater represents a culmination of the constant exploratory endeavor going on in this form. Moreover, the purpose of this work is not to list all the successful examples of the various theater forms produced to date but to discuss some of the distinctive efforts and accomplishments of architects and directors who have contributed to the development of the theater.

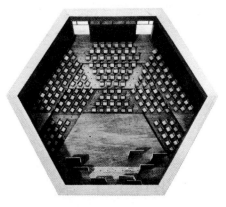

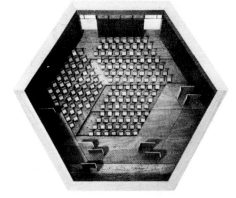

Figure 211. The Podium: some stage and auditorium arrangements, with the floor raised or lowered as required. (By permission and courtesy of Fritz Schäfer, the architect.)

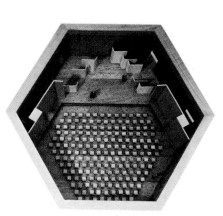
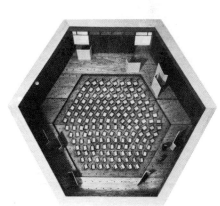

Figure 212. Ben Schlanger: space-form design for a proscenium theater.
(Credit: Ben Schlanger.)

Part Four

RESULTANT TREND IN THE EVOLUTION OF THE CONTEMPORARY THEATER

16
Resultant Trend in the Evolution of Function and Form

Separation of Functions

The art of the theater is by its very nature ephemeral. Whereas in the visual arts the expression imprinted by the artist on canvas or marble remains unchanged and unaffected by the passage of time, a permanent achievement ever reflecting the style and character of its period, in the performing arts things are different and more complex.

In the theater the expression of the artist-performer, whether actor, dancer, or musician, cannot be forever imprinted or even repeated with identical stress and value a second time. Regardless of the fact that the same script, choreography, or score is used, the expression and artistic quality of the first performance will be different from that of the second or any subsequent rendering. "Two theatrical creations at a different moment of time," asserts Ben Schlanger, "are never identical."[231]

Art in the theater lasts only as long as the time required for its performance.

The performer's art changes according to the conditions prevailing at the moment of expression.

Art in the theater is directly affected by its relation to the environment.

It is also strongly affected by the place in which it is performed.

It is a composite art. It embraces drama, musical comedy, opera, operetta, dance, music. Each of these art forms has its own requirements—requirements as to scale, function, relation to the audience. Each demands a different relationship with its surroundings, a particular, specific architectural structure that meets all those requirements.

The basic criterion for the design of such a structure, which is itself an art form, is that it should provide a suitable space in which the performers can express themselves freely and effectively, a space in which the spectators can receive that expression without obstruction.

This criterion and the effort to meet it produced the three contemporary theater forms described. And we have seen how each of these was created specifically to serve one form of performing art alone and possibly a second but related form as well.

Thus the Italian proscenium was devised to serve the opera and later the big spectacle, operetta, and musical comedy. In the course of the evolution of the theater the open stage and the theater-in-the-round appeared, their purpose being to serve the different forms of drama and the ideas of the dramatic playwrights and directors. Last came the experimental, adaptable theater, which dynamically combined all three forms in a single space and proved suitable only for small-scale productions.

No single one of these forms can be used for every kind of performing art, each of which has its own functional requirements that differ sharply from the others. To elucidate these functional differences, it is useful to take a separate look at each of the performing arts and the conditions required for it to function properly in the space of the theater.

An Analysis of Functional Requirements

It is generally acknowledged that when people go to a performance they want the greatest possible comfort and the least possible disturbance of their enjoyment; they want mental or audiovisual entertainment, and they want complete safety. The producer wants ease and convenience in preparing the show, good conditions for the performance itself, proper organization—in short, a creditable presentation at the lowest possible cost. Last, the artists of the theater—the playwrights, directors, actors, composers, musicians, dancers, stage designers—want the kind of conditions that will permit them to make the best of the abilities and talent.

Each type of performance is defined by its own limits.

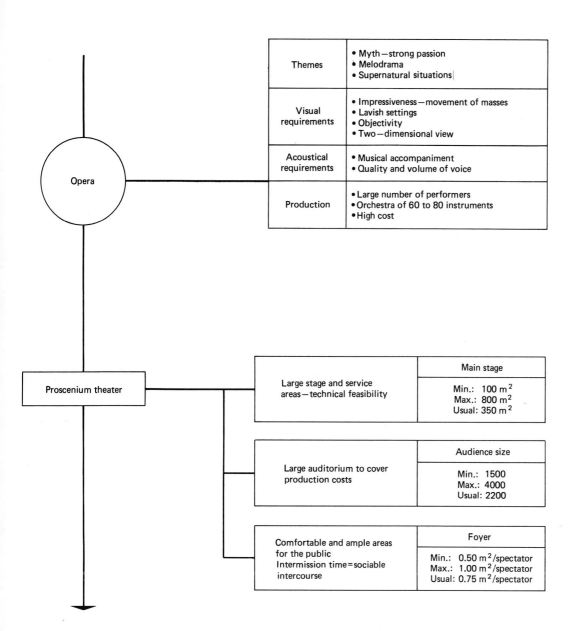

			Themes	• Myth—strong passion • Melodrama • Supernatural situations

Opera

	Themes	• Myth—strong passion • Melodrama • Supernatural situations
	Visual requirements	• Impressiveness—movement of masses • Lavish settings • Objectivity • Two—dimensional view
	Acoustical requirements	• Musical accompaniment • Quality and volume of voice
	Production	• Large number of performers • Orchestra of 60 to 80 instruments • High cost

Proscenium theater

Large stage and service areas—technical feasibility	Main stage Min.: 100 m² Max.: 800 m² Usual: 350 m²
Large auditorium to cover production costs	Audience size Min.: 1500 Max.: 4000 Usual: 2200
Comfortable and ample areas for the public Intermission time=sociable intercourse	Foyer Min.: 0.50 m²/spectator Max.: 1.00 m²/spectator Usual: 0.75 m²/spectator

Typical examples		Distribution of areas (%)			Audience size
		Stage & service areas	Auditorium	Public areas	
Paris Opera	1874*	24 (Main stage 416 m²)	17	59	2150
N. Y. Metropolitan Opera	1966	48 (Main stage 825 m²)	14	38	4000
Hamburg Opera	1955	44 (Main stage 213 m²)	24	32	1680

*According to Roderick Ham

Diagram 1.

Traditional opera's main theme is myth, strong passion, and the individual's romantic struggle with the supernatural. It requires impressive settings, striking color contrasts in lighting and costumes, and the movement of massive numbers of actors over the stage. Music plays the primary role, speech is lyric, and the libretto secondary. The performers depend for expression not on the spoken word but on the volume and quality of their voices, which almost always must dominate the music. In opera the space pertaining to each function must be as large as

233

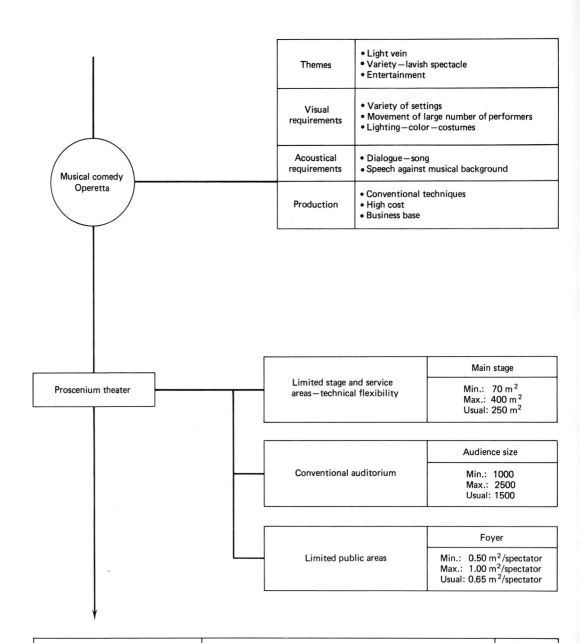

		Main stage
Themes	• Light vein • Variety—lavish spectacle • Entertainment	
Visual requirements	• Variety of settings • Movement of large number of performers • Lighting—color—costumes	
Acoustical requirements	• Dialogue—song • Speech against musical background	
Production	• Conventional techniques • High cost • Business base	

Musical comedy
Operetta

Proscenium theater

Limited stage and service areas—technical flexibility	Main stage
	Min.: 70 m^2 Max.: 400 m^2 Usual: 250 m^2

Conventional auditorium	Audience size
	Min.: 1000 Max.: 2500 Usual: 1500

Limited public areas	Foyer
	Min.: 0.50 m^2/spectator Max.: 1.00 m^2/spectator Usual: 0.65 m^2/spectator

Typical examples		Distribution of areas (%)			Audience size
		Stage and service areas	Auditorium	Public areas	
Drury Lane, London	1812*	48 (Main stage 305 m^2)	19	33	2283
Municipal Theater, Münster	1956	18 (Main stage 247 m^2)	12	70	955
Municipal Theater, Bohn	1965	50 (Main stage 370 m^2)	10	40	896

Diagram 2.

*According to Roderick Ham

possible. The stage with its orchestra pit, wings, and backstage areas must be so designed as to accommodate the massive and varied scenery, to permit ample movement of a host of performers, and to provide room for a large orchestra. A vast auditorium is needed—something encountered in nearly all eighteenth- and nineteenth-century theaters—to provide for the largest possible audience. This is essential to cover the high production costs of grand opera. Moreover, because most operatic performances are lengthy, everything connected with the audience—the foyers, the seats—must be carefully designed for convenience and comfort. Intermissions are impor-

234

tant. The subscription system adopted during recent years in most countries has turned the opera house into a center for social intercourse to the point where it is no exaggeration to say that the intermission is often more important to the operagoer than the performance. It is all but impossible to use a building of this kind for any other purpose. This is why modern opera houses are built mostly for reasons of prestige, usually with government financing and only in major cities, and they are nearly always part of large cultural centers containing smaller theaters that serve the other performing arts (Diagram 1).[232]

Musical comedy, light opera, and operetta deal with lighter themes. Here speech is more important, but it is always accompanied by music, song, and the movement of the dance. Their aim is to provide a pleasing and lavish spectacle—easy and superficial entertainment for the eyes and ears. Settings are more functional and more varied. As in opera, extensive technical facilities are needed to shift the scenery quickly, creating impressive visual effects. There must be plenty of room for the onstage presence and movement of large numbers of performers, but the size of the orchestra pit can be reduced: Twenty instruments are generally sufficient. There is a fair amount of dialogue, and the need to communicate the actors' expression calls for a closer relationship between audience and performers. This means that the house must not be too big, although production costs are high and require sizable audiences to cover them. Buildings of this kind are to be found in practically every medium-sized city in the more advanced countries and are constructed and maintained by local governments. Their size permits them to be used also for *variety shows* and *vaudeville*, both types having the same characteristics as musical comedy (Diagram 2).

The *concert*'s sole theme is music. Music of every kind, from classical to modern, from symphonic works requiring large orchestras to recitals by a single performer. Scenery here is nonexistent and technical facilities are completely useless. The prime requirements are acoustic perfection and a flexible auditorium.[233]

The great popularity of classical music in recent years spurred construction of a large number of buildings exclusively for concerts in large and middle-sized cities (Figure 213).[234] These concert halls, of course, are unsuitable for any

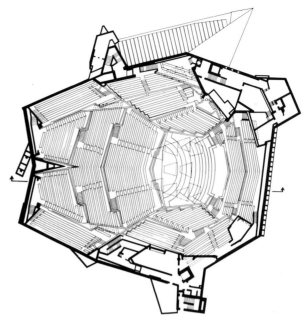

Figure 213. Berlin Philharmonic Hall: plan. Design by Hans Scharoun, 1963. (By permission of George Izenour.)

other purpose, but this does not bother their organizers. Music is so popular that they are constantly in use. In many cases a city can do without a costly edifice devoted solely to concert performances. Any opera house or operetta theater will do, provided it has good acoustics, a wide proscenium arch, and a forestage that will allow it to be converted without difficulty to a concert hall (Diagram 3).

Drama has the primary purpose of projecting the spoken word. Drama comes in many shapes and forms, according to the trend espoused by the playwright.

The presentation of drama requires the use of every artistic inspiration and technical aid serving a dramatic purpose, for the audience must be induced to shed its disbelief and assess the actors and plot exactly as presented. The importance of speech and expression and the actors' kinetic three-dimensional relation to the space in which they perform call for a small auditorium, where the distances between actors and audience do not exceed tolerable natural visual and acoustic limits. The public that goes to see drama in its proper form is usually a cultured public, whose

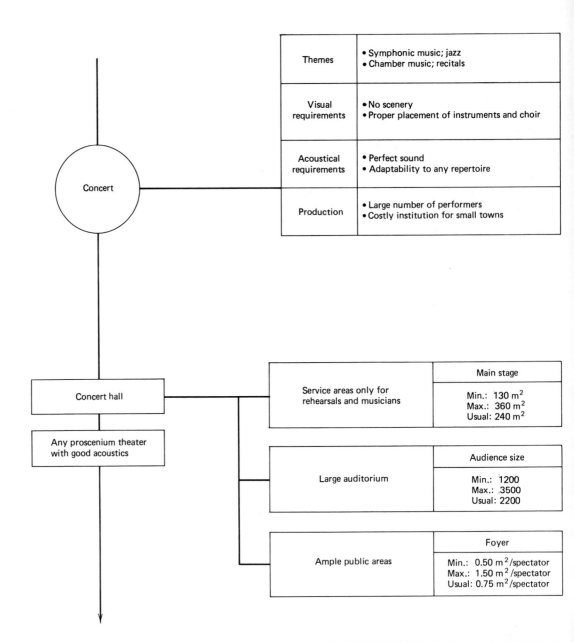

	Themes	• Symphonic music; jazz • Chamber music; recitals
Concert	Visual requirements	• No scenery • Proper placement of instruments and choir
	Acoustical requirements	• Perfect sound • Adaptability to any repertoire
	Production	• Large number of performers • Costly institution for small towns

Concert hall

Any proscenium theater with good acoustics

		Main stage
Service areas only for rehearsals and musicians		Min.: 130 m² Max.: 360 m² Usual: 240 m²

		Audience size
Large auditorium		Min.: 1200 Max.: 3500 Usual: 2200

		Foyer
Ample public areas		Min.: 0.50 m²/spectator Max.: 1.50 m²/spectator Usual: 0.75 m²/spectator

Typical examples		Distribution of areas (%)			Audience size
		Stage and service areas	Auditorium	Public areas	
Berlin Philarmonic	1963	10 (Main stage 330 m²)	40	50	2200
Pavilion, Los Angeles	1964	22 (Main stage 360 m²)	45	63	3250
Festsaal, Ingolstadt	1966	6 (Main stage 135 m²)	50	44	4350

Diagram 3.

expectations from a performance of this developing art form are high.

One must not confuse the drama repertory theater with the commercial Broadway or boulevard theater. The latter could safely be described as a form that has no connection with the performing arts, since it is not itself an art. Per-

haps some of the more talented actors performing on a Broadway stage rise to the level of expressing a form of art, but theirs is no more than a conscious individual effort and is not a collective one. The other factors that go to make a commercial theater are all reduced to a common level. The playwright, resorting to farce or melodrama, uses the easy expedient of repetition; the director, usually a businessperson, is interested in low costs and high returns; the settings are confined to the conventional box-set type, a room with the necessary furniture. The architectural and building requirements of the commercial theater are not demanding. Any design that provides a classic proscenium and a comparatively large auditorium is acceptable.

True drama, however—the drama of Aeschylus, Sophocles, and Euripides, of Shakespeare and Lorca, of Brecht and Beckett—caters to a discriminating public that demands collective art, the result of the efforts of the playwright, the actor, the director, the stage designer, and, last but not least, the architect. It is the architect's creative effort that has produced the right theater forms for true drama. The open stage, the theater-in-the-round, even the conventional proscenium theater updated and adapted to modern requirements—all made their appearance in the theater world as the result of efforts to improve the presentation of this particular art. Almost all of these drama theaters are small, designed on a human scale to ensure a high degree of communication between the actors and the audience. The actors communicate through facial expression, body sculpture, and three-dimensional relation to space. The larger the house, the less effectively they can communicate; in a theater designed for opera or musical comedy the presentation of drama is completely impossible. Any attempt to combine the two is doomed to failure; drama requires its own exclusive temple: one of the three contemporary theater forms or the latest, most developed form of experimental adaptable theater (Diagram 4).

The *dance*, which used to make do with any hall available for public events, in recent years has tended to be performed in theaters designed specifically for this art form alone. However, the popularity it enjoyed in the past has dwindled, and it is confined today to a few major cities. A theater constructed exclusively for dance is doomed to certain financial failure; consequently such facilities are to be found only in a very few cities, their existence justified by tradition or reasons of prestige. Financial feasibility aside, a modern dance theater must provide an extremely flexible stage, a spacious orchestra pit, and a steeply amphitheatrical auditorium where the audience can experience a three-dimensional sense of space (Figure 214).[235] Dance is an art form that acts upon the audience through movement and the composite pattern of the dancers in space; therefore, a three-dimensional view is essential to the success of a performance. Anybody who had the opportunity to see and compare performances by Margot Fonteyn and Rudolf Nureyev at the outdated and uncomfortable Covent Garden in London and at the Theater of Herod Atticus in Athens (Figure 31) will readily understand how important the third dimension is to an appreciation of the dance. Yet, because theaters devoted exclusively to dance are unprofitable, this art form is compelled, despite the visual disadvantages, to resort to traditional opera houses and concert halls. The open stage and arena can often be used to good effect, but the area of the stage is too small to allow ample development of the choreography. However, these stages are quite suitable for solo or small-group performances (Diagram 5).

Figure 214. Proposal by Seth Hiller for a theater exclusively for dance. (Credit: Seth Hiller.)

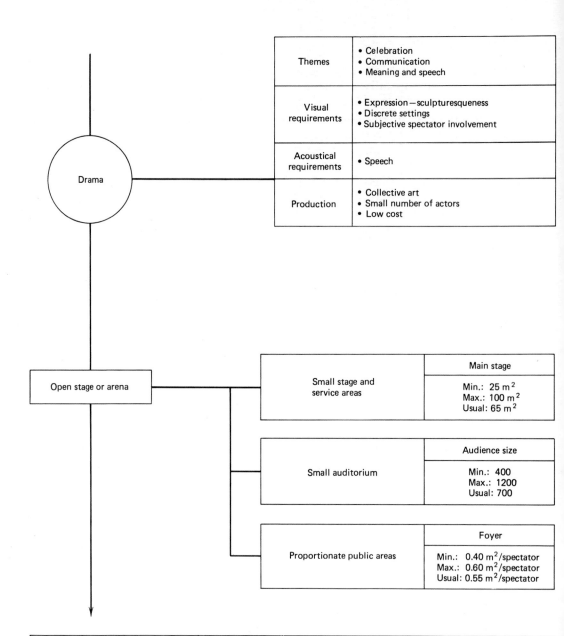

	Themes	• Celebration • Communication • Meaning and speech
	Visual requirements	• Expression — sculpturesqueness • Discrete settings • Subjective spectator involvement
	Acoustical requirements	• Speech
	Production	• Collective art • Small number of actors • Low cost

Drama

Open stage or arena

	Main stage
Small stage and service areas	Min.: 25 m^2 Max.: 100 m^2 Usual: 65 m^2

	Audience size
Small auditorium	Min.: 400 Max.: 1200 Usual: 700

	Foyer
Proportionate public areas	Min.: 0.40 m^2/spectator Max.: 0.60 m^2/spectator Usual: 0.55 m^2/spectator

Diagram 4.

Typical examples		Distribution of areas (%)			Audience size
		Stage and service areas	Auditorium	Public areas	
Crucible, Sheffield	1971*	28 (Main stage 25 m^2)	42	30	1018
Tyrone Guthrie, Minneapolis	1963	20 (Main stage 62 m^2)	36	42	1437
Arena Stage, Washington, D. C.	1962	8 (Main stage 99 m^2)	60	34	752

*According to Roderick Ham

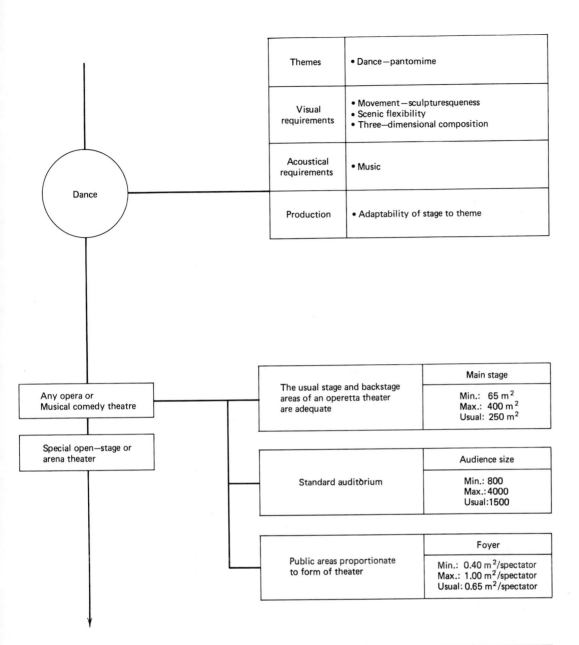

Themes	• Dance—pantomime
Visual requirements	• Movement—sculpturesqueness • Scenic flexibility • Three—dimensional composition
Acoustical requirements	• Music
Production	• Adaptability of stage to theme

Dance

Any opera or Musical comedy theatre

Special open—stage or arena theater

The usual stage and backstage areas of an operetta theater are adequate	Main stage Min.: 65 m² Max.: 400 m² Usual: 250 m²
Standard auditorium	Audience size Min.: 800 Max.: 4000 Usual: 1500
Public areas proportionate to form of theater	Foyer Min.: 0.40 m²/spectator Max.: 1.00 m²/spectator Usual: 0.65 m²/spectator

Typical examples	Distribution of areas (%)			Audience size
	Stage and service areas	Auditorium	Public areas	
Covent Garden, London* 1858/1964	47 (Main stage 270 m²)	28	25	2110
New York State Theater* 1964	30 (Main stage 228 m²)	21	49	2729
Open—stage proposal**	25 (Main stage 150 m²)	60	15	1100

*According to Roderick Ham   **Ideal Theater, p. 50

Diagram 5.

This analysis of the different functional requirements of each of the performing arts gives rise, logically enough, to the following questions.

How can theaters meet the cultural needs of a city? Is it possible in an average-sized metropolis of 2 or 3 million people—or in a smaller city where the theatrical and cultural level is highly developed—to build five different theaters, one for each of the five basic performing arts?

How can such theaters survive, such expensive projects with enormous maintenance and production costs, projects that, to be viable must operate 200 to 250 nights a year?

Can a city provide such attendance levels? Are the cultural needs and intellectual level of its citizens so great that all these theaters will be filled almost every night?

One could point to New York, Paris, and London and say such things are possible there, but that does not answer the question for the countless other big cities whose character is less comprehensive and complex. The answer may well lie in two new approaches that have developed in recent years, two theatrical forms that constitute the resultant trend in the future evolution of the theater. The goal of this trend is to make of the performing arts a cultural asset belonging to the greatest possible number of people.

The first of these approaches is the multipurpose or multiple-use theater. The second is the organized civic theater center or cultural center.

Evolution of the Form

In arriving at its contemporary state, the theater has traveled a long evolutionary course. Starting, as we have seen, from the classic prototypes of ancient Greece, it was influenced by changing social and political conditions, and it developed its forms in conformance with the trends and cultural climate of the periods it passed through.

In endeavoring to identify and define the resultant trend of this evolutionary course, it is helpful to consult Diagram 6, which is a graphic compilation of the most distinctive examples of the various theater forms from ancient times to the present. The plans shown have been drawn to the same scale (1 : 1000) to make comparisons easier, and the auditorium–stage relationship, the actor–audience relationship, which had a determining influence on the development of the architectural form, has been indicated by different shadings.

Essentially, the evolutionary process started in the fifth century B.C. with the classic Athenian theater, the Theater of Dionysus in Athens, where the actor–audience relationship was direct. It was the period when drama, the integrated form of what we call meaning and speech, was at its height. This direct relationship was carried forward into the Hellenistic and the Greco-Roman theater with a few minor differences, mainly in the position of the orchestra and the size of the scene-building. In the Greco-Roman theater the Roman influence became apparent when the main acting area was moved to the proscenium and the orchestra gradually lost its importance. This can be seen distinctly in the plan of the Theater of Magnesia (Diagram 6), which has been drawn comparatively to show the arrangement during the Hellenistic period and the later arrangement of the theater during the Roman period. In all three types of Greek theater the form was the same, regardless of the reduction in size or the different shape—semicircular or elliptical—of the auditorium.

The form underwent a basic change with the advent of the Roman theater proper. The change in the audience–actor relationship eliminated the orchestra by converting it to a gladiatorial ring and resulted in an enlarged scene-building. Technical requirements necessitated thick bearing walls to support the edifice now that the theater had moved from the natural slopes of the hillsides to the heart of the city, where it stood as an independent building. These changes altered the theater's original form. It became inflexible, heavy, functionally awkward, and cumbersome; the actor stood facing the audience, and the relationship that had united them in direct communication for four centuries was gone.

The Middle Ages brought a complete and final severance of every link between the theater and the public. The evolutionary process thus came to a standstill, not to be resumed until the Renaissance, when it picked up again based now not on the Greek pattern but on the Roman. The Teatro Olimpico came first; it was followed by the Teatro Farnese and in turn by the Italian court theaters of the baroque era and the eighteenth century, representing the triumph of the Italian stage and the proscenium theater.

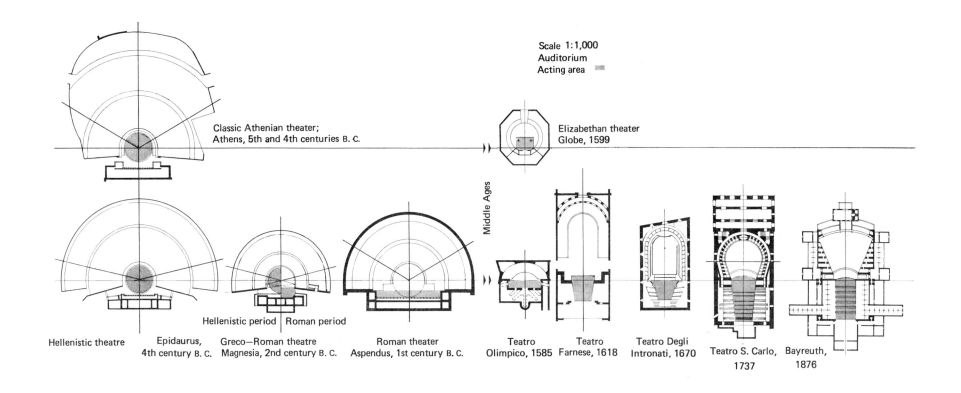

Classic Athenian theater;
Athens, 5th and 4th centuries B.C.

Elizabethan theater
Globe, 1599

Middle Ages

Hellenistic theatre

Epidaurus,
4th century B.C.

Hellenistic period | Roman period

Greco—Roman theatre
Magnesia, 2nd century B.C.

Roman theater
Aspendus, 1st century B.C.

Teatro
Olimpico, 1585

Teatro
Farnese, 1618

Teatro Degli
Intronati, 1670

Teatro S. Carlo,
1737

Bayreuth,
1876

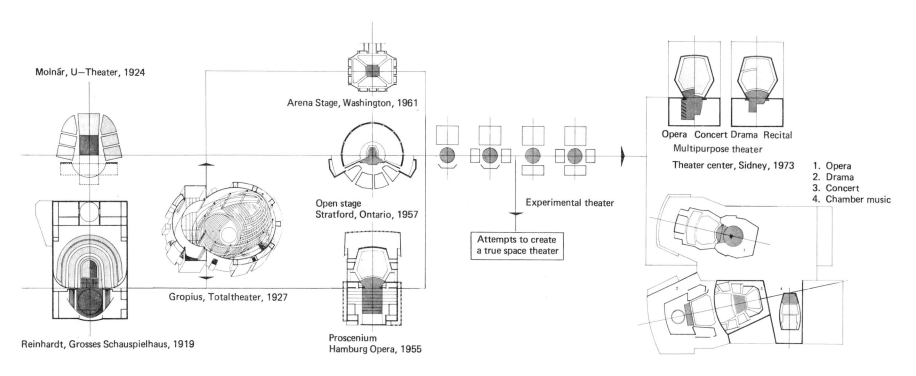

Molnár, U—Theater, 1924

Arena Stage, Washington, 1961

Opera Concert Drama Recital

Multipurpose theater

Theater center, Sidney, 1973

1. Opera
2. Drama
3. Concert
4. Chamber music

Open stage
Stratford, Ontario, 1957

Experimental theater

Attempts to create
a true space theater

Gropius, Totaltheater, 1927

Reinhardt, Grosses Schauspielhaus, 1919

Proscenium
Hamburg Opera, 1955

Diagram 6. Resultant trend in the evolution of the plan.

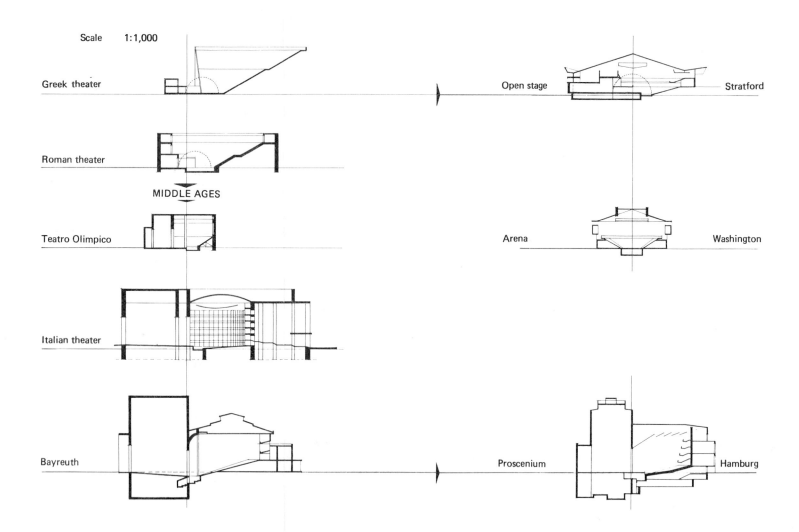

Scale   1:1,000

Greek theater

Roman theater

MIDDLE AGES

Teatro Olimpico

Italian theater

Bayreuth

Open stage   Stratford

Arena   Washington

Proscenium   Hamburg

Diagram 7. Evolution of the section.

The audience–actor relationship remained divided into a confrontation from opposite sides. The form changed only insofar as the auditorium, size, and stage facilities were concerned. The diminished importance of the spoken word in conjunction with the equally diminished cultural sophistication of those times made the proscenium theater the reigning form, in fact the only form. There is one shining exception: the Elizabethan stage, which, though not based on the Greek prototype, nevertheless attained the same result. It achieved that result because of a similar need for communication between audience and actor that only speech of surpassing power can inspire—yet another proof of the determinative importance of speech in developing the architectural form of the theater.

Wagner, with his Festival Theater in Bayreuth, and Reinhardt, with his Grosses Schauspielhaus, tried to rescue the theater from its stagnant state but without notable result. Wagner managed to create an auditorium simple and Doric in design by eliminating the tiered loges and baroque fussiness, but he stuck faithfully to the formula of the Italian stage. Reinhardt, strongly influenced by the revolutionary trends of the early years of our century, tried to revive the classic orchestra, but he saw it only as an extension and complement of the traditional Italian proscenium arch, serving the grandiose and the spectacular.

The Bauhaus era was a milestone in the evolutionary progress of the theater. Molnár's U-theater ushered in the open stage and made space theater a realizable concept, while Gropius, with his "total theater," was the first to pose the problem inherent in the notion that the theater should be not monolithic but flexible, that it should serve not merely one of the performing arts but all of them.

Gropius' theater was never built, but what is important is that it prompted architects and theater people to explore and experiment. The *Totaltheater*, in combination with the Bayreuth effort, led to the advanced proscenium theater of today. In conjunction with the enduring tradition left by the Greek and Elizabethan theaters, it culminated in the open stage, in the successful designs of the Stratford and Tyrone Guthrie playhouses, and also in the theater-in-the-round, which from its modest and tentative beginnings on the small stages of the post–World War II period developed into an organized form with the construction of the Arena Stage in 1961.

When we study Diagram 6, it becomes clearly apparent that the original form, the classic Theater of Dionysus, was split into three components. The first took a path that led to the degeneration of this form and that paralleled the degeneration of theatrical art and the decline of drama. As a result, a totally different form was produced: the proscenium theater. The second, based on true drama, retained intact all the elements of the Greek theater except the size of the playhouse. As it passed through the Elizabethan period, it arrived at the open-stage theater. And the third, as a development of Gropius' proposal continuing the evolutionary process of the second, produced the theater-in-the-round and the arena, where pure drama found new possibilities of expression.

Diagram 7, also drawn to the same scale to allow comparative examination of the development of the theater section, leads to the same conclusion. We can discern here still more clearly the transition from the Greek theater to the Italian, marked by the progressive shrinking of the auditorium and followed at the same time by an increase in scenic elaboration. One could, in fact, express this phenomenon in mathematical terms: *In the theater the extent of scenic elaboration is inversely proportional to the importance of speech.* Thus we notice that the increased importance of speech in recent years has reestablished a direct proportion in the relation between auditorium and stage (open stage and arena). Conversely, when speech is considered a secondary element, this relationship remains the same as formed by the Italian stage (opera).

The experimental theater cannot be considered a fourth form nor can it be contended that its roots go deep; basically it is an attempt to combine the three recognized forms in a single bare space. It is, however, the best and only stimulus to further theatrical progress. It could become a worthwhile form in the future if an effort is made to develop it as a really organized space theater, a form that will integrate the theatrical function, the spectator, and the actor in a unity without the imperfections of the existing experimental theaters.

When we study the functional needs of the performing arts today, we wonder what the future trend will be in the evolutionary course of the theater and to what extent the three component forces defined can lead to a resultant trend, a new and determining form free of conventions and compromises.

This probably will not happen for many years to come, primarily because the evolution of the theater is too slow. It is a process measured in centuries and affected by radical social and political rearrangements and upheavals that delay or accelerate it accordingly. The twentieth century has undergone its own rearrangements. Everybody is—or pretends to be—"content," at least in whatever concerns the theater and its development. Any drive toward further progress in organized theater space is not based on radical innovations but on partial improvements and the pursuit of greater financial gains.

Drama is no longer strong enough to create new forms by itself, whereas the commercial theater, which does have the power to innovate, is perfectly satisfied with things as they are now—or, rather, as they have been for four centuries.

What can unequivocally be identified as a resultant development are the current efforts leading toward compound forms such as the multipurpose theater readily adaptable to all functional needs and the theater center containing theaters of various forms, each designed to serve one or more of the performing arts. These theaters and centers, the purpose of which is to serve, promote, and popularize those arts and to serve the combined needs of modern civic centers, are the subject of Chapter 17.

17
The Compound Forms

The Multipurpose Theater

To avoid any semantic confusion between the terms *adaptable* and *multipurpose*, I begin by defining the distinction. We have seen that the adaptable or experimental theater allows the relations between stage and auditorium to be changed by mechanically or manually shifting component elements so that one and the same space can be adapted to any of the three forms discussed. The term *adaptable* corresponds more closely to *multiform*, denoting the multiplicity of shapes an auditorium and acting area can assume. A multipurpose theater or place of assembly, by contrast, is a building of fixed design and form that can have more than one use.

Whereas the adaptable, experimental theater was a product of the philosophical need to find and develop means of expressing theatrical art, the multipurpose theater was spawned by the practical need of increasing the profitability of a building that is costly to construct and expensive to maintain. The first has an experimental and cultural base, the second a practical, business one.

This may be the reason the multipurpose theater is a product born and developed mainly in the United States, a country where every project must serve a practical purpose and yield financial returns commensurate with the investment. This business approach in an area so genuinely artistic and cultural is completely justified when one considers the relation between theater and state in America; it is, however, rather difficult to consider since no such relation exists.

This may seem odd to a European accustomed to the notion of state, national, or municipal theater and to the idea that the theater is an important institution well within the province of government sponsorship. Yet, in the United States the theater, like a great many other social institutions and functions, has been left entirely to private enterprise and the initiative of the citizens. None of the thousands of American theaters of various forms and sizes, from the smallest college studios to New York's Metropolitan Opera House and Lincoln Center, its parent complex, was built with government backing or planning. All were created by the initiative of civic or community groups, by private donation and subscription, and by the strong competitive urge that drives each group to produce something better, more original, and more impressive than the other.

High construction costs, soaring land values, and huge maintenance expenses compelled sponsoring groups to combine practical expediency with culture and seek the best possible result at the lowest possible cost.

Speaking about his own creation (the famous Jesse H. Jones Hall in Houston) in the spring of 1966, George Izenour said that not more than five American metropolitan centers can afford to house each kind of musical or dramatic performance in a separate hall. For example, New York's Lincoln Center, with its separate buildings for symphony, opera, ballet, and theater cost $164 million, and 99.9 percent of American cities do not have anything like that kind of money. This has meant combination halls in most cities, but these usually require compromises on size and acoustics. By trying to be everything acoustically, they too often ended up being nothing.[236]

In an interview, Izenour added:

The impossibility of getting such large sums of money led to the need for multipurpose halls in most cities. The saving is considerable. We must remember that the major cost of a theater center is in the construction of its shell—that is, its total "architectural volume." At Jones Hall, that "volume" cost us $6 million. The special equipment required to give this theater its multipurpose capability, in both stage and auditorium, did not cost more than $600,000. This means that for an additional outlay of 10 percent, Houston acquired not one but five different halls.[237]

Dynamic in design and architecturally outstanding, the Houston theater is justly considered the pioneer multipurpose theater in America in size and value and perhaps one of the best examples of modern theater architecture (Figure 215). Created by architects Caudill, Rowlett, and Scott and by Izenour, it is distinguished by a simplicity of design unusual in a building intended for this kind of function. A careful study of the plan reveals "an outstandingly admirable design, which is why the building is considered the most refined theater of its kind in the world."[238]

Figure 215. Jesse H. Jones Hall, Houston, 1966: view and plan. (By permission of George Izenour.)

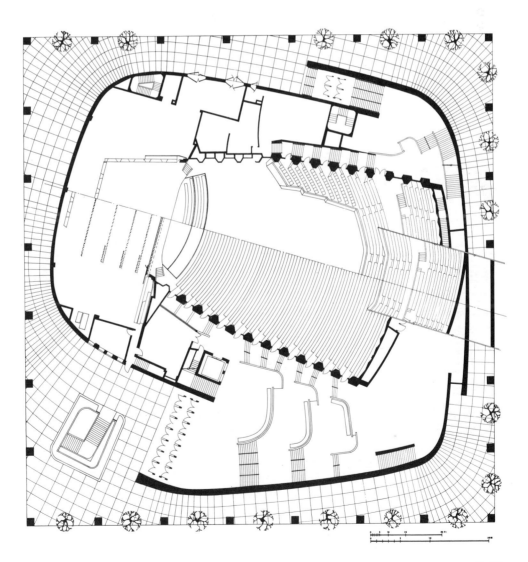

But if Jones Hall is a pioneer, the Edwin Thomas Performing Arts Hall at the University of Akron, Ohio, may be considered the most sophisticated multiple-use building for the performing arts in the world. Designed by the same team as Jones Hall—architects Caudill, Rowlett, and Scott and Izenour—its free design contrasts with the clean-cut cubical shapes in the exterior masses and plan of Jones Hall. For the theater-design and engineering consultant it was the culmination of a long-range plan in the United States that achieved ultimate environmental control over the auditorium and stage, where a system of variable seating geometry, auditorium volume, and acoustics are integral with architecture.

The primary structure is a massive in situ reinforced-concrete system of walls, beams, and folded plates (Figure 216). In overall plan the building consists of the auditorium, lobbies, plazas, and an underground parking structure wrapped around a parallelogram-shaped stage house (Figure 217). The focal point of the complex is the auditorium, which at its maximum capacity seats 3,008 spectators and can be converted in a very short time from concert hall to opera theater, recital hall, or intimate drama theater.

Both sides of the auditorium are enveloped by an impressive glazed lobby terminated at the rear by a buttressed great wall (Figure 218). This wall serves as one of two structural supports (the stage tower is the other) for spanning the lobbies and the auditorium. The roof is a reinforced-concrete, post-stressed cable, valley beam, and folded-plate structural system. The secondary inside auditorium wall is a combined steel-framed block-masonry system from floor to roof. The basic feature that makes the Edwin Thomas Hall a multipurpose theater is the conceptual originality of the ceiling, which can be adjusted to suit every performing art.

Figure 216. Edwin Thomas Performing Arts Hall, Akron, 1974: facade at night. (By permission of George Izenour.)

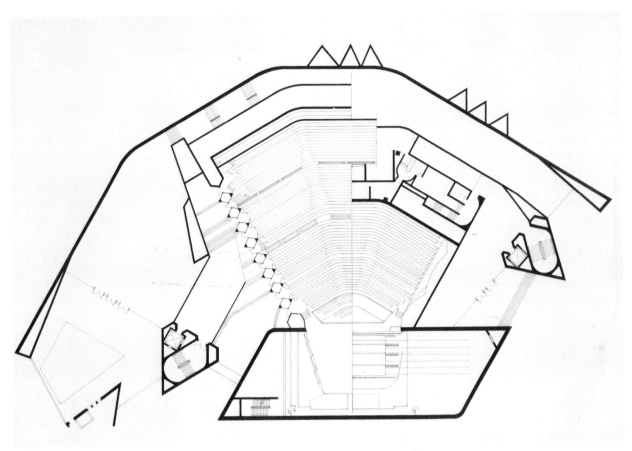

Figure 217. Edwin Thomas Hall: plan. (By permission of George Izenour.)

Figure 218. Edwin Thomas Hall: lobby and tension sculpture (counterweights). (By permission of George Izenour.)

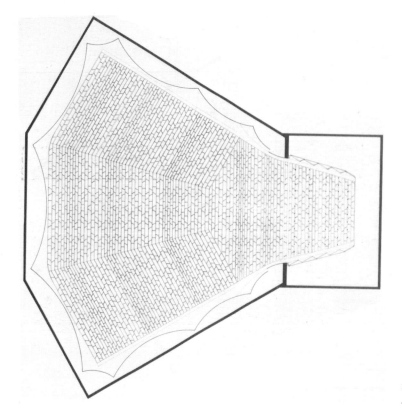

A series of catenary cables are restrained at either end by steel frames and suspend 3600 acoustically dampened steel plates (Figure 219). These constitute in the aggregate an auditorium ceiling system that is hung by still another cable supporting system from a steel interfacing structure connected to the roof.

The sound-reflecting-steel auditorium ceiling and matching stage acoustical-steel shell ceiling float free of the walls. These are of exposed transsondent steel mesh woven in situ. In the auditorium, behind this steel mesh but invisible, are hard-plaster, convex, splayed, sound-reflecting walls. On the stage the acoustical shell consists of dampened-steel, sound-reflecting walls. Between the woven steel and sound-reflecting surfaces are interposed 12,000 square feet of programmed absorption. This massive movable ceiling weighs 44 tons and utilizes six closed-loop, clew-stabilized, electromotive winch drives, connected to 27 lead-filled chrome-plated steel cylinders (counterweights weighing approximately 47 tons) hung in the main lobby as a tension sculpture (Figure 219). The total visual effect of the ceiling is that of a continuous, geometrically abstract, mosaiclike drapery hung in slightly overlapping, mitered catenary folds. The movable ceiling sections are grouped in arrays, group counterweighted and electromotively driven linearly (up and down) as well as radially displaced. Movement of the structure is synchronized by means of an analog computer and interlocking switching logic.

In concert position, the movable-ceiling catenary-panel arrays articulate between the fixed catenary-panel arrays over the flying balcony at the rear of the auditorium and the fixed-ceiling arrays within the acoustical shell, itself preerected within the stage house (Figure 220), yielding a series of convex modulations that direct evenly diffused first-energy reflections over the spectators. Angular displacement of the group of three mitered catenaries directly ahead of the flying balcony, with stage acoustical shell stored and with either full- or small-sized orchestra pit, yields an opera or musical comedy

Figure 220. Edwin Thomas Hall: concert hall mode. (a) View from auditorium to stage;
(b) longitudinal perspective section. (By permission of George Izenour.)

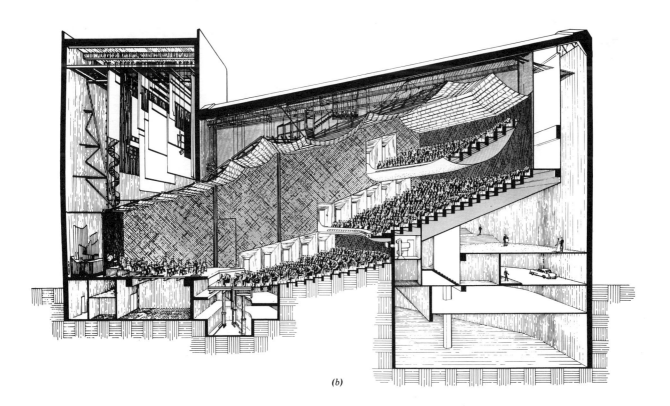

(b)

249

Figure 221. Edwin Thomas Hall: opera and musical comedy mode. (a) View from stage to auditorium; (b) longitudinal perspective section. (By permission of George Izenour.)

(a)

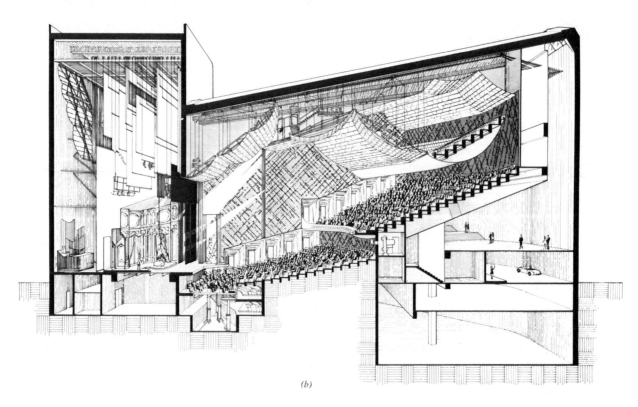

(b)

theater seating 2,400 (Figure 221). The six sections immediately in front of the proscenium, including the light-bridge (also with stage acoustical shell stored), when angularly displaced and lowered 15 feet at the proscenium and 48 feet to the grand-tier balcony rail, yield an intimate drama theater with or without an apron stage or orchestra pit, or, with the small stage acoustical shell erected, a recital hall seating 850 to 900 (Figure 222). Separate angular articulation of the single trapezoidal ceiling leaf on the stage side of the light bridge opens the ceiling in front

Figure 222. Edwin Thomas Hall: drama theater or recital hall mode. (a) View from stage to auditorium; (b) longitudinal perspective section. (By permission of George Izenour.)

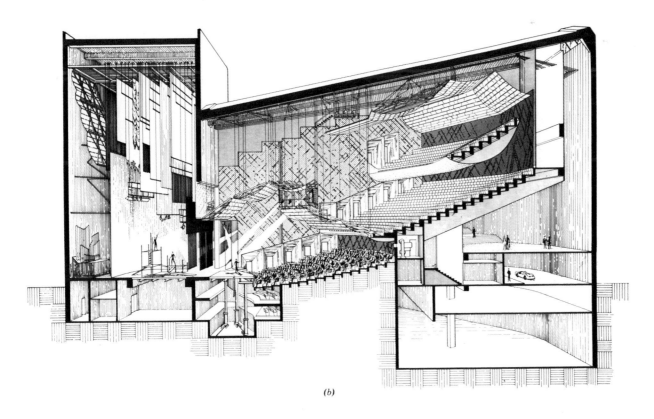

(b)

251

Figure 223. Edwin Thomas Hall: overall view of the auditorium, with all houselights on, showing the movable ceiling from the rear in the drama theater mode. (By permission of George Izenour.)

of the bridge for front lighting the opera, musical comedy, or theater mode (Figures 221*b* and 222*a*). An overall view of the auditorium from the left side of the flying balcony, in the intimate theater mode (Figure 223), shows dramatically the massive reduction in both volume and seating capacity achieved by lowering the movable ceiling.

To appreciate the vastness of this 3,008-seat auditorium when it functions as a concert hall, one has only to compare it with the three leading halls in the world: the Boston Symphony, 2,289 seats; the Grosser Musikvereinssaal in Vienna, 1,680 seats; and the Concertgebouw in Amsterdam, 2206 seats.

Compared, again, with the world's classic opera houses, the Edwin Thomas Hall has no cause to envy the famous La Scala in Milan (2,289 seats), the Vienna State Opera (1,658 seats), or the Paris Opera (2,150 seats), except perhaps for the glamor of tradition. The acoustic achievement, on the contrary, is much better at Edwin Thomas Hall, thanks to the flexibility of the ceiling and the technical sophistication of the design, features that were beyond the capability of eighteenth-century technology. Finally, in the drama theater mode the reduced volume of the hall effortlessly serves the principal func-

tion required by drama: actor–audience communication and identification.

All the conversions, the lighting control and the required stage conversions, are programmed into an electronic control center designed by Izenour, which operates the changes in minimum time without the help of human hands.[239]

A measure of the success of this multipurpose theater is that ever since it opened, except for a few brief vacation recesses, it has been in use constantly, night and day, serving not only the performing arts but also various social and cultural events, such as lectures and forums. It is a remarkably successful and vital institution that for adherents of the multipurpose concept could be the ideal answer to a problem confronting many cities, particularly those that have no organized theater at all.

Another distinctive multipurpose theater, built on a smaller scale and designed to serve not a big city but a university, is the Loretto Hilton Center at Webster College, St. Louis, Missouri.[240] Constructed in 1967 by architects Murphy and Mackey in collaboration with Izenour, it can be used for any of the performing arts or converted into separate lecture halls and classrooms (Figures 224, 225).

Figure 224. Loretto Hilton Center, St. Louis, 1967: auditorium and stage. (By permission of George Izenour.)

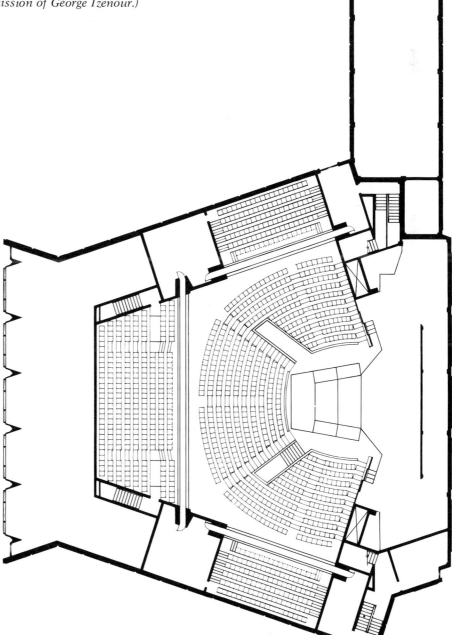

Figure 225. Loretto Hilton Center: plan. (By permission of George Izenour.)

The theater was conceived as a solution to the problem faced by a college that could not afford to build a number of special-purpose edifices but that was intensely interested in teaching and cultivating the fine arts. This interest inspired the architects and Izenour, with the cooperation of directors Tyrone Guthrie and Jo Mielziner, to create a building that can serve 21 different functions.[241]

Guthrie's contribution is apparent in the characteristic choice of the basic form of the auditorium, which bears a striking similarity to the Stratford and Minneapolis theaters. The open-stage arrangement differs only in the angle of inclination of the end walls behind the seating tiers. After the discussion of Jones Hall and Edwin Thomas Hall, in which we saw how a proscenium theater can be designed to serve multiple purposes, the Loretto Hilton Center provides us with an illustration of what can be done with a typical open-stage theater.

Surrounding the auditorium are three alcoves that can be cut off from the main space by a mechanical system of movable double partitions to form three independent lecture rooms. The partitions are soundproofed so that all the areas can be used simultaneously without acoustical interference (Figure 227). With the three alcoves excluded, the main auditorium has a 500-seat capacity (Figure 226a) and is suitable for dramatic performances or lectures. The same arrangement can be used for musical performances, in which case the front sections of the double partitions are slid open to expose polished plywood surfaces for maximum sound reflection.

With two of the alcoves excluded and the third joined to the main auditorium (Figure 226b), the seating capacity increases to 750, and the theater is suitable for musical comedy, drama, opera, and ballet. When all three alcoves are joined to the auditorium and additional seating installed on the rear stage, the house seats an audience of 1,200 (Figure 226c); with the open stage accommodating a full symphony orchestra, the theater becomes a concert hall.

These two examples are sufficient to convey a clear idea of the working of a multipurpose theater, a functionally simple form that, nevertheless, serves the theater and the community in multiple ways. There are many who support the view that once the people concerned with the

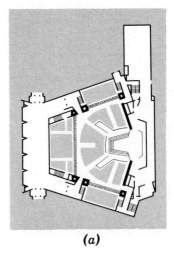

(a)

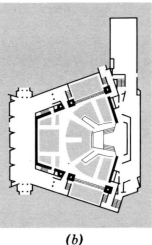

(b)

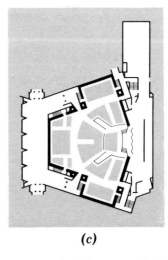

(c)

Figure 226. Loretto Hilton Center: variations of the auditorium. (a) Space arranged for drama, lectures, and music recitals, 500 seats; (b) space arranged for ballet, musical comedy, and opera, 750 seats; (c) space arranged for concerts, 1,200 seats. (By permission of George Izenour.)

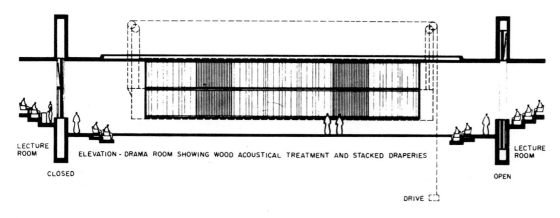

LECTURE
ROOM

ELEVATION - DRAMA ROOM SHOWING WOOD ACOUSTICAL TREATMENT AND STACKED DRAPERIES

LECTURE
ROOM

CLOSED

OPEN

DRIVE

Figure 227. Loretto Hilton Center: section, showing how the partitions of the alcoves move. (By permission of George Izenour.)

theater are convinced that this form is the only rational and financially feasible trend, the medium-sized city will have found the right solution to its theater problems. There are others who contest this view, claiming that multipurpose theaters affect the social structure of the community and deflect theater art from its very raison d'être. The truth lies midway between these two arguments. What we may take for granted is that, with the major technological advances that can reasonably be expected in the future, the multipurpose theater could well expand into another compound form, a form approaching Gropius' vision of "total theater."

On the other hand, there are utopian proposals, like those of Paolo Soleri (Figures 228, 229),[242] which come close to the notions produced by the fertile imagination of futurist Antonio Sant'Elia in the early years of our century.[243] Such proposals, produced by pure futuristic fantasy with little or no sense of rhythm and proportion, have never found an area in which they could be applied, and it is improbable that they ever will, particularly in an era when all traces of romanticism have vanished under the weight of technological pragmatism.

Figure 228. Paolo Soleri: proposal for a theater for the Institute of Indian Art, Santa Fe. (Credit: L'Architecture d'aujourd'hui, No. 152, 1970.)

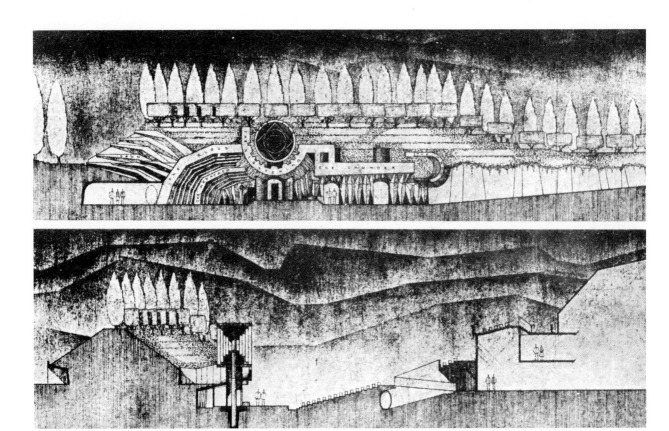

Figure 229. Soleri's theater: view and section. (Credit: L'Architecture d'aujourd'hui, *No. 152, 1970.)*

The Theater Center

If the multipurpose theater could be the future trend in the evolution of contemporary theater within the limited scope of a medium-sized city, the theater center is unquestionably the current trend in the major metropolis with its multiple theater needs.

Recognizing their citizens' constantly growing desire for cultural advancement and their eagerness for greater contact with the theater, most big cities in recent years have started giving such a center serious consideration, integrating it in the structure of their city plans and studying the costs of construction.

A theater, as a unit, is an important civic structural element in the urban pattern of a city or town, requiring due study and a careful approach to the problems involved: environment, traffic access, service facilities, parking, and all the other problems created when large numbers of people converge on one place. The experience gained from the existence of large and grandiose eighteenth- and nineteenth-century theaters in many modern big cities and the extremely difficult problems they cause have forced town planners to view the theater not as an independent unit but as a unity directly connected with the master plan of the city. Instead of spreading the problems by constructing four or five separate theaters in different places, it was considered wiser to concentrate them on a single site, where they would be easier to deal with and the linkup with other urban functions more effective. The result was the theater center. Erected either on a suitably arranged site inside the existing city plan or as part of planned regional expansion, the center contains several theaters, each with a different function, and provides facilities to serve the public and the theaters themselves. Depending on the intentions and preferences of their sponsors—the state or private foundations—and on local conditions and restrictions, the complexes built so far differ in size and name; they are variously known as cultural centers or music centers or centers of arts.

256

The basic pattern of such centers is a single site containing two or more theaters, drama schools or schools of music; workshops and service areas; parking lots; and other public facilities. Apart from the urban convenience of such a plan, the savings in construction and maintenance costs are considerable—concentration of facilities is always more economical than fragmentation and dispersion. Nevertheless, though consolidating the facilities may save money, a cultural center is a costly project that only affluent cities can afford.

A big proscenium theater, an opera house, is usually the dominant unit in a performing arts center. A drama theater and an experimental theater primarily for educational purposes generally complete the complex. This pattern, however, is by no means universal; it varies accord-ing to the needs of the city, the size of its population, its traditions, and its history. In Ottawa, for instance, the National Arts Center, built in 1969 by architects Affleck, Desbarats, Dimakopoulos, Lebensold, and Sise (Figure 230), is considered an eminently successful institution and an impressive achievement for a city with a population that does not exceed 300,000. Built in the heart of the city, the complex includes a 2300-seat opera house used also as a concert hall, a 900-seat drama theater convertible to proscenium or open stage, and a 300-seat experimental theater-workshop for pilot productions and avant-garde performances.[244] To round out the complex there are conference rooms, offices for the center's staff, and shops. An underground level provides parking space for 900 cars, a vital facility in a cultural center of any size.

Figure 230. National Arts Center, Ottawa. (Above) (a) *General view of the complex;* (on pages 258–260) (b) *master plan;* (c) *the opera house;* (d) *the drama theater;* (e) *the experimental studio. Architectural design by Affleck, Desbarats, Dimakopulos. (By permission of the National Arts Center, Ottawa, and courtesy of the Canadian Embassy in Athens.)*

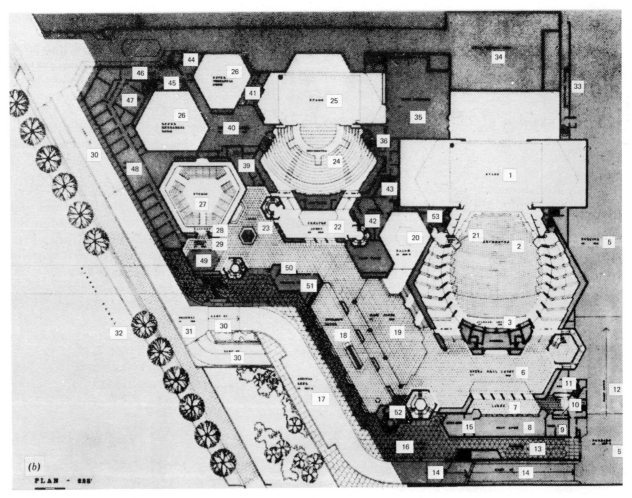

Figure 230b. Master plan.

1. Stage	19. Main foyer	36. Offices
2. Orchestra	20. Salon	37. Coat room
3. Standee area	21. Royal box	38. Controls
4. Control	22. Theater lobby	39. Rest rooms
5. Parking	23. Lobby	40. Repertory office
6. Opera hall lobby	24. Orchestra	41. Washrooms
7. Lobby	25. Stage	42. Lobby
8. Coat room	26. Upper rehearsal room	43. Servery
9. Rest room	27. Studio	44. Library
10. First aid	28. Balcony	45. Lobby
11. Store	29. Studio lobby	46. Reception
12. Ramp down	30. Ramp up	47. Conference
13. Passage	31. Roadway	48. Administrative offices
14. Ramp up	32. Rideau coanl	49. Open
15. Rest room	33. Pedestrian passage	50. General office
16. Loading area	34. Upper trucking area	51. Ticket office
17. Arrival area	35. Upper workshop	52. Lobby
18. Entrance foyer		53. Lobby

Figure 230c. The opera house.

Figure 230d. The drama theater.

(d)

Figure 230e. The experimental studio.

New York City, the great metropolis with its 10 million inhabitants, chose a project of impressive proportions and splendor, commensurate perhaps with the city's fame: the much talked about and also much criticized Lincoln Center for the Performing Arts, an example of mediocre neoclassicism and collaborative disharmony. Looking at the general view and master plan of the center (Figures 231, 232), we see the New York State Theater by architect Philip Johnson (Figure 233), a 2,729-seat house for ballet and every kind of musical comedy or operetta.[245] The heart and center of the complex is the famed Metropolitan Opera House (Figure 234), designed by architect Wallace Harrison, an overgrown building with a 4,000-seat auditorium, the product, possibly, of an attempt to create theatrical tradition, something America did not have before the twentieth century (Figure 235).

At the top right of Figure 232 is the beautiful Vivian Beaumont Theater (Figures 236, 237), Eero Saarinen's last masterpiece and the only independent, noncommercial drama theater in New York City. In the same building mass, and with due deference to Saarinen's personality, architects Skidmore, Owings, and Merrill (the SOM Group) have incorporated their own project, the Library and Museum of the Performing Arts.

Completing the design (Figure 232, bottom right) is the Avery Fisher Hall (Philharmonic Hall) (Figure 238) by architect Max Abramowitz, a theater built exclusively for concerts.

Lincoln Center took 10 years to build, from 1957 to 1967; in 1970 another building was added, which houses the Juilliard Schools of Music. Because there was no space left in the same block, it was built on the other side of the street and connected to the main complex by an overhead footbridge.

Figure 231. Lincoln Center for the Performing Arts, New York City: general view. (Courtesy of the American Embassy in Athens.)

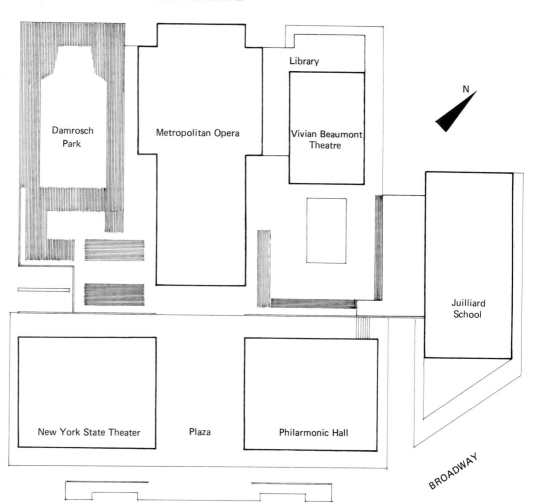

Figure 232. Lincoln Center, master plan. (Drawing by author.)

Figure 233. Lincoln Center: (above) main plaza with its
fountains and the New York State Theater in the background; (right) view from stage to audience of the
2,729-seat auditorium of the New York State Theater.
(Courtesy of the American Embassy in Athens.)

262

Figure 234. Metropolitan Opera House, Lincoln Center: view of the auditorium, with the golden curtain of the proscenium. (Courtesy of the American Embassy in Athens.)

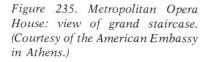

Figure 235. Metropolitan Opera House: view of grand staircase. (Courtesy of the American Embassy in Athens.)

Figure 236. Vivian Beaumont Theater, Lincoln Center: auditorium. (Courtesy of the American Embassy in Athens.)

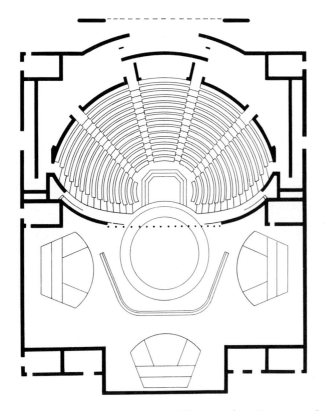

Figure 237. *Vivian Beaumont Theater: plan. (Courtesy of the American Embassy in Athens.)*

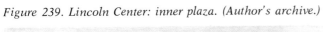

Figure 238. *Avery Fisher Hall, Lincoln Center. (Author's archive.)*

Figure 239. *Lincoln Center: inner plaza. (Author's archive.)*

Although I have tried in this work to avoid negative comment on the examples cited, I cannot avoid it in the case of Lincoln Center because it underscores a vital point: that in a project of such importance a spirit of concordance among the cooperating architects is absolutely essential.

When I mentioned earlier that the center is a typical example of "collaborative disharmony," I intended it as a reference to the working methods and relationships that prevailed among the architects of the three main theaters—namely the Metropolitan Opera House, the New York State Theater, and the Avery Fisher Hall—and to my own experience with the subject. Here was an opportunity, perhaps unique in history, for architects to cooperate in creating what could well have become one of the wonders of the world, yet they responded to the challenge in a spirit of narrow-minded self-interest. They chose, by their own admissions,[246] to compete against each other rather than to suppress their professional vanity in the interests of a composite unity. Each regarded his building as an independent project, a means of projecting his own personality and enhancing his own reputation rather than as part of an overall design. The result was a neoclassical composition glaringly out of step with the spirit of our times: three massively weighty and outsize buildings, each struggling to find its place and character around a nondescript fountain or two, a design suffering from elephantiasis, as Marcel Breuer once aptly described it.[247]

On first seeing the center, one is disturbed by its overt and pronounced disharmony. But as one advances within it, leaving the mammoth buildings behind, one discovers at the back of the site a different world, a world created by cooperative effort and the power of composition. That is the effect produced by the result of cooperation between the two groups assigned to design the Vivian Beaumont Theater and the library and museum.

Instead of competing for the starring role, the Saarinen Group and the SOM Group decided to work jointly toward a common goal and an integrated design. So successful was the outcome that this section of the complex, with its inner plaza and sculptures by Henry Moore, is an island of escape from the oppressive ambience of the main complex (Figure 239).

The overall failure, aggravated by a number of technical blunders such as the execrable acoustics of Avery Fisher Hall, which cost a huge sum of money to correct, made Lincoln Center the target of an avalanche of criticism. A characteristic comment and one that reflects a pertinent theory came from theater critic Robert Brustein:

Lincoln Center is what America produces instead of art . . . we ought to stop building culture centers until we have built a culture. . . . Good theatre, or good art of any kind, does not spring forth fully grown in a marble building before audiences who spill champagne over their black ties and diamond pendants during the intermission.[246]

The same spirit, with even unhappier results, pervades Edward Durell Stone's design for the John F. Kennedy Center in Washington, D.C., which opened in 1972. Any effort to create a harmonious composition was evidently considered superfluous (Figures 240, 241); the three theaters are aligned in a single massive building, where the tone is set by Italian marble, sumptuous chandeliers, and vast halls, producing an unbelievably monotonous environment.

Figure 240. John F. Kennedy Center. (Courtesy of the American Embassy in Athens.)

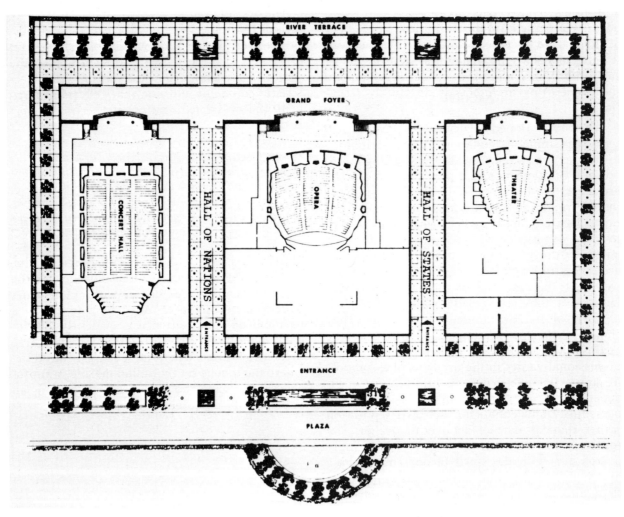

Figure 241. John F. Kennedy Center, Washington, D.C.: plan. (Author's archive.)

Figure 242. Los Angeles Music Center. (Courtesy of Welton Becket and Associates; author's archive.)

An incomparably better composite effect is achieved by Welton Becket's Music Center in Los Angeles (Figure 242), where the three different theaters form an architecturally integrated whole. The complex blends successfully with its urban environment and is efficiently linked to the surrounding traffic arteries, thanks largely to its very well-designed four-level parking garage (Figure 243), which holds 2,000 cars and can be vacated in a few minutes.

Figure 243. Los Angeles Music Center: (a) general section; (b) plan. (Courtesy of Welton Becket and Associates; author's archive.)

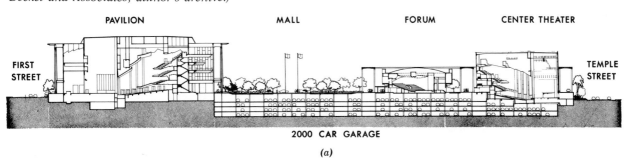

(a)

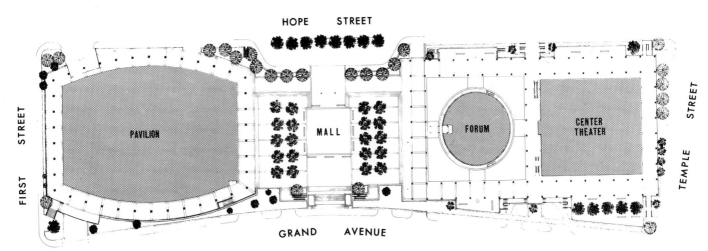

(b)

The center is made up of the Pavilion (Figure 244), a 3,250-seat theater for opera and concerts; the 750-seat Mark Taper Forum, discussed in Chapter 13 (Figures 160, 161); and the 2,100-seat Ahmanson Theater (Figure 245), which is designed mainly for musical comedy and operetta but can also be used for drama, ballet, light opera, or any other musical event that does not require the elaborate facilities of the Pavilion.

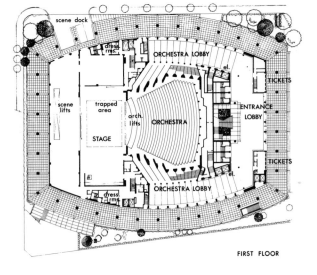

FIRST FLOOR

Figure 244. Los Angeles Music Center Pavilion: plan. (Courtesy of Welton Becket and Associates; author's archive.)

Figure 245. Ahmanson Theater, Los Angeles Music center: plan. (Courtesy of Welton Becket and Associates; author's archive.)

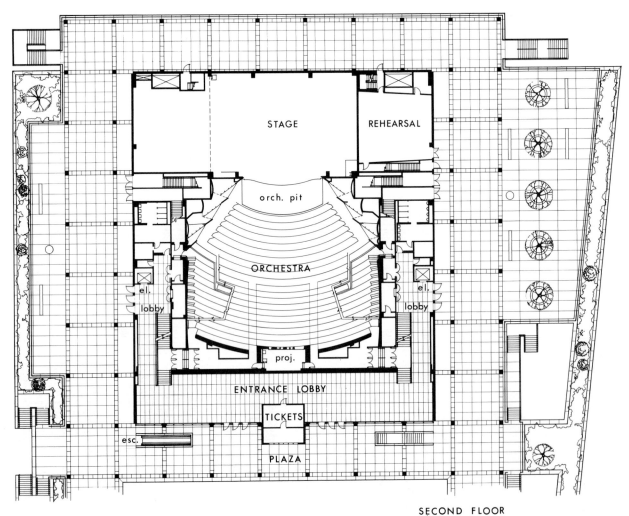

SECOND FLOOR

In contrast to the United States, Europe, perhaps for reasons of tradition, has not gone in for the overgrown complex. It has opted for simple and compact designs on a human scale, which are effortlessly incorporated into the urban surround. It is not elephantiasis one encounters in the theater centers of Europe but the purely functional, the product of culture and tradition. One can see that nearly all European complexes have been designed and built to serve the spirit and not as commercial establishments; that is why none of the theaters in these centers exceeds a capacity of 1,000 or at most 1,200 seats. The smallness of these theaters seems to be a determinative indicator of the difference between America and Europe in the area of general theater policy. In the United States, land of private business enterprise, with a nouveau-riche tendency toward ostentation, the life of a theater center is entirely dependent on box-office receipts and on the number of spectator-consumers. In Europe, by contrast, a deep-seated theater tradition and different standards of cultural learning, combined with sponsorship by the state, determine the planning and operation of its centers. The seats in a theater must not exceed a number consonant with the proper performance of its function, determined by the human scale. Whether a theater operates profitably or at a loss is not important; what matters is that it is there, in the town, along with the church and the school, all of them considered indispensable in forming the character and cultural background of the citizen.

A case in point is the National Theatre in London (Figures 246–249), designed by architect Denys Lasdun and built in 1971 on the bank of the Thames. It comprises the Olivier Theatre, a 1,165-seat fan-shaped auditorium (Figure 248), used principally for drama; the Lyttleton Theatre, a 900-seat traditional proscenium theater (Figure 249); and the Cottesloe, a 200- to 400-seat experimental theater, that indispensable component of every modern center.[248] What is distinctive about the London complex and a point worth noting is that the drama has been restored to a leading role. Whereas in the United States and even in Germany the main theater in a center of this kind would be the opera house, in England the spoken word has been reinstated. Thus in the Olivier Theatre, modeled on the corner stage taught by Norman Bel Geddes in 1914 (Figure 148) and developed by Frank Lloyd Wright at the Kalita Humphrey Theater in 1960 (Figure 153), the ancient word and the words of Shakespeare and modern drama reign once more.

However, the auditorium is rather too deep for a drama theatre. With its total of 21 rows of seats—15 in the main auditorium and six in the balcony—it fails to keep the audience in close proximity to the stage and the actors, thus falling short of the desired functional requirement of drama for a close actor–spectator relationship. Perhaps this is why the Olivier has been having functional problems from the very beginning.

Figure 246. National Theater, London. (Photo by author.)

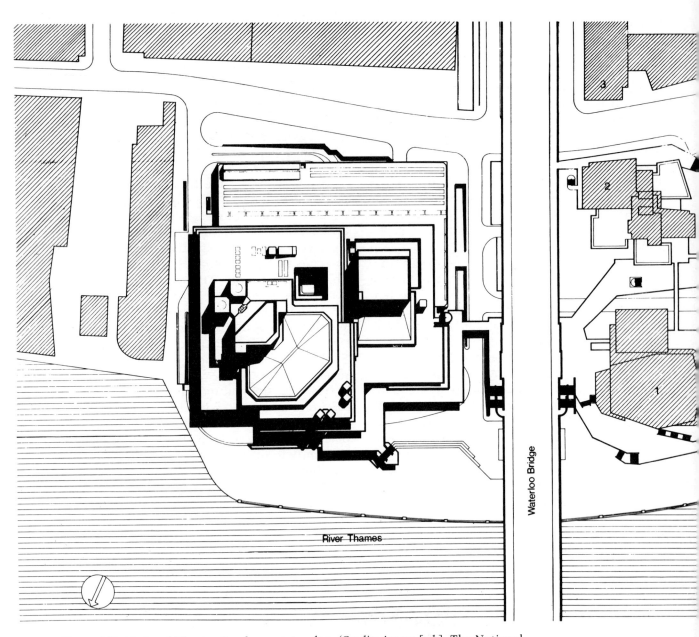

Figure 247. National Theatre, London: master plan. (Credit: Amery [ed.], The National Theatre, p. 17.)

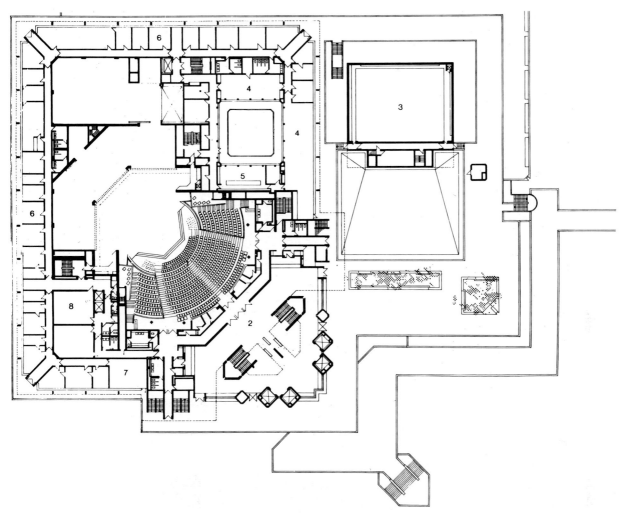

Figure 248. National Theatre, London: plan at the level of the Olivier Theatre. (Credit: Amery [ed.], The National Theatre, p. 20.)

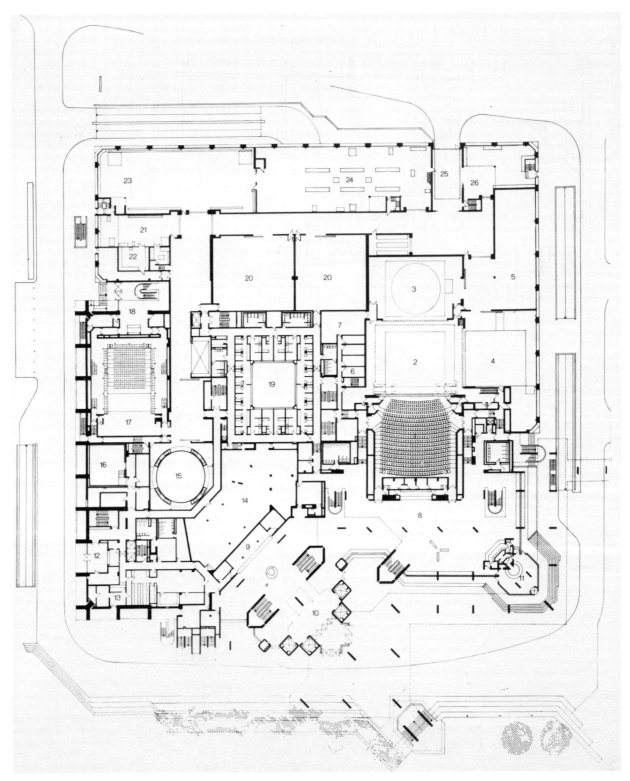

Figure 249. National Theatre, London: plan of the Lyttleton Theatre (1); plan of the Cottesloe Theater (17). (Credit: Amery [ed.], The National Theatre, p. 18.)

272

Also intended for drama is the Lyttleton Theatre, but it can be used for other performances as well. Its stage facilities allow the presentation of opera, operetta, or spectacular musical comedy. Last, the Cottesloe reflects everything that could be desired by a director in search of new techniques; it is designed to be a workshop for the future and can convert easily to any theater form.

In Germany one can see another example of a theater center that has shed all superfluous tradditional features and adopted revolutionary designs both in the pattern of its building masses (Figure 250*a*) and in the arrangement of its interiors (Figure 250*b–d*). Entirely modern, the Theatre Center in Düsseldorf (1969), designed by architect Bernhard Pfau, should, in my opinion, serve all architects as the answer to the problem of using modern techniques to create new architectural forms unfettered by conventional established prototypes. This can be distinctly felt when one is inside the unusual auditorium (Figure 250*b*) or the beautiful and spacious foyer that reflects the structure of the auditorium (Figure 250*d*) or when one contemplates the easy graceful curves of the exteriors.

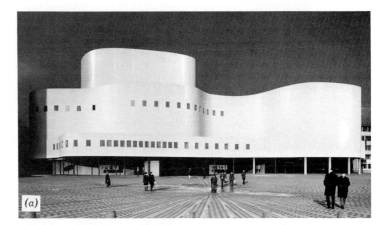

Figure 250. Düsseldorf theater center: (right) (a) *southern view from the main plaza;* (below) (b) *auditorium of the main house;* (on succeeding pages) (c) *experimental theater;* (d) *foyer of the center. (By permission and courtesy of Bernhard Pfau, the architect.)*

Figure 250c. Experimental theater.

Figure 250d. Foyer of the center.

274

Not surprisingly, the main theater, conforming to German tradition, is fully equipped for the production of opera or any other big spectacle, but its basic purpose is to present drama, which is why its capacity has been limited to 1,000 seats. Closely linked to it is an experimental theater (Figure 251) in arena form, seating approximately 300; its integration into the overall design of the center not only kept construction costs low but makes it economical to operate.

The Düsseldorf center bears out my comments concerning the situation in the United States: the stage has been given greater weight than the auditorium, reiterating the principle adopted by Max Littmann when he created the Prinz Regent Theater in Munich (Figure 102) with its great stage area. If one compares the 4,000-seat Metropolitan Opera House with the Düsseldorf theater, one is struck by the different emphasis in the stage–auditorium relation; although the German theater has only one-fourth the capacity of the Metropolitan, its stage and stage-service facilities have roughly the same area and volume.

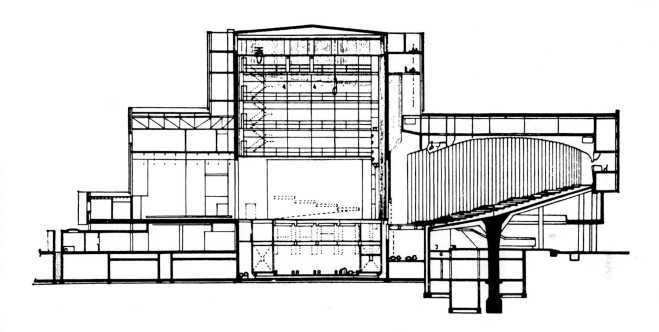

Figure 251. Düsseldorf theater center: (above) *section;* (right) *plan. (By permission and courtesy of Bernhard Pfau, the architect.)*

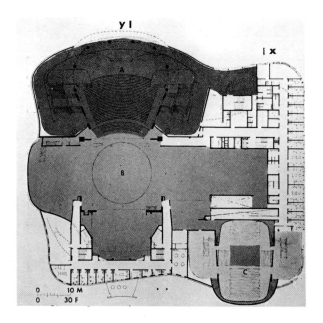

The Düsseldorf complex, along with the Ulm and Mannheim theater centers, are the outstanding examples and I think the ones most indicative of the future evolution of the theater in a country with such a rich theatrical past and such a strong current drive to build more and more theaters.

In Greece, to depart for a moment from the beaten path, the old National Theater in Athens is currently being expanded into a theater center for drama; its goal is to provide its artists with every opportunity for experimentation in new techniques of drama production, interpretation, and expression. The solution adopted (Figures 252–257) is an attempt by the architect of the project (who happens to be the author of this book) to give the new theater and the whole complex adaptability, flexibility, and independence, without ignoring the human scale. To ac-

complish that result, it was necessary to make use, in comparative measure of course, of all the information and experience available today, avoiding the mistakes of the past, mistakes that are apparent in many modern theaters in other parts of the world. In this the architect has had the valuable help of George Izenour, who, as consultant for the acoustics and stage technology, made the proposals practicable.

The complex will include, directly adjacent to the old traditional nineteenth-century Italian-stage theater built by German architect Ernst Ziller, an open-stage theater readily adaptable to the modern requirements of dramatic expression and a small experimental theater for use by the National Theater's School of Drama. Thus this expansion project, when completed, will provide all the requisites—the material requisites at least—for a complex that will be self-sufficient in

Figure 252. National Theater, Athens, 1979: (below) *master plan in model;* (opposite page) *general view in model. (Author's archive.)*

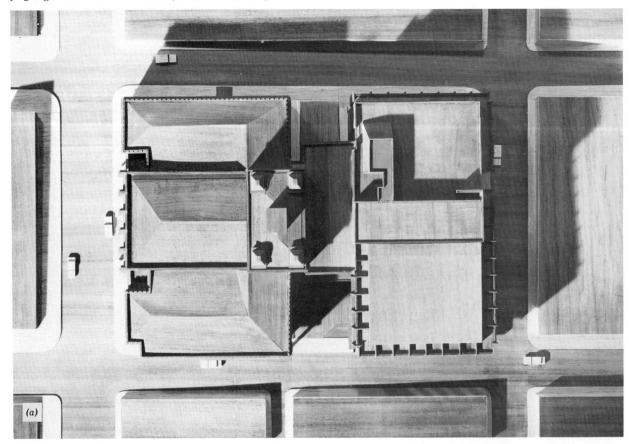

(a)

(b)

operation, both as a building and as a theatrical institution. It will contain the classic proscenium theater, a flexible and easily adaptable new stage, and a small experimental studio; it will also have an organized assortment of workshop and technical facilities and equipment that will enable the actors and students to make their own costumes and wigs, for instance, or to create the layouts they think best and to see and comment critically on one another's work.

The floor of the new theater's apron-orchestra-stage (Figure 253), consists of a modular system of movable platforms, simple and speedy to operate, which is the basic means of achieving adaptability and flexibility. With appropriate arrangement of these platforms, the interior can be converted to one of the three contemporary theater forms or any other variation required by the performance (Figure 255). Its physical flexibility is thus assured to a greater degree than in many modern theaters of this type; with a little help from the people working in it, it could well operate as a true space theater.

Izenour's determinative influence is clearly apparent in the designs and models of the final proposals by the architect and the consultant, whose threefold aim was functional operation, efficient organization of space, and rational use of technology.

The stage technology has no dazzling or far-fetched features. The floor of the orchestra and stage consists of a modular system of 12 movable traps; each module is 1.20×3.00 ($4M \times 10M$, $M = 0.30$), mechanically operated to move vertically from the level of the stages (+0.50) to the operating technical level below the orchestra (−2.75). Each section moves independently and can stop at any position along its travel (Figure 256a).

Because of the modular design, the acting area can be converted and adapted to satisfy operations in three different modes. All of these are subject to further modification by means of a submodular system that is a geometric function of the modular system. With the help of the three-dimensional elements of the submodular system, the geometry of the orchestra can easily change (Figure 256b), and the space can be quickly and smoothly converted from open-stage to proscenium theater.

A large trap-platform covering the rear half of the stage has two basic functions. One is to serve as the principal mechanical means of vertical communication between the stages and the workshops on the lower level. The other is to carry the movable elements that form the seat-banks, by means of which the space is converted to theater-in-the-round.

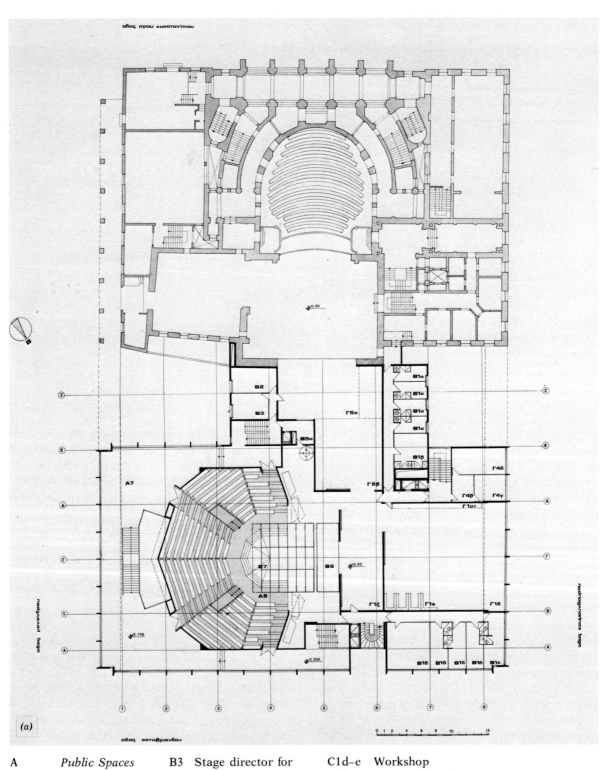

(a)

A	*Public Spaces*	B3	Stage director for	C1d–e	Workshop
A7	Foyer		new stage	C1f	Trap
A8	Auditorium	B5	Stage equipment	C1g	Scenery store
B	*Performance*	B6	Stage with trap-	C4b–d	Production offices
	Spaces		platform	C5	Old stage's sets
B1	Performers' ac-	B7	Apron stage (or-	C5a	Back stage
	commodations		chestra)	C5b	Scenery store
B1a–1e	Dressing rooms	C	*Production Spaces*		
B2	Stage director	C1	New stage's sets		
	for old stage				

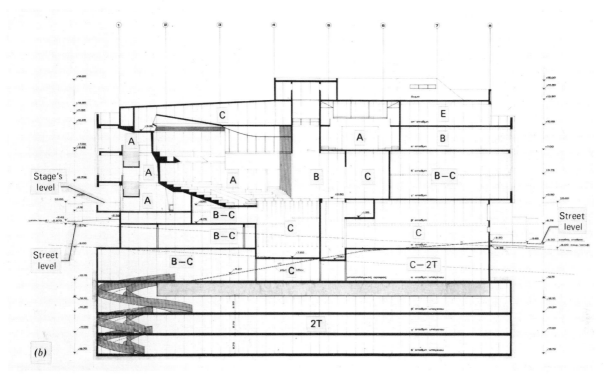

A   Public spaces
B   Performance spaces
C   Production spaces
D   Drama school
E   Administration
2T   Garage

Figure 253. National Theater, Athens, extension to a theater center: (a) *plan at level* c, *auditorium and foyer (+0, 50);* (b) *longitudinal section. (Author's archive.)*

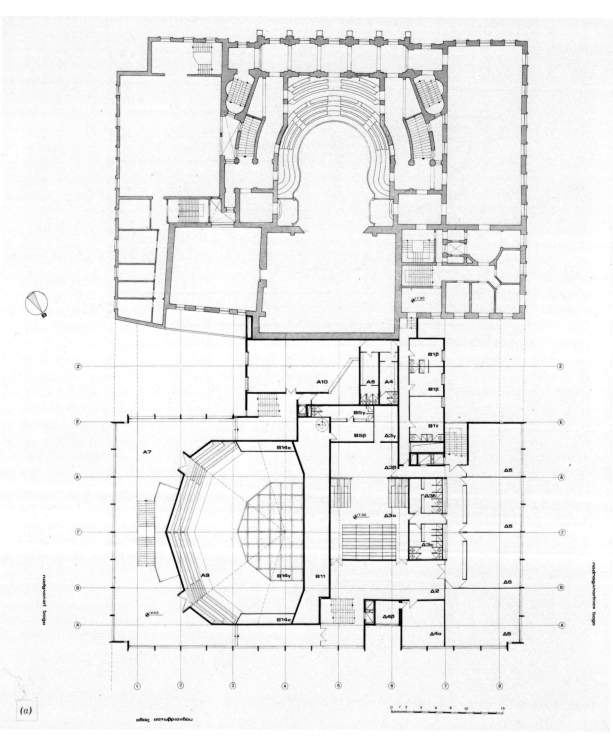

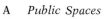

A	*Public Spaces*	B	*Performance Spaces*	D	*Drama School*
A4	Lavatories for men			D2	Foyer
A5	Lavatories for women	B1	Performance accommodation	D3	Experimental studio
A7	Foyer			D4	Library
A9	Balcony	B1b–g	Dressing rooms	D5	Classrooms
		B5	Stage equipment		
		B11	Fly tower		
		B14	Lighting for orchestra		

280

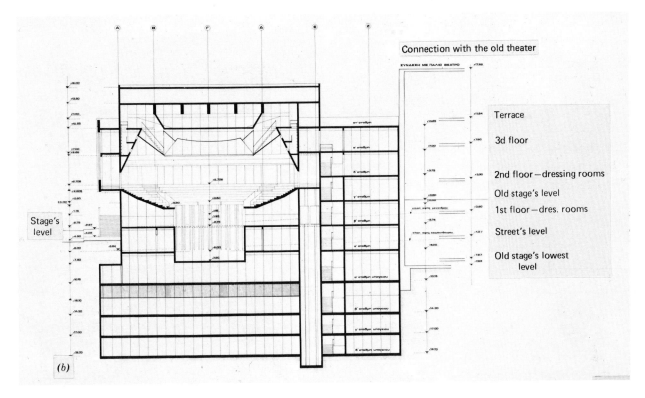

Terrace

3d floor

2nd floor—dressing rooms

Old stage's level

1st floor—dres. rooms

Street's level

Old stage's lowest
level

Stage's
level

(b)

A   Public spaces
B   Performance spaces
C   Production spaces
D   Drama school
E   Administration
ET Garage

Figure 254. National Theater, Athens, extension to a theater center: (a) *plan at level* e,
balcony and studio (+7,00); (b) *longitudinal section. (Author's archive.)*

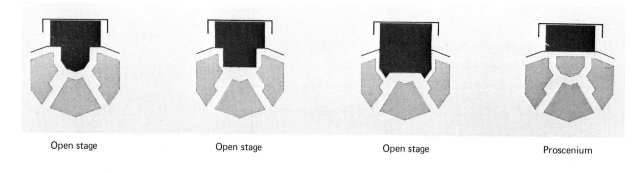

Open stage   Open stage   Open stage   Proscenium

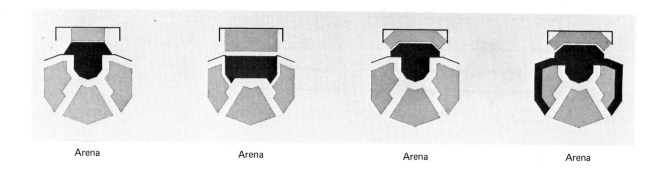

Arena   Arena   Arena   Arena

Variations of the new stage or (adaptability and flexibility)

Figure 255. National Theater, Athens: variations of the new auditorium. (Author's archive.)

An auxiliary level (−1.95) serves as storage space for the elements when they are not in use. The arena and the open stage can be arranged in four and three alternative layouts, respectively (Figures 255, 257c).

The limited area of the site necessitated a vertical development of functions. It is self-evident that vertical development, as opposed to any horizontal arrangement, poses serious problems, mainly in the shifting of heavy properties or settings. In the new Greek National Theater many of these problems are overcome by using the platform as a lift for vertical transportation.

The drama school is organized to operate in accordance with international standards. Its main spaces are developed at the same level as the balcony of the new theater (Figure 254). For the sake of autonomy of operation, it has a separate and independent entrance. The most distinctive feature of the school premises is its small studio, which, in combination with the ballroom, operates as a true experimental theater, seating 120 to 150 spectators. Conversion of its space will be accomplished with the help of a simple system of portable 0.90 × 1.80 modular elements fitting into the basic module of the design ($M = 0.30$, $3M = 1.20$), the ballroom that converts to a stage, and the lighting system.

Production and performance spaces are so organized as to provide the complex with all the service areas needed for self-sufficient operation: an institution able to produce on its own everything the performance needs, from the settings to the actors themselves.

Figure 256. National Theater, Athens: flexibility of orchestra and stage. (Above) *Model of the orchestra modular system; (below) some of the variations possible in the geometry of the orchestra. (Archives of the author and George Izenour.)*

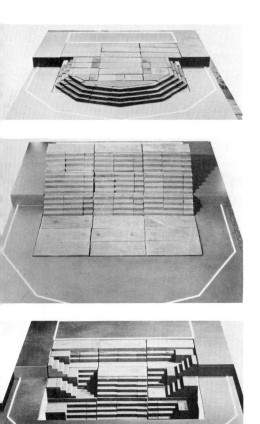
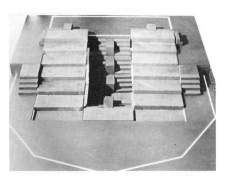
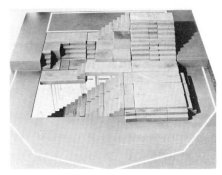
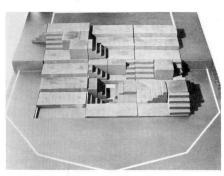
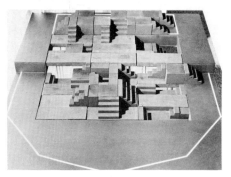

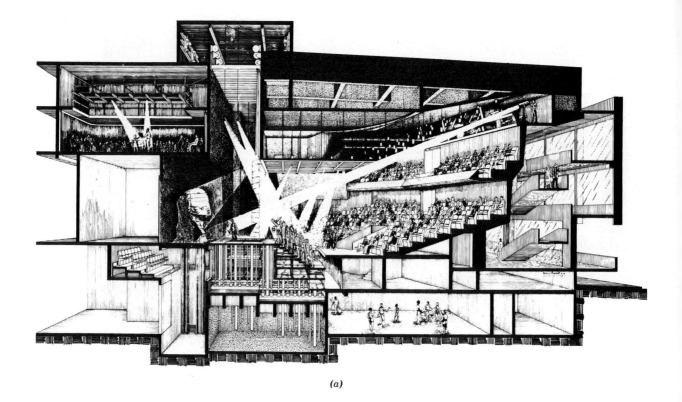

(a)

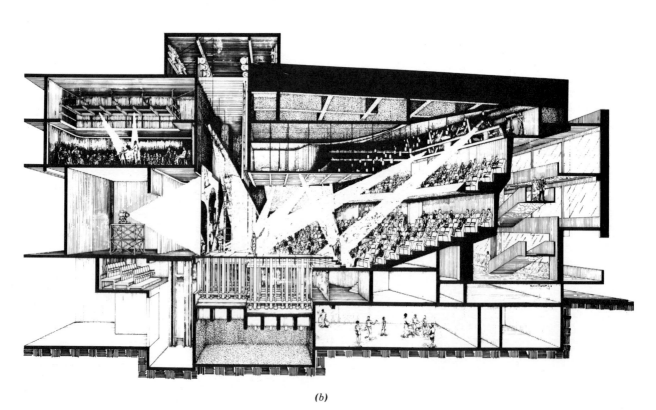

(b)

Figure 257. National Theater, Athens: longitudinal sections. (Above) (a) Open-stage theater form; (b) open stage with projection integration; (opposite page) (c) proscenium theater form; (d) arena theater form. (Archives of the author and George Izenour.)

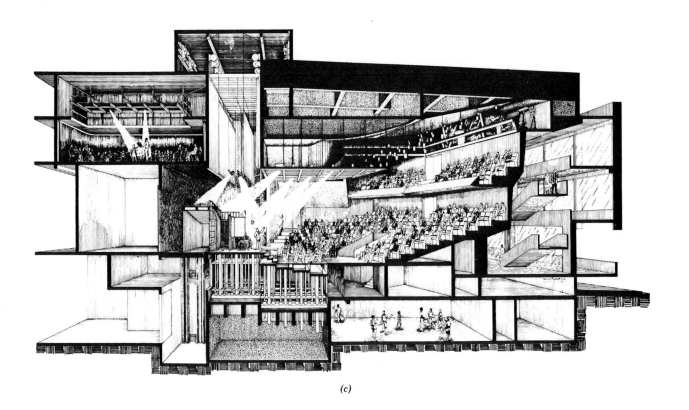

(c)

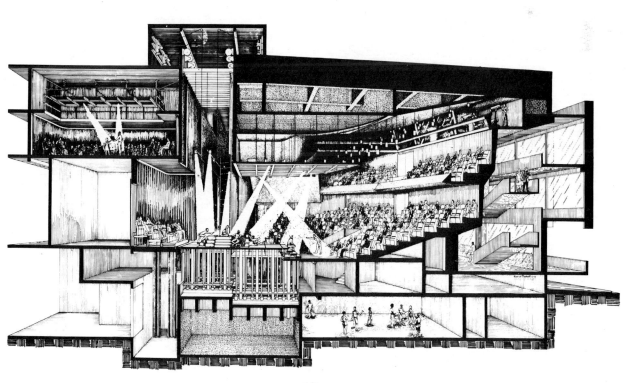

(d)

285

Switzerland, finally, is the home of a notable example of modern architecture, based, as at Düsseldorf, on the removal of all superfluities and the application of geometrical forms uninfluenced by convention. As in Ottawa and Ulm, the theater center in St. Gall (Figures 258–261) has abolished the right angle and adopted the hexagonal grid, resulting in a new sense of space and a new functional concept.

Standing in the middle of the city's park, the center serves all the performing arts and, since its opening in 1968, has become the city's salient point of interest and the pride of its community.

Designed by architects Claude Paillard and Hansjörg Gugler, it consists of a small (771 seats) main theater, an experimental playhouse, and a little outdoor theater, harmoniously integrated in the overall design. However, probably because of the climate, the outdoor theater has remained unused (Figure 261). The stage of the main theater, basically a proscenium form, has a fairly large forestage that can be lowered to the level of the auditorium floor, thereby increasing its capacity to 855 seats. Both arrangements favor drama, but the stage has ample facilities for the production of opera whenever desired.

Figure 258. Municipal Theater Center, St. Gall, Switzerland. (Photo by author).

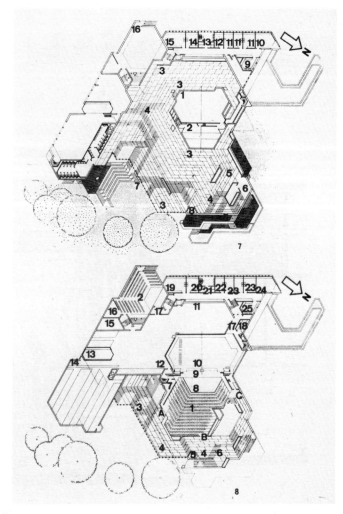

Figure 259. Municipal Theater Center, St. Gall: ground floor plan, upper floor plan. (Courtesy of the city of St. Gall.)

Figure 260. Municipal Theater Center, St. Gall: auditorium of the main house. (Courtesy of the city of St. Gall.)

Figure 261. St. Gall: abandoned outdoor theater. (Photos by author.)

As in the Düsseldorf center, the experimental stage is directly and efficiently linked to the stage of the main theater, while the outdoor theater is a unifying element that integrates the composition of the center's free spaces.

This small provincial town's successful answer to the problem of providing a home for the theatrical spirit at moderate cost should cause the skeptics, for whom the theater is an expensive luxury of doubtful value, to pause and reflect; it should cause those in countries and cities where the theatrical spirit has been neglected and shelved to have second thoughts, for it

broadcasts the heartening message that everything is possible given the will, the proper planning, and the inspired creator. There is no point in aspiring to magnificence or waiting to accumulate huge sums of money for behemoths of dubious architectural merit like Lincoln Center or the Opera Center in Sidney[249] (Figures 262, 263). Cities that aspire to such ostentation are cities without tradition or cultural background, capitals attempting to cloak a sad lack of spirituality and character behind a facade of pretentious splendor.

Figure 262. Opera Center, Sidney, 1973: general view. (Courtesy of the Australian Embassy in Athens; author's archive.)

Figure 263. Opera Center, Sidney: plan of first level. (Courtesy of the Australian Embassy in Athens; author's archive.)

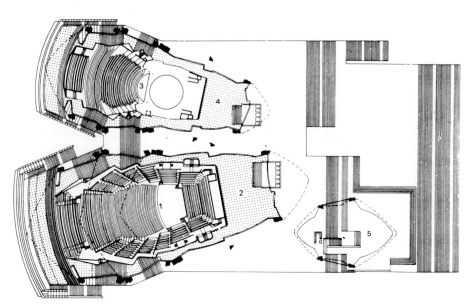

18
The Space Theater
of Our Era

The Established Space

The Italian Renaissance, with its culture, with the rules it imposed, the tradition it created, and the style it bequeathed to future generations, had a twofold effect on the evolution of the theater. In the first place, it resuscitated an art form that had lain dormant for a thousand years, breathed life into it, and gave it vitality, color, and dimension. It also endowed that form with a physical frame, a space that was static and fixed, that steered architecture and the theatrical function in a direction offering very little latitude for development of the building form and mode of expression.

The architectural form assumed a standard pattern. The building, imposing, solid, and stately, enclosed a cubic space with one of its six sides opening to reveal a picture—a picture one had no alternative but to view in two of its dimensions: height and width.

The theatrical function was separated into two parts: one was the picture, consisting of the stage and the actor on it; the second was the cube containing the audience. That was the basic requisite: actor and audience facing and looking at each other, judging and being judged, each in his own assigned space. Any notion of interlinking the two spaces was, for four centuries, inconceivable.

What counted above all was the visual effect, the illusion of the stage picture, the magic of a mysterious lighted space facing the audience. This happened because the scenography—which now we can safely call classical—used a purely geometrical approach, the premises of which could not be tailored to the natural human stature. For one thing, its basis was Renaissance art, which, in its pursuit of objective visual reproduction, applied to painting what Pierre Francastel has described as "a realistic system of perspective representation drawn from the mathematics of Euclid and from careful observation of the ruins of antiquity."[250] This notion, with the help of Serlio and his disciples, was transferred chapter and verse to the theater.

This, in my opinion, was the point where error and misconstruction of the rules of perspective crept in, error that started the renascent theater off on the wrong foot; the perspective of a painting or by extension a photograph is by no means the same as natural perspective, the perspective effect perceived by a person moving in three-dimensional space. An object in space always has a form; this "form," according to Panagiotis Ladopoulos, is a three-dimensional figure; therefore, it has a "geometrical structure" and, to the observer, "perspective aspects." Professor Ladopoulos adds: "To perceive the structure of the memorized image of an object it is not enough to see it from one angle only; one must see it from all its aspects. The sum of those aspects form a succession of geometric transmutations which I call perspective."[251]

This view, of course, is at variance with the Renaissance notion of theater and axial perspective scenography as put forth by Serlio, who advocated viewing the stage from one and only one position, and it shows how wrong was the premise on which the notion originated. This view is confirmed and elucidated by Jacques Polieri's analysis of the fallacy of "Italian perspective":

In "Italian perspective" the picture is the cross-section of a plane perpendicular to the optical cone created by the spectator's eye and the radii connecting it with all points of the stage area. This principle, however, is based on an erroneous assumption: the assumption of a single motionless eye. The visual field of our one eye covers a sector of approximately 150 degrees, inside which we see every object projected on a single plane.

When we use both eyes, however, we cover a 200-degree visual field which allows us to see objects situated to the left and right and even a little behind us; moreover, when our eyes move they explore the visible space "spherically."

These concepts are all incompatible with the notions of the Renaissance theorists.[252]

To insist, therefore, on the Renaissance notion of space—on photographic, realistic representation—is to accept that there is only one kind of vision, "the vision of a Cyclops, not of a human being," as Francastel aptly puts it.[253]

Nonetheless, these notions were accepted as correct both by the people of the theater and by the public for hundreds of years. Illusion, optical effect, cyclopean vision became a habit that endured, that still endures and will die hard—preserved by tradition, by the conservative spirit of a section of contemporary society, by the stagnating, nonevolving commercial theater.

Theater, however, was born of the union and communion of two elements, the spectator and the actor.

The close association of those elements made it into an art, the most social of all arts but an eclectic one that chooses from the others what it wants.

It selects from literature, architecture, painting, sculpture, and dance the ingredients it needs and combines them to produce a new creation.

There have been times in its centuries-long history when one or another of the arts fell into decline, but the theater never ceased to live. It survived without the word, without its architectural frame, without color or movement. But it never stopped evolving, not even in the Middle Ages, because at all times and in all places there was that preexistent relation between actor and spectator and the need for communication between them.

Communication was greatly reduced by the notion of placing the two primary elements in separate, facing spaces. It was reduced and kept down for a long time, but it never wholly disappeared, because the actor and the spectator both felt that there must be something else, something stronger and more exciting to the relationship between them, something more than an audience just watching and listening.

Inevitably, after the centuries-long interval there came a time when the search started anew—the search for communication, participation, identification. It came about when the human spirit finally emerged from the inanition that accompanies ignorance and acquired the keenness, thinking power, and intellectual curiosity produced by education.

We have seen how in the early years of this century actors tried to move out of their appointed area but were frustrated by the spatial arrangement of the traditional theater. The same frustration was felt by the director, whose creative scope was cramped by the two-dimensional stage, and the architect, who now realized that the use of the third dimension was a solution that would provide the theater with a broader field of development. The efforts of the Bauhaus, Gropius' total theater, Weininger's spherical theater, and Schlemmer's theories of space all reflected this conviction. Although these proposals never materialized, they nonetheless provided the stimulus that led to the development of

the contemporary theater forms, the forms that discarded the spatial arrangement institutionalized by tradition and that brought the actor in touch with the audience once more.

The concept of the third dimension had a significant effect on everybody concerned with the theater. The space theater in its open-stage and arena forms propagated the merits of movement and the sculptured human figure so convincingly that this was accepted as the line along which theatre architecture must develop. The Bauhaus ideas, faithfully reflected by Molnár's U-theater, were carefully and consistently studied, leading to the creation of the forms discussed thus far, which reunited the theater's two basic component elements and restored it to its natural environment: space.

Molnár's U-Theater

It is essential at this point to take a look at a proposal made by Farkas Molnár, as a Bauhaus student, for a true space theater in which the actor becomes a moving element in space and the action is visible from every point in that space (Figure 264). The ideas incorporated in his

Figure 264. Farkas Molnár's U-theater in operation. (From Gropius and Schlemmer, Theater of the Bauhaus, *p. 72. By permission of Mrs. Walter Gropius.)*

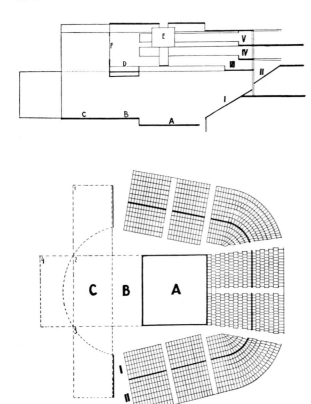

A. First stage
B. Second stage
C. Third stage
D. Fourth stage
E. Elevator and
    lighting ap-
    paratus
F. Mechanical,
    sound, lighting
    effects
G. Suspended
    bridge, stage
    machinery, cat-
    walks

I, II. Two U-shaped
        rings built in the
        form of the am-
        phitheater
III.   A single balcony
        connected with
        the suspended
        stage (D) (150
        persons)
IV, V. Two rows of
        loges: total 240
        seats; the divid-
        ing walls are
        movable or can
        be variously rear-
        ranged

Figure 265. U-theater: section and plan. (From Gropius and Schlemmer, Theater of the Bauhaus, *p. 75. By permission of Mrs. Walter Gropius.)*

proposal have since been used repeatedly by architects and have helped the theater acquire its contemporary forms as we see them today.

The distinctive features of the U-theater are its five different stages and the layout of its auditorium (Figure 265), which is a standard assumption today for certain theater forms but in 1924 was a revolution against every established feature.[254]

The first stage (*A* in Figure 265), 11 × 11 meters, can be raised or lowered whole or in sections. In space this stage gives prominence to human movement in dance, acrobatic, or vaudeville performances. The action can be viewed from three sides if desired. The audience seating surrounds the action area in a 270 degree arc, steeply amphitheatrical for better visibility. This form of layout was used years later in the open-stage theaters in Stratford, Ontario, and Minneapolis.

The second stage (*B*) is a platform level with the front row of audience seats. It can be moved both vertically and horizontally (backward and forward) and is used for three-dimensional stag-

ing. Scenery can be set up, unseen by the audience, behind a curtain and then carried into the action area by means of this movable platform.

The third stage (*C*) is in classic German proscenium form, surrounded on three sides by supplementary areas, with its back-scene in the form of an arc. The combined use of all three stages provides true communication between actors and audience. What enhances this communication still further are the other two stages: the fourth (*D*), a cantilever platform directly over the second stage and joined to the first balcony, and the fifth (*E*), a cylindrical structure in the center of the ceiling that can move in any direction. The cylinder, used for lowering persons or objects to the action area, has two platforms at its base, which serve as bridges linking it with the two balconies.

How the different stages connect with one another and with the auditorium can be seen in the isometric plan (Figure 266). The plan also shows the layout of the house where two U-shaped banks of seating tiers (I and II in Figure 265)

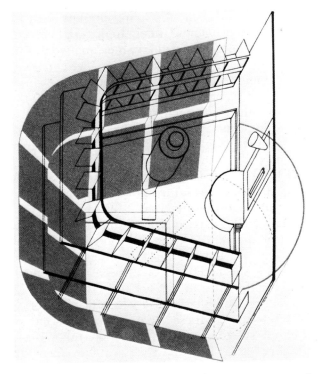

Figure 266. U-theater: isometric. (From Gropius and Schlemmer, Theater of the Bauhaus, *p. 77. By permission of Mrs. Walter Gropius.)*

determine the form of the auditorium. Adjustable and revolving audience seats allow comfortable and unobstructed viewing of any form and kind of performance, from any point. The first balcony (III) is level with the fourth stage; by means of projecting platforms it can be used in a performance in combination with the movable, fifth ceiling-mounted stage (Figure 264). That Molnár could not entirely escape from the established usages of his time is shown by the two tiers of boxes (IV and V), an alien and jarring element in this revolutionary and original design.

Contemplating the examples discussed here (and the many others in various countries that have the exclusive aim of solving the problem of space and establishing contemporary theater forms), one can assert that very few of the things Molnár proposed more than 50 years ago have changed. It is in fact easy to see that his U-theater is still way ahead of us and his theories as revolutionary as ever.

Trends of Our Time

The various examples of contemporary theaters cited so far may be regarded as those most characteristic of the trends of our time in the development of the theater form. In the course of my research, I concluded that the search for a true space theater, such as those proposed by Gropius, Molnár, and Weininger, is today of less than consuming interest to the researcher and, of course, to the financial sponsor. The theater in our era lacks the ardent support it enjoyed in the past, the eager followers whose fruitful efforts, particularly in the 1920s and 1950s, revitalized the traditional form and discovered new configurations and arrangements.

In most countries today, notably those that contributed most to the theater's development, the theater is subject to strong financial and social pressures, which are anything but an incitement to research and experimentation. The developments of the past decade are conclusive evidence that the organized groups are following trends oriented primarily toward the predominant form of the traditional proscenium, with research and exploration left to the small studio theaters. This, as we have seen, is true of the major complexes in the United States, with their mammoth multimillion-dollar theaters for audiences of thousands. If there had indeed been any disposition to create a theater along the lines proposed by Gropius or Molnár, the funds were abundantly available and so was the technology. But the financial pressures work against such experiments. Experimentation and exploration are confined to the limited domain of the experimental theater, the studio, which was affixed to the big theaters and theater centers as a functional complement—an adjunct like the workshops and other backstage facilities—and not as a primary theater with the self-sufficiency to be a source of revenue for its operator. It does not even rate the name of "theater"; it is mostly known as "studio" or "workshop," as in Ulm or at the Young Vic and the Cottesloe in London.

The erroneous notion that the theater is entertainment rather than education and edification led to its division into civic theater and art theater. The first has moved slowly but surely to the stagnant state that characterized the theaters of the eighteenth and nineteenth centuries. Technological facilities may meanwhile have changed and the settings may have grown more sophisticated and splendid, but the substance is the same, and so is the mental approach. The problem of unity in space has not affected the civic theater, where other things are more important, such as entertainment, socializing, fashion, and glamor.

The experimental art theater had to go where it was really needed, where there were individuals of restless spirit and active mind. It is found on university campuses where a strong desire for learning and exploration prevails, in drama schools and little theater companies where every theatrical expression, from Chekhov's to Albee's, is studied down to its smallest detail.

We find it, too, in the new expressive forms of political or militant theater, as a function directly related to the time and place where it is happening. This function has been variously called documentary theater, living theater, happening, cafe-theater, and fringe theater. It moved out of its traditional home, the playhouse, to real-life settings: the school, the factory, the vacant lot, the street, the square. Its

time is the present, the living present with its immediate problems, timely topics, and current issues of concern to ordinary men and women. It is contemporary political theater—we can see it developing today in many countries—whose message is generally impossible to express in the classic and traditional space of a theater; it is more appropriate in a natural social environment, reverting to medieval and renaissance forms such as the booth stage and the stand at the local fair. It is theater that aspires to create and stimulate a mature political awareness of current issues, events, and trends.

One such theater is Ariane Mnouchkine's Theater of the Sun (Théâtre du Soleil) in France. Since it started in 1964, its aim has been to create a spectacle free of illusion, in a neutral and indifferent space.[255] For its performances, it uses any available shed, in which five platforms are set up; on these "stages," reminiscent of lighted street corners, the action takes place (Figure 267). The audience watches from all sides, either from outside where they sit on benches placed to one side of the stage area, or from inside, in the space between the stages,

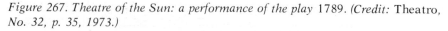

Figure 267. Theatre of the Sun: a performance of the play 1789. *(Credit:* Theatro, *No. 32, p. 35, 1973.)*

where they stand or move about freely during the performance. Whether they stand or move in the center of the stage area, they become, as Bernard Dort wrote, "an integral element of the spectacle."[256] This is actor-audience communication and identification at its most pronounced.

Similar ventures have sprung up in several other countries. A great many such groups took part in the Ninth International Theater Festival at Nancy, France, in 1973, an event that assembled some of the most radical trends in the contemporary theater. Director Katerina Thomadaki, a visitor at the festival, described it as "a mosaic of experiments moving in every direction."[257]

Political theater, ever in search of the appropriate space for its activity and the right form of communication with its public, has gone well beyond the experiments of the Theater of the Sun. During the 1960s many countries saw the emergence of "street theater," which aspires either to play the role of political opposition or to present issues in a frugal theatrical way to the people they concern. Here the theater moves out of its appointed space to seek out the spectators in their own surroundings (Figure 268).

Figure 268. Street theater: (above) *scenes from a performance on the Spielstrasse, Munich;* (right) *the Scala de la Ragione. (Photo by the author.)*

Street theater is not a sort of "antitheater": it is not against the legitimate theater; its true mission is to concern itself with the things that affect the common people. The methods it uses are distinctive: singing and dancing in folk or pop style, narrating a simple story and acting it out in such a way as to create the kind of activation sought by Brecht, only more directly; apostrophizing the spectators with direct questions and urging them to state their opinions on the subject. It uses these methods to make the audience reflect on its own condition.[258]

A number of recognized playwrights write for the street theater, including Edward Bond and John Arden in England and Peter Weiss in Germany. In West Berlin, in 1969, the Kreuzberg Strassentheater dealt with an urban renewal program for the district of the same name. In Munich, during the 1972 Olympic Games, a new variation of this theatrical expression used the occasion to make itself known: the mixed media, also encountered in Verona, Italy, in the summer of 1973 (Figure 268).

In Munich the space used was a natural one—the Olympic Park—and the development was linear. The audience, that is to say the spectators at the games, moved along a line in that space, encountering in turn the different street-theater groups arrayed along the Spielstrasse.[259] They stopped, talked with the actors, exchanged views and ideas with them, watched performances on themes connected with the games or themes protesting recent political events, and watched the audiovisual media installed next to the park's artificial lake. In Verona the environment was different: the enclosed space of a medieval square, the Scala de la Ragione. Here the audience was seated, while the actors moved around and among it or performed on a platform with the aid of some simple stage props. In both cases, along with the characteristic street-theater methods, use was made of various technical aids distinctive of the mixed-media technique.[260]

What distinguishes mixed media as a concept and a specialized technique of communication is the mixed use of artistic methods and technical aids in such a way that they interact directly. It is now possible, first, to stage a performance using various artistic and other techniques; second, to discuss it and record the debate on videotape; third, to play back the debate on a large screen through closed-circuit television, so that the spectators see themselves as part of a motion picture; fourth, to discuss reactions with the people who took part in the debate. All these things together make for a level of reflection that could not be achieved by any other means. It is a truly activating effect, such as Brecht only dreamed of, since the spectators, seeing themselves talk and share in the action, are now able to *judge* their own reactions by juxtaposition and comparison with the theme.

Although at first glance it may seem that mixed media might be the logical future form of contemporary theater, the fact is that it never went beyond the stage of a theatrical manifestation to become what could be considered a theater form. Recent attempts to stage mixed-media theater in conventional playhouses and public squares are really no more than an extension of known esthetic methods and techniques of show production. Nor can one say that any serious effort has been made, so far at least, to create a suitable permanent space for it.[261]

This and all other unconventional current theatrical movements are prevented by lack of funds from advancing beyond the mere search for new staging and acting techniques. Any thought of solving problems of organized space must be ruled out since it would involve construction, and construction means money, which just is not there. The search for a form of organized space theater is confined to small-scale projects and applications, like the Podium at Ulm or the Cottesloe in London, where the simplest of means have been resorted to. And there are others that, as we discuss later, use film projection as a means of unifying space, actor, and audience.

Under these circumstances and conditions, the "ideal theater" would seem to be as far away as ever. Without, of course, accepting Brecht's pessimistic prediction that the theater will disappear in the next 50 years,[262] one should, nevertheless, not hope for an early advent of the theatrical Messiah, the inspired creator and guide who will overcome all social and financial obstacles to give the theater its new form, a form appropriate to its era.

Film Projection as an Element of Space

Although the people whose profession is the theater are reluctant to trust the judgment and influence of the public when a new and completely radical theater form is tried, it is, nevertheless, a fact that the spectators' sense of vision is no longer satisfied with the flat picture they are offered. This is partly due to the experience gained from the open stage and arena but mostly due to the two-dimensional picture that is the daily fare fed to them by movies and television. They have begun to look for something new in the theater, something other than their usual experience, a sharper sense of awareness that they are in a theater and not in their neighborhood movie house or in their living room facing the television set. They want to feel part of a whole. This feeling has been aptly described by Peter Larkin:

It is always interesting to discover what the audience identifies with. In the theater a great many individuals make up the audience, but audience is a singular noun. Many into one, one set of empathetic reactions. In a movie, however, the viewer remains isolated from his fellow—wrapped in air conditioning, alone. Why is it no one claps in a movie? They do in theaters.[263]

The answer to the question is given by Michelis, in his exploration of the principles of esthetic communication:

The audience is the community itself on a small scale, in all its plenitude and complexity. When the play is liked, esthetic enthusiasm breaks out spontaneously and the spectators react as a whole, they all become one and each represents a force for all. That is to say, unity is established among the variety of spectators just as unity binds together the variety of feelings in the soul of each individual. To arrive, however, at such a result, the play must have already been judged; moreover, as it was being judged by all together, it was also being judged by each separately. Each spectator experienced whatever his cultural substance and character let him feel. Then he found others who shared the same experience and they, the few among the many, joined in a partial manifestation of applause thereby revealing their common feeling. The same happened to other small groups among the whole who did the same until, in a kind of reflex interaction, all together conformed to an overall unity.[264]

This disposition and response on the part of the spectator made it necessary to revise certain notions and views. The rise of the motion picture and the development of its techniques influenced the thinking and viewpoints of directors, designers, and architects, who thought they had found a way to create a space theater by using simple means and without necessarily departing from conventional building forms. Film projection would provide those simple means. With its help they would try to unify the performers' space and audience's space by enclosing one or the other in constant motion produced by projecting slides or films.

Paul Rudolph, then dean of Yale's School of Architecture, in collaboration with stage designer Ralph Alswang, produced a proposal for an "ideal theater" (Figure 269) where projection would be used as a basic element of the architectural design in an attempt to convert what was essentially a proscenium theater into a space theater.

Figure 269. Paul Rudolph's 2,000-seat theater for simultaneous film projection and live action. (Credit: Professor Paul Rudolph, the architect.)

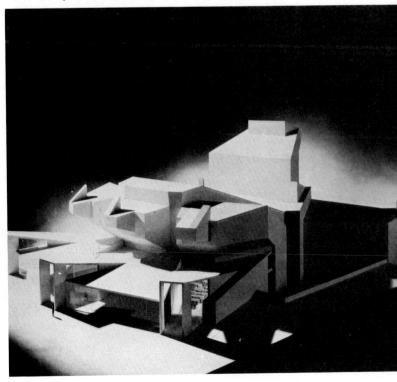

In pursuit of this aim they designed a 2,000-seat theater, the form of which was determined by projection angles more than by architectural discrimination. This is readily apparent in the building's masses; each interior function is reflected in the exterior design and in the plan layout (Figures 270, 271), where the projection angles define the form of the space.

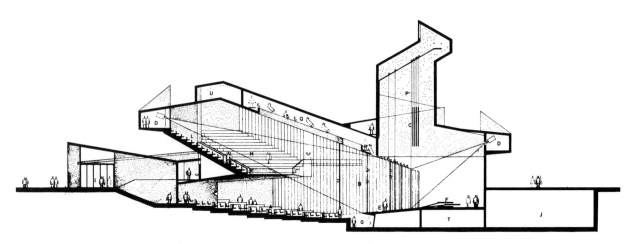

A Seats in groups separated by up-holstered rails
B Translucent screens adjustable for stage, auditorium lighting and movie projection
C A combination of three-dimensional elements flown from fly-tower used with lighting and movie projection
D Six projection booths located to give maximum flexibility
E Sliding doors on ramped stage
F Revolving cantilevered platforms
G Orchestra shell
H Sound and lighting control centers
I Foyer—audience enters between the main floor and balcony levels
J Workshops
K Freight elevator

L Balcony seating between main structural piers
M Side tiers bringing audience nearer stage
N Main access to balcony directly from foyer
O Side access to balcony directly from foyer
P Fly tower with gridiron for flying screens and flats
Q Lighting gallery
R Front light bridge
S Toilets
T Dressing rooms
U Air conditioning
V Catwalk space
W Courtyard

Figure 270. Rudolph's theater: section (Credit: Professor Paul Rudolph, the architect.)

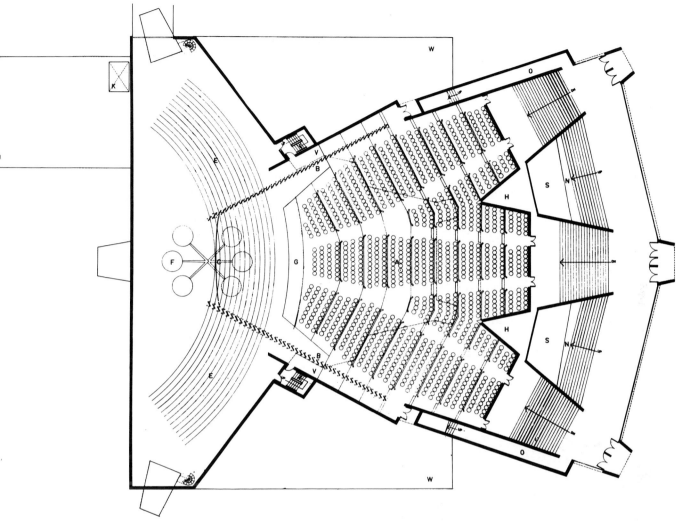

Figure 271. Rudolph's theater: plan. (See Figure 270 for key.) (Credit: Professor Paul Rudolph, the architect.)

Except for the free composition of its levels, the structure is neither more nor less than a typical proscenium theater. The only difference is in the shape of the stage; since traditional settings are not used, it conforms to the requirements of projection. There is no proscenium arch; two continuous translucent louvered panels, with catwalks behind, flank the auditorium and stage and are adjustable for stage lighting, movie projection, and acoustical variation (Figure 272). Obviously their deep thrust into the auditorium is intended to act as a unifying link connecting it with the stage. The ramped stage indicates a sliding floor and platforms on moving arms. The moving floor is intended to give the actor fluidity of motion and allow the use of conventional props and scenic units. Rudolph believes that the integration of all these elements would create a relationship between the shape of the screen, the design of the motion picture, the lighting, and the actor moving through space. "Thus will be created a fluid imagery which will make limitless the horizons of the theater."[265]

We cannot wholly share Rudolph's and Alswang's optimistic expectation of successfully linking a three-dimensional actor and a two-dimensional picture in space. The cinema is an art entirely different from that which is generated on a stage. It is an art produced not solely by the presentation of a well-photographed picture but by the combined successful efforts of the actor, the director, the cameraman, and the writer; to appreciate this art, one must first grasp the meaning of those combined efforts. This is impossible to do in a theater where the actor intrudes into this art, confuses it, and disrupts it with his own three-dimensional sculpturesqueness. In my opinion, the cinema and the theater are incompatible, and any attempt to weld the two-dimensional mobility of the one to the three-dimensional sculpture of the other is doomed to failure. The future of the theater should not be sought through amalgamation with extrinsic elements but in the theater itself, in its own domain and by its own people, aided by the great heritage of the past and the contemporary evolutionary effort to develop its form.

Figure 272. Rudolph's theater (model): views of the interior, showing film projected (above) on the stage background and (right) on the side walls. (Credit: Professor Paul Rudolph, the architect.)

Perhaps a measure of cooperation can be achieved if and when the mixed-media concept comes into wider use, because mixed media is an offspring of the theater itself. It uses technical aids not passively but organically; it seeks not to create an effect but to emphasize the message that the theater as an institution aspires to convey to its public.

A much more interesting and much more feasible project is the proposal put forward by architect Ben Schlanger and designer Donald Oenslanger for a theater without proscenium, where projection is used merely as a scenographic aid and not as a determinant of the entire form of the theater. Indeed, their proposal is an attempt to create an entirely new form of space theater quite unlike any we have encountered in our consideration of the arena or the open stage (Figures 273–275).

In this proposal unity of space is sought through parallelism, not encirclement. The designer's aim is to enable the spectator to walk into a space that is seemingly shapeless and endless in form and thus to occupy a seat in a pattern that deliberately does not suggest a focal point of interest, as do the arced rows of seating in most theaters. From that place, they reason,

spectators would be less conscious of physical confinement by the surrounding walls and ceiling of a proscenium-theater auditorium, since they would be a good distance away from the intrusive but necessary limits and very near, almost inside, a stage area that extended the full width of the theater.

The arrangement of the seats in straight lines on a sharply sloping, stepped floor gives every member of the audience a sense of looking in almost any direction, a sense of "leftness" and "rightness" of space that arced seating does not permit. The entire audience is face to face with the stage; the spectator is not forced to look at spectators opposite; his or her gaze ranges over the stage area—a more interesting sight, to say the least, than a cluster of anonymous faces.

The elongated stage form is a real challenge to directors, designers, and actors to devise new figures, styles, and modes of expression. The amplitude of available space makes it possible to establish several points of interest at once, especially if all the stage pictures have been set up beforehand. A rapid sequential alternation of the action, made possible by this setup, heightens the audience's interest; it keeps the actors at high pitch by eliminating the pauses for scene

Figure 273. Ben Schlanger's theater without proscenium. (Credit: Ben Schlanger.)

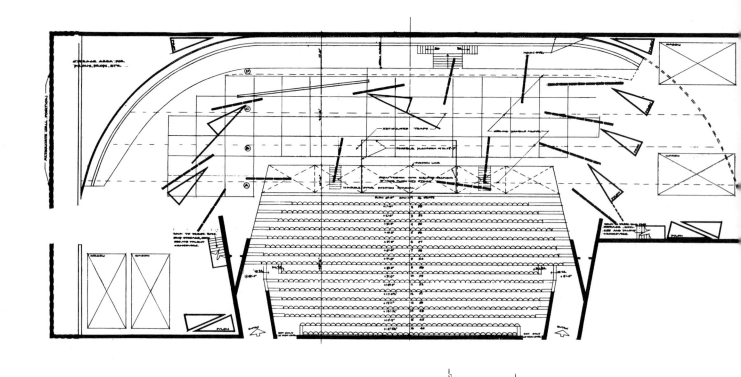

Figure 274. (Above) Schlanger's theater: plan. (Credit: Ben Schlanger.) (Below) Theater of Thoricon in Attica: plan. (According to Dörpfeld and Reisch Das Griechische Theater; author's archive.)

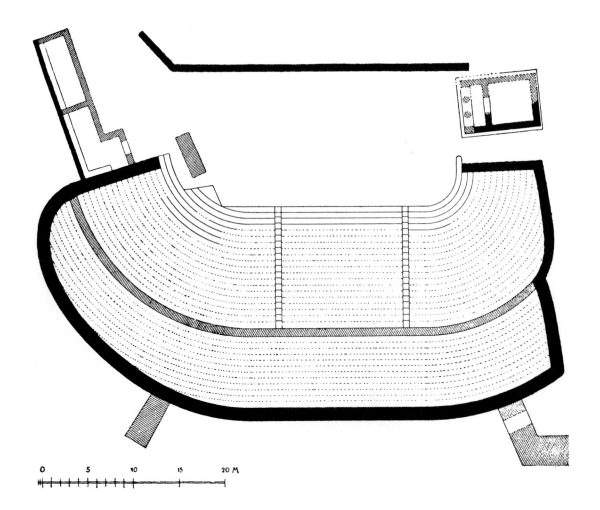

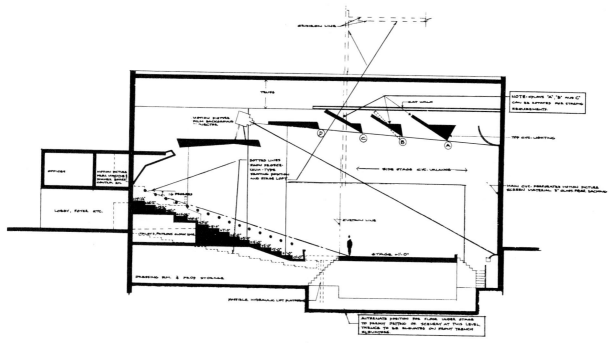

Figure 275. Schlanger's theater: section. (Credit: Ben Schlanger.)

changes, which interrupt the stream of their inspiration and concentration.

The parallel arrangement chosen by Schlanger is by no means disruptive of audience participation in the action and communication with the performer. On the contrary, the spectators should experience a heightened sense of space, with the stage practically surrounding them and covering their entire field of vision. The stage, which could well be designated the "spatial stage," is the dominant element; in order not to break the continuity of the space, the architect has even gone so far as to dispense with the balcony tier, despite the box-office loss involved.

Studying the section of the design, one observes that film projection has an entirely ancillary role, not a dominant one as in Rudolph's proposal. Its purpose is to provide a projected stage background rather than to play a part in unifying the space. Major importance has been given to lighting, which the architect has arranged along novel lines. He proposes equal brightness for stage and auditorium throughout the performance, thereby avoiding the inevitable breakup of spatial unity caused by the contrast between a brightly lighted stage and an auditorium plunged into darkness.

This is an interesting proposal that could contribute invaluably to the efforts to find new and more useful nonproscenium forms that will give the playwright, the director, the scenic artist, and the patron the opportunity for a new experience in the living theater.[266] While theater evolution requires exploration of every new notion, the notion must be truly effective and must spring, as Nicoll very rightly points out,[267] from a clear acknowledgment and acceptance of the premise that the art of the theater should not be confused with any other art, such as that of film. The right motivation for development must come from reexamination and reexploration, from a fresh angle of every theatrical success and failure in the past, from a rejection of modernism for the sake of modernism, and from a difficult but resolute effort to forge a way through the chaotic eclecticism of our era.

What seems surprising enough is that Schlanger may have had this motivation while designing his proposal, because the result of his efforts does not look different from that of the early Greeks. They too were trying to reexamine the old forms, to find new ways of organizing the space. In the fourth century B.C. they constructed the theater of Thoricon, in Attica (Figure 274b), trying to establish a new notion, a new trend toward "rightness" of space.

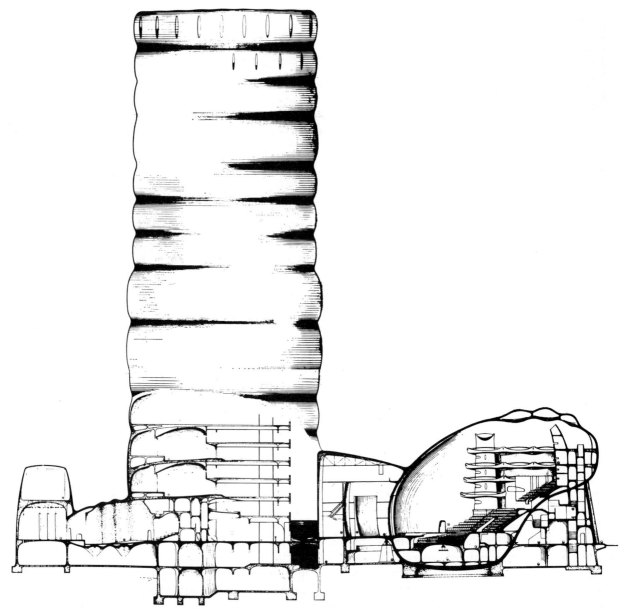

Figure 276. Frederick J. Kiesler's "Universal"; a proposal for a civic theater center. (Credit: Frederick Kiesler.)

Efforts such as those of Frederick Kiesler (Figures 276, 277) or Paolo Soleri (Figure 228), who believe that the theater should be left free to find forms of building totally different from anything accepted and established, have offered nothing but a vague, eclectic, and modernistic architectural shell. The problem is how to diversify, not the exterior of the theater, but its interior, that part of it which we acknowledge to be a function and a force for cultural and intellectual development. Perhaps if mixed media manages soon to overcome the inevitable opposition and difficulties attending the emergence of all innovative efforts, it could, combined with an organized space, produce a building that would act as a center of communication for the public.

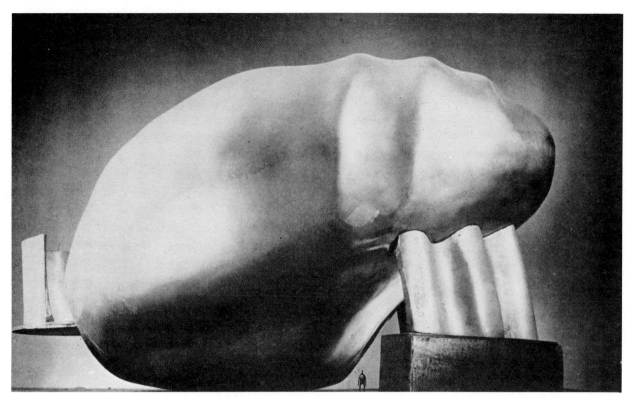

Figure 277. Kiesler's "Universal": part of the model. (Nicoll, Development of the
Theatre, *p. 249. Reprinted by permission.)*

Such a building should be designed in a way that ensures optimal expression of the different forms that make up a true mixed-media production—namely, coherence of the theater arts, visual information, sound and light effects to enhance the performance, musical and rhythmical stimulants, free open-end debate, and projection of the meditation's function itself. This kind of mixed-media theater would finally do what our traditional theaters have not managed to do, perhaps much more effectively than one would expect from a street theater. It would become truly a place of "creative communication," where the gap between actors and audience has been bridged, where people would overcome their diffidence and hesitation and talk to each other; they would be in contact, they would get to know one another, they would get to know the actors, the playwright, the producer. It would be a place, in short where a genuine, interesting exchange of ideas generated on the spot would be possible.

19
The Importance of Meaning and Speech

Dominant Role of the Playwright

Meaning and speech created theater. If we accept this axiom, it follows that we must acknowledge that theater began with the dramatist. Luis Kahn, the eminent architect, once said:

Nothing will ever change my conviction that theater was created by the dramatist. He defined the various forms of the past; it is he who will determine every new form in the future. As long as meaning and speech are inherent in the concept of theater, the playwright will always be the dominant component in its evolution.[268]

This conviction, emphatically stated by an expert of such stature, should not be overlooked. However exaggerated this opinion may seem in our era, if we look at the history of theatrical evolution we will see that all dramatists (referring of course to the literary giants of the theater) bequeathed to the art a form of theater relevant to the development of their own particular word. We have encountered this characteristic all the way from antiquity to the present.

We have seen how the theater—theater grounded on meaning and speech—was born in an improvised setting, a space that the dramatist sought as a place in which to develop their art. They needed that space because, unlike painters or sculptors who are confined to expressing themselves on and through an object, dramatists required physical space as their vehicle. They needed space to demonstrate their art because it is the nature of drama that it must be presented to many people together; it cannot be presented independently to separate individuals, as can painting and sculpture.

The dramatists began, accordingly, by using the slope of a hill on which they placed the audience, and a flat space at the foot of the hill where they could develop their words and meanings and the movement of the actors who expressed them. Later dramatists adapted their needs to a medieval church, a Spanish plaza, an Elizabethan courtyard, or a royal antechamber. The dramatist went on from there, as we are told by A. Terjakis, "to try and reconstruct, in an architecturally organized whole, the functional elements of the cradle of his art."[269]

Thus, in the beginning there was the play, the word; afterward came the building created specifically for it. We have seen how the Attic theater of Aeschylus, the Elizabethan playhouse of Shakespeare, and the *corral* of Lope de Vega came into being as the appropriate forms devised by their dramatist-creators to achieve the best possible communication with their audiences, the judges of their art.

Every art form, according to playwright Elmer Rice, comprises two phases. The first is self-expression—an idea, a vision, a conception that artists feel the need to externalize, to bring out from their inner selves and make the property of all. The second phase is communication, the sharing of this art with others, to make them communicants.[270] These two basic desires for self-expression and communication are the same in all the arts, but the way they are realized in each art differs greatly.

When painters, for instance, finish a canvas they feel that their expression has been imprinted and their work completed, ready to be communicated to individuals or groups at that very moment or at any time thereafter. Playwrights, however, are faced with a much more complex problem, one that makes the achievement of such communication a very difficult task. In their case communication is a process that cannot be addressed to one individual; it needs many people. Nor can it be achieved as soon as expression has been completed, but only after much preparation involving an arduous series of actions. Playwrights do have the satisfaction of a completed cycle of expression and communication until they have made the actors memorize the written word, shown them how to speak the lines and move as required by the action and the plot, until they have found the right space where all this can be combined and presented to the people who wish to communicate with the result of their art.

Whenever in the course of its history the theater found itself deprived of a great classic poetic dramatist, it was transformed into mere spectacle; the desire for communication either waned or disappeared altogether. We have seen how this happened during the period of Roman power, during the Middle Ages, and during the Italian Renaissance, when the absence of a towering creative intellect left the field open to all the lesser theatrical talents; incapable of creating something new, they rehashed the old forms.

We have seen this situation at its most characteristic during the Italian Renaissance, when the absence of a dramatist as a guiding spirit led to a theater form that became predominant, the Italian proscenium, a form utterly unsuited to drama and the spoken word and that made communication impossible. This same absence of a controlling dramaturgical spirit changed the theater into a spectacle that had no use for speech and meaning. By contrast, in the renascent England of Elizabethan times and in Spain, where the names of Shakespeare and Lope de Vega are inseparably connected with the period, the evolution of the theater form followed an entirely different direction.

Action and Plot

In a play two concepts predominate that have been widely misunderstood and misinterpreted: "action" and "plot." We quote P.A. Touchard, director of France's National School of Drama, on the subject:

Action in the theater is generated by the inner force that impels everybody—whether an individual or a collective expression—towards freedom. The greater the obstacles encountered by that force, the more vigorous the action becomes. What causes the spurious controversies among the different schools is that they confuse action with plot—the last being nothing but the sequence or conjuncture of the episodes. . . . The action becomes either tragic or comic, depending on whether satisfaction of the drive for freedom is considered vitally important or not.[271]

Touchard goes on to explain what the concept of freedom means as used here. For Racine's Andromache, freedom means remaining faithful to her dead husband and saving her child, while for Pyrrhus, her captor, freedom means loving Andromache and compelling her to marry him. To take an example from comedy, for Molière's Misanthrope, freedom means marrying the young widow Célimène, while for her it means enjoying her new-found independence. The action stems from these conflicting drives.

Such are the situations that generate action in the theater, and action gains momentum and intensity as the desires and drives grow more specific and more conflicting. There is always one single line of action for each character in a play, whereas the plot is—but not always—the aggregate of those individual lines of action. I say not always, because it is possible for action to have no share in a plot. Sometimes a plot may contain no trace of action at all. I have enlisted the help of Touchard in this difficult analysis because my purpose is to show that meaning and speech cannot exist without action in the plot.

The classic tragedies—Aristophanes' comedies, Shakespeare's verse-dramas, Ibsen's masterpieces—none of these would have seen the light of day but for this inner force, which Touchard calls a "drive for freedom." It is the driving force that made those works immortal, while the farces, the melodramas, and most of the modern boulevard romances have vanished into oblivion because they were plays of "words" and plots, without action and therefore without meaning and speech.

A complete absence of action as defined by Touchard is characteristic, up to a point, of the contemporary theater. It is not something recent; it has been many centuries in the making. This is the onerous heritage that thinking playwrights tried so bravely to throw off in the early years of our century; but their mastery was not great enough to enable them to create something new. We have seen how Antoine with his Théâtre Libre tried to restore the primacy of meaning and to produce thought-provoking plays instead of the popular romances of the day, which had plot but nothing else. We have seen the extreme positions taken by Piscator, who tried through his political theater to give the audience an experience and, more, to extract from his audience a certainty that that experience would lead it to form specific conclusions. Touchard notes that "the stage has become a tribune. Action has become external. It has been treated almost as an educational aid that could bring some vitality to the reassessment of ideas."[271]

This, then, was the situation that produced the two major theater trends of the first half of our century: the theater of "positions," where people obey the playwright's injunctions and not their own inner impulses, and the theater of "words," otherwise known as the boulevard theater.

The boulevard theater, changeless and unhindered by anxieties or problems, continued on its chosen course right up to the present, attracting the same public, people who, as Selden observes, are hard put to give you a reply when you ask them what they are feeling as they come out of the theater; they will talk, perhaps, about every small detail, but it will be impossible for them to tell you what was "generally" the meaning of the things they heard and what they "generally" liked about the things they saw.[272] For them the theater will never be anything but just another place of entertainment.

The theater of positions, on the other hand, developed remarkably and became the intellectual medium of every thinking person. But it committed one major error, as a result of which meaning and speech lost their ascendancy in the contemporary theater.

The Playwright's Status Today

The error of the theater of positions was that it developed into a theater of ideas devoid of any form of theatrical action as taught by the great dramatists. Meaning is expressed now only through words and abstract concepts, not through the strivings of individuals engaged in a real struggle. The spectator is called upon to cast out all emotion and to judge. Brecht once declared that traditional theater arouses the spectator's emotion (*ermöglicht ihm Gefühle*), while contemporary theater urges him to make decisions (*erzwingt von ihm Entscheidungen*).[273]

Brecht was a great theater figure. Profoundly influenced by Piscator's theories, he emerged as the great reformer of theatrical meaning. His plays were indeed invested with a form of the struggle for freedom defined by Touchard. But it was freedom for the spectator, not for the hero of the play.

Brecht strictly excluded all illusion. This produced the fundamental notion of "epic theater" (*epischen Theaters*): the stage does not pretend, it presents; it asks from the spectator not sensitivity but criticism.[274] He created epic theater in an attempt to prove that any endeavor to revise the classic dramatists is vain and contrary to every form of development.

This, of course, is true up to a point, and it applies to all art forms. But any new creation must acquire self-sufficiency and a character purely its own. This was true of the transition from academic to nonobjective cubist painting;

it was true of the change in architecture from neoclassicism to the strong geometric designs made possible by modern materials. These arts, however, are not as complex as the theater, or as social. If an individual does not at once accept a new trend, it does not mean that the trend will cease to exist. When people see modern sculpture or an ultramodern building and are not attracted by its style, all they have to do is turn their glance away a few times until they finally get used to it and accept it as an essential feature of their environment. But when they are offered theater full of abstract concepts, words that are often disheartening or displeasing, without heroes or action, without reflective thought, then you may be sure they will not give you their contribution a second time. And that contribution, moral and material, is what keeps the theater alive.

When Brecht with his epic theater and basically valid theories, or Jean-Paul Sartre with his existentialist theater, or Samuel Becket with his theater of the absurd appealed to their public to sustain them in their efforts to revive meaning and speech, a majority failed to respond. These innovators, for their part, failed to relate their endeavors to the fact that the theatergoing public is largely made up of people of an older generation who are not too eager for strenuous mental exertion, while the young are engaged in the pursuit of interests that are much more exciting to them. Thus the contemporary spoken word gradually lost its ascendancy. When playwrights failed to find theatrical inspiration equivalent to that of the great periods of the past, when their abstract and obscure ideas evoked little or no response from the public, the theater had to turn for salvation to other expedients, other creative forces within itself. They ceded the dominant role to the director, the technical consultant, the architect. They abandoned the power of the spoken word in favor of the magic of lighting, color, and scenery. They downgraded the modern playwright and forced him or her to do the bidding of others, to fit the words to the available theater form, whatever it might be. They went so far as to give some contemporary theater people the right to claim that the theater can exist without the playwright, that, according to Renco Casali, "a naked man in a public square is enough to create theater, that one can have theatrical drama without a playwright."[275]

The process, then, began to work in reverse. Now it was the instrument, the specific architectural structure, that awaited the right repertory. Playwrights must write scripts suited to the form of the theater in which their plays are to be staged; they must accept the director's corrections and changes and move their characters in a space predetermined by the architect. They are left with no recourse but to reflect nostalgically on the exalted status of the dramatist in bygone times; and if they are among those who still believe in the spoken word, their reflections may well run along the lines of the thoughts expressed more than two centuries ago by Denis Diderot as he pondered a similarly sad situation:

To change the form of the dramatic genre, I would ask only for a very open, very expansive theater showing, when the theme of the play calls for it, a spacious square with its surrounding buildings, such as the colonnade of a palace, the entrance to a temple, various spaces distributed in such a way that the audience would experience all the action, while on the other hand part of it would be hidden from the performers.

Such once was, or could have been, the stage for Aeschylus' Eumenides . . . . Will we ever do something like that in our own theaters? We are never able to show more than one action, while in real life there are nearly always several concurrent actions, a convergent reenactment of which would mutually reinforce them and have a terrifying impact upon us.

Then we would tremble to go to a show, yet we would not be able to stop ourselves from going; then instead of the transient little emotions, that cold applause, those rare tears that are enough to satisfy the poet, he would instill turbulence and terror in our souls and we would see those eminently probable and scarcely credible happenings of Ancient Tragedy coming to life before us. . . .

We would learn to combine pantomime with the spoken word, to interpolate a talking scene and a silent scene intermingled, and to achieve an effect through the fusion of the two scenes.[276]

A Chronology of
Theater Forms
and Trends

	Trends–Developments	Theater Forms	Scenographic Developments	Playwrights	Architects–Directors	Distinguishing Features
Before the sixth century B.C.	Primitive ceremonial rites Motion as a means of expression Egypt: Coronation ceremonies in the thirtieth century B.C.—Abydos Passion plays, from the twenty-fifth to the sixth century B.C. Greece: Games and ritual ceremonies at Knossos and Phaestos, from the twentieth to the fifteenth century B.C.	Egypt: Temple courtyards and squares Greece: Theaters of Knossos and Phaestos, Minoan theater	Egypt: Reenactment of battles, processions of priests Greece: No scenic devices	Rudimentary form of dialogue		Worship of the dead, nature worship
Sixth century B.C.	Birth of tragedy Emergence of ancient Greek drama Worship of Dionysus	Preclassical (pre-Aeschylean) theater			Thespis	Spiritual harmony Strong religious feeling Teaching
Fifth century B.C.	Greek drama at its peak Tragedy and comedy	Classic Athenian theater	Stage (*skene*) and proscenium (*proskenion*) appear First scenographic attempts	Aeschylus Sophocles Aristophanes		All social classes participate Austerity and economy of speech
Fourth to third century B.C.	Decline of tragedy and comedy Introduction of expression in speech Complex action Middle and New Comedy	Hellenistic theater	Development of the acting area Scenic conventions Machines *periakti*	Euripides Menander	Polyclitus	Gradual departure from religious themes Social themes Variety Introduction of magnificence
Second century B.C.	Change in social concepts Importance of the theater decreases Ancient Greek theatre spreads to the colonies Roman-type drama appears	Greco-Roman theater	Acting area becomes imposing Orchestra eliminated Semicircular form develops	Plautus Terence		Elegant recitation Impressive spectacle Religious element discarded entirely Display of power and wealth
First century B.C.–First century A.D.	Roman tragedy and comedy The theater turns to spectacle and farce	Roman theater	*Proscaenium* *Scaenae frons* Gladiatorial arena	Seneca		Entertainment

	Trends–Developments	Theater Forms	Scenographic Developments	Playwrights	Architects–Directors	Distinguishing Features
Second to twelfth century	Disappearance of all forms of drama Byzantine liturgical drama Precursor theater forms	The hippodrome as theater The Byzantine church as theater	Cubicles (*cubicula*), fifth-century Byzantium	Gregory of Nazianzus Romano		Fanaticism Hostility toward the theater Dominance of the church
1200–1500	Western liturgical drama Mystery plays Theater guilds Confrérie de la Passion	The church and its grounds as theater Mansions, wagon stages, pageants	Mansions			
1500–1550	Development of the mystery plays Appearance of popular playhouses Return to classicism Italian Renaissance Search for traditional elements	Booth stages Court theater The theater of Serlio (1539) Hôtel de Bourgogne (1548)	Geometry in the theater Introduction of perspective Vistas		Peruzzi Serlio	Sociality The theater as the preserve of a small, privileged minority Court theater Misconstruction of the classic prototypes
1550–1600	Emergence of Italian opera Renaissance in France, Spain Elizabethan period: English drama reaches its peak (1558–1603) Commedia dell'arte in Italy, France	Teatro Olimpico (1585) Elizabethan stage Corrales	Development of vistas English stage bare of all scenery	Shakespeare Lope de Vega	Palladio Scamozzi De Witt	England, Spain: Revival of spoken word through Shakespeare and Lope de Vega
1600–1700	Emergence of baroque Private and court theater-masques Peak of Italian opera Puritan England, restoration of the English theater First English opera (1656) Theater returns to the bourgeois class Cretan theater develops	Development of the proscenium theater, Teatro Farnese (1618) Opera house English proscenium theater Proscenium theater develops in the rest of Europe	Scène à l'italienne *Periakti* Frontispiece, shutters Italian stage prevails in all of Europe	Shakespeare Lope de Vega Ben Jonson Corneille Killigrew Davenant Racine Molière	Aleotti Inigo Jones Furttenbach Webb Wren Torelli	Playwright's dominant role and position in the theater begins to decline

	Trends–Developments	Theater Forms	Scenographic Developments	Playwrights	Architects– Directors	Distinguishing Features
1700–1800	Evolution at a standstill–the big spectacle, era of great acting Emergence of commercial theater Sturm und Drang First theater activity in the United States Rococo, neoclassicism	Elaboration of the form Italian stage influences English theater	Importance of scenic magnificence and splendor	Voltaire Diderot Marivaux Garrick Goethe Schiller	Juvarra Carasale Alfieri Morelli Piermarini Bibbiena	The theater as an entertainment medium of bourgeois society Importance of the spectacle The theater as an escape from everyday life
1800–1870	Melodrama Romanticism, realism Commercial theater prevails	The architecture of repetition	Illusion Naturalistic settings Box set (1840)	Dumas Hugo		Dominance of the commercial theater Stagnation
1870–1914	Period of peace, first reactions against the established theater Theatrical revolution, neorealism Antoine's Théâtre Libre (1887) Freie Bühne, Berlin (1889) Independent Theatre, London Théâtre Antoine (1896–1906) Moscow Art Theater (1897) World War I	Paris Opera (1876) Wagner's Bayreuth Festival Theater (1876) Broadway and boulevard theater Influence of Bayreuth on German architecture	Development of stage technology– Lighting (1879) Scenic naturalism developed by Antoine "Fourth wall" Appia's and Craig's new esthetic trend in scenography	Ibsen Tolstoy Chekhov Zola Strindberg Shaw Hauptmann	Garnier Brückwald Semper Littman Kaufmann Antoine Stanislavski Reinhardt Appia Craig	Monotony Earnest efforts by amateurs to rescue the theater from stagnation The director assumes a creative role
1918–1939	The period between the wars Political theater Theater and technics Production develops as an art Bauhaus (1919–1928) "Golden Decade" of the theater	Grosses Schauspielhaus (1919) Vieux-Colombier (1913–24) Weininger's spherical theater and Molnár's U-theater (1924) Gropius' "Total theater" (1927) Meyerhold's "biomechanical" theater (1935)	"Anti-illusionist" scenography: expressionism, surrealism, constructivism, dadaism, formalism	Pirandello Eliot O'Neill Mayakovski Brecht I	Gropius Schlemmer Copeau Meyerhold Vakhtangov Tairov Jessner Piscator Bel Geddes	Period of exploration and new principles The theater as a political medium Cerebration as an element of the spoken word

	Trends–Developments	Theater Forms	Scenographic Developments	Playwrights	Architects–Directors	Distinguishing Features
1945–1960	Search for new forms Building of theaters Concurrent development of all the performing arts Epic theater	Contemporary theater Open-stage theater Theater-in-the-round (arena stage) Adaptable or experimental theater	Neo-constructivism "Anti-illusionist" scenography Lighting as the dominant scenographic element	Brecht II Anouilh Camus Sartre Ionesco Miller	Joseph Mielziner Guthrie E. Jones Villiers Otto	Distinct separation of entertainment and intellectual or "cerebral" theater
1960 to the present	The theater in the city Separation of the performing arts, development of compound forms Explorations for a space theater Theater of the absurd, development of modern drama Living theater, marginal theater Street theater, mixed media Development of radical trends	Multipurpose theaters Theater centers Theater without proscenium	Film projection as a scenographic element Space stage The natural environment of the community as a scenographic element	Becket Frisch Dürenmatt Weiss Albee Osborne Pinter Williams Grass Arden	Mnouchkine Gropius Mies van der Rohe Wright Saarinen Izenour Breuer Schlanger Pfau	Theater of "positions" and theater of "words" Political theater, militant theater

Notes

1. Cheney, *Theatre*, pp. 11–13.
2. Nietzsche, *Birth of Tragedy*, p. 17.
3. Ibid., p. 11.
4. Herodotus, *Histories*, Vol. 2, pars. 59–63.
5. Roberts, *On Stage*, p. 18. See also Kakouri, *Pre-Asthetic Forms*, pp. 79–81, concerning Osiris.
6. Nicoll, *World History of the Theatre*, vol. 1, p. 10.
7. The stage designer Jo Mielziner once said, "When you study the history of theatre architecture you cannot better their concept of the relationships in that wonderful two-way communication of the audience with the actor." Mielziner, "The Future of Theatre Architecture," p. 16.
8. Cailler and Cailler, "Les théâtres Gréco-Romains," p. 32.
9. Allen, *The Greek Theatre of the Fifth Century B.C.*, p. 3.
10. Nietzsche, *Birth of Tragedy*, p. 36.
11. Ibid., p. 47.
12. Lascaris, *Lectures in the History of Ancient Greek Theatre*, vol. 1, p. 113. Nicolaos Lascaris was a professor of drama. See also Mouzenidis, *Ancient Greek Theatre*, pp. 9–49, 112. Takis Mouzenidis was a famous Greek stage director. Nicoll, *World History of the Theatre*, pp. 59, 121, 212. For Nietzsche, these characters were simply "Dionysian masks"; cf. Kakouri, *Pre-Aesthetic Forms*, p. 89.
13. Cailler and Cailler, "Les théâtres Gréco-Romains," p. 31.
14. Allen, *Greek Theatre of the Fifth Century B.C.*, p. 10, maintains that the Theater of Dionysus in its fourth-century form could seat 14,000. However, if we accept Dörpfeld's contention (see fn. 15, p. 44) that each spectator occupied 41 centimeters of lateral space, then the seating capacity of this theater must have been approximately 17,000.
15. Dörpfeld and Reisch, *Das griechische Theater*, p. 27. See also Allen, *Greek Theatre of the Fifth Century B.C.*, p. 21
16. Nicoll, *Development of the Theatre*, p. 11.
17. Fiechter, *Die baugeschichtliche Entwicklung des antiken Theaters*, p. 35. Fiechter asserts that this structure rarely exceeded two stories. Although his study of Greek theaters is an admirable and noteworthy work, many of his conclusions are no longer accepted today. See also Fiechter, *Antike griechische Theaterbauten*, nos. 6–8.
18. Dörpfeld and Reisch, *Das griechische Theater*, p. 28. The orchestra was moved in the fourth century b.c. (ca. 328–326 B.C.), when the Theater of Dionysus was given its final form during the administration of Lycurgus. Dörpfeld estimates that the diameter of the new orchestra was 19.61 meters, which is the equivalent of 60 "Aeginetan," or Attic, feet (0.327 meters equals 1 foot). This discovery led him to conclude that the orchestra was the cornerstone and center of gravity of the entire design. Dörpfeld and Reisch, *Das greichische Theater*, p. 59; Flickinger, *The Greek Theater and Its Drama*, p. 69; also A. Varvaringos, "The Theater of Dionysus in Athens," *Thespis*, no 7 (December 1973), p. 18.
19. An interesting and detailed description of the proscenium is given by Dörpfeld and Reisch, *Das griechische Theater*, p. 218, based on the *Onomasticon* (IV; 130) of Julius Pollux, "from the theologeion which was above the stage as viewed." See also Lascaris, *Lectures*, vol. 2, p. 230; vol. 3, p. 131.
20. Allen, *Greek Theatre of the Fifth Century B.C.*, p. 60. See also Flickinger, *Greek Theater and Its Drama*, p. 70.
21. Aesychlus; "episceneum; the compartment over the stage." Vitruvius, *De Architectura*, VII; 5,5, "episcaenium." See Allen, *Greek Theatre of the Fifth Century B.C.*, p. 58. See also Dörpfeld and Reisch, *Das griechische Theater*, p. 299; Pickard-Cambridge, *Theatre of Dionysus in Athens*.
22. Lascaris, *Lectures*, vol. 2, p. 204. See also Mouzenidis, *The Ancient Greek Theatre*, p. 86.
23. Lascaris, *Lectures*, vol. 2, p. 183. See also Nicoll, *World History of the Theatre*, pp. 121–124.
24. Nietzsche, *Birth of Tragedy*, p. 56.
25. Cheney, *Theatre*, p. 78. See also Nicoll, *World History of the Theatre*, p. 261.
26. Nietzsche, *Birth of Tragedy*, p. 57.
27. Mouzenidis writes that in the plays of Euripides "the gods abound but they lack divinity." Mouzenidis, *Ancient Greek Theatre*, p. 65.
28. Concerning these and almost all the other theaters of this period, see Dörpfeld and Reisch, *Das griechische Theater*, pp. 100–144; Fiechter, *Antike griechische Theaterbauten;* 1930 Oropos (part 1), Megalopolis (part 4), Sicyon (part 3), Eretria (part 9), Epidaurus (part 10). See also Orlandos, *Excavations at Sicyon*, p. 393. Anastasios Orlandos was an Academician and Professor of the National Technical University of Athens—School of Architecture and Professor of Archaeology at the University of Athens.
29. Dörpfeld and Reisch, *Das griechische Theater*, part 9, p. 32.
30. Lascaris, *Lectures*, vol. 2, p. 237.
31. Werner, *Theatergebäude*, pp. 12–24.
32. Dörpfeld and Reich, *Das griechische Theater*, p. 144. The Delos theater is believed to have been built in 250 b.c., but it shows strong Roman influence.

33. Cailler and Cailler, "Les théâtres Gréco-Romains," pp. 112–115. See also Orlandos, "Messène, Chronique des fouilles en 1957," pp. 714–716.

34. Lascaris, *Lectures*, vol. 2, pp. 170–190.

35. Mouzenidis, *Ancient Greek Theatre*, p. 86. See also Lascaris, *Lectures*, vol. 2, p. 204.

36. Allen, *Greek Theatre of the Fifth Century B.C.*, p. 60.

37. Dörpfeld and Reisch, *Das griechische Theater*, p. 222. See also Pollux, *Onomastikon*, vol. 4, p. 126, or Vitruvius, *Ten Books on Architecture*, vol. 6.

38. The *Onomastikon* of Pollux, particularly vol. 4, has been used as a source by almost all students of the ancient Greek theater. See also Dörpfeld and Reisch, *Das griechische Theater*, pp. 60–65; Lascaris, *Lectures*, vol. 3, pp. 130–145; Mouzenidis, *Ancient Greek Theatre*, p. 129.

39. In Aeschylus' *Eumenides*, verse 64, we read: "rotated apparatus"; in Aristophanes' *Clouds*, verse 184: "when the eccyclema was turned"; in Pollux' *Onomastikon*, vol. 4, p. 128: "and the eccyclema on wooden planks." See also Allen, *Greek Theatre of the Fifth Century B.C.*, p. 64.

40. Pollux, *Onomasticon*, vol. 4, p. 128, "the machine lies toward the left parodos above the stage in height." See also Dörpfeld and Reisch, *Das griechische Theater*, pp. 230–233.

41. Lascaris, *Lectures*, vol. 3, pp. 157–172.

42. Hadas, *Imperial Rome*, pp. 35–39.

43. Tidworth, *Theatres*, p. 23.

44. Cheney, *Theatre*, p. 90. See also Hadas, *Imperial Rome*, p. 45.

45. Cheney, *Theatre*, p. 79. In this context, interestingly, Alexis Solomos writes that when the Roman fleet entered the port of Tarentum not a citizen was to be seen in the town because they were all at the theaters. Solomos, *Bacchus the Saint*, p. 38. Alexis Solomos is a director and was for two years, 1980 and 1981, General Director of the National Theatre of Athens.

46. Lascaris, *Lectures*, vol. 1, p. 336. See also Nicoll, *World History of the Theatre*, pp. 283, 317, 329.

47. Nietzsche, *Birth of Tragedy*, p. 59.

48. Cheney, *Theatre*, pp. 80–82.

49. Roberts, *On Stage*, p. 67. See also Werner, *Theatergebäude*, p. 27.

50. Dörpfeld and Reisch, *Das griechische Theater*, pp. 385–395.

51. Lascaris, *Lectures*, vol. 2, p. 229. See also Dörpfeld and Reisch, *Das griechische Theater*, p. 387.

52. Vitruvius, *Ten Books on Architecture*, p. 146.

53. Nicoll, *World History of the Theatre*, p. 284. See also Werner, *Theatergebäude*, pp. 25–41 on details of Roman theaters.

54. Strong, *Classical World*, p. 132.

55. Tertullian, *De Spectaculis*. See also Cheney, *The Theatre*, p. 134.

56. Papadopoulos, *Religious Theater of the Byzantines*, p. 7. A very interesting dissertation for those who wish to study in depth the theater of this period. See also Solomos, *Bacchus*.

57. Tidworth, *Theatres*, p. 35.

58. Koukoules, *The Byzantines*, vol. 6, p. 111. The author mentions that in the fourth century A.D. Methodius, Bishop of Patara, wrote the "Symposium of Ten Virgins" and that mimes first appeared in the fifth century. See also Cottas, *Le théâtre à Byzance*, p. 50. At this point it is worth noting the existence in those times of yet another Greek folkway of a theatrical nature, the *Momogeria* in Pontus, part of the festivities celebrating the first day of the year of the Roman and Byzantine calends. See Samouilides, "The Momogeri of Pontus," *Theatro*, vol. 6, no. 33 (May–June 1973), pp. 36–40. See also Solomos, *Bacchus*, p. 120.

59. Nicoll, *Development of the Theatre*, p. 48.

60. Cheney, *Theatre*, p. 137.

61. Papadopoulos writes that the church's war against the theater was waged on two fronts; one target was the Christians who frequented playhouses and the other the actors themselves, who were refused baptism and communion. See Papadopoulos, *Religious Theatre*, p. 8. Some interesting information about the church's active opposition is given in Solomos, *Bacchus*, chap. 3.

62. The history of the true strolling actor is lost in the Dark Ages between the sixth and twelfth centuries. By contrast, the originators of the rhapsodic poem, the minstrels, the singers, and the reciters, can be traced everywhere—in France, England, and Germany. They were employed as entertainers at banquets in feudal castles and royal courts. Both Tidworth, *Theatres*, p. 35, and Nicoll, *World History of the Theatre*, p. 344, mention a German nun named Hroswitha who staged a form of play in the tenth century. See also Cheney, *Theatre*, p. 138.

63. The troubadour in France, variously known elsewhere as the *giocolatore* or *goukelaere* or *jongleur*, may have been a source of mere amusement and entertainment to his audience, but his chosen occupation was something that can be likened to dramatic art, a substitute for the theater in the darker centuries.

64. Cheney, *Theatre*, pp. 141–145.

65. According to Papadopoulos, *Religious Theatre*, p. 25, Theophylactus was the first Patriarch of Constantinople to allow the theater to enter the great church of Saint Sophia, with an orchestra

consisting of actors from the temporal theater. This event, which occurred in the tenth century, was the culmination of a long and arduous struggle that started at the time of the iconoclasm struggle, as a result of which Byzantine drama reached its high point in the tenth and eleventh centuries.

66. The date of this work has not been determined; the prevailing view is that it was written in the tenth century to be read rather than performed. See Papadopoulos, *Religious Theatre*, p. 27; also Cottas, *Le théâtre à Byzance*, p. 197. Solomos, *Bacchus*, p. 77, maintains that this work was not written by Gregory; he dates it in the fourth or fifth century, p. 109. Cheney, *Theatre*, p. 143, considers it as having had a limited influence on the Western mystery plays. It is of value chiefly because it incorporates bodily several hundred lines out of Euripides' plays, including passages nowhere else preserved.

67. Papadopoulos, *Religious Theatre*, p. 79. Koukoulés, *Byzantines*, p. 111, and Kakouri, p. 104, *Pre-Aesthetic Forms*, p. 104, both relate that when Luitprandi, Bishop of Cremona, attended a liturgical drama during a visit to Constantinople in 968, he derided the Byzantines, writing that "the frivolous Greeks celebrate the Assumption of the Prophet Elijah with staged performances."

68. Tenth and eleventh centuries. See Papadopoulos, *Religious Theatre*, p. 57. The *nipter* performance (foot-washing ceremony) is preserved to this day on the Greek island of Patmos and in Jerusalem. See Kakouri, *Pre-Aesthetic Forms*, p. 113. Koukoulés, *Byzantines*, p. 112, writes that the custom was formerly also observed on the Greek island of Zante.

69. Although their ritual is not known, these dramas must have been performed in the church of Saint Sophia in the twelfth century. See Papadopoulos, *Religious Theatre*, p. 78; Solomos, *Bacchus*, pp. 165–180.

70. The religious drama influenced not only Christian art and multiplied the rituals of church services; it also influenced religious hymnology. The mass was divided into parts: recitatives, sung parts, and parts of pure acting. From a narrative intoned by a single priest, recitation of the service evolved into a dialogue. The dialogue, with two or three priests taking part, developed notably and was very well received by the society of that time. See Papadopoulos, *Religious Theatre*, p. 61.

71. Papadopoulos, *Religious Theatre*, p. 87. Concerning the *nipter*, the author maintains that it was introduced to the royal households of Europe directly from the court of Byzantium and not by the Western church (p. 106). However, many Western scholars either ignore or do not accept the fact that the Byzantine liturgical drama directly influenced the West.

72. Some of the confréries produced farces with no object other than amusement and satire, the latter sometimes bitter and aimed at the church. It was an early and gross form of later French vulgar comedy and Italian commedia dell'arte, both of which fertilized the genius of Molière. See Cheney, *Theatre*, p. 163; Nicoll, *Development of the Theatre*, p. 50.

73. Roberts, *On Stage*, p. 94. See also Tidworth, *Theatres*, p. 40; Nicoll, *Development of the Theatre*, pp. 50–61.

74. Werner, *Theatergebäude*, pp. 42–45. See also Nicoll, *World History of the Theatre*, pp. 349–363.

75. The plan dates from 1425, in the reign of Henry VI. The text of the play itself proves that the circular layout was used in parts of Cornwall and contains valuable interpretative comments. See also Tidworth, *Theatres*, p. 39.

76. Like permanent scenery, these movable sets were symbolic representations of the place or picture required by the play and were fairly easy to handle. The flat surface mounted on wheels was the acting area. When the plot called for a greater amount of room, the actors would step down to the ground, as they did from the mansions in the permanent settings. Roberts, *On Stage*, p. 98. See also Kakouri, *Pre-Aesthetic Forms*, p. 118; Nicoll, *Development of the Theatre*, p. 59.

77. Kakouri, *Pre-Aesthetic Forms*, p. 121. See also Nicoll, *Development of the Theatre*, p. 60.

78. Nicoll, "The Theater," *Collier's Encyclopedia* (1962), vol. 22, p. 247. See also Tidworth, *Theatres*, p. 48, citing Fra Giocondo (1511), Cesariano (1521), Serlio (1551), and Barbaro (1556).

79. Werner, *Theatergebäude*, p. 51. See also Nicoll, *World History of the Theatre*, p. 402.

80. "*Cenera autem sunt scaenarum tria: unum quod dicitur tragicum, alterum comicum, tertium satyricum.*" Vitruvius, *De Architectura*. See also Lascaris, *Lectures*, vol. 3, p. 64; Nicoll, *Development of the Theatre*, p. 70; Tidworth, *Theatres*, p. 49.

81. Martindale, *Man and the Renaissance*, p. 34.

82. Roberts, *On Stage*, p. 120. See also Werner, *Theatergebäude*, pp. 52, 53.

83. Cheney, *Theatre*, p. 197. See also Tidworth, *Theatres*, p. 50.

84. Tidworth, *Theatres*, p. 51, mentions that the one existing report of the opening ceremony at the Teatro Olimpico reveals that it could comfortably seat 3,000 spectators who would sit and

watch an 11-hour performance without tiring. See also Werner, *Theatergebäude*, p. 53.

85. Werner, *Theatergebäude*, pp. 54–56. See also Tidworth, *Theatres*, pp. 65–68; Roberts, *On Stage*, p. 122.

86. Werner, *Theatergebäude*, p. 49. See also Nicoll, *Development of the Theatre*, p. 89.

87. Southern, *Seven Ages*, p. 161.

88. Nicoll, "The Theater", *Collier's Encyclopedia*, (1962), vol. 22, p. 248. See also Tidworth, *Theatres*, p. 37.

89. Roberts, *On Stage*, pp. 183–184.

90. Nicoll, *World History of the Theatre*, p. 447.

91. Roberts, *On Stage*, p. 158. See also Werner, *Theatergebäude*, p. 47. Werner writes that the theater was also called the Blackfriars Theater.

92. Werner, *Theatergebäude*, p. 46. See also Nicoll, *Development of the Theatre*, p. 97.

93. Southern, *Seven Ages*, p. 173.

94. Kitson, *Age of Baroque*, p. 8.

95. Southern, *Seven Ages*, p. 223.

96. This is the only available evidence of any significance concerning this stage system, and it should be studied in combination with Figures 58 and 59. See also Southern, *Seven Ages*, p. 226.

97. See earlier discussion of the Italian Renaissance stage.

98. Nicoll, *Development of the Theatre*, p. 117.

99. *Columbia-Viking Desk Encyclopedia*, (1966), p. 916.

100. The masques were a form of court entertainment stressing music and spectacle, entirely different from the popular Shakespearean theater. See also Roberts, *On Stage*, p. 515.

101. Jones brought back from Italy some of the Parigi's designs. See Southern, *Seven Ages*, pp. 188, 196; Tidworth, *Theatres*, p. 63.

102. Southern, *Seven Ages*, pp. 196, 197. A painted proscenium arch frames the stage the same way as an illustration may frame the first page or title page of a book.

103. Nicoll, *Development of the Theatre*, p. 108.

104. Arnott and Woodruff, *Drama and the Theatre*, p. 23.

105. For a more detailed description of the theaters mentioned, see Nicoll, *Development of the Theatre*, pp. 172–180; Tidworth *Theatres*, pp. 65–68; Werner, *Theatergebäude*, pp. 57–65.

106. Southern, *Seven Ages*, p. 232.

107. Nicoll, "The Theater." In *Collier's Encyclopedia* (1962), vol. 22, p. 248.

108. Tidworth, *Theatres*, p. 64.

109. It is not certain whether the drawing is of the original building erected in 1632 or its later reconstruction.

110. Nicoll, *Development of the Theatre*, p. 164.

111. Ben Jonson, the celebrated poet and dramatist, a contemporary and friend of William Shakespeare, was the principal creator of the court masque.

112. Southern, *Seven Ages*, pp. 235–237.

113. Roberts, *On Stage*, p. 230.

114. Nicoll, *History of Restoration Drama*. See also Roberts, *On Stage*, p. 238.

115. Southern, *Seven Ages*, p. 238.

116. Roberts, *On Stage*, pp. 254, 262; Nicoll, *Development of the Theatre*, p. 159.

117. Tidworth, *Theatres*, pp. 74, 78.

118. Bouboulidis, *Cretan Theatre*. See also Protopapa-Bouboulidou, *Theatre in Zante*, pp. 17–20; Kakouri, *Pre-Aesthetic Forms*, pp. 141, 177, 179.

119. Cheney, *Theatre*, p. 380.

120. An interesting analysis of romanticism is made by Nicoll, *World History of the Theatre*, pp. 289–292.

121. Arnott and Woodruff, *Drama and the Theatre*, p. 30.

122. Cheney, *Theater*, p. 415.

123. Sturm and Drang (storm and stress) is an eighteenth-century period of German literary romanticism that began with Gotthold Ephraim Lessing (1729–1781), and includes the work of a group of ardently romantic writers from which the two immortals, Goethe and Schiller, stand out. See Garten, *Modern German Drama*, p. 13; also Melchinger, *Theater der Gegenwart*, p. 176.

124. Nietzsche, *Birth of Tragedy*, p. 107.

125. Cheney, *Theatre*, p. 464.

126. Nicoll, *Development of the Theatre*, p. 253.

127. Roberts, *On Stage*, p. 364.

128. Nicoll, *Development of the Theatre*, p. 203.

129. Arnott and Woodruff, *Drama and the Theatre*, p. 38.

130. Roberts, *On Stage*, p. 366. See also Nicoll, *Development of the Theatre*, p. 200.

131. Roberts, *On Stage*, p. 379.

132. The Paris Opera was the work of Charles Garnier and opened in 1875. See Tidworth, *Theatres*, pp. 157–164. Nineteenth-century theaters in the neoclassical style of the period are also described in Werner, *Theatergebäude*, pp. 66–72, 102–123.

133. Roberts, *On Stage*, pp. 356, 363, 496. See also Werner, *Theatergebäude*, p. 120.

134. Despite the austerity and the "democratic" form of the theater, Wagner did not omit the royal boxes, the *Furstengallerie*, which, as in the court theaters, are a main feature of the design. The royal boxes, moreover, are the only points from which there is an unobstructed view of the whole stage, while the orchestra is completely hidden. See also Tidworth, *Theatres*, p. 173.

135. In 1879 Zola introduced the strict discipline of

natural science to fiction with his essay on the experimental novel, maintaining that the writing of fiction should become one of the experimental sciences. See also F.W.J. Hemmings, "Emile Zola." In *Collier's Encyclopedia* (1962), vol. 23, p. 768.

136. Sabine, *History of Political Theories*, pp. 806–854.
137. Denis Bablet, "La remise en question du lieu théâtral au vingtième siècle." In Centre National, *Le lieu théâtral*, p. 16.
138. Cheney, *Theatre*, p. 454.
139. Roberts, *On Stage*, p. 412.
140. Arnott and Woodruff, *Drama and the Theatre*, p. 107.
141. Cheney, *Theatre*, p. 458.
142. Rendle, *Everyman and His Theatre*, p. 9.
143. Roberts, *On Stage*, pp. 420, 425, 446.
144. Cheney, *Theatre*, p. 491.
145. Arnott and Woodruff, *Drama and the Theatre*, p. 108.
146. Nicoll, *Development of the Theatre*, p. 230.
147. Roberts, *On Stage*, p. 430.
148. Bablet. In Centre National, *Le lieu théâtral*, p. 16.
149. Nicoll, *Development of the Theatre*, p. 212.
150. Cheney, *Theatre*, p. 524.
151. Bablet. In Centre National, *Le lieu théâtral*, p. 20.
152. Piscator, *Politische Theater*, p. 33.
153. Piscator, *Politische Theater*, pp. 37–39.
154. Erwin Piscator, "La technique nécessité artistique." In Centre National, *Le lieu théâtral*, p. 182.
155. The chronological order of the development of Piscator's theater was 1919–1920, the Tribunal, Königsberg; 1920–1921, Theater of the Proletariat, Berlin; 1923–1924, Central-Theater, Berlin; thereafter in the same city: 1924–1927, the Volksbühne; 1927–1929, the Piscator-Bühne. See Piscator, *Politische Theater*, p. 39.
156. The cyclorama is a scenic feature still in use today as a stage background. It is generally a construction of stretched canvas, metal, or wood, with a panoramic open curvature; it is also called "sky."
157. Southern, *Seven Ages*, p. 271.
158. Vittorio De Feo, "Architecture et théâtre," *VH* 101, Nos. 7–8 (1972), p. 103.
159. *Ibid.* p. 95; see reprinted Meyerhold's program from V. Quillici's magazine, *L'architettura del Costruttivismo*, footnote 58.
160. Rendle, *Everyman*, p. 19.
161. Whiting, *Introduction to the Theatre*, pp. 287–288.
162. Rowell, *Stage Design*, p. 21.
163. Meyerhold insisted that "we must destroy the

box-stage once and for all. . . . The new stage will have platforms that can be moved horizontally or vertically and will permit the use of methods to convert the spoken word and operate the movable structures." De Feo, "Architecture et Théâtre." In *VH* 101, nos. 7–8 (1972), p. 95.

164. Bablet. In Centre National, *Le lieu théâtral*, p. 19.
165. Robert Edmond Jones, "Towards a New Stage." In *Theatre Arts Monthly* (March 1941). See also Mously, *Contemporary Theater*, p. 35.
166. Southern, *Seven Ages*, p. 269.
167. Izenour, "Building for the Performing Arts," p. 99.
168. Interview with Izenour at Yale University, October 1967.
169. Information provided by Mrs. Walter Gropius.
170. The basic message and summons of the Bauhaus school were publicized in its first manifesto: "The ultimate aim of all formative endeavor is 'the Structure' [*der Bau*]. To adorn it was formerly the primary duty of the fine arts. Today those arts are segregated, each enclosed in totally self-contained isolation from which they will never be able to escape unless all artists cooperate with each other again. Architects, painters, sculptors must again become acquainted with and learn to understand the complex form of the Structure, in its entirety and in its every detail; and then their works, of their own accord, will be full of the architectural spirit they have lost in the artistic salons.

. . .

"Architects, painters, sculptors—we must all turn back to craftsmanship! There is no such thing as 'professional art.' There is no difference between the artist and the craftsman. The artist, who must possess the basic skills of the craftsman, is but one rung above him on the ladder.

"Let us therefore create a new 'craftsmen's guild' without the class arrogance they have tried to build like a towering overbearing wall between the craftsman and the artist! We must desire and pursue the creation of a new Structure of the future that will represent, in an integrated form [*Gestalt*], architecture, sculpture and painting and, with the help of a million craftsmen's hands, will soar like a crystal symbol of the coming new creed." Gropius, Gropius, and Bayer, *Bauhaus 1919–1928*, p. 16.

171. Gropius, "Introduction." In Gropius and Schlemmer, *Theater of the Bauhaus*, p. 17.
172. Schlemmer, "Man and Art Figure." In Gropius and Schlemmer, *Theater of the Bauhaus*, pp. 19, 22–25, 81.

173. Schlemmer, "Theater (Bühne)." In Gropius and Schlemmer, *Theater of the Bauhaus*, p. 89.

174. Analyzing the reasons he decided in favor of this theater, Piscator explains: "After I had staged various plays at the Volksbühne and the state theater, I had formed a definite and clear-cut notion of a theater so designed as to resemble a machine, or more precisely a typewriter, where from Aeschylus or Shakespeare to Chekhov and Brecht . . . it would be able to satisfy every need." Piscator, "La technique nécessité artistique." In Center National, *Le lieu théâtral*, p. 181.

175. Gropius, "Introduction." In Gropius and Schlemmer, *Theater of the Bauhaus*, pp. 12–14.

176. "It was a time when such a concept could easily have been realized. Everything was thought out and designed, down to the smallest detail. We were all living a feverish period of exploration and intellectual restlessness; we all wanted to accomplish something new, a characteristic cachet. . . . One would think we had a presentiment of the approaching end." Gropius, in an interview with the author.

177. One of Gropius's innovations in his *Totaltheater* was the integration of movie and slide projection in the theater as an element of the setting and as a means of unifying space. See also Melchinger, *Theater der Gegenwart*, p. 36.

178. It is called so by Jean Jacquot, who also said: "To enjoy the perfect illusion, the privileged spectators of noble lineage had to be seated in the royal box, which was situated on the perspective axis. Moreover, it was paradoxical that the semicircular or horseshoe arrangement of the house, with its multistoried rows of boxes, which prevailed from the very first in opera houses built to accommodate large audiences, corresponded to a social class distinction reflected in the scale of ticket prices and the degree of comfort and good visibility. It also conformed to the notion of the theater as a meeting place where the public gathered to see and be seen, a place where the spectacle of the house was no less diverting than the spectacle on the stage." Jacquot, "Le lieu théâtral et la culture." In Centre National, *Le lieu théâtral*, p. 226.

179. Stage designer Peter Larkin made a characteristic comment: "The only way the old forms will disappear from theater production is when they become too expensive to operate. Again the only way you can get people to use new tools in the theater is not to give them the old ones." In American Federation of Arts, *Ideal Theater*, p. 9.

180. Melchinger, *Theater der Gegenwart*, pp. 34–35.

See also Nicoll, *Development of the Theatre*, p. 234.

181. Percy Corry proclaimed in 1949 that "the competent actor finds no technical difficulty in establishing that unity from behind a proscenium arch. It is his job to do so and he is, in fact, aided by the separation of this world of 'realism' from the reality of the auditorium. . . . The emotional response is actually heightened by remoteness; a darkened auditorium and concentration on a lighted acting area induce greater emotional sensitivity and help to suspend rational judgment." Corry, "That Intimate Stage." In *Tabs*, 7, no. 3. See also Mously, *Contemporary Theater*, p. 42.

182. Pierre Francastel, at a convention in Royaumont, in 1961, took the same approximate position: "But I do not believe a greater degree of communication can be required, because the mere fact that the audience and the actors are there together in one and the same space is sufficient. The Italian stage appeared, at a given time, to be the ideal type for communication, particularly after it became the practice to darken the house." Francastel, "Le théâtre est-il un art visuel?" In Centre National, *Le lieu théâtral*, p. 81.

183. This is also the opinion of critic Robert Brustein, who wrote the following in 1960: "Much as the spatial separation of the two different worlds, the auditorium and the stage, has helped to bring about technical progress, it fails to draw the spectators physically into the orbit of the play; being on the other side of the curtain or the orchestra pit, he remains beside the drama, not in it. The theater is thereby robbed of one of its strongest means to make the spectator participate in the drama." Brustein, "Scorn Not the Proscenium." In *Theatre Arts* (May 1960), p. 82.

184. André Villiers, for one, summed up the situation in replying to Francastel at the Royaumont gathering: "We note that the Italian stage very often breaks away from its original function, from the notion of a frame and an 'optical box.' Most directors, when faced with the prospect of working for a pretty 'Italian picture frame,' try to escape from it, to develop their creation in front of it, to convert it, to bring forth the actors from the opposite and of the auditorium." Villiers, "Rapports de l'acteur et du spectateur comme conditions d'une architecture." In Centre National, *Le lieu théâtral*, p. 85.

185. Southern, *Seven Ages*, pp. 279–281.

186. Among them was Eugène Ionesco, who argued: "We must and can do everything. Nothing should be excepted and every kind of thing

should be tried. But just as the violin does not destroy the saxophone, which in turn does not destroy the flute, in the same way the new architecture, the new stages, the new theater structures should not weaken the old. That would be a shame." Berhnard Pfau, "Reflections sûr le théâtre et la scène." In *L'Architecture d'aujourd'hui*, no. 129 (1966), p. 44. See also Ionesco, in *Werk*, no. 9 (September 1960).

187. Max Frisch, the German director, said: "The stage of a modern theater should be adaptable to the existing theatrical literature. Save for the ancient drama which is very seldom presented in a modern theater, the entire body of that literature, including the avant-garde, was written for the Italian-type stage. The most knowledgeable experimenter of our time, Bertolt Brecht, used nothing but the Italian stage when he managed to get his own theater. Efforts toward a future expansion of the stage area are always desirable, but they should not destroy the architectural unity of the natural stage of the picture-frame and the limelights." Pfau, "Reflections sûr le théâtre." In *L'Architecture d'aujourd'hui*, no. 129, p. 44. See also *Bauwelt*, no. 44, 1964.

188. Thomas de Gaetani, "Theatre Architecture." In *A.I.A. Journal*, vol. 36, no. 2 (August 1961), p. 76. See also Gussmann, *Theatergebäude*, p. 46.

189. Information given by the architect, Gerhard Weber.

190. Information given by the architect, Fritz Bornemann.

191. Information given by the architect, Harold Deilmann.

192. Southern, *Seven Ages*, p. 283.

193. Information given by one of the architects, W. Beck.

194. Information given by the city of Bochum.

195. Wright, *Grady Gammage Memorial Auditorium*, p. 11.

196. Southern, *Seven Ages*, p. 287.

197. Southern, *Seven Ages*, p. 283. See also Brecht, *Plays*, vol. 1.

198. Harwell Hamilton Harris, "The Architecture." In the *Dallas Theater Center, Brochure*, 1967 p. 26. See also "A Theatre by Wright." *Architectural Record*, March 1960, p. 163.

199. Jones, *Marcel Breuer, 1921–1962*, p. 207.

200. Southern, *Seven Ages*, pp. 291–293. See also Ontario Theatre Study Report, *The Awkward Stage*, pp. 89–108.

201. Becket, press release, 1967, and explanations received by the author in a personal interview with staff members of Welton Becket and Associates, Los Angeles, October 1967.

202. Howell, Killick, Patridge, and Amis, "Old Vic."

In *L'Architecture d'aujourd'hui*, no. 152 (1970), p. 92.

203. Tyrone Guthrie, reexamining the importance of illusion, also said: "It has always seemed to me that people do not submit to illusion in the theater much after the age of ten or eleven. They are perfectly aware that the middle-aged lady uncomfortably suspended on a wire is not Peter Pan but an actress pretending to be Peter Pan. For a performance to attempt to create an illusion is . . . gallant but . . . futile." Guthrie, "A Director Views the Stage." In *Design Quarterly* 58, (1963), p. 4.

204. Ralph Rapson, "The Architect's Design." In *Design Quarterly*, 58 (1963), p. 6.

205. Southern, *Seven Ages*, p. 284.

206. Corry, *Planning the Stage*, p. 85. See also Tidworth, *Theatres*, p. 205.

207. Southern, *Seven Ages*, p. 285.

208. Corry, *Planning the Stage*, pp. 86–89.

209. Nicoll, *Development of the Theatre*, p. 234.

210. Selden and Sellman, *Stage Scenery and Lighting*, p. 198.

211. Burris-Meyer and Cole, *Theatres and Auditoriums*, p. 272.

212. Ham, *Theatre Planning*, p. 115.

213. Joseph, *Planning for New Forms of Theatre*, p. 30.

214. Burris-Meyer and Cole, *Theatres and Auditoriums*, p. 130.

215. For further details concerning acoustics and other technical matters connected with the theater, see Izenour, *Theater Design*; Ham, *Theatre Planning* (footnote 212); and Burris-Meyer and Cole, *Theatres and Auditoriums* (footnote 211). See also Papathanasopoulos, *Echo-Proofing of Buildings*. For conventional theaters, see Gussmann, *Theatergebäude* (footnote 188).

216. Supporting her ideas, Zelda Fichandler said: "I did not want to waste time arguing with an architect about the respective values of the proscenium versus the arena stage. I made up my mind on that issue a long time ago and have set my stakes with that form which reunites the audience and the play in the same 'room,' where historically they used to be and where they belong in today's world." Review: "New Image, Old Plan for Arena Stage Theater." In *Architectural Record* (February 1952), p. 123.

217. Geoffrey Brooks, "Octagon Theater, Bolton." In *L'Architecture d'aujourd'hui*, no. 152 (1970), p. 91.

218. Schubert, *Moderner Theaterbau*, pp. 180–181.

219. Corry, *Planning the Stage*, p. 190.

220. Nicoll, *Development of the Theatre*, p. 237.

221. Norman Bel Geddes, "Symposium on Theatre Planning." In *Educational Theatre Journal*, 11, no. 1 (March 1950).

222. André Veinstein, "Les Théâtres expérimentaux-organisation-architecture." In *L'Architecture d'aujourd'hui*, no. 129 (1966), p. 62. See also the same author's *Le théâtre expérimental*.

223. Student Theater in Tampere, 1962. In *Bauen-Wohnen*, no. 2 (1964), p. 219.

224. Schubert, *Moderner Theaterbau*, p. 66. See also Nicoll, *Development of the Theatre*, p. 236.

225. Izenour, "Building for the Performing Arts," p. 101.

226. Izenour, "Drama School Complex." In American Federation of the Arts, *Ideal Theater*, p. 75.

227. Review: "Drama Center for Harvard." In *Architectural Record* (September 1960), p. 152.

228. Hämer, "Stahlkonstruktionen im Theaterbau," pp. 46–57. Also information given by the architect, Gerhard Weber.

229. Peter Moro, "Gulbenkian Center in Hull." In *Mehrzweckgebäude, E + P. Entwurf und Planung*, pp. 80–81. Also information given by the architect.

230. Fritz Schäfer, "Théâtre Ulm." In *L'Architecture d'aujourd'hui*, no. 152 (1970), p. 74. See also *Ulmer Theater-Neubau 1969*, pp. 5–18.

231. Ben Schlanger, "Multipurpose Places of Assembly." In *A.I.A. Journal*, 42, no. 2 (December 1964), p. 66.

232. Diagrams 1 to 5 show the functional requirements and the most suitable theater form for each performing art. They also give general figures for the size of each space in a typical theater and comparative examples of how these spaces are distributed in some existing theaters. The source of these figures are (*a*) my estimates and measurements made and (*b*) a comparison of the assumptions accepted by Burris-Meyer and Cole, *Theatres and Auditoriums*, and Ham, *Theatre Planning*. The plans and sections shown in Diagrams 6 and 7 have been designed by me to a common scale (1:1000) for the sake of easy comparison of forms and shapes.

233. The famous Swiss pianist Rudolph Ganz once said: "Sounds from instruments located at the farthest ends of the stage take slightly longer to reach the conductor than those from the closest instruments. When this happens, one must adjust to it or the orchestra isn't playing together. Can you imagine how hard it is to play good music under these conditions? There's a theater in Paris where you play one note and hear two. I performed in a hall something like this in San Francisco; when I played 'plunk,' the audience heard 'plunk, plunk.' Since the audience heard twice, I asked the manager to pay me twice." Ganz, "Interview." In *Talmanac* (November 1964), pp. 10–11.

234. Jürgen Joedicke, "Architekturkritik—Musik im Mittelpunkt, Philarmonie Berlin." In *Bauen—Wohnen*, no. 12 (1963), pp. 497–504.

235. Barrie Greenbie, "A Theater for Dance." In American Federation of the Arts, *Iaeal Theater*, p. 44.

236. Izenour, "Design a Sound Idea for Combination Hall." In *Engineering News-Record* (November 3, 1966), p. 45.

237. Interview with Izenour, Athens, February 1968.

238. Review: "The Jesse H. Jones Hall." In *Architectural Record*, (February 1967), p. 131.

239. Information provided by Izenour. See also Izenour, *Theater Design*, pp. 374–382.

240. Information and plans given by Izenour.

241. Comment: "The Loretto Hilton Center for the Performing Arts." In *Architectural Record* (February 1967), p. 149.

242. Paolo Soleri, "Théâtre à Santa Fé." In *L'Architecture d'aujourd'hui*, no. 152 (1970), p. 17.

243. Antonio Sant'Elia (1888–1916) was a young Italian futurist who was killed in World War I. Influenced by Wagner, he proposed a scheme for a skyscraper connected with subways and elevators and with traffic lanes at different levels, brought together in architectural unity. This scheme was in accord with the futurists' love of motion and interest in its artistic possibilities. See also Giedion, *Space, Time and Architecture*, p. 319.

244. Information given by the National Arts Center, Ottawa, and the Canadian Embassy in Greece.

245. Ham, *Theatre Planning*, p. 252.

246. Wolf von Eckardt, "Capital Could Learn from Lincoln Center." In *The Washington Post* (February 19, 1967).

247. Interview with Breuer, New York City, November 1967.

248. Amery, *National Theatre*, 1977.

249. The Sidney Opera Center, which is in fact a complete theater center, was designed in 1957 by Danish architect Joern Utzon; he resigned from the project in 1966 as a result of disagreement. The project was continued by a team of four Australian architects and opened in October 1973. It comprises a 2,700-seat concert hall, a 1,500-seat opera house, a 550-seat proscenium theater for drama, and a 420-seat chamber music hall. See also "Opernhaus Sidney." In *DBZ* no. 1 (1974), p. 33.

250. Francastel, *Peinture et société*, p. 11.

251. Ladopoulos, *Visual Arts and Geometry*, p. 21. Ladopoulos is professor of Geometrie at the National Technical University of Athens.

252. Polieri, "L'espace scénique nouveau." In Centre National, *Le lieu théâtral*, p. 132.

253. Francastel, "Le théâtre est-il un art visuel?" In Centre National, *Le lieu théâtral*, p. 77.

254. Molnár, "U-Theater." In Gropius and Schlemmer, *Theater of the Bauhaus*, pp. 72–77.

255. An extensive analysis of the Theater of the Sun is found in *Theatro* 6, no. 32 (March–April 1973), pp. 33–82. Mnouchkine also presented her work with this project in a lecture at the French Institute in Athens, November 25, 1974.

256. Dort, review of the plays *1789* and *1973*, staged by the Theater of the Sun. In *Theatro* 6, no. 32 (March–April 1973), p. 73.

257. Thomadaki, "Nancy Festival 1973." In *Theatro* 6, no. 33; 6, 34/36 (1973); 37, 38/39 (1974). A very interesting analytical and critical review of a theater project that in the past nine years has been presenting some of the most revolutionary trends in the theater.

258. Rainer Taeni, "New Forms of Communication."

259. The Spielstrasse is a pedestrian walk in Munich's Olympic Park connecting the main stadium with the open-air theater, the Theatron. It runs along the south bank of the artificial lake.

260. Description based on my own experience.

261. Taeni mentioned in his lecture that such attempts were made at the Hamburg Opera and in public squares in Bonn.

262. Teo Otto, "Interview." In *Theaterausstellungskatalog*, p. 93.

263. Larkin. In American Federation of the Arts, *The Ideal Theater*, p. 13.

264. Michelis, *Architecture as Art*, p. 32. Panagiotis Michelis, was a philosopher and professor of the Theory of Forms at the School of Architecture of the National Technical University of Athens.

265. Rudolph and Answang explained the rationale that led them to their proposal: "Although the ability to play without proscenium, or in-the-round, is an important advance in theater flexibility, it, too, does not provide the excitement theater offered us before the age of space. Where is that excitement today, and how can it be achieved? . . . A potential for achieving this is offered through the use of film combined with live stage action in one complete blending. By so doing, the two techniques of theatrical presentation are synthesized into a new form of theater. This form utilizes a new motion picture screen which has no frame. Film for this would be shot so that its composition is in relationship to the live actors on stage." Rudolph and Answang. In American Federation of the Arts, *Ideal Theater*, pp. 15–19.

266. Schlanger and Oenslager. In American Federation of the Arts, *Ideal Theater*, p. 129.

267. Nicoll, *Development of the Theatre*, p. 251.

268. Interview with Louis Kahn, Philadelphia, September 1967.

269. A. Terjakis ["Eranistis"], "Theater Architecture." In *To Vima* (March 16, 1968). Angelos Terjakis was a famous writer and Academician.

270. Whiting, *Introduction to the Theatre*, p. 149.

271. Touchard, "Racine, Andromache." In *Le Monde*, (June 5, 1968).

272. Selden, *Theatre Double Game*, p. 19.

273. Southern, *Seven Ages*, p. 274.

274. Comment: "Die Vielfalt der Deutschen Theaterlandschaft." In *Theaterausstellungskatalog*, p. 91.

275. Katerina Thomadaki, "Ninth Nancy Festival." In *Theatro* 7, no. 37 (January–February 1974), p. 66. Casali is one of the founders of a theater group in Argentina called The Baires Community. It was established in 1969.

276. Denis Diderot, "Dissertation." Reprinted in *Theatro* 6, no. 32 (March–April 1973), p. 50.

Bibliography

BOOKS

Allen, James Turney. *The Greek Theatre of the Fifth Century B.C.* Berkeley: Semicentennial Publications of the University of California, 1918. Brooklyn, N.Y.: Haskell House, 1969 reprint.

American Federation of Arts. *The Ideal Theater: Eight Concepts.* New York: The Federation, 1962.

Amery, Collin (ed.). *The National Theatre: The Architectural Review Guide.* London: Architectural Press, 1977.

Arnott, J.F., and Woodruff, Graham. *Drama and the Theatre.* London: John Russell Brown, 1971.

Becket, Welton. Press release. Los Angeles: Welton Becket and Associates, 1967.

Bouboulidis, Phaedon K. *Cretan Theatre.* Athens: I. D. Kollaros, 1970.

Brecht, Bertolt. *Plays,* vol. 1. London: Eric Bentley, 1959.

Burris-Meyer, Harold, and Cole, Edward C. *Theatres and Auditoriums,* 2nd ed. New York: Reinhold, 1967.

Cailler, Pierre, and Cailler, Diky. "Les Théâtres Gréco-Romains de Grèce." *Style,* no. 1 (autumn 1966).

Centre National de la Recherche Scientifique. *Le lieu théâtral dans la sociétè moderne.* Paris: Editions du C.N.R.S., 1966.

Cheney, Sheldon. *The Theatre: 3000 Years of Acting and Stagecraft.* London: Vision, 1963.

Corry, Percy. *Planning the Stage.* London: Pittman, 1961.

Cottas, Venetia. *Le théâtre à Byzance.* Paris: Librairie Orientaliste Paul Geuthner, 1931.

Dallas Theater Center. *Dallas Theater Brochure.* Dallas, 1967.

Dörpfeld, W., and Reisch, E. *Das griechische Theater.* Athens: Barth und Von Hirst, 1896.

Drama Lecture Series. *Futures in American Theater.* Dept. of Drama, University of Texas, 1962–1963.

Fiechter, E. *Antike griechische Theaterbauten,* parts 1–10. Stuttgart: W. Kohlhammer Verlag, 1930.

Fiechter, E. *Die baugeschichtliche Entwicklung des antiken Theaters.* Stuttgart, 1914.

Flickinger, Roy C. *The Greek Theater and Its Drama.* Chicago: University of Chicago Press, 1918; 4th ed., 1960.

Francastel, Pierre. *Peinture et société.* Paris: Gallimard, 1965.

Garten, H. F. *Modern German Drama.* London: Methuen, 1964.

Giedion, Sigfried. *Space, Time and Architecture,* 3rd ed. Cambridge, Mass.: Harvard University Press, 1959.

Gropius, Walter, Gropius, Ise, and Bayer, Herbert. *Bauhaus 1919–1928.* Teufen, Switz.: Verlag Arthur Niggli, 1955.

Gropius, Walter, and Schlemmer, Oskar. *The Theater of the Bauhaus.* Middletown, Conn.: Wesleyan University Press, 1961.

Gussman, Hans. *Theatergebäude.* East Berlin: VEB Verlag Technik, 1954.

Hadas, Moses. *Imperial Rome.* Morristown, N.J.: Silver Burdette, 1965.

Ham, Roderick. *Theatre Planning.* London: Architectural Press, 1972.

Hämer, H. W. "Stahlkonstruktionen im Theaterbau." Merkblätter no. 289. Düsseldorf: Beratungsstelle für Stahlverwendung.

Herodotus *Histories,* vols. 1–9. Translation by A. Theophilos. Athens: Epistimonike Ekdoseis Papyros, 1953.

Izenour, George. "Building for the Performing Arts." *Tulanè Drama Review,* vol. 7, no. 4, June 1963.

Izenour, George. *Theater Design.* New York: McGraw-Hill, 1977.

Jones, Cranston. *Marcel Breuer,* 1921–1962. Stuttgart: Gert Hatje Verlag, 1962.

Joseph, Stephen. *Planning for New Forms of Theatre.* London: Standard Electric and Engineering Co., 1961.

Kakouri, Katerina I. *Pre-Aesthetic Forms of Theatre.* Athens: Fili tou Vivliou, 1946.

Kitson, Michael. *The Age of Baroque.* Greek translation. Athens: Chrysos Typos E.P.E., 1967.

Koukoulés, Phaedon. *The Byzantines: Their Life and Civilization.* Athens: Institut Francais (no. 90), 1955.

Ladopoulos, Panagiotis. *Visual Arts and Geometry.* Reports of the Academy of Athens, vol. 43, 1968.

Lascaris, Nicolaos I. *Lectures in the History of Ancient Greek Theatre,* vols. 1–3. Athens: Acropolis, 1928.

Martindale, Andrew. *Man and the Renaissance.* Greek translation. Athens: Chrysos Typos E.P.E., 1967.

Mehrzweckgebäude. *E+P Entwurf und Planung.* Munich: Verlag Georg D. W. Callwey, 1967.

Melchinger, Siegfried. *Theater der Gegenwart.* Frankfurt: Fischer Bücherei, 1956.

Michelis, Panagiotis A. *Architecture as Art,* 4th ed. Athens, 1973.

Mielziner, Jo. "The Future of Theater Architecture." In *Futures in American Theater,* Drama Lecture Series, Dept. of Drama, University of Texas, 1962–1963.

Mously, Abdel-Fattah. *The Contemporary Theater.* Washington, D.C.: The Catholic University Press, 1965.

Mouzenidis, Takis. *The Ancient Greek Theatre (Tragedy and Comedy).* Athens: National Tourist Organization, 1970.

Nicoll, Allardyce. *The Development of the Theatre.* London: Harrap, 1966.

Nicoll, Allardyce. *History of Restoration Drama.* Cambridge, Eng.: Cambridge University Press, 1923.

Nicoll, Allardyce. *A World History of the Theatre*, vols. 1–3. Greek translation by Maria Economou. Athens: Pnoi, 1962.

Nietzsche, Friedrich. *The Birth of Tragedy*. Greek translation. Athens: Govostis.

Ontario Theatre Study Report. *The Awkward Stage*. Toronto: Methuen, 1969.

Orlandos, Anastasios K. *Excavations at Sicyon*. Athens: Reports of the Archaeological Society, 1952.

Orlandos, Anastasios K. "Messène, chronique des fouilles en 1957." *Bulletin de la correspondance hellénique*, vol. 82, nos. 1,2. Athens: Ecole Francaise d'Athènes, 1958.

Papadopoulos, Athimos A. *The Religious Theatre of the Byzantines*. Athens: Syllogos Ofelimon Vivlion (no. 40), 1927.

Papathanasopoulos, Vasilis. *Echo-proofing of Buildings, Space Acoustics*. Athens: Pyrsos A.E., 1940.

Pickard-Cambridge, A.W. *The Theatre of Dionysus in Athens*. Oxford, Eng.: Clarendon, 1946.

Piscator, Erwin. *Das politische Theater*. Hamburg: Rowohlt Verlag GmBH, 1963.

Pollux, Julius. *Onomastikon*, vols. 1–10. Frankfurti: Apud Cl. Marnium, 1968.

Protopapa-Bouboulidou, Glykeria. *The Theatre in Zante from the Seventeenth to the Nineteenth Century*. Doctoral thesis. Athens, 1958.

Rendle, Adrian. *Everyman and His Theatre*. London: Pittman, 1968.

Roberts, Vera Mowry. *On Stage: A History of Theatre*. New York: Harper and Row, 1962.

Rowell, Kenneth. *Stage Design*. London: Studio Vista, 1968.

Sabine, George H. *History of Political Theories*. Greek translation by M. Krispis. Athens: M. Pechlivanidis, 1967.

Schubert, Hannelore. *Moderner Theaterbau*. Stuttgart-Bern: Karl Krämer Verlag, 1971.

Selden, Samuel (ed.). *Theatre Double Game*. Chapel Hill: University of North Carolina Press, 1969.

Selden, Samuel, and Sellman, Hunton D. *Stage Scenery and Lighting*. New York: Appleton-Century-Crofts, 1959.

Solomos, Alexis. *Bacchus the Saint*, 2nd ed. Athens: Pleias O.E., 1974.

Southern, Richard. *The Seven Ages of the Theatre*. London: Faber and Faber, 1968.

Strong, Donald. *The Classical World*. Greek translation. Athens: Chrysos Typos E.P.E., 1967.

Taeni, Rainer. "New Forms of Communication—from Street Theater to Mixed Media." Lecture. Athens: Goethe Institut, 11 February 1974. Published in *Theatro* 7, no. 37 (1974); translation by Rita Stamos.

Theaterausstellungskatalog. Munich: Goethe Institut, 1969.

Tidworth, Simon. *Theatres: An Illustrated History*. London: Pall Mall Press, 1973.

Ulmer Theater-Neubau 1969. Ulm: City of Ulm, 1971.

Veinstein, André. *Le théâtre expérimental*. Brussels: Collection Dionysos. La Renaissance du Livre, 1968.

Vandersleyen, *Das alte Aegypten*. Propylaen Kunstgesichte, 19.

Varvaringos, A. "The Theater of Dionysus in Athens." *Thespis*, no. 7 (December 1973).

Vitruvius, Pollio, *De architectura I–X*. Amstelodami: Apud Lud. Elzevirium, 1649 (National Library, Athens).

Vitruvius, Pollio. *The Ten Books on Architecture*. Translated by Morris Hicky Morgan. Cambridge, Mass.: Harvard University Press, 1914.

Werner, Eberhard. *Theatergebäude*. East Berlin: VEB Verlag Technik, 1954.

Whiting, Frank. *An Introduction to the Theatre*. New York: Harper & Row, 1954.

Wright, Frank Lloyd. *The Grady Gamage Memorial Auditorium*. Tempe: Arizona State University Press, 1964.

ENCYCLOPEDIAS

Americana, vol. 26. New York: Americana, 1966.

Collier's Encyclopedia, vols. 3, 22, 23. New York: Crowell-Collier, 1962.

Columbia-Viking Desk Encyclopedia, 2nd ed. New York: Columbia University Press, 1966.

Papyros-Larousse 7. Athens: E.E.E., 1964.

NEWSPAPERS

La Monde (Paris), January 5, 1968.

To Vima (Athens), March 16, 1968.

The Washington Post (Washington, D.C.), February 19, 1967.

PERIODICALS

A.I.A. Journal 36, no. 2, August 1961; 42, no. 6, December 1964.

Architectural Record, March 1960, September 1960, February 1962, February, 1967.

L'Architecture d'aujourd'hui, no. 122, 1965; 129, 1965; 152, 1970.

Bauen—Wohnen, no. 12, 1963; no. 2, 1964.

Bauwelt, no. 44, 1964.

DBZ (Deutsche Bauzeitschrift) 1, 1974.

Design Quarterly (Walker Art Center, Minneapolis), 58, 1963.

Educational Theatre Journal, 11, no. 1, March 1950.

Engineering News-Record, November 3, 1966.

Tabs 7, no. 3.

Talmanac, November 1964.

Theatre Arts, May 1960.

Theatre Arts Monthly, March 1941.

Theatro, 6, no. 32, March–April 1973; 6, no. 33, May–June, 1973; 6, no. 34/36, July–December 1973; 7, no. 37, January–February 1974; 7, no. 38/39, March–June 1974.

Thespis, 7, December 1973.

VH 101, no. 7–8, 1972.

Werk, no. 9, September 1960.

Yale Scientific Magazine, 29, no. 8, May 1955.

Index